**PEYOTE
POLITICS**

New Directions in Native American Studies
Liza Black and Colin G. Calloway, General Editors

PEYOTE POLITICS

THE MAKING OF THE NATIVE AMERICAN CHURCH, 1880–1937

LISA D. BARNETT

UNIVERSITY OF OKLAHOMA PRESS : NORMAN

Library of Congress Cataloging-in-Publication Data
Names: Barnett, Lisa D., 1963– author.
Title: Peyote politics : the making of the Native American Church, 1880–1937 / Lisa D. Barnett.
Other titles: New directions in Native American studies ; v. 24.
Description: Norman : University of Oklahoma Press, [2025] | Series: New directions in Native American studies ; volume 24 | Includes bibliographical references and index. | Summary: "A history of the rise of Peyotism and the Native American Church (founded 1918) from the 1880s to the 1930s, this book details the struggle to secure constitutional protections for the Peyotist religion and its rituals and how that struggle reshaped the faithful's identity as 'Native' and 'American' and established their place in the American political and legal systems"—Provided by publisher.
Identifiers: LCCN 2024040468 | ISBN 9780806195384 (hardcover)
Subjects: LCSH: Native American Church of North America—History—20th century. | Peyotism—History—19th century. | Peyotism—History—20th century. | Indians of North America—Religion.
Classification: LCC E98.R3 B255 2025 | DDC 970.004/97—dc23/eng/20241228
LC record available at https://lccn.loc.gov/2024040468

Peyote Politics: The Making of the Native American Church, 1880–1937 is Volume 24 in the New Directions in Native American Studies series.

The paper in this book meets the guidelines for permanence and durability of the Committee on Production Guidelines for Book Longevity of the Council on Library Resources, Inc. ∞

Copyright © 2025 the University of Oklahoma Press, Norman, Publishing Division of the University. Manufactured in the U.S.A.

All rights reserved. No part of this publication may be reproduced, stored in a retrieval system, or transmitted, in any form or by any means, electronic, mechanical, photocopying, recording, or otherwise—except as permitted under Section 107 or 108 of the United States Copyright Act—without the prior written permission of the University of Oklahoma Press. To request permission to reproduce selections from this book, write to Permissions, University of Oklahoma Press, 2800 Venture Drive, Norman, OK 73069, or email rights.oupress@ou.edu.

To the TCU History Department, which welcomed me as a student in the doctoral program from Brite Divinity School and helped shape my identity as a historian.

CONTENTS

Preface – ix
Acknowledgments – xi

Introduction – 1

Part I. The Politics of Religious Identity
1 Peyotism: A New Native American Religion – 15
2 The Push for Peyote Legislation: The Thin Line of Separation between Church and State – 38

Part II. The Politics of Racial Identity
3 From the Borderlands to the Bordered Lands: The Commercial Trade of Peyote – 63
4 Another Indian War: Race, Drugs, and the War on Peyote – 81

Part III. The Politics of Political Identity
5 Evading the "White Man's" Law: Peyotists' Use of the Legal and Political Systems – 105
6 "Let Us Keep Our Worship": Peyotists and the First Amendment – 127

Afterword – 147

Notes – 153
Bibliography – 205
Index – 233

PREFACE

My interest in peyote and the Native American Church began as a student at Brite Divinity School, working on my master's in theology focusing on American religious history. I had read *Spirit and Resistance* by George E. Tinker and encountered his reference to the Native American Church and peyote among many of the Osage people. I grew up in north central Oklahoma just a county away from Osage land and had taken Oklahoma history, yet had never heard of the Native American Church. My curiosity as a religious historian led me to research and learn so much that had not been taught to me as part of Oklahoma history or American history.

My interest in Native American history also comes from familial cultural connections lost over time. As a person of Indigenous descent, I am unable to claim anything beyond a genealogical connection to people who lived hundreds of years ago in the area of McMinn County, Tennessee, because language and cultural rituals were lost in the process of assimilation. I am claimed on the tribal roll of a non-federally recognized tribe. Because of my affiliation only through genealogy and not culture, I do not use Native American identity in a public or profitable way but only to talk about the tragedy of the loss of cultural identity within my family history. This inspires me as a historian to preserve the history and culture of Native America in the work that I do.

ACKNOWLEDGMENTS

The Peyotist Indians, as well as their supporters, believed they engaged in a religious path that promoted cultural aspects of Indianness important to preserve in a period of societal change and transition. Their pleas for religious freedom and their struggle to maintain their identities as Peyotists coalesced around a cultural contestation of "appropriate" forms of religious practice. I feel fortunate that this work allows for the voices of Native Americans to be heard from their testimony at state hearings in Oklahoma in 1908, federal congressional hearings in 1918, writings in the journal for the Society of American Indians, and the enormous amount of press coverage devoted to the peyote controversy where their comments were included as part of the story. My interest in Peyotism as an "outsider" comes from a belief in religious liberty and a desire to share their historical struggle as active participants in shaping Native Americans' entrance into the twentieth century.

Listing only my name as the author of this book does not fully acknowledge all those who have aided in its completion. My motto has been "it takes a village to write a book," and I am grateful to so many people. This project began at Brite Divinity School as a thesis and at Texas Christian University as my dissertation. My gratitude extends first to my advisor, Todd Kerstetter. He provided constructive criticism and much needed infusions of ideas and feedback to encourage a high level of production and quality. I am grateful for the support of my dissertation committee members—Rebecca Sharpless, Alan Gallay, Alex Hidalgo, and Jeff Williams—who never ceased to challenge me in the best of ways. Members of my writing group in the TCU History Department helped me immensely in completing this project by helping me think through ideas and offering suggestions. Much appreciation goes to Beth Hessel, Kendra DeHart, Sherilyn Farnes, Reilly Hatch, Joe Schiller, with a special note of thanks to Brett Dowdle, Mike Burns, and Kallie Kosc, who read and commented on the bulk of this project.

Fruitful conversations have also come with many in scholarly fellowship. Special thanks to Thomas Kavanagh, assistant professor of anthropology at Seton Hall University and the consulting anthropologist for the Comanche Nation; Carney Saupitty Jr., a cultural specialist with the Comanche National Museum and Cultural Center in Lawton, Oklahoma; Elsie Whitehorn, an Otoe who is a First Born Church Peyotist and a Peyotist in the Otoe-Missouria chapter of the Native American Church; and Jade Roubedeaux, an Otoe who is a First Born Church Peyotist and a roadman with the Otoe-Missouria chapter of the Native American Church.

I am also indebted to my colleagues at Phillips Theological Seminary (Tulsa, Oklahoma) who have encouraged my work and engaged me in conversation over this project, especially Warren Carter, Joe Bessler, Lisa Davison, Kathy McCallie, Briana Wong, Peter Capretto, and Sarah Morice Brubaker. Special thanks to Avery Phillips, the reserves, electronic resources, and serials librarian, who helped me with producing some of the images and research.

I appreciate the support given by the University of Oklahoma Press. Alessandra Jacobi Tamulevich, senior acquisitions editor, has done an outstanding job guiding this book from proposal to production with helpful feedback from the peer review process. Special thanks to Upili DeSilva for getting files to production. I am grateful to Steven Baker, managing editor, and Helen Robertson, project editor, for shepherding the work through copyediting and typesetting. Freelance copyeditor Katie Smith did a fantastic job. It was also great working with Tom Jonas, who produced the maps.

Thanks to my siblings and their families—Brenda, Greg, and Matthew Finn, and Ed Barnett and his daughter Bethany Barnett—for their support and confidence in me. Special thanks go to my mom, Judy Barnett, for her belief in me and encouragement along this journey, and especially for her willingness to engage my enthusiasm for history by accompanying me on many historical tours around northern Oklahoma—no doubt that my dad, Bill Barnett, would have loved joining us in these excursions if he were still with us. To all the "villagers" in the kin-dom that surrounds me, I am truly grateful. However, while I believe strongly in the value of cooperative scholarship, as the author of this book I bear full responsibility for any shortcomings, errors, or omissions.

INTRODUCTION

When Peyotism emerged as a new Native American religion among some of the Southern Plains tribes in the latter half of the nineteenth century, it spread quickly into other parts of Indian Territory and Oklahoma Territory and then throughout Indian Country.[1] When James Mooney, a white ethnologist working for the US Bureau of Ethnology, witnessed a Kiowa peyote ceremony in 1891, he highlighted peyote, a mild hallucinogenic agent found in the tops of cactuses that grow in northern Mexico and south Texas, as a valuable medicine, and he noted, "The ceremonial eating of the plant has become the great religious rite of all the tribes of the southern plains."[2] Several Peyotists, including Quanah Parker (Comanche), spoke at a session of the Oklahoma constitutional convention in 1906–7 and reiterated the value of peyote as both a medicine and a means to worship God.[3] Parker addressed that body in 1907 about Native Americans' use of peyote, saying, "All my Indian people use that for medicine.... It is no poison and we want to keep that medicine.... My people are citizens of the United States, and my people keep the right way; they go to school and teach school. I wish you delegates will look after my people.... My delegates will look after my people, look after my Indians. My Indians, just the same as you people, are citizens of the United States."[4] Notable in Parker's address is the naming of peyote as a valuable medicine for Native Americans and his declaration that his people were already citizens of the United States, whether recognized legally or not at that time. This contention of citizenship status fueled the ongoing arguments by Peyotists for their right to religious freedom in their worship practices utilizing the plant.

Beginning in 1903, the characterization of peyote by non–Native Americans underwent a dramatic change. Newspapers soon reported on an investigation undertaken by Francis E. Leupp, commissioner of Indian Affairs (1904–9), on Native American use of peyote and noted that "Uncle Sam" was becoming "excited over the Saturday night sprees of his Indian wards, fearing that the former lords of the American continent are giving themselves over to the slavery of a dope habit."[5] Soon non–Native American reformers linked peyote to other drugs such as opium, cocaine, and marijuana, thereby secularizing the sacred medicine in the public imagination so that federal legislative efforts could begin to criminalize and prohibit the use of peyote.

The concern on the part of white missionaries, Indian agents, and other "friends" of the Native American that peyote caused moral and physical harm spread. Not all Native Americans adopted Peyotism; in fact, many vehemently opposed it and worked with white reformers to attempt to eradicate the religious practice, including some leaders of the Society of American Indians (SAI), an organization formed in 1911 by Native intellectuals who favored the acculturation of Native Americans into American society. In 1916, the SAI officially took an anti-peyote position, though some members of the organization were Peyotists. SAI secretary Gertrude Simmons Bonnin (Yankton Nakota / Sioux, who also went by the name Zitkala-Ša) led the anti-peyote faction, becoming one of the most visible and outspoken opponents of the religious practice. In 1918 Bonnin's statement "Peyote Causes Race Suicide" was included in a congressional report concerning anti-peyote legislation; in it, she advocated for prohibition, declaring peyote to be "the twin brother of alcohol, and first cousin to habit-forming drugs."[6] Native Americans who were not associated with the SAI also opposed the use of peyote in religious practices. Many evangelical Christian Native Americans aligned themselves with the white social reformers' methods and reasons to oppose Peyotism.

Motivated primarily by concerns over the nature of citizenship status for Native Americans, both non–Native Americans and non-Peyotists waged a full-fledged assault on the religious freedom of Peyotists throughout the first three decades of the twentieth century. Their strategy to rid Native American society of the perceived uncivilized, un-Christian, and pagan practices included drawing peyote into the emerging racialized war on drugs to ensure federal prohibition against the peyote religion; in short, turning the "sacred" into the "profane."[7] However, Peyotists had their own understandings of Native and American identity and adopted their own strategies of resistance to protect their religious freedom. Peyotists fought to preserve the sacredness of their religious use of peyote, and the culmination of their efforts was the 1918 establishment of the Native American Church (NAC) in Oklahoma. In this process, Peyotists also reconstructed a new understanding of Native American identity.

A variety of first-order questions emerge from this trajectory of events. What did it mean to be a Native American in the early twentieth century, and whose authoritative power made this decision? What did it mean to be a "good" American citizen? Concerning the peyote religion, second-order questions also arise. How did peyote intersect with and affect these levels of identity construction? Why did some Native Americans vehemently oppose the peyote religion? How much religious freedom do mainstream (white Christian) Americans actually support, and who decides what constitutes legitimate religious practices and beliefs?

The terminology used to categorize Native Americans during this time period has also complicated these questions. Historians frequently fall into the binary of framing the cultural battle over Peyotism (and other issues) as one between "traditionalists" and "progressives"; the term "progressive Indian," especially with reference to the Society of American Indians, whose members were dubbed "red progressives," became associated with "modern professionals and intellectuals" or, at the very least, Native Americans who were educated.[8] This simplistic dichotomy masks the reality that many adherents of the peyote religion were younger, educated Native Americans and were even members of the SAI. Peyotism transcended generational and ideological lines and incorporated a diversity of religious experiences and practices within the pan-Indian religion. Accordingly, this work uses "Peyotists and non-Peyotists" to demarcate these two groups of Native Americans. In addition, the binary of "Native American" versus "white" often emerges in the history of Peyotism and the Native American Church, which overshadows the fact that one of the leading supporters of the peyote religion was a white ethnologist who also advised Native Americans on strategies of resistance.[9] And the complicated notions of American identity and citizenship that many immigrants to the United States were forced to navigate also extended to the consideration of Native Americans for citizenship status. In many ways, the unofficial requirement of American Christianity (particularly the Protestant version in American culture) as a qualification for US citizenship framed much of the controversy around the new Native American religion of Peyotism that many (though certainly not the majority of) Native Americans were adopting.

This work is both a social history encompassing the political and legal events surrounding Peyotism and its practitioners and a narrative of social identities centered on the controversy over peyote, particularly related to the terms "Native" and "American." The complex social construction of identities around peyote frames this work. Scott Richard Lyons (Ojibwe/Dakota) defines identity as "the assemblage of *meanings* that a group holds as important signifiers of identity, and they [those meanings] say something about what that group values."[10] The peyote religion of the late nineteenth and early twentieth centuries became a highly contested issue over social identities, and opponents (both non–Native Americans and Native Americans) sought to prohibit the religious practice by transforming peyote into a narcotic, thus drawing Native Americans into the emerging, racialized war on drugs. However, as this book argues, those Native Americans who were Peyotists resisted this secularization of their religious practice by using the American political and legal systems, ultimately incorporating in 1918 as the Native American Church to secure their religious freedom, and by forming a new, hybrid cultural identity, namely, "Native American," that emphasized the real possibility of honoring Native identity as well as American identity on the path to citizenship status. The book's time frame of 1880–1937 focuses on the rise and spread of Peyotism throughout Indian Country, as well as on federal and state efforts to suppress and prohibit Native use of peyote, with 1937 being the last year congressional representatives attempted to pass peyote legislation. It was not until 1965 that the federal government was able to act with an amendment to the federal Food, Drug, and Cosmetic Act, which declared peyote to be a dangerous drug. The 1970 Controlled Substance Act listed peyote as a Schedule I hallucinogenic substance with a high potential for abuse. The years for this study also coincide with the incipient racialized war on drugs affecting other minority groups in the United States, as well as social attempts at Americanization for the growing immigrant population of the country.

An intentional focus of this study is on the intersection of race and religion, where the politics of identity also relate to issues of power.[11] An examination of both the construction of identities and the performance of identities is important to this analysis, in order to identify the power relationships involved in the peyote controversy. The articles of incorporation for the NAC also illuminate identity construction, especially the hybridity of a Native American identity at a time when many Native Americans did not possess US citizenship status. The contested cultural space of identity, with its racial, ethnic, and political dimensions, led Peyotists to assess their own understanding of Native American identity and to preserve their religious freedom within the spheres of American democracy, which professed to value the First Amendment right to religious freedom. This becomes noticeable in Peyotists' shift in rhetoric in discussing peyote in different cultural contexts. Within the cultural context of a religious ceremony, peyote is referred to as a "sacred medicine" and extolled for its healing and protective properties for both individuals

Lophophora williamsii, also known as peyote cactus. Photo by Peter A. Mansfeld. Reproduced under CC BY 3.0.

and the Native community that practices the religion. So revered is the cactus that "Grandfather Peyote" sits atop an altar during the religious ceremonies as a reminder of the gift of the cactus given by the Creator. Within Native American cosmological worldviews, the plant itself is also seen as an ancestor, a living relative that helps bring balance and healing within the community, so Peyotists often refer to peyote with a familial language of respect as a way to reinforce their Native identity. However, discussions outside of the context of the NAC community bring forth the language of "religion," "church," and "sacrament," which equate to concepts understood within Christian contexts. Peyotists' use of Christianized rhetoric demonstrates their ability to hold both/and views of religious practice but also reveals a strategy of using rhetoric as a way to combat the restriction of their religious freedoms. In many ways, Peyotists, many of whom were not yet American citizens, were the ones who truly valued this constitutional ideal and worked tirelessly through the legal and political systems to protect their religion.

While this book operates on the assumption that both race and religion are social constructions attempting to formulate meanings, these constructions have social realities with consequences.[12] After Barbara J. Fields's seminal historical pronouncement in 1982 that "the notion of race, in its popular manifestation is an ideological construct and thus, above all, a historical product," other works have deepened our understanding of racial categorization and formation within the larger social fabric.[13] Ian Haney-López posits, "Race exists alongside a multitude of social identities that shape and are themselves shaped by the way in which race is given meaning. We live race through class, religion, nationality, gender, sexual identity, and so on."[14] Historically, this idea resonates with the issue of the peyote religion in the early part of the twentieth century and the conflation of peyote with the use of alcohol and dangerous narcotics, the implication being that, like alcohol, peyote use threatens the ability of Peyotists to participate in full social and political citizenship, at least according to most non–Native Americans and some Native folks. For many, this meant giving up the new Native American religious practice of worshiping with peyote. Many in American society felt that Peyotism also did not fall within the parameters of acceptable religious practice that were necessary to gain the full guarantee of religious freedom.

The second precept in this analysis focuses on the social construction not only of race, but also of religion. In his sociological study of religion, Peter Berger argued, "Religion is a product of the society from which it springs . . . it is the 'sacred canopy' which every human society builds over its world to give it meaning."[15] Religious historian Robert Orsi also elaborates on the cultural constructionist approach to religion in his groundbreaking work on lived religion, writing, "Religions arise from and refer back to discrete social and cultural worlds and they are inevitably shaped by the structures and limits of these worlds as they engage them. This is the dialectic of religion, which takes place within and in complex relationship with the dialectics of culture."[16] Since the introduction of this approach and the rise of religious studies in the field of lived religion, definitions reflect a more thorough understanding of religion's relationship with culture. Thomas Tweed's definition provides a more accurate framework with which to assess Peyotism: "Religions are cultural processes whereby individuals and groups map, construct, and inhabit worlds of meaning. They involve power as well."[17] Peyotists of the late nineteenth and early twentieth centuries understood this approach to religion.

Problematic in the understanding of Peyotism are cultural differences in religion. The Western-centered dichotomy provides a cosmological distinction between two separate spheres, heaven and earth, which define the parameters for identifying the specialness equated with religious experience. This is in contradistinction to a Native American worldview where the sacred exists in every part of existence, both personal and communal. In one of the earliest published works on Peyotism, anthropologist Weston La Barre offered a socioreligious analysis of the peyote religion. He wrote, "Peyote is the only plant toward which the Kiowa and other typical non-agricultural Plains tribes have a religious attitude and from which they can get 'power.' . . . Peyotism functions in all ways as a *living religion.*"[18]

Most of the early accounts of the peyote experience come from anthropologists whose intentions were to try to psychologize why some Native Americans were drawn to Peyotism, to translate the ceremony to a white audience, or to trace the diffusion of Peyotism among the various Native American peoples.[19] Their books offer a prescriptive listing of factual events, sometimes accompanied by anecdotal sources, but they provide limited analysis to fit Peyotism into a broader historical narrative. Only limited contextualization of the time period occurs in their works, with the exception of connecting the rise of Peyotism to the perceived declension of the Ghost Dance movement following the Wounded Knee massacre in 1890 and the federal Indian policy shift to relocate tribes to assigned reservations. Some studies attempted to interpret the concomitant disruption of cultural life as a singular event.

This work seeks to place the challenges to Peyotism within the historical context of Progressive Era politics and the social reforms taking place in the early decades of the twentieth century. The push for national alcohol prohibition, as well as America's participation in World War I, factor in to the cultural contestation over peyote. The inclusion of Native Americans in the early twentieth century as those exerting agency continues to fill a previous void in the historical record, where Native Americans disappeared from history after 1890 (and Wounded Knee), only to possibly reemerge in the historical record after World War II in the shift to urbanization, or even later in the 1960s with the emergence of the Red Power movement. The conflict over peyote intersected with several societal paradigm shifts. The modern era embraced scientific investigation as a means for classification, witnessed nativist responses to the influx of immigrants to the United States, and saw significant shifts in federal Indian policy from the reservation system to the allotment era and then to the Indian New Deal. Each had an impact on the religious freedom of the Native American people. This work seeks to place the political and legal struggles over Peyotism within the larger historical context to show that despite their minority status in the American religious landscape, Peyotists saw their religion as worthy of constitutional protection and sought to use the American systems to protect their right to practice their specific worship rituals.

This book consists of three parts, each one related to a particular aspect of identity and its relationship to peyote. The chapters proceed in a generally chronological order, though overlaps in the chronological narrative appear, as each section relates to larger themes and historical contexts. A theme running throughout each of the chapters is the politics of identity that appear at the intersection of race and religion, as well as the ability of peyote and Peyotists to cross cultural, economic, political, religious, and social borders.

Part 1 deals with the politics of Peyotist religious identity and focuses on the social construction and meaning of religion, especially in the transition from the reservation to the allotment era. Unlike the earlier works of anthropologists, who focused on the reservation system and the spread of Peyotism, this study places more emphasis on the cultural changes occurring during the allotment era. Chapter 1 traces the emergence of Peyotism as a new Native American religion among some of the peoples on the southern plains, and then examines its rapid spread throughout Indian (later, Oklahoma) Territory and on to the Native peoples of the northern plains and further into the American West. The chapter also deals with the variations in the peyote ceremony that developed as the religion spread. In spite of the differences—including the addition of Christian elements in some cases—Peyotism provided a distinct Native American religious identity. Chapter 2 examines the opposition to the Native American identities associated with the peyote religion. The chapter explores the oppositional stance taken by non–Native American government officials and Protestant Christian missionaries as well as non-Peyotists, specifically those associated with the Society of American Indians due to the prominence of their work and the abundance of sources they created. The tensions between religious freedom for Peyotists and their assimilation into American religious society became noticeable in early attempts to suppress the religious practice.

Part 2 focuses on the politics of racial identity in relation to peyote. This section notes a shift in oppositional strategy against peyote beginning in 1903. Previous attempts at suppression based on the liquor laws governing Indian Country proved ineffective, so opponents began discursively trying to change the meaning of peyote, categorizing it as a narcotic with effects equal to those of opium, cocaine, and marijuana. By secularizing peyote (or turning the "sacred" into the "profane"), federal authorities could begin a full-fledged assault on the religious practice. Chapter 3 focuses on the commercial connection to peyote in the US-Mexican borderlands. Peyote grows in northern Mexico and south Texas in areas around the Rio Grande, and peyote supplies from Mexico were making their way into Indian Country via commercial trading houses in Laredo, Texas, as well as Eagle Pass and El Paso in Texas. Federal officials became alarmed at the "drug" trafficking in peyote and took steps to eradicate the borderlands trade. Chapter 4 turns to the shift in rhetoric that equated peyote with cocaine (primarily associated with Blacks in the South), marijuana (perceived as a problem among Mexicans), and opium (associated with the Chinese), and the ensuing federal congressional legislative efforts to prohibit its use. Attempts to categorize peyote as a drug made efforts to criminalize the religious practice easier to pursue. Yet Peyotists still found ways to resist these efforts by invoking the sacred and religious nature of peyote.

Part 3 investigates the politics of political identity, particularly in relation to the issue of Native American citizenship status and ideas of "Americanness." Chapter 5 examines Peyotists using the framework of the American legal system to advocate for the right to express their religious identity. In doing so, their efforts reveal aspects of a nascent pan-Indian identity developing around organized efforts to protect their right to religious freedom. This chapter also highlights organized lobbying efforts in favor of peyote and the political supporters that Peyotists gained in the cultural battle. Chapter 6 focuses specifically on the 1918 incorporation of the Native American Church in Oklahoma. It investigates the idea of Peyotists utilizing the political and legal discourses in American religious society that are now outlined in the NAC articles of incorporation, specifically the references to "church" and to peyote as a "sacrament."

Historical contexts and positioning factor into identity construction and the politics of identity that ensue, which is why Philip Deloria, in his book *Indians in Unexpected Places*, encourages historical reflection to "situate Native people in relation to their particular historical moment."[20] The controversy around peyote use by some Native Americans reveals new efforts by white Americans to colonize Native peoples, but it also shows the Peyotists' success in resisting these new forms of oppression, as well as their power to form an identity of "Native" and "American" around their religion in the early twentieth century.

NOTES ON TERMINOLOGY

The contentious nature of rhetoric and particularly the linguistic elements of the colonization of Native American peoples require historians to be aware of the power of discourse. Language is "a place of struggle," a place where the oppressed work to "resist colonization, to move from object to subject."[21] In this linguistic struggle over reality, identity, and history, words are not without significance, particularly when "Native Americans have been dominated through an oppressive use of language by the European invaders and settlers."[22] Therefore, I submit the following caveats on the use of language in this book.

NATIVE AMERICAN VERSUS INDIAN. "Native American" is the preferred term, especially when discussing the efforts to create the Native American Church. References to specific tribal identities will also appear when applicable. Occasionally, the term "Indigenous" is used to refer to larger groupings of Native peoples across North America. I do utilize the term "Indian" in direct quotes from contemporary sources as a historical reference for readers. I also use this term to refer to the Anglo government policies that resulted from the colonial experience and are still in use today. This applies as well to the phrase "Indian Country." In 1882, Congress called for clarification of the term "Indian Country" as used in the Revised Statutes and other laws of the United States. A report prepared by the Office of Indian Affairs concluded that the "words 'Indian Country' referred to the portions of the public land allotted to the use and occupation of the Indians."[23] By 1918, when the Native American Church of Oklahoma was incorporated, the term Indian Country" had also been enlarged "so as to include many classes of lands owned or occupied by Indians or located within the exterior boundaries of the reservations," including "any lands owned by Indians individually or as communities, whether allotted or not, Indian settlements, Indian school lands, and Indian pueblos."[24]

RELIGION. Scholars in the field of religious studies may object to my use of the term "religion" when speaking about Native American traditions because of the Eurocentric assumptions attached to this word with its ideological support of colonialism. This, too, shall become a theme addressed in this work to suggest a cross-cultural historical understanding of religion.[25] This work recognizes that religion is also a "category of discourse, whose precise meanings and implications are continually being negotiated in the course of social interaction."[26] Added to the discussion is the hegemonic status of Christianity within American society. The "near equation of Christianity with religion remains a commonplace" in culture, write religious historians Catherine A. Brekus and W. Clark Gilpin. They note, "Christians have infused American society with an extensive repertoire of stories, symbols, and ethical ideals that have been among the defining terms of American cultural debate."[27] Included as well are constructed notions of race, with whiteness as a systemic basis for Christianity in the United States. The hope of attaining white privilege came with a socioreligious requirement of promoting the moral ideals of "Christian citizenship" for a variety of groups—thinking and behaving like a particular version of white Christianity. This idea of "Christian citizenship" also impacted Native Americans at the time of disputes over Peyotism.

PEYOTISM, PEYOTISTS. These terms refer to the Native American religion and its practitioners. As such, my use of the term "Peyotists" only refers to Native Americans. In the sources used in this work that quote Peyotists, male voices are notable, as is reflective of the time period. Some have assumed that women were excluded from the use of peyote and the religious ceremonies because of the absence of female Peyotist voices in direct quotes in the press and in testimonies at state and congressional hearings. Many scholars emphasize that the increased presence of women actively involved in Peyotism came with the expansion of the Native American Church of North America throughout the late 1920s and into the 1930s and with the international charter of the Native American Church in the 1950s. However, evidence does exist that women were involved in Peyotism during the period covered in this book. An early document of surveillance sent to an Indian agent on a reservation in Oklahoma Territory by James Deer (Caddo) on October 2, 1895, contained a list of names of those who came together to "eat mescal [peyote]." While most were men, there were seven women listed: "Mrs. Do-Kish, Mrs. Sam Slick, Mrs. Paul Griffin (former Mrs. Deer), Miss Shawonotty, Mrs. Big Trees, Mrs. Win-you, and Mrs. Billie Bowleg."[28] A newspaper reporter wrote in July 1906 that "six men and three women of the Cheyenne tribe went to Ponca City to introduce the mescal bean feast [peyote ceremony]."[29] Though these references to women at the peyote ceremonies do not explicitly indicate their participation, their presence does imply a connection with Peyotism. Indian agents also began to note women's use of peyote on their reservations.[30] Arthur Bonnicastle (Osage) made a statement in 1915 that was entered into the peyote hearings of 1918, claiming that "in their religious ceremonies, women are allowed to use not over five and the men seven of these peyotes."[31] Finally, James Mooney, the ethnologist studying Peyotism among on the Kiowa-Comanche reservation, testified before Congress in the 1918 hearings on peyote, "I understand that in the tribes that have adopted it, more recently women take part with the men, the result probably of the spread of education."[32]

PART I

THE POLITICS OF RELIGIOUS IDENTITY

1 PEYOTISM

A NEW NATIVE AMERICAN RELIGION

In expressing his opposition to the use of peyote by Native Americans, US representative Harry Gandy of South Dakota referred to these sensory experiential effects of peyote as "creating an artificial paradise for its addicts." He commented to the press, "The lure of the substance lies in its ability to produce beautiful visions, in which there are wonderful sights and sounds, and beautiful colors. . . . Common sounds seem wonderful, so that one note struck on the piano seems like a whole chord . . . but it is the colors constantly coming and going that make the most satisfying and fascinating appeal."[1] Gandy's description of what Peyotists consider a sacred religious experience was antithetical to religion in the opinion of many Protestant Christians. Opposition to the new Native American religion of Peyotism stemmed in part from different approaches to understanding cultural religious practices. By the time Peyotism emerged in the United States in the latter part of the nineteenth century, Christianity's influence throughout Indian Country even led some Indigenous Christians to question the validity of a religious experience aided by the use of peyote. In hearings before Congress in 1918, Chester Y. Arthur (Assiniboine) testified through an interpreter (Gertrude Bonnin), "In our present state of enlightenment, it is very strange that the Bible on which Christianity is based says nothing whatever about peyote."[2] Arthur was an elder in the Presbyterian Church, largely responsible for building the Mni-Sda Presbyterian Church, known as the Chelsea Church, on the Fort Peck Indian Reservation. He was later ordained to the ministry of Word and Sacrament in 1929.[3] Arthur represented a significant population of Native American Christians who lived in the cultural context of religious division between approaches to biblical interpretation, known in religious circles and the popular press as modernism versus fundamentalism. For evangelicals like Arthur who espoused the doctrines of biblical inerrancy and biblical infallibility, the written text of the Bible provided an authoritative worldview on how to live. The importance of a sacred text deemed authored by God over the personal mystical religious experience of a human individual, especially an experience induced by a mind-altering substance, formed a significant paradigm for evaluating Peyotism and its religious value in connecting to the sacred.[4]

For centuries, many Native peoples have known about the usefulness of plants, herbs, and their derivatives to produce altered states of consciousness that connect individuals to a holy or sacred "Other." An encounter with the Divine also has social dimensions consistent with the cosmological worldview of Native peoples, where the elements of the supernatural and the natural world communicate with one another to inform daily life in tribal communities. This broad view of lived reality is a definition of religion for Native Americans.[5] The use of natural botanical substances as an aid to this encounter with a "holy Other" is consistent with Native American views on religious experience, which often stand in contradistinction to Western-centered views of religion that focus on a system of institutionalized beliefs, practices, and written texts and have a narrow conception of religious experience.[6] The dominant Western Protestant version of Christianity tends to view mystical states of consciousness, especially when brought about by the use of mind-altering substances, as suspicious with regard to the validity of the religious experience. Many view the use of these substances (often labelled as "drugs") to obtain a religious experience as concomitant to worshiping the natural world rather than the divine deity emanating from the Bible-based religion preached in Western churches.[7] The failure of many Euro-American Christians to accept the differences between the metaphysical schemes of the two cultures continues to marginalize the significance of this "lived religion" for members of the Native American Church.

Entheogens—literally signifying "God-containing" or "God-enabling"—are natural substances considered sacred by many cultures that are taken within the context of a religious ceremony to enable a person to tap into another state of consciousness to experience God.[8] A misunderstanding of entheogens and their ability to contribute to authentic religious experience comes from a dichotomous worldview categorization between sacred and profane, which has become the hallmark of Western religious thought. The dismissal of the significance of entheogens into the realm of "profane" comes from a cultural misinterpretation of their sacred nature. For Native

Dried peyote cactus and buttons prepared for ingestion. Photograph from *Annual Report of the Bureau of American Ethnology to the Secretary of the Smithsonian Institution* (Washington, DC: Government Printing Office, 1895).

Americans, entheogens function as mediators between the mind and the environment, serving as a tool to communicate with the Divine, thus blending the realms of the sacred and profane. The substances have the power to defy the division between the physical and the spiritual worlds, thus allowing an individual to experience a sacred perception of reality through a direct participation with the Divine.

Peyote, a small, spineless cactus that grows exclusively in areas along the US-Mexican border around the Rio Grande, is one such entheogen for Native Americans. The cactus produces small "buttons" on its top, which are ingested in either their green or dried state. The buttons contain some psychoactive alkaloids, and foremost among these is mescaline, which produces a feeling of immobility from a slowing of the pulse rate that leads to a sense of serenity. A range of different visual effects can also result in response to the chemical in the cactus.[9] Another effect of peyote is a state of synesthesia, a phenomenological experience where sensory information from unrelated senses is rerouted by the brain so that one might hear color or see sound. Religious studies professor Robert C. Fuller notes that in a spiritual dialectic with the "Ineffable Other," the participants in a peyote ceremony "see visions that speak, feel words that comfort, and even taste their surroundings. This phenomenal experience, commonly referred to as synesthesia, feels absolutely *authentic* (as opposed to hallucinatory) for those undergoing the event."[10] There is, according to Christopher Vecsey, a scholar of religion and Native American studies, "the feeling in using peyote of being taken over, overwhelmed by a force greater than oneself, or receiving power directly and personally from something grand.... Peyote use triggers religious experience, a perceived contact with an awe-inspiring holiness."[11]

As appealing as the effects of peyote may sound, the means to achieve them are not always as pleasant. The peyote button has an exceedingly bitter taste, and, when eaten or brewed into an infusion of peyote tea and drunk, it produces a sour taste that can be nauseating.[12] Vomiting is common with the ingestion of peyote; in fact, participants in the religious ceremony often carry a cup or a can because this also became part of the religious practice, as it was considered a way for a person to rid himself or herself of poisons, both physical and spiritual, another distinctive cultural worldview related to the concept of religious experience.[13] Regarded as a sacred medicine with healing powers, the use of peyote by Native Americans conveys a broader understanding of theological concepts. Healing is not just a release from physical symptoms, but more importantly, healing means the ability to accept one's life and circumstances and find ways to readjust one's attitude to embrace happiness and hope.[14] Peyotist Paul Boynton (Southern Arapaho) testified to this at the 1918 congressional hearings: "I could see that there was something greater than the medicine itself. I saw that God planted the herb that I was using so I says, 'I am going to use God's herb.... I am going to take God's blessing.'... It [peyote] cures sin, spiritually."[15] The reverence for the peyote cactus as a gift of the Creator became an important expression of Native American religious identity in the various forms of peyote ceremonial practice that emerged among many of the Plains tribes in the late nineteenth and early twentieth centuries. However, a clash of cultures would begin to challenge the Native American interpretation of sacred religious practice concerning the use of peyote.

The medicinal and religious use of peyote had been commonplace among various Indigenous tribes in Mexico for centuries, but only came into regular use by Native peoples in the United States sometime prior to the 1880s. It was only in the 1880s that Indian agents working on the reservations became aware of the use of peyote and the spread of a religious ceremony around its use. Once Peyotism—a Native American religion based on the ritual consumption of peyote—emerged among the tribes of the southern plains, it quickly spread to others throughout the Oklahoma and Indian

Territories, making Oklahoma the "cradle of Peyotism," so dubbed because of the large concentration of peyote practitioners within the borders of its territory. Quickly though, the peyote religion spread northward and westward through intertribal visits. The introduction of a new Native American religion brought ritual changes from the ceremonies in Mexico. Though not adopted on a widespread basis among all Native peoples, the rapid diffusion of the religious practice brought different varieties of peyote ceremonial practices, although the foundational use of peyote provided the basis for Peyotism to become a pan-Indian religion.

A multitude of changes affecting Native peoples coincided with the rise of Peyotism during the latter part of the nineteenth century. Following the Civil War, many Americans believed that a concentrated federal effort to "win the West" for white settlers might help restore a sense of national unity to recover from the brutal effects of division that still remained following the war.[16] Unfortunately, progress toward this end meant the continued disruption of the Native American peoples who already inhabited the American West and their cultures. The continual question, "What will become of the Indian?" led reformers and federal officials to enact policies to transform Native people into American Indians or Indian Americans, another racial identity subsumed by a larger American identity.[17] Thus began a sustained federal policy to reconstruct Native Americans in the image of white American citizens. Reservations were to serve as a holding location and training ground in the journey to assimilate Native Americans into the dominant mainstream society. Federal efforts to transform the younger generation of Native Americans came in 1879 with the opening of the first off-reservation boarding school, a policy that continued into the twentieth century that aimed to save Native peoples by destroying their Native cultural identity. The government hoped to do the same with the older generation of Indians through the implementation of the Dawes Allotment Act in 1887, a policy designed to dismantle the reservations and tribes and promote individual ownership of land accompanied by American citizenship status.[18] The conversion of the Native person into an American would require an erasure of the vestiges of the former life that impeded progress into the modern life, which included religious practices not consistent with white Christianity.[19] In 1883, the Office of Indian Affairs established the Court of Indian Offenses to eliminate various cultural and religious practices of Indians. The implementation of a Religious Crimes Code specifically prohibited certain rituals such as the Sun Dance (a ceremony of renewal and cleansing involving a test of pain and sacrifice by piercing the skin with skewers and attempting to dance while bound to a pole) and the giveaway (a practice of Indigenous abundance where personal possessions are shared with others in the community). Agents of the government could use forceful means, such as imprisonment or withholding rations, to stop any Native American religious practice that they deemed immoral, resistive to government authority, or that became a hinderance to the acceptance of white civilization.[20] Federal efforts to eliminate the Ghost Dance, another new Native American religion of the late nineteenth century, resulted in the 1890 massacre of Lakota practitioners at Wounded Knee. Peyotism also became a religious practice targeted for eradication by the dominant culture. Yet despite efforts to rid the Native Americans of their Indigenous identity, they found ways to resist and continued to practice cultural and religious ceremonies deemed important to them.

The story of the advent and rapid spread of Peyotism is an important part of the history of American religion. Yet many scholars of American religious history frequently fail to add Peyotism to the pantheon of new and innovative religious movements appearing in the nineteenth and early twentieth centuries and instead relegate its significance to the field of Native American history, due in large part to its uniqueness as a Native American religion.[21] Even with a Western emphasis on the institutionalization of religion, the 1918 incorporation of the Native American Church often fails to be included in the accounting of other denominational histories. This chapter demonstrates how Peyotism fits into the larger scholarly assessments of religion, especially in the study of American religious history.

A NATIVE AMERICAN RELIGION FROM MEXICO CROSSES THE BORDER

When ethnologist James Mooney began his study of Peyotism among the Kiowa and Comanche in the late nineteenth century, he traced the roots of the religious practice to the pre-Columbian Indigenous peoples of what is now northern and central Mexico.[22] Further anthropological and archaeological work has confirmed the pre-Columbian use of peyote. In ancient sites along the Rio Grande, archaeologists have found peyote tops and dried peyote buttons strung together on a cord to wear as a necklace that date to 5000 BCE. Rock art from cave shelters in the Lower Pecos Canyonlands of Texas reveal images interpreted to be representations of peyote experiences and beliefs, and archeologists date these rock paintings to be 2,950–4,200 years old. The discovery of similar imagery found in other locations such as Oaxaca, Mexico, date to 400–200 BCE.[23] Early textual documentation concerning peyote use in the Spanish borderlands also exists.

At the time of European contact with Indigenous cultures in what is now Mexico, the Spanish encountered a Native pharmacopeia of plants used for both medicinal and spiritual purposes. Spanish clergy and chroniclers took note of peyote—called *peyotl* in Nahuatl—and documented its extensive use by Indigenous peoples.[24] The earliest reference to peyote came from the writings of Franciscan missionary Bernardino de Sahagún who began conducting research into Indigenous cultures in the 1540s, which he compiled into the *Historia general de las cosas de la Nueva España* (General history of the things of New Spain).[25] Sahagún wrote that "it was the Chichimeca Indians of the north who first discovered the properties" of peyotl, and that "those who eat or drink it see visions either frightful or laughable." The Native peoples believed that the plant "protects them from all danger."[26] An Indigenous doctor at Tlatelolco named Martín de la Cruz made an explicit claim in 1552 that peyote posed no harm to its users and advocated the use of "indigenous *yerbas* ('grasses' or 'herb,' a category that generally includes peyote) as powerful healing tools."[27] Francisco Hernández de Toledo, a naturalist and court physician to King Philip II, embarked on a mission to New Spain in 1570 to study the region's medicinal plants and animals. For seven years, Hernández gathered information throughout the Valley of Mexico, learning Nahuatl, recording local medical customs, studying Indigenous medicines, and writing down all his observations. In his comments on the use of peyote, he wrote, "Ground up and applied to painful joints it is said to give relief. Wonderful properties are attributed to this root (if any faith can be given to what is commonly said among them on this point)."[28] Others would also write about the medicinal benefits of peyote, but the religious teachings of the Catholic Church would soon grow stronger in their opposition to the use of peyote. In 1591, Juan de Cárdenas listed peyote as one of several fantastic yerbas in his taxonomy of the New World. However, Cárdenas also saw a nefarious side to such substances used by "foolish and stupid people." Peyote "allowed those who took it to lose their inhibitions, caused them to see demons and to believe that they could speak with the Devil, and divine the future."[29] The Catholic Church's construction of peyote as an agent of evil allowed Church officials (acting as agents of the nation-state) to take steps to eradicate its use by Native peoples as part of a systematic policy to Christianize and conquer.

Catholic priests denounced peyote as *una raíz diabolica* (a diabolic root) that served as an agent of the devil to keep the new Christian converts from embracing their total allegiance to the church. Ironically, this is the same claim that later would be made by Protestant missionaries in the United States in their efforts to stamp out peyote use among Native Americans.[30] The early Catholic missionaries opposed peyote because of its connection with what they perceived to be superstitious and pagan religious practices, not because of any health benefits derived from its use.[31] The constructed division between legitimate and illegitimate religiosity made by those in positions of power contributed to a religious campaign to reinforce a caste system that organized Spanish rule in the Americas.[32] The ultimate expression of the Church working to impose colonial rule on subjects of the state was the use of Church pronouncements and Inquisition hearings to enforce the decrees against peyote use. In 1571, Spaniards introduced the Inquisition into Mexico. The functions of the Holy Office included not only the punishment of perceived heretical beliefs and practices deemed contrary to Catholic teachings, but also included the power to police all behaviors of daily life to meet the responsibility to care for the moral ethics of the community within the larger nation-state enterprise.[33] Concerned that the use of peyote was spreading to other racial populations in colonial Mexico, Church officials classified peyote as a heresy against the Holy Catholic Faith in the interest of the public welfare.

The decision to ban peyote came in 1620 with an official edict issued by the Inquisitors. The edict declared peyote use an act of superstition over and against the sacredness and holiness of the Catholic faith. The Inquisitors connected the use of peyote to "the Devil, the real author of this vice, who first avails himself of the natural credulity of the Indians and their tendency to idolatry" and cautioned other racial groups, denouncing the potential spread of peyote to "many other persons too little disposed to fear God and of very little faith."[34] While the Inquisition lacked legal authority to go after Indigenous Peyotists because Native peoples (*Indios*) were placed in a distinct legal category protecting them from prosecution in colonial Mexico, the power of the Inquisitors was able to curb the use of peyote among non-Indigenous groups and to signal the Church's general dissatisfaction with peyote use.[35] The edict, along with many documented Inquisition hearings throughout Mexico, demonstrates the seriousness of the Church's commitment to eliminate the use of peyote.[36] It also shows the power of the Spanish Empire, as the Spanish began to impose their cultural and religious values on Indigenous peoples through the establishment of settler colonialism.

The Inquisition's fear of the contagious aspect of peyote spoke to the dualistic nature of the sacred and the profane, specifically in "the transmission of indigenous things into nonindigenous realms," according to historian Alexander S. Dawson.[37] After the 1620 edict of the Holy Office, peyote use, or even the mere mention of the substance, would be criminalized with a variety of degrees of punishable offenses.[38] Father Bartholome Garcia even developed a catechism for use by missionaries serving the peoples of San Antonio and other locales in the Rio Grande area, which asked the penitents, "Has comido el peyote?" (Have you eaten peyote?) as part of the confessional act.[39] Yet, despite the Church's attempts to suppress peyote, its use continued to flourish, and in some areas it even syncretized with Catholic religious practices, as evidenced particularly by the Christian Tarahumara Indians who would make the sign of the cross in the presence of their sacred peyote cactus.[40]

Anthropologists have traced the use of peyote in early Mexico to a variety of peoples. Indigenous peoples attributed to this divine plant sacred powers for healing, wholeness, the purification of mind, body, and spirit, and protection against instances of sorcery.[41] The Huichols, or Wixáritari people, are the most studied Native group outside of North America in regards to their relationship to peyote. Historians such as Thomas Maroukis claim the Huichols "have the strongest pre-Columbian spiritual practices of any Indigenous group in Mexico," with their current practices remaining very similar to peyote rituals described in the sixteenth century.[42] Today, some Cora, Tepehuano, and Tarahumara still use peyote, but only the Huichol Peyotists continue to make an annual pilgrimage to the peyote desert in the San Luis Potosí as part of their religious practice.[43]

The Huichol's "peyote hunt," a key part of their sacred peyote ceremony, is an annual pilgrimage under the direction of a *mara'akame*, a guide or medicine person (both genders can assume the role), who has a special relation with the peyote, or *hikuri* as it is known to the Huichol people. Participants prepare for the pilgrimage with rituals of confession and purification, and throughout the peyote hunt they must be celibate and remain humble. Under the mara'akame's direction, the Huichols collect peyote and ritually ingest it in a ceremony around a fire. Visions from peyote's use are to be enjoyed, but only the visions given by the mara'akame are considered important for guidance.[44] It seems that the authority of the office or role carries significant weight for religious purposes. Carl Lumholtz, a Norwegian ethnologist, conducted expeditions in Mexico from 1890 to 1910 (financed by the American Museum of Natural History), and he wrote of both the Huichol and Tarahumara cultures, including their ritual use of peyote. He noted similar performative functions of their peyote ceremonies, including the sacred pilgrimage to harvest peyote, the importance of the ceremony around a fire, and the role of the spiritual leader in the ritual. Another feature of the peyote rite among the Mexican practitioners was the importance of dancing. In his account of the Tarahumara ceremony, Lumholtz recorded, "The night is passed in dancing. . . . The [peyote] feast consists mainly in dancing, which, of course, is followed by eating and drinking."[45] The elements of the peyote ceremony in Mexico addressed here are significant because, as the religious complex migrated across the border to Native Americans in the United States, these features either transformed or disappeared entirely in the creation of an Americanized version of Peyotism.

Peyote usage in nineteenth-century Mexico began to decline as cultural and political changes swept across the region. After achieving independence from Spain in 1821, Mexico soon became embroiled in conflicts with the United States, resulting in changes to the landscape. The war with Texas in the 1830s brought loss of land in the northeastern part of the country, with additional land losses resulting from the 1848 US-Mexican War. The 1860s brought another war for Mexico, this time with France, as the latter attempted to usurp the country's sovereignty.[46] Although Mexico was successful in its resistance, the following period left the country vulnerable to internal political strife, which culminated in the beginning of the Mexican Revolution in 1910. The significant expansion of a national identity in Mexico during the nineteenth century often came at the expense of Indigenous cultures. Catholicism also continued to expand and became the dominant religious identity of many Native peoples. Peyote use continued to some extent as an important folk remedy for physical healing, but ceremonial usage only continued in the more remote areas among a small number of tribes.[47] The American imperial expansion into northeastern Mexico in the nineteenth century also corresponded with the Comanche Indians' expansionist desires on the southern plains. In his book *The Comanche Empire*, Pekka Hämäläinen writes that the Comanches were also "powerful actors who had the capacity to remake societies and reshape histories," and they built an imperial Comanchería empire on the plains that remained until after the American Civil War.[48] Contact and relationships with the Comanches and other tribes integrated into their alliance (as well as Native Americans who the Comanches considered enemies) led to the dissemination of Peyotism in the United States in the latter part of the nineteenth century.

Anthropologists have studied Peyotism extensively in an attempt to identify the specific tribe responsible for its importation into the United States, but conclusive evidence to trace the Mexican-American connection remains elusive. Most scholars narrow the choices of potential tribes as the transnational cultural conduits for the religious practice to those peoples living close to the border before their resettlement onto reservations—the Carrizo, Lipan Apache, Mescalero Apache, Tonkawa, Karankawa, and Caddo—as well as those who had extensive contact with Indigenous peoples in Mexico through raids and trade—the Kiowa, Comanche, and Kiowa-Apache. However, the network of diffusion varies among anthropological studies and among Native Americans themselves in their tribal stories and histories.[49] Ethnographical work tends to view the borderlands connection as beginning with the Carrizos then spreading to the Lipan Apaches, who brought it to the tribes in Oklahoma.[50] However, the fascination of previous anthropological histories of peyote with identifying which tribe brought peyote over the border and into the United States results from a nationalistic approach to viewing the diffusion of Peyotism. Peyote possesses no nationality as it grows on both sides of what has become the international boundary line between Mexico and the United States. Additionally, the fluidity of the early border between the two nation-states would have aided the transnational dissemination of the religious practice. The demarcation of the international border did factor into the cultural contestation over peyote once it began to spread throughout the western United States.

The introduction of Peyotism into Native American tribes in the United States coincided with cultural changes also affecting Indigenous populations. Just as Mexico underwent political changes impacting Mexican national identity, so, too, did the United States encourage an American national identity extending into the West in order to reunite the nation in the aftermath of the Civil War. Unfortunately, the imperial identity of white Americans frequently conflicted with Native cultural identities. In seeking to preserve those cultural identities, Native peoples often found themselves in violent conflict with US military forces. Federal officials resolved to solve the so-called "Indian problem" in 1851 by expanding the concentration policy of moving Indians onto reservations.[51] Alterations to Native Americans' ways of living through the slaughter of buffalo and military pressure eventually made it necessary for them to move onto government-designated lands to survive, much of it in Indian Territory (including present-day Oklahoma). Peyotism accompanied some of the Native American tribes to the reservations in Indian Territory, and with a wide variety of Native peoples living in close proximity to one another, the religion spread quickly. The attempts to "Americanize" Native Americans also contributed to a new form of religious worship involving the use of peyote. The irony of the reservation system imposed upon Native Americans by whites was that it contributed to the transmission of Peyotism, as Indigenous peoples were brought into closer contact with each other through decreased distances for intertribal visitations.[52] A 1922 government report on peyote revealed that the religion went "from one reservation to another by visiting Indians whose principal object is to pass along something new, something of interest."[53] Modern technology also contributed to its rapid expansion when Native Americans took advantage of the railroad, and later automobiles, to attend intertribal gatherings; in short, the "civilized" use of technology assisted the pan-Indian development of Peyotism.

A NEW NATIVE AMERICAN RELIGION EMERGES

The popularity of Peyotism among some tribes in the United States began in Oklahoma, but the religion quickly spread to Native Americans living in other states. The religious ceremony around the use of peyote changed as it moved north of the international border, a jurisdictional divide constructed by nation-states and bounded by lines on a map. Native Americans transformed the religious ritual from that practiced in Mexico to suit the unique transformations of their own culture taking place in the American West. Innovative modifications to Native American peyote ceremonies took place in the US development of Peyotism throughout the late nineteenth and early twentieth centuries. Many Peyotists continued to participate in other religious traditions simultaneously with Peyotism—both other Native American religious practices such as the Sun Dance and the Ghost Dance as well as Christian denominational affiliations. However, even the addition of Christian theological beliefs and practices to the peyote ceremony often reflected an Indigenous Christianity.

The development of US Native American versions of Peyotism began in Oklahoma among the Comanche, Kiowa, and Kiowa-Apache, who lived on reservation land established on October 21, 1867. Federal officials first noted and reported on the use of peyote in 1886 when Indian agent J. Lee Hall informed the Office of Indian Affairs that "the Comanches and a few of the Kiowas secure the tops of a kind of cactus that comes from Mexico, which they eat, and it produces the same effect as opium.... The Comanches call it wo-co-wist."[54] However, the use of peyote by the Comanche, Kiowa, and Kiowa-Apache had gone unnoticed by whites for many years prior to this official report. Quanah Parker testified before the Oklahoma state legislature in 1908 that the Comanches had used peyote for fifty years, which would put the date around 1858, and that he had been using peyote for the last forty years.[55] The familiarity of peyote to the Comanche and Kiowa came, no doubt, from their pre-reservation time of raids through Texas to the border of Mexico, where the plant grows naturally.[56] Credit for the source of the modern peyote ceremony that emerged in Oklahoma goes to two Lipan Apaches named Chiwat and Pinero who married Comanche women and lived among the Comanches in the late 1870s.[57]

The shared reservation space inevitably meant the spread of the religion among those tribal groupings, but the proximity of the reservation to other Native peoples assigned to reservation lands produced an even greater distribution of Peyotism. Though it is difficult to determine its precise chronological diffusion through Oklahoma, anthropological work done on specific tribes can offer insights into the timing and extent of Peyotism's circulation. Between 1880 and 1900, some members,

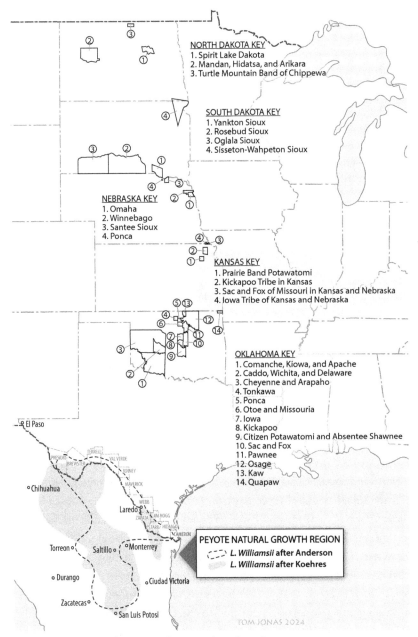

Peyote's natural-growth region and its spread northward

27

though not the majority, of the following tribes adopted the religion as part of their cultural tradition: Southern Cheyenne, Southern Arapaho, Wichita, Caddo, Delaware, Quapaw, Osage, Tonkawa, Kaw, Otoe-Missouria, Ponca, Pawnee, Iowa, Sac and Fox, Kickapoo, Citizen Potawatomi, Shawnee, Absentee Shawnee, and Seneca-Cayuga.[58] Ironically, the greatest numbers of Native Americans living in Indian Territory (Oklahoma) were members of the relocated Five Southeast Tribes—the Cherokee, Chickasaw, Choctaw, Muscogee (Creek), and Seminole, who had been the first to relocate to Indian Territory in the 1830s—yet relatively few of these tribal members adopted Peyotism. While these larger Native American nations did not practice Peyotism, little evidence indicates they opposed the religion. In fact, peyote's greatest legislative supporters came from mixed-blood members of the southeast tribes who were elected to both the Oklahoma state legislature and to Congress. Yet because of the tribal affiliations of many practicing Peyotists, the religion developed an association of affinity with the "blanket tribes" in Oklahoma.[59] Despite this moniker, the importance of Peyotism for some Native Americans led ethnologist James Mooney to testify of its close connection with Native American life, which is why he chose to go to Oklahoma to study the religion.[60] Just as the borders of the reservation lands could not stop the spread of this new Native American religion, neither could the border of the state.

Peyotism quickly spread throughout the American West. By 1914, the Kansas tribes of Sac and Fox, Prairie Potawatomi, Kickapoo, and Iowa, who lived on adjoining reservations in the northeastern corner of the state, had members who adopted the religion, as did some Winnebago of Nebraska and Wisconsin, Omaha of Nebraska, Fox of Iowa, Menominee of Wisconsin, Chippewa (or Ojibwe) of Minnesota and North Dakota, Northern Ponca of Nebraska, Sioux (Lakota, Dakota, and Nakota) of North and South Dakota, Northern Cheyenne and Crow of Montana, Northern Arapaho and Shoshone of Wyoming, Ute of Colorado and Utah, and Taos of New Mexico. It was not until 1929 that Peyotism came to the Indians living in the Far West, where it emerged among a minority group of Gosiute (or Goshute) and Shoshone of the western Great Basin, Washo, and Northern Paiute. Sometime in the 1930s, the religion reached the Navajo, the largest tribe in the United States. The acceptance of Peyotism by the Southern Paiute and by Native American tribes located in the state of Washington would not occur until the latter part of the twentieth century. Within a span of fifty years, Peyotism became an important part of the religious culture of many Native peoples throughout the American West.[61]

When the peyote religion emerged in the United States, the religious practice began to deviate from its Mexican origins. A different form of the peyote ceremony first appeared among the Kiowa and Comanche in Oklahoma in the mid-1870s, and this ceremony formed the basis of the new Native American religion.[62] There were, however, some similarities between the peyote ceremony that developed on the southern plains and its Mexican precursor, with the retention of some of the elements involved in the worship service. Daniel C. Swan, a cultural anthropologist and museum curator, observed that Native Americans also made use of "drums and rattles, ritual corn-husk cigarettes, fire and incense as cleansing agents, meat and corn as ceremonial foods, and most importantly, peyote."[63] Ethnologists have also noted a parallel in the sacredness of the number four—a dedication to the four directions common among Peyotists, beginning with the Huichols, who shot four arrows over the first peyote they found on their annual pilgrimage. Water, also considered a sacred element, played a key role in the cultural context of the ceremony across borders. The Huichol Peyotists also practiced an all-night ceremony around a fire, and a designated peyote feast followed the end of the ritual.[64] Despite these commonalities, the differences between the Mexican and American peyote ceremonies are significant enough to conclude that Peyotism in the United States was a manifestation of a new religious practice.

One change made to the Native American ceremony in the United States brought a shift in the leader-based practice of medicine. The ceremony practiced in Mexico remained in control of the spiritual leader, who directed the experience of the participants and provided meaningful visions for the community. The adaptation of Peyotism by the Kiowa-Comanche in Oklahoma, according to Robert Fuller, shifted the focus from the spiritual leader "to every participant's quest for power. Doctoring was still an important feature but was subordinated to the more general goal of enabling individuals to seek blessing and prosperity through establishing harmony with supernatural power."[65] The ritual leader of the ceremony became the "roadman," though no claim of spiritual power was associated with this position, as the peyote itself served as the repository of power from the Creator. Peyote transposed the traditional ritual hierarchy found in most Indigenous cultures by replacing it with a religion of egalitarianism. Those who in the past had to go through a spiritual medium to gain divine insight into their lives and heal various ailments could now attain spiritual introspection and healing without any intermediary.[66] Within the context of ritual practice, in Mexico only the leader sang during the ceremony, whereas on the southern plains all participants had opportunities to sing and offer prayers.[67]

Another significant change to the Native American peyote ceremony was the elimination of dancing in exchange for a contemplative form of communication with the Divine through music, quiet meditation, and prayer that involved sitting through the all-night ceremony.[68] Dancing was a prominent part of the ceremony in Mexico but disappeared entirely in the Native American peyote ceremonies on the US side of the border.[69] This was a notable cultural shift according to anthropologist Thomas W. Kavanaugh, because music and dance were "integral parts of the social and cultural life of the native peoples of the Southern Plains" and represented "the dynamic and creative expressions of Indian identity and pride, both for individuals and communities."[70] Yet, Peyotists were willing to give up this aspect of cultural identity and adapt the ceremony to new social realities. During the reservation era, the Indian Office vigorously opposed Native American rituals as elements of an uncivilized culture and targeted dances specifically in light of that view.[71] Reports of Indian agents and missionaries included in the yearly report of the commissioner of Indian Affairs contain numerous incidents of dances taking place on the reservations, often accompanied by a judgment of contempt for the practice.[72] Native Americans on the reservations were well aware of the increased state surveillance scrutinizing them and their cultural practices. The substitution of dancing for contemplative meditation reflected a strategy to avoid the panoptical gaze of white reformers.

Likewise, a similar explanation accounts for the Peyotists' choice to hold their peyote meetings in a tepee instead of the open-air environment for worship that often accompanied dances. In Mexico, the peyote ritual took place yearly in an outdoor patio setting where participants gathered in a square formation.[73] The transition to the tepee by the Plains Indians meant a circular formation for a smaller gathering of participants, which also contributed to an increased frequency of peyote meetings to accommodate all who wanted to take part in the ritual. Whether intentional or not, the relocation of the ceremony to an indoor setting provided more cover from the watchful eyes of white agents and missionaries.

By the 1880s, a standardized ceremonial structure developed for Peyotism as the religion spread. Core elements of a homogenized ritual that began with Kiowa-Comanche Peyotists included common practices in an order of worship, designated roles of service in the ceremony, and accompanying ritual paraphernalia. The ceremony usually took place on Saturday night, but not necessarily on consecutive weekends.[74] Some, like anthropologist James Mooney, even speculated that Peyotists selected Saturday night for their all-night peyote ceremony "in deference to the white man's idea of Sunday as a sacred day and day of rest."[75] When a member of the community called for a peyote meeting, they erected a tepee for the ceremony and transformed a mound of dirt inside, near the center, into an altar space for the peyote. The sponsors who asked for a meeting were responsible for the financial costs of the peyote and meals. They also assisted with other practical preparations for the meeting.[76] Before the ceremony began, the necessary supplies of wood for the fire, water, drums, gourd rattles, cedar, and peyote buttons were gathered. Food for the feast held at the dispersal of the ceremony was also prepared. The ceremony began around nine o'clock at night as participants entered the tepee and sat in a circle around the fire. The order and content of a peyote ceremony varied from tribe to tribe.[77] However, the basic ceremonial structure included a pattern of burning cedar incense, consuming peyote, and rounds of singing and praying. At midnight, there was a pause in the service to stand and walk around. When the service resumed, there was a ritual for the consumption of water, followed by the burning of cedar, the consumption of more peyote, and then the ritual pattern of song and prayer began again and continued until dawn.[78]

In addition to the roadman, the chief official responsible for conducting the peyote service, there were other officials who assisted in guiding the ceremony. Other principal roles included the drum chief, who accompanied the singing; the fire chief, who tended the fire through the all-night ritual; and the morning water woman, who brought blessed water into the meeting at dawn along with a breakfast of corn, fruit, and meat. The role of the morning water woman fits well with many of the tribes' mythic origin stories of "Peyote Woman," who was the first person chosen by the Creator to receive the gift of peyote. James Mooney recorded the oral tradition of the origin of peyote as conveyed to him in 1897 by his Kiowa informant, Gaapiatan (meaning, "The man who strikes with a feathered lance"; he also had a Comanche name, Haitsiki).[79] Mooney was told the story of two young brothers who went out on the warpath but did not return. Their sister assumed they were dead and went into the mountains to mourn for them. As she fell asleep that night, she heard a voice in a dream saying her brothers were still alive. The voice also told her that when she awoke, she would encounter something that would help her. She found a peyote plant and took it home with her. After she told the elders what had happened, they erected a tepee with a crescent-shaped mound inside, following the directions given to her in the dream. The people prayed, sang, and ate the peyote, which had miraculously multiplied. During the ceremony, the people envisioned the two brothers still alive and sent out a rescue party to find them. The people continued to eat peyote and honor the "Peyote Woman."[80] Mooney later learned that this was the core story of peyote's beginnings shared by many Plains Indian tribes. Though the origin stories had variations among the tribes who adopted Peyotism, Mooney noted that "certain consistent themes emerged: someone lost (usually a woman) who experiences spiritual distress, hunger, and thirst and finds physical and spiritual comfort through peyote personified." As Peyotism developed, "the woman came to be represented by the Morning Water Woman" who brought the sacred water and food to the participants.[81] However, the similarity in the basic structure and content of the peyote service among its varied tribal practitioners did not mean uniformity in the expression of their religious beliefs.

All forms of organized religion are subject to transmutations as individuals live their religious beliefs and practices and use religion as a way to make meaning for their lives. As an organized religion centered around a core ritual complex, Peyotism also underwent alterations in its conceptual views concerning religious experiences, and soon varieties of peyote experiences emerged around influential Peyotist leaders. The original Kiowa-Comanche peyote ceremony, advocated by influential figures like Quanah Parker, came to be known as the "Half Moon" or "Little Moon" ceremony, so named for the raised, crescent-shaped mound that served as the ceremonial altar. The open end of the tepee faced east, and the mound sat near the western end of the structure. A large Chief Peyote button (also called Grandfather Peyote) rested in the center of the mound and remained there all night. The ritual elements of the Half Moon Way were uniquely Native American in their religious identity. However, the pan-Indian appeal of Peyotism soon allowed for the incorporation of other religious identities in the ceremony, especially the representation of a variety of Christian views.

Around 1880, a Caddo-Delaware medicine man named John Wilson became familiar with Peyotism and introduced variations to the peyote ceremony that differed from the Half Moon ceremony. Wilson elongated the arms of the crescent altar, making it more horseshoe-shaped, and added a small dirt mound east of the fire to represent the sun, leading to the identification of his variation as the "Big Moon" ceremony. A straight east-west line ran from the entrance of the tepee to the peyote on the altar. This line intersected with a line running from north to south to create a cross.[82] John Wilson also added new songs to the ritual and concrete ethical teachings preaching abstinence from alcohol and gambling, as well as greatly reducing the role of tobacco in the service. His inclusion of Christian symbolism in the peyote ceremony appealed to many who soon became converts to Wilson's Big Moon ceremony, particularly Peyotists among the Delaware, Osage, Wichita, Winnebago, Kickapoo, Omaha, and Potawatomi.[83]

Other Peyotists continued to make changes to the peyote ceremony that reflected their religious worldviews. With the spread of Peyotism to the northern plains, a Winnebago named John Rave continued to modify the Big Moon ceremony with the overt addition of Christian symbols and meaning. His peyote ritual, the "Cross Fire" ceremony, became more recognizable by Native American Christians, and whites often referred to it as the "Indian form of Christianity."[84] The Cross Fire ceremony banned the use of tobacco by participants and continued the addition of preaching and exhortation in the meetings. According to Robert Hall's 1918 report on peyote, Rave added a peyote baptism for a new convert, where he dipped his hand in a "dilute infusion of peyote and rubbed it across the forehead of a new member, saying, 'I baptize thee in the name of God, the Son, and the Holy Ghost, which is called God's Holiness.'"[85] Christian texts and language also characterized many of the songs in the peyote ceremony. An entirely new element added by Winnebago Peyotists was the presence of the Bible in the peyote service. In the Cross Fire ceremony, Chief Peyote is placed directly on an open Bible displayed on the altar. Credit for this material change in the arrangement of the altar space goes to Winnebago Peyotist Albert Hensley, who "posited the dogma that the peyote opened the Bible to the understanding of the people."[86] Interestingly, around 1911, a schism developed between Rave and Hensley and Hensley withdrew from the original group of Winnebago Peyotists. The differences between the two men centered on the function of the peyote ceremony. A 1914 article revealed that "Rave believed primarily in the use of [peyote] for its curative purposes, and Hensley, apparently, for its application to religious exhortation."[87] Despite the differences in Winnebago Peyotism, since about 1900 the Christianized Cross Fire peyote ceremony has also been adopted by some Peyotists of Chippewa, Menominee, Sioux (Lakota, Dakota, Nakota), Shoshone, Ute, Gosiute (or Goshute), and Navajo tribal affiliations.[88] The alterations of the peyote ceremony demonstrated the hybridity of religious worldviews that could make Peyotism attractive, allowing adherents to further modify elements of the service to express their unique tribal cosmology. For example, the Osage leader Black Dog II, who began practicing Wilson's Big Moon Peyotism, placed Osage symbols of the morning star on the peyote altar and drew lightning symbols on its apron. According to Willard Hughes Rollings's historical account of the Osage people, Black Dog II also "turned the altar to face the west, unlike all other Peyote altars that faced east. Black Dog insisted that an Osage could not look east for spiritual direction, but must look west where the sun was leading, not where it had been."[89] The "Navajo V-way" ceremony takes place in a hogan structure that is hexagonal and constructed of logs. The ceremonial space has a much less elaborate altar for the peyote and uses hot coals and ashes in a V-shaped arrangement rather than a fire within the room. This ceremony also emphasizes an individualized confession of one's sins to a greater extent than the Big Moon ritual.[90]

No matter what form the peyote ritual took, the ceremony was an honest and reverent religious expression where the use of peyote was for religious and physical healing purposes.[91] The varieties of peyote experience that emerged in the late nineteenth and early twentieth centuries reflected a new Native American way of expressing one's spiritual existence at a time when significant cultural shifts were taking place. In 1918, all the variations of Peyotism came to exist within the umbrella of the Native American Church, emphasizing the pan-Indian appeal of this new Native American religion.

CONTROVERSY DEVELOPS OVER PEYOTISM AS A RELIGION

As Indian Affairs officials and social reformers became aware of the popularity and spread of the new religion among some Native Americans, conflicts emerged in the early twentieth century over the appropriateness of using peyote in a religious setting. Concerns about Peyotism reflected the desire to bring Native Americans into the modern era through the enactment of the allotment policy in 1887, which promised eventual citizenship status to those who accepted the individual allotments of land and eschewed tribal relationships. Government officials viewed Peyotism as a vestige of tribal ways that prevented Native Americans from fully assimilating into an Americanized way of life. Additionally, Indian officials in the early twentieth century recalled the rise and popularity of the Ghost Dance religion from the latter part of the nineteenth century and governmental attempts to eradicate it, which resulted in the massacre at Wounded Knee in 1890. Interestingly, the incident at Wounded Knee did not end the Ghost Dance religion as it continued to be practiced by many Native Americans in Oklahoma throughout the early part of the twentieth century. Many of the practitioners of the Ghost Dance religion also came to practice the peyote religion.[92]

For federal officials and white religious reformers, Peyotism represented another barrier to Native Americans' full inclusion in an American way of life. As attempts to prohibit peyote emerged, including state and federal efforts to legislate its elimination, questions about the nature of religion and religious practice emerged in the discussions, particularly within the framework of America as a country that protected religious liberties. The ultimate question for policymakers was whether Peyotism was a "real" religion, and the ensuing debates over Peyotism demonstrated the vastly different worldviews about the nature of religion held by whites and Native American Peyotists.

Christian reformers conceded that Native Americans were a religious people, but the specific argument involved the appropriate methods for achieving a spiritual state in worship.[93] Peyotism's critics tried to discredit the ceremonial practice by arguing that the peyote cactus became the object of worship, making the religion a "semireligious movement with peyote as a fetish."[94] Peyotists, however, responded to these allegations with testimony at the 1918 congressional hearings, declaring that "peyote people have faith as any other Christian or religion [sic] people in the world toward the Great Spirit, which is above all," and that peyote was simply an aid to connect with this higher being.[95] For Peyotists, the peyote produced an altered state of consciousness but did not cloud the consciousness. It was only with peyote that a revelatory experience was possible. The insights that came from this religious experience provided the cosmological connection between the human and spirit world. Adding validity to the Peyotists' claim was William James's 1902 work *Varieties of Religious Experience*, in which he submitted "that personal, mystical experience is the core of authentic religion."[96] James recognized that normal waking consciousness, or rational consciousness, was only one type. Speaking about the metaphysical significance of his experience with nitrous oxide intoxication, James wrote, "No account of the universe in its totality can be final which leaves these other forms of consciousness quite disregarded.... To me the living sense of its reality only comes in the artificial mystic state of mind."[97] James reconceptualized authentic religious experience to allow the inclusion of expanded states of consciousness. In writing about what he terms "mystical states," he said, "Mystical states of a well-pronounced and emphatic sort *are* usually authoritative over those who have them.... Mystical experiences are as direct perceptions of fact for those who have them as any sensations ever were for us."[98] Yet opponents of peyote were not as willing to accept the argument that religious experiences using peyote counted as legitimate religion.

The notion of what separates "real" religion from "false" religion is itself a Western construction concerned with the functional categorization of religion; it is an attempt to define meaning rather than to explore the varied phenomena of religious experience and is an effort to engage religiosity from ritualistic and ideological facets rather than experiential components. Social reformers opposed to Peyotism, such as Dr. Harvey Wiley, argued it was "a religion, which is based upon an illusion or an unnatural stimulus" and was "about as far from real religion as one can get." This understanding of religion narrowed the definition to "a state of mind based on faith and works and not upon any unnatural stimulus."[99] Indian Affairs officials maintained that the "religious significance" of Peyotism did not place it in the same category as genuine religious faith, for the Peyotists' understanding and use of the word "religion" only equated to a cultural custom or habit. Therefore, in the minds of federal agents, a ban on Peyotism could be based on the same justification given for attempts to eliminate Native American dances.[100] Supporters of Native American religious experiences disputed this line of reasoning with a broader view of religion that was inclusive of all forms of religion, including the varieties of Native American religious practices. In refuting the idea of a Christian "monopoly on spiritual truth," ethnologist Stansberry Hagar, representing the views of many proponents of Peyotism, wrote in a letter to Herbert Welch, the co-founder of the Indian Rights Association, "No one spiritual master, and no sacred book has ever possessed such a monopoly. Not one, but a thousand paths lead to the spiritual goal. No one path is much, if at all, superior to many others. Forms of religion are unimportant. Therefore, interference with Indian religion is indeed a serious wrong."[101] However, in the early decades of the twentieth century, views concerning religion remained wrapped in a national commitment to an American identity centered on capitalism and its Puritan religious heritage, which extolled the virtues of efficiency and productivity.[102] Peyotism became embroiled in the Western resistance to religious experience and the emphasis on core religious beliefs that supported a national agenda of progress.

The introduction of Peyotism as a new Native American religion in the latter half of the nineteenth century soon led to a cultural divide between Peyotists and white Christians in the twentieth century, where the politics of peyote in the Progressive Era would result in legislative attempts to ban the religious practice. The view that the religious practice interfered with concentrated attempts to "Americanize" Native Americans coincided with a larger cultural shift during the era of a growing, nationalistic American cultural identity.[103] Peyotism signified to its opponents an adherence to "barbaric" and "heathenish" practices of the past, the antithesis of the progress required for Native Americans to become absorbed into the body politic as members of the American race who exhibited moral ideas of Christian citizenship as espoused by white reformers.[104] Just as the Spanish in Mexico, determined to stamp out the evil, pagan practices of the Indigenous habitants, tried to eradicate peyote use through the Inquisition, so, too, did many American Christian reformers try to do the same in the twentieth century. The Indian Office and Christian missionaries perceived Peyotism as a threat in their efforts to Christianize and further civilize Native Americans, and they worked together to restrict the use of peyote.

Beginning in 1916, federal congressional legislative efforts began to criminalize the religious practice, and a cultural war over the peyote religion ensued. Reformers continued to divide religion into a Western-centered dichotomy of sacred and secular and put Peyotism in the latter category. Opponents of the religion failed to see peyote as a religious adjunct to help one to achieve a special experience with the Divine, similar to other practices like prayer, fasting, and trance, which are found in a variety of other religious contexts, including Christianity.[105] Peyotists, though, were willing to fight to preserve the sacredness of their religion, as well as to advance their own interpretation of racial and religious identities consistent with American identity and the rights and privileges of citizenship. In their cultural battle with government officials and religious reformers, the efforts of Peyotists to organize a church to preserve their own unique religious practices showed that they could be both productive American citizens and Native American Peyotists.

2 THE PUSH FOR PEYOTE LEGISLATION

THE THIN LINE OF SEPARATION BETWEEN CHURCH AND STATE

Appearing at the senate hearings on mescal as part of the first legislative session of the state of Oklahoma in January 1908, a Southern Arapaho Peyotist named Paul Boynton gave the following testimony in support of the Native American religion:

> It is known that there is a great many denominations but let us call this [Peyotism] one of them—let us try to recognize it as one of the ways the Great Spirit is talking to the Indians. . . . Just because a few men do not like this at all why do you go to work and make a law? No, you have no reason whatever—common sense will always tell us that any religion that might be existing among the Indians would be constitutional. If you think they have a religion of their own, give them a right—that is what I am after—if my people think they have a religion of their own, give them a right. . . . I do not think you got any right whatever, or any other denomination to interfere with this right. Let my people have a right—let them have their right because I have seen that it does them good.[1]

Boynton had become a Peyotist when he joined the Comanche peyote group in 1884. He had also been a student intermittently at Carlisle, attended a Presbyterian Church, and was an adherent of the Ghost Dance religion.[2] Boynton, like many other Peyotists, represents the complexity of Native American religious beliefs that can adopt multiple cosmological views and religious practices simultaneously. This ability runs counter to Western religious thought within white Christianity, which espouses a single way to practice religion, within the denominational structures of a church. White Christianity, particularly within evangelical or fundamentalist paradigms, promotes rigid exclusion and eschews the blending of Christian dogma with other religious views. Boynton's statements also revealed the heart of the controversy that ensued between Peyotism and white Christianity—competition for followers and cultural dominance. By elevating Peyotism to the rhetoric of denominational status and arguing the Native American religion had a constitutional right to exist, Boynton touched a nerve among leaders in the Protestant church-state alliance wanting to assimilate Native Americans into an American identity that practiced Christianity exclusively.

Peyotism not only satisfied the religious needs of many Native Americans, but also instilled a sense of pride in practicing a distinctively Native American religion.[3] It should come as no surprise, then, that Christian missionaries and religious leaders opposed the rapid spread of Peyotism among Native peoples. Missionaries and Christian reformers composed a Christian establishment that had a long history of involvement in the policy making of the Office of Indian Affairs.[4] Now in the early decades of the twentieth century, the Protestant religious hegemony interpreted this new form of Native American worship as an additional threat to the fabric of national identity in the modern era. The goal of federal Indian policy now shifted to incorporate the nation's Indigenous inhabitants into national life as independent citizens, not as Native Americans.[5] From the promise of US citizenship associated with the Dawes Act in 1887, the modification of that promise in 1906 with the Burke Act (viewed by many government officials as an apprenticeship track toward civic responsibilities), to the final passage of the Indian Citizenship Bill in 1924, Native Americans found themselves entwined in a confusion of bureaucratic efforts to demarcate Native identity and American identity.[6] Native Americans could only gain the rights and privileges of citizenship by adopting certain social practices that policymakers deemed appropriate for a civilized society. In 1885 (two years before the passage of the Dawes General Allotment Act), John D. C. Atkins, the commissioner of Indian Affairs, presented a list of requirements to measure the progress from wardship to American citizenship: the "Indian must own a homestead, abandon tribal relations, learn to labor and rear their families as white people, learn their obligations to the government and to society, possess a knowledge of the English language that is essential to their comprehension of the duties and obligations of citizenship," and "give up their superstitions, forsake their savage habits and learn the arts of civilization."[7] It was this last requirement of giving up "superstitions ... [and] savage habits" that proved problematic in the cultural contestation over peyote.

To the Christian missionaries and reformers, Peyotism was more than a physiological or social problem; rather, it was a form of pagan worship, antithetical to the tenets of Christianity. More precisely, said Dr. Robert E. Newberne in a report prepared for the commissioner of Indian Affairs in 1922, the use of peyote was "paganism arrayed against Christianity—the power of a drug against the elevating influence of the Cross." Just as the "Roman Catholic Church in Mexico exerted its influence against the peyote habit since the day of the coming of the first missionaries from Spain," the same declaration and commitment would need to come from the churches of all denominations doing missionary work among the Native Americans in the United States.[8] Christian workers committed themselves to assisting the government to suppress the evil of peyote, which to them seemed to undo all the government's efforts of education and preparation for citizenship.[9]

The symbiotic relationship of church and state has a long history in the policy of Indian affairs. Encouraged by the formalization of Grant's "peace policy" that allowed church officials from various denominations to have extensive official participation in Indian policy, an unofficial alliance continued long after the formal abandonment of Grant's policy. A variety of Christian church-state activities to suppress Native American religious expressions coincided with the rise of the peyote practice during the latter part of the nineteenth century and continued into the twentieth century. However, by the start of the twentieth century, the policy was not just to Christianize and civilize, but to make the Native American fit for citizenship in a Christian nation.[10] The specific charge was to move Indians from "heathenism" to American citizenship, to merge them into a white nationality and religion.[11] Amid the legislative efforts to define citizenship status for Native Americans, Charles Burke, the commissioner of Indian affairs, noted in 1921 the importance of the Christian denominations in the process of preparing the nation's wards. He praised Christian missionaries for their "spiritual conceptions" that "hold a fundamental place in our civilization" and for their work in Indian country to promote the "moral ideals of Christian citizenship."[12] Peyotism represented a serious threat to this church-state alliance by challenging the non-Native prescribed ideas of Christian identity and citizenship. Christian missionaries feared the impact Peyotism had on their own efforts to evangelize to Native Americans. Mission workers constantly complained to government officials that the peyote religion threatened their evangelism efforts, and they encouraged policymakers to act to suppress the practice.

From 1916, federal congressional representatives began trying to criminalize the religious practice, and a cultural war over the peyote religion ensued. Between 1916 and 1937, congressional leaders made nine attempts to pass significant legislation prohibiting peyote. Public support for legislation came not only from white, Christian reformers, but also from non-Peyotist, Christian Native Americans, many of whom were associated with the Society of American Indians (SAI), an organization founded in 1911 by Native American professionals and intellectuals who had been educated at government-run schools. Though the SAI proclaimed itself to be an organization representing all Native peoples, the SAI leadership began to see Peyotism as a cultural barrier to attaining their ultimate goal of US citizenship for all Native Americans. Citizens were to be self-sufficient and economically independent, qualities irreconcilable with the use of peyote, as characterized by anti-Peyotists.[13] Arthur Parker (Seneca), executive secretary of the SAI and editor of its quarterly journal, wrote in 1916, "The future of the Indian is with the white race.... They must adjust themselves to this civilization and understand its ways, or the Indian must perish from the face of the earth."[14] Just a few months after Parker penned these assimilative sentiments, the gathering at the Sixth Conference of the SAI officially and publicly proclaimed their opposition to peyote, urging Congress to pass federal legislation to prohibit its commercial trade and use.[15]

Despite support from Christian reformers, federal efforts to ban peyote and its accompanying religious beliefs were unsuccessful. Peyotists fought to preserve the sacredness of their religion, as well as to advance their own interpretation of racial and religious identities consistent with American identity and the rights and privileges of citizenship. Despite the nebulous character of their citizenship status—possessing no legal standing as citizens—Peyotists argued for their First Amendment constitutional right to the free exercise of their religion. Adding additional support to their argument was the decision in 1918 to incorporate legally as the Native American Church of Oklahoma. Peyotism found support from among both non-Natives and non-Peyotists, including influential Oklahoma congress members who hoped their support of Native American religious freedom might translate into to a Democratic voting constituency when they became enfranchised citizens. The subsequent failure of Christian reformers to obtain anti-peyote legislation revealed the weakening of the church-state alliance, and the politics of peyote exposed the erosion of the Protestant hegemonic status in the early twentieth century.

PEYOTISM VERSUS CHRISTIANITY: MISSIONARIES PERCEIVE A THREAT

As Peyotism emerged and developed in the United States in the latter part of the nineteenth century, it was not long before the dominant Protestant religious culture became aware of its influence and began to take measures to eradicate both the item used in worship and the religious beliefs associated with it. The ensuing cultural contestation over Peyotism coincided with larger societal challenges to Anglo-Saxon Protestantism and the hegemonic influence it enjoyed over American culture throughout the "Age of Empire" (1803–98). The growing presence of other faiths and other forms of Christianity, as well as the increased prestige of science, challenged the nature of religious authority that had once been the exclusive domain of evangelical Protestantism. Demographic changes through immigration patterns began to threaten the established Protestant majority in America as immigrants arrived with different languages, religious affiliations, and cultural values and practices. In 1850, only five percent of the total population in the United States was Roman Catholic, but around 1870, an upsurge in Irish, German, and Italian Catholic immigration began to weaken the dominant status formerly enjoyed by Anglo-Saxon Protestants. By 1898, one out of every three church members in America belonged to the Catholic Church.[16] The perceived threat to the cultural identity of a Protestant Christian America did not stem solely from the growth of Catholicism; the influx of immigrants also multiplied the Jewish communities in the United States. Between 1880 and 1900, more than half a million Jews entered the country, fleeing the anti-Semitic pressures directed against them in their homelands.[17]

Modernity also had an impact on the Protestant establishment in America, due to forces both secular and religious. Technological advancements in science provoked social change and engendered social tensions. Increasing industrialization, cyclical economic depressions, and a widening of the gap between rich and poor resulted in violent labor unrest as the United States transformed from a primarily agrarian to industrial economy, with large influxes of people moving into urban settings. Religious innovation also flourished in this modern world. Mary Baker Eddy's Christian Science combined a metaphysical view of the human spirit with modern notions of science, purportedly to reinstate the lost art of healing that was part of the primitive church. Her publication of her 1875 book *Science and Health with Key to the Scriptures* was seen by many to be a direct challenge to the scriptural authority of the Bible. In 1901, a Bible student from Topeka, Kansas, began the religious practice of speaking in tongues, evidence of a baptism by the Holy Spirit, and thus beginning the modern Pentecostal movement. According to religious historian Kathryn Lofton, in 1913, "George Hensley introduced snake handling to the ritual cue of southern evangelicals; a year later, Jehovah's Witnesses were sure the world would end." The early modern period was also "the age of Edward Bellamy's Christian socialism, Sinclair Lewis's religious cynicism, and Robert G. Ingersoll's atheism."[18]

Radical changes in the intellectual climate of the country also raised crucial theological issues concerning the authority of the Bible that provided the basis for the conflict between Protestant liberalism/modernism and fundamentalism. Protestants had clung to the sole authority of biblical scripture, but the introduction of new biblical studies based upon scientific or higher criticism coming from the German universities in the latter part of the nineteenth century, along with Darwinian biology, led to the questioning of biblical inspiration that was threatening to many Protestants. The conservative theological response to this new scientific study of the Bible was the publication of *The Fundamentals*, a twelve-volume series of books (1910–1915) written to codify the conservative position and re-inscribe a set of fundamentals of the Christian faith that evangelicals could unite on in theological belief.[19]

External threats to American Protestantism also came from the increased immigrant population of the mid-nineteenth century, including large numbers of Chinese and Japanese who came to the American West. By the late nineteenth century, many Russian Jews fleeing pogroms had also immigrated to America, along with others from southern and eastern Europe escaping violence and oppression who were predominately Catholic or Jewish in religious affiliation. Peter W. Williams argues that although Roman Catholics had become the single largest religious denomination, they "could not compare in numbers or social influence with the *combined* ranks of the Protestant denominations."[20] However, the Protestant establishment still found itself competing for power with Roman Catholics throughout Indian Country in the transition to the twentieth century, particularly over issues of federal funding for educating Native Americans.[21] The perception of a religious threat to the Protestant establishment that supposedly made America a "Christian nation" only reinforced the dominant culture of American imperialism. The perception from white culture of a challenge to their hegemonic status by the "Others" created a climate of social apprehension and hostility towards difference. A manifestation of this social unease appeared in the United States in the late nineteenth century, when a resurgence of nativist sentiment arose in response to an influx of immigrants into the country.

Race became the unifying factor sustaining the Protestant enterprise in the church-state alliance on Indian affairs. More specifically, working to save the Native American race became a significant uniting feature of Protestant mission work. As scientific theories about race emerged, these social models of evolutionary development influenced federal Indian policy in the transition from reservations to allotment, with the ultimate goal of citizen membership in American society.[22] It was the publication of Lewis Henry Morgan's work *Ancient Society: Or Researches in the Lines of Human Progress from Savagery through Barbarism to Civilization* in 1877 that provided a framework for social evolution theory as it applied to the Native American peoples. Morgan, an anthropologist and social theorist, described a progression through varying degrees on a scale ranging from states of savagery to barbarism and on to civilization. Depending upon specific tribal groupings, Native American societies were classified on a hierarchical structure ranging from lower barbarism to upper savagery, with middle barbarism also a possible category of classification. According to Morgan, in no instance had Native people ever achieved the status of civilized.[23]

This idea deeply concerned federal policymakers after the passage of the Dawes Act in 1887, which tied citizenship to allotment. The act proclaimed "that every Indian born within the territorial limits of the United States who has voluntarily taken up within said limits his residence, separate and apart from any tribe of Indians, and has adopted the habits of civilized life is hereby declared to be a citizen of the United States, and is entitled to all the rights, privileges, and immunities of such citizens."[24] In terms of political identity, writes historian Alan Trachtenberg, "Indians would learn to think of themselves no longer as tribal Indians but as national Americans, individuals whose goal was to 'rise.'"[25] Citizenship status would be the achievement of progress toward a condition that represented real Americanness, a standard set by the dominant white culture. To overcome the social forces that had hindered the allegedly less-fortunate red race, the "American race" and the federal government as its agent would need to help Native Americans move to a state of "Christian civilization," as the commissioner of Indian Affairs described it.[26] The goal of Indian affairs at the beginning of the twentieth century was to settle for all time the "Indian question" by educating Native Americans "to work, live, and act as a reputable, moral citizen." Indian commissioner William Jones wrote that the Native American would transform from the "painted, feather-crowned hero of the novelist" into a "self-supporting, useful member of society."[27] The anthropological concept of race made it conceivable to promote an idea that all races should learn to think and act like white Protestants. In changing to assimilate into this preferred identity, the view among social reformers was that white privilege would soon follow.[28] Achieving this task would require Protestant missionaries to work with the Native Americans and to serve as intermediaries between them and American society.

Openly supported by federal policymakers, Christian mission work in Indian Country had long sought to convert Native peoples in order to end the ongoing wars between Native Americans and white settlers.[29] In their discussions concerning the so-called "Indian problem" and the proposed solution of allotment, the Board of Indian Commissioners noted in their 1869 annual report that the government had an obligation to the Native Americans "to protect them, to educate them in industry, the arts of civilization, and the principles of Christianity," and that the "establishment of Christian missions should be encouraged" because "the religion of our blessed Savior is believed to be the most effective agent for the civilization of any people."[30] In the transition of federal Indian policy following the enactment of the allotment program, Thomas Jefferson Morgan, the commissioner of Indian Affairs (who was also a Baptist minister and former seminary professor), believed that to bring Native peoples off the reservations and into the modern age they, like immigrants to America, would need to assimilate into American society with a common language (English) and a commitment to mutual national cultural values, which included a common religion.[31]

Similar to social scientists employing theories of scientific racism, the Protestant establishment used frameworks from the anthropology of religion to establish a hierarchy. White Protestant Christianity was at the top, serving as the model of true religion by which to judge all others. This hierarchy also afforded Anglo-Saxon Protestants the opportunity to determine the ethical standards of morality that they deemed important criteria for American citizenship.

True religion cultivated "civilized" standards of conduct and morality, understood in exclusively Anglo-Protestant terms, and made its adherents fit for American citizenship. As religious historian Tisa Wenger writes, "In this sense, only Christianity—and often only Protestant Christianity—qualified."[32] Although the Indian Office could take no direct part in the religious training of Native Americans, it cooperated willingly with each of the Christian denominations doing mission work in Indian Country.[33] Church-sponsored work among the Native Americans continued to be a tool of colonialism even in modernity. Not surprisingly, then, the Protestant establishment began to perceive a threat to their hegemonic status brought by the development of Peyotism among some Native peoples. The expanding use of peyote alarmed Christian churches, philanthropic reform organizations, and government officials. They believed that the peyote religion threatened their attempts to "save the Indian" and they were ready and willing to do battle with this "agent of the devil." For those advocating assimilation into the dominant culture, Peyotism represented primitive beliefs and heathenish practices; Peyotism could not help the Native American peoples civilize. As immigrants to America faced pressure to divest themselves of their ethnic cultures and Americanize themselves, so, too, did Native Americans.

Missionaries working among tribes in Oklahoma Territory first reported the use of peyote to Indian Office officials in 1892. In his official report to the commissioner of Indian Affairs, Rev. J. J. Methvin, a missionary from the Methodist Episcopal Church South to the western tribes, wrote, "Gambling and mescal [peyote]-eating are common among the Indians, and if some wholesome law against these could be enacted and enforced so as to make these evils among them disreputable it would be a wise step."[34] On the Kiowa, Comanche, and Wichita Agency, Indian agent E. E. White issued his own order on June 6, 1888, forbidding Native Americans on his reservation to eat or possess peyote.[35] However, the efforts of the Court of Indian Offenses to stop the various cultural and religious practices of Native Americans deemed "uncivilized" by white officials failed to stop the spread of Peyotism. On the Kiowa-Comanche reservation, Peyotists dominated the Court of Indian Offenses, including Quanah Parker (Comanche), Lone Wolf (Kiowa), and Apiatan (Comanche).[36] Interestingly, Quanah Parker, who served as chief judge of the court, lost his position in 1897, not because he was a practicing Peyotist but because he was a practicing polygamist.[37] When he took his seventh wife in 1894, the commissioner of Indian Affairs wrote him that he would have to either give her up or lose his judgeship. Quanah pledged to return the seventh wife to her family, but later, after a trip to Washington, Quanah told the reservation agent that the commissioner of Indian Affairs had given him permission to keep his latest wife. They had five children together. Quanah continued to serve on the court until 1897, when a new commissioner ordered him removed over the issue of having multiple wives.[38] Because of his importance to the local Indian agent, Quanah remained on the federal government payroll as a farmer. Other notable Peyotists also served in official government capacities on the reservations and received pay from the federal government. These included Otto Wells (Comanche), Willie Ahdosy (Comanche), Stanley Edge (Caddo), Pe-wo (Comanche), Marcus Poco (Comanche), and Charles Daily (Otoe-Missouria), the latter three individuals serving as members of the Indian police force on their respective agencies.[39] While Indian agents observed that the use of peyote was beginning to interfere with the work of missionaries, the tangled web of bureaucracy surrounding the Office of Indian Affairs precluded effective enforcement mechanisms to stop the spread of Peyotism.

As peyote continued to remain unregulated in Indian Country, Christian missionaries began to complain about its impact on their own evangelization efforts. Rev. B. F. Gassaway, a missionary for the Methodist Episcopal Church South, complained to the Indian Affairs Office that not enough action was occurring on the Kiowa, Comanche, and Wichita Agency to stop the proliferation of Peyotism.[40] Gassaway noted that the all-night Saturday ceremonies where Native Americans used peyote left them "in such a state of stupefaction that it is utterly impossible to teach them anything from the word of God" on Sunday mornings during Christian worship services. In his view, Peyotism was the "chief hindrance to the efforts of the missionaries."[41] Christian workers perceived Peyotism as a threat to their efforts to convert and Christianize Native Americans in order to bring them into the Christian nation as productive and moral citizens.[42] For Christian missionaries, the soul of the nation was at stake in their efforts, and Peyotism was not only incompatible with the Christian faith, but it also severely hindered their work. Rev. W. C. Roe, a missionary for the Reformed Church of America who ministered to the Southern Cheyenne and Arapaho nations at Seger's Colony, Oklahoma, testified at congressional hearings over proposed peyote legislation in 1918 and employed a taxonomic anthropological categorization of religion. He placed "Christianity, the accepted religion of most civilized races of the earth," at the top of the religious hierarchy, superior to "the pagan or hybrid forms of religion practiced by aboriginal peoples," and argued that "anything that prevents the acceptance of the better and the retention of the worse is a detriment" to the Native Americans.[43] In the view of Christian missionaries, Peyotism was supplanting their efforts to bring Native peoples into the Christian faith. The cultural battle lines became clear—Christianity versus Peyotism—and the two religions could not coexist.[44]

The idea of competition for church members had been a part of American religious history since the disestablishment of religion in the formation of the early republic, and denominations became used to competing with one another for members. However, the introduction of Peyotism and the subsequent creation of the Native American Church provided a new and serious danger to the mainline Protestant establishment. Some Christian missionaries witnessed a decline in church membership among Peyotists and argued it was a waste of time and denominational monies to invest in work among the Native Americans who used peyote.[45] Other Christian workers, such as Rev. T. J. Davis, called for an organized Protestant assault on peyote "to show the Indian that the missionary has the denomination behind him, and opposes peyote because the denomination requires it of him."[46] The dominant Protestant churches also wanted to organize against peyote in order to ward off competition from other alternative denominations that might be more willing to accept Peyotists into their churches. For example, Baptist missionary F. L. King wrote to the secretary of the Baptist Home Mission Society about his work among the Arapahos in Oklahoma and claimed, "The Mormon church is lurking at our doors (they are with the Cheyennes). They encourage the use of Peyota [sic]. They would be only too glad to step in and take over a work and encourage all of these old ways."[47]

A more significant rationale for the ensuing religious showdown between Peyotism and Christianity came from of a Westernized view of religion, which placed Christianity in a mutually exclusive relationship with competing religious views. This was a contrast with Native American cosmological ideas of religion as a fluid process with hybrid expressions that could be simultaneously Native and Christian. In reality, many Peyotists were also Christians, and with the emergence of John Wilson's Christianized "Big Moon" ceremony and John Rave's "Cross Fire" ceremony, the number of Christian Peyotists increased due to the religious use of peyote.[48] Yet, a hybrid Christianity was not an acceptable option for Protestant missionaries, who had an all-or-nothing attitude. For the Protestant establishment, religiosity, expressed in terms of institutional church membership, was a zero-sum concept where one could not be a member of two churches at the same time. Certainly, Protestant missionaries could not permit people to be a member of a Protestant church and a peyote church at the same time.[49] Even as certain features of Christianity blended with Peyotism, Protestant missionaries considered the Native American religion to be a superstitious, pagan practice antithetical to the goals of Christianity and Christian citizenship.[50] Just as peyote created concerns among the Spanish missionaries in early Mexico not because of its narcotic effects but because the use of the cactus prevented the conversion of Native peoples to Christianity, so, too, did Peyotism raise similar concerns among Protestant missionaries in the United States in the early twentieth century. Efforts to eradicate peyote would require the church-state alliance to collaborate in bringing colonizing policies into the modern era.

MIXING RELIGION AND POLITICS AROUND PEYOTISM

The first attempt to legislate peyote beyond the authority of the Office of Indian Affairs came in 1899, when the Oklahoma Territorial legislature enacted a law prohibiting the use of "Mescal Beans" among Native Americans and provided excessive penalties, including a fine of twenty-five to two hundred dollars and/or up to six months in jail, for its violation. Problematic for the enforcement of this policy was the wording in the statute. While legislators intended the statute to prohibit peyote, the early rhetorical confusion from anthropologists, and then Indian agents, who referred to peyote as a mescal bean became codified in the Oklahoma Territory law.[51] When officials attempted to prosecute Peyotists, the legal strategy focused on the inaccuracy of language in the statute. Additionally, the statute remained unenforceable because while peyote was considered to be illegal in Oklahoma Territory, there were no federal statutes that applied to reservations under federal supervision that made peyote illegal.[52] As statehood status came for Oklahoma, efforts to correct the imprecise language in the law followed. Hearings on amending the mescal bean bill to prohibit peyote took place in 1908. Indian agents, Christian missionaries, and Peyotists all testified before the committee on Public Health, Sanitation, and Practice of Medicine, which had control over Oklahoma House Bill No. 49. After days of testimony from all parties interested in the legislation, the committee recommended discontinuing the legislative matter because the press reported many of the Oklahoma legislators "thought it advisable not to interfere with the religious ceremonies of the Indians."[53] The 1908 hearings on peyote legislation in Oklahoma witnessed, said one reporter, on one side "the missionary, ever prevalent with advice that was not asked for—the [Indian] agent of a department who wishes to hold his position," and on the other side, "the one governed." The defeat of state legislation to prohibit peyote in Oklahoma by a successful lobbying effort from Peyotists represented a new era of resistance in the "struggle between the government by department and government by right of consent given by the governed."[54]

Following the defeat of anti-Peyotists to obtain state legislation, Indian Office officials, Christian reformers, and other "friends" of the Indians began a concentrated push for federal legislation to stop the use of peyote among Peyotists throughout the United States. Rev. H. L. Price of the United Evangelical Church in El Reno, Oklahoma, suggested that all "civic leagues, ministerial unions, and temperance societies jointly unite" to petition for legislation against peyote, and he encouraged "every minister in the state of Oklahoma to present this matter to his congregation in its true light and preach at least one sermon upon this subject."[55] Indian agents also believed prohibitory legislation was imperative due to the increasing menace of what they began to deem the peyote habit. Some officials wanted to lobby Congress to enact appropriate legislation.[56] Others suggested that missionaries should ask Congress for legislation.[57] The culmination of both views came to fruition in 1912 when the Board of Indian Commissioners, a group of Christian philanthropists appointed to oversee the Bureau of Indian Affairs, voted to favor legislation or executive action restricting the use of and traffic in peyote. The board began to lobby for a strong federal law against peyote.[58] Directing this lobby effort was Robert D. Hall of the YMCA.[59] In March 1913, anti-Peyotists attempted a legal maneuver to stop peyote use by requesting that Congress approve an amendment to add peyote to the financing of the Indian prohibition law against intoxicating liquors, which had been in effect since 1897. However, the Senate Committee on Indian Affairs voted to strike the words "and peyote" from the appropriation bill.[60] It became apparent to those who opposed peyote that a stronger mechanism for peyote prohibition would be necessary.

The first federal legislative attempt to criminalize peyote came in 1916 with the introduction of bills introduced by Representative Harry L. Gandy (D) of South Dakota and Senator William H. Thompson (D) of Kansas. Senate action blocked the Thompson bill (S. 3526), so efforts to pass legislation focused on the Gandy bill (H.R. 10669), which sought to prohibit the traffic in peyote, "including its sale to Indians, introduction into the Country, importation and transportation," with penalties for trafficking peyote that included "imprisonment for more than sixty days and less than one year, or by a fine of not less than $100 nor more than $500, or both."[61] Support for the Gandy legislation came from several white Christian sources, including the YMCA, the Indian Rights Association, the Lake Mohonk Conference of the Friends of the Indian, and the National Indian Association.[62] Interestingly, support for the Gandy bill also came from anti-Peyotists who were Native Americans and also felt the need to organize and lobby to stop the spread of Peyotism. The Third National Indian Student Conference that met in 1916 adopted a resolution in which the first plank strongly denounced the "use of the drug peyote by our Indian race," and appealed to "all loyal Christians and non-Christian members of our race" to unite to "destroy this traffic in peyote, which is destroying our people, both body and soul."[63] The resolution urged the passage of the Gandy bill to accomplish this task. Yet, ironically, in the very next section of the resolution, the National Indian Student Conference supported the efforts to allow any Native American pupil who was over eighteen to choose their own religious affiliation. This suggested a strong commitment to honoring the American principle of religious liberty, though the point of the resolution made it clear that this privilege did not extend to Peyotism.

The most vocal Native American support for the Gandy legislation came from the leadership ranks of the Society of American Indians (SAI). Founded in April 1911 by a group of Native American intellectuals, the SAI wanted to be a unified voice of American Indians and to pursue controversial political goals without appearing to be radical or too political. Organizers believed in a central purpose of speaking up for Native American peoples. Unfortunately, the leadership of the SAI began to support the racial assimilationist agenda advocated by white American culture. Arthur Parker frequently commented in correspondence that "the Indian cannot always remain in the old way," because modernity required competition with whites; therefore, Native Americans "must learn the same ways that the white man learns in business, in mind, and in all the activities of life."[64] The illustration from the *Denver News* depicted the SAI leader as a "whitened" Indian dressed in "citizens' clothes" holding a lamp of

Illustration featuring an imagined leader nurtured in the Society of American Indians. From the *Quarterly Journal of the Society of American Indians*, October–December 1913. Courtesy of HathiTrust.

knowledge and books as the way to solve the "Indian problem" in the United States. The SAI leadership often made condescending remarks about Native Americans in the smaller tribes, who they argued refused to work but rather chose to merely get lands and annuities from the government.[65] In many respects, the SAI ultimately became a paternalistic extension of government policy, using Native Americans in its leadership ranks—often characterized as the "red progressives"—to work to assimilate other Native Americans—deemed to be "backward Indians"—into white American society. The reason for the opposition to peyote by this Native American organization lay in differing legislative goals for federal Indian policy.

The principal platform planks that united the SAI leadership were "advocacy for U.S. birthright citizenship for all American Indians and tribal access to the

U.S. Court of Claims."[66] While the SAI was an organization formed by and for Indians, its leadership recognized that to achieve their ultimate aims of citizenship status for all American Indians, it would require the support of white constituents who supported their causes. Peyotism ultimately became a political liability to the achievement of their goals.

The membership of the SAI included many Peyotists and supporters of Peyotism, some of whom served in leadership capacities for the organization. Oliver Lamere (Winnebago), a well-known Peyotist, served on the SAI advisory board. Active SAI member Francis La Flesche (Omaha) was also a supporter of Peyotism. Thomas Sloan (Omaha) had been the chair of the temporary Executive Council and served as the first vice president after the second annual conference until he stepped down because of rumors of questionable activities in his past as an attorney. However, the SAI appointed Sloan as its first attorney.[67] Sloan would become the key figure that ultimately forced the SAI to take an official stance against peyote in order for the organization to secure the white Christian support it sought for other legislative goals.

Less than a year after the formation of the SAI, Executive Secretary Arthur C. Parker (Seneca) noted in correspondence sent to him that some people feared that the SAI "may, in priding ourselves as Indians, be too pagan in our policy and sympathize with the mescal-peyote element. This is one reason why Mr. Sloan is feared by some."[68] Parker wrote just a few days later concerned about a distrust among people as to what the SAI could turn into, and specifically cited the fear of Sloan among the various missionary workers. Parker commented that both A. L. Riggs and Thomas C. Moffett of the Presbyterian Church were engaged in fighting Peyotism and charged Sloan of sympathizing with the Peyotists. Of particular concern for Parker was that "these white interests have a large influence" and their views represented the "Christian and missionary antagonism to Mr. Sloan and thus to the Society."[69] Thomas Moffett, the secretary of the Board of Home Missions for the Presbyterian Church, wrote to Parker in 1916 to express dissatisfaction that Thomas Sloan opposed the passage of the Gandy bill. Moffett identified Sloan as an active member of the SAI who was a detriment to the organization because of his support for peyote.[70] Later that following year, at the sixth annual conference of the SAI held in September in Cedar Rapids, Iowa, the Society of American Indians officially passed a resolution urging Congress to pass the "Gandy bill to prohibit the commerce in and use of peyote among our people, because of its known baneful effects upon the users in mind and morals."[71] The SAI's official position on peyote had the appearance of political acquiescence to white Christian constituents rather than a true belief in the harms of peyote, at least for members like Arthur Parker, who hinted at such a view three years before the resolution passed. In 1913, Parker admitted that he thought peyote seemed harmless in its physical effects upon the community and was certainly not as dangerous as alcohol. However, his main objection to peyote was that it was "a form of heathen practice, which tends to confuse the minds of the people and turn them from associating with the various missionaries who have jurisdiction over their reservations."[72] The white Protestant establishment had successfully divided the SAI.

In spite of all the support for the Gandy bill from various Christian enterprises, it failed to be enacted in 1916. Representative Gandy resubmitted the bill in 1917 as H.R. 4999, at the time Senator Henry F. Ashurst (D) of Arizona submitted his legislation to prohibit peyote (S. 1862). Both pieces of legislation failed to be enacted into law. The next significant attempt at peyote legislation came in 1918 with a bill (H.R. 2614) proposed by Representative Carl Hayden (D) of Arizona. Hayden's bill actually came from a request made by the Office of Indian Affairs and resulted in extensive hearings before a subcommittee of the House of Representatives. These hearings generated a tremendous amount of publicity over the peyote issue and, once again, brought an organized peyote lobby to Washington to testify against the proposed legislation. The hearings featured Gertrude Bonnin, representing the SAI in support of the bill, and ethnologists James Mooney, Francis La Flesche, Truman Michelson, and William Safford defending peyote alongside the Peyotists. The 1918 hearings resulted in a bitter schism between the Bureau of American Ethnology and the Office of Indian Affairs as Indian officials and Christian missionaries accused the ethnologists of supporting Peyotism in order to exploit Native Americans for cultural studies by encouraging them to remain in an uncivilized state practicing their heathenish customs.[73] Although the Hayden bill did not make it out of committee, just months after the congressional hearings ended Peyotists in Oklahoma formally incorporated as the Native American Church in an attempt to resist further legislative attempts to eradicate their religion.

Despite this legal maneuver to protect their religious practice, continued legislative attempts to ban peyote persisted, but all failed in Congress. In 1919, Representative Gandy attempted one more time to get a bill passed but could not. In 1921 and 1922, Congressman Hayden again introduced legislation to ban peyote, but neither passed. In 1924, Senator Charles Curtis (R), a Native American (Kaw) from Kansas, introduced a bill to prohibit peyote that failed to pass. In 1926, it was Representative Scott Leavitt (R) from Montana who attempted to get legislation passed but like the others was unsuccessful in his efforts. The last attempt at anti-peyote legislation before successful criminalization in 1970 came in 1937 from Senator Dennis Chavez (D) of New Mexico.[74]

State legislatures were more successful in passing peyote prohibition laws. In 1917, Utah, Colorado, Nevada, and Kansas enacted anti-peyote state legislation. Arizona, Montana, North Dakota, and South Dakota all passed similar state laws in 1923. Iowa successfully prohibited peyote in 1925, followed by New Mexico and Wyoming in 1929, and Idaho in 1933. However, the state laws were largely futile efforts to prohibit peyote, as state courts had little jurisdiction on reservations. Anthropologist Omer Stewart noted that Peyotists were "shrewd enough to hold their meetings on some man's allotment, which is held in trust by the United States government, over which the state has no jurisdiction, and there is no federal law prohibiting the use of the bean, so the users go unmolested."[75] The failure of the federal legislature to ban peyote is surprising at first; why was Congress unable to stop the spread of Peyotism, especially when the Protestant establishment so vehemently opposed the practice? Perhaps the support of white Protestants may not have served the federal government as much as it did in the nineteenth century. A closer examination of the peyote issue reveals the declension of the church-state alliance for Native American affairs in the twentieth century.

CHALLENGES TO WHITE CHRISTIANITY AND THE CHURCH-STATE ALLIANCE

Missionaries and religious leaders on the reservations had sought to preserve and maintain their status as the hegemonic religious force. James Mooney alluded to this issue of power when he wrote that Peyotists are "opposed, persecuted, and vilified by interested missionaries and officials who fear the development of Indian initiative as a danger to their own monopoly of religious and economic control."[76] A quote from a Peyotist appearing in a journal article also framed the argument in terms of an issue over power: "Some pale faces who claim to be our friends are fighting our religion.... It's these missionaries and some government officials who are making this complaint. It's nothing but jealousy that the missionaries have against the Indians, since they can't drive the red people with an iron rod to join their churches."[77] Peyotism became embroiled in controversy around a Western resistance to the varieties of religious experience and emphasis on core religious beliefs that supported a national agenda of progress. However, in the cultural battle over Peyotism that occurred in the early decades of the twentieth century, Peyotists and their supporters made compelling challenges to the conception of white Christianity and its imposition of homogeneity upon Native peoples. Unwilling to forsake their Native American religion, they sought to resist the dominant religious culture attacking Peyotism. In addition, Peyotists found the necessary political support to separate the church-state alliance that had long been active in Indian affairs.

Indian policy in the United States operated in a hierarchical fashion, with a commissioner of Indian Affairs at the top (operating, after 1849, from the Office of Indian Affairs in Washington, DC), followed by regional superintendents, then by agents, who were responsible for a single tribe or a group of tribes. The agents, in turn, supervised all the agency employees, such as teachers, blacksmiths, and farmers. Many Native peoples and white social reformers were suspicious of the sincerity of the Indian agents' desire to solve the "Indian problem," as they might fear losing their government-paid positions. Additionally, according to historian David Wishart, many agents "were corrupt, taking advantage of the remoteness of their situations by skimming their charges' annuities, or by colluding with settlers to steal Indian lands."[78] Fraud in the Indian Bureau had become a serious problem and took away the meager appropriations allowed by Congress for Native peoples. The term "Indian Ring" was coined to describe "a corrupt group, which had become interested in the Indian for purposes of private gain."[79]

In the early twentieth century, supporters of Peyotism accused Protestant missionaries of being part of a corrupt "Indian Ring," and using Native Americans for their own personal gain, both in terms of financial gain and religious status and control. In 1908, during the Oklahoma state legislature hearings on peyote, Otto Wells (Comanche) declared "the twin curses of the Indian race" to be "the missionary who begged for the Indian and used the money for selfish purposes, and the dishonest agents who wanted their positions retained."[80] Wells's testimony at the Oklahoma peyote hearings revealed the financial corruption of Protestant missionaries serving the Native American populations and their hypocrisy in not practicing what they preached, as he highlighted the missionaries' efforts to take up a financial offering from the Indians, but instead of using the money on churches, they used it on themselves.[81] While opponents of Peyotism had consistently levied charges of Peyotists being duped into purchasing peyote from unscrupulous traffickers in the peyote trade, practitioners of Peyotism countered that, in reality, Peyotists did not profit from their religion, unlike their white Protestant counterparts, who received big salaries for preaching to the people.[82] An Osage Peyotist commented on the profit motivation of Christian missionaries and some government officials who were fighting Peyotism when he claimed, "They are with the Indian for the mighty dollar just the same as anyone else. If they were not drawing a salary, they would not be with us for just love."[83] Members of the Protestant establishment sought to maintain their religious status in their perceived competition with Peyotism, but peyote's supporters directly engaged the issue of power and hypocrisy surrounding the desire to maintain Protestant control in federal Indian affairs.

Peyotists viewed attempts to suppress their religion through legislative efforts as another means to promulgate the establishment of Christianity among Native peoples and impose a white Christian identity on Native Americans. In his support for Peyotism, Francis La Flesche (Omaha) observed that the new peyote religion taught the sense of morality that Christian missionaries sought from the Native Americans in order to transform into them productive citizens. Though not a Peyotist, La Flesche witnessed those who had taken up the new religion striving to live upright, moral lives.[84] Morality as a part of religion also became an issue with peyote's opponents. Rev. Lyman Abbott promoted the "religion of good morals," proclaiming religion to be "living a pure, honest, upright, kindly, and reverent life," something that he claimed the use of peyote did not promote.[85] La Flesche's testimony supporting Peyotism emphasized that the religion "taught the avoidance of stealing, lying, drunkenness, adultery, assaults, [and] the making of false and evil reports against neighbors," and that Peyotists were "taught to be kind and loving to one another."[86] In short, Peyotism taught the "religion of good morals" that Protestant Christians like Abbott emphasized, so the conflict between Christians and Peyotists was not necessarily about how to define religion, but rather, the "right" way to practice those religious beliefs.

Control over the religious experience of Native peoples was a part of the church-state alliance. Former Oklahoma Territorial representative J. W. Hadley, who had fought against early attempts to prohibit peyote, framed the beginning of the cultural controversy over Peyotism as originating with bigoted fanatics who wanted to meddle with the natural rights of Peyotists simply because they worshipped God in a different way. In his opinion, the battle over Peyotism was an unnecessary interference with the religious rights of the Native Americans.[87] In spite of public declarations made in 1918 by commissioner of Indian Affairs Cato Sells, announcing a policy direction to preserve certain valued aspects of Native American culture, including music, handicrafts, and religion, the peyote religion seemed to fall outside the parameters of acceptable Native American culture.[88] The Indian Bureau's persecution of Indigenous religions came because they stood in the way of Christian missionaries. The actions of the Indian Office to wage war on Native American religious practices in order to appease Christian missionaries further defined the status of Native Americans as wards of the government "who are denied the possession of souls."[89]

Harsh criticism against Protestant missionaries who opposed peyote also came from ethnologist James Mooney, the son of Irish Catholic immigrants. Mooney's mother came from Meath, Ireland, and his father was from West Meath, Ireland. His parents immigrated to the United States in 1852 and became US citizens in 1859, while residing in Richmond, Indiana.[90] Though born in America, Mooney "always had a deep love for the country of his ancestry." When he was eighteen, Mooney became an officer and local organizer in the Land League, an "Irish agrarian movement that quickly became the most popular Irish nationalist movement of the nineteenth century." Branches emerged across the United States, and thousands of Irish Americans participated in "transatlantic Irish nationalism."[91] Mooney was also influential in the formation of the Gaelic Society of Washington, where he served as president from its establishment in 1907 until 1910. Ethnologist John Swanton observed that during Mooney's life, he "wrote a number of articles on Irish customs, gave considerable attention to the study of the Irish tongue, and followed the home rule and republican movements with the utmost sympathy."[92] Mooney also remained acutely aware of the tensions between Protestants and Catholics, both in Ireland and in the United States, and the violence and oppression that Catholics often suffered for their religious beliefs.[93] Though a nominal Catholic in his own religious practice, Mooney espoused religious liberty for both Christian and Native religions, and became an ardent defender of Peyotism.

Mooney considered the agitation to deny the religious rights of the Peyotists as coming from "poorly informed fanatics who see no good in any religious forms that are not their own."[94] Unfortunately for Mooney, the Protestant missionaries he criticized began complaining about his work among the Native American peoples. Rev. Bruce Kinney sent a letter to Matthew Sniffen of the American Baptist Mission Society, saying, "We were told repeatedly that Mr. Mooney of the Smithsonian Institute at Washington, was working down there among the Indians and distinctly encouraging their old tribal customs, particularly the use of peyote."[95] Officials also accused Mooney of being prejudiced against the missionaries.[96] Following Mooney's testimony in support of Peyotism at the 1918 congressional hearings, Sniffen voiced his concern over Mooney, as a representative of a government agency—the Ethnological Bureau—encouraging the peyote practice among Native Americans and denouncing the efforts of missionaries who had their welfare in mind. Sniffen alleged that Mooney wanted to keep Native Americans in their most barbaric state in order to make them ethnological specimens for study by scientists. He urged that Mooney's superiors instruct him to abandon his support of Peyotism.[97]

Shortly after the 1918 hearings ended, Mooney returned to his work in Oklahoma when the Department of the Interior requested the director of the Bureau of Ethnology to recall Mooney because of his interference in the work of the Indian Service.

Mooney returned to Washington, banned from doing fieldwork in Oklahoma ever again. The superintendent of the Cheyenne and Arapaho Agency informed the missionaries of the action, writing, "Mr. Mooney made quite a lot of trouble here for us as he was openly and avowedly in favor of the use of peyote. His actions were so repugnant to me that I finally secured authority from the Indian office to order him to leave the reservation."[98] In appealing his banishment from the field, Mooney later wrote that he had been singled out for sacrifice.[99] After his vocal support for Peyotism cost him his career doing ethnological fieldwork, Mooney continued to correspond with officials of the Native American Church to encourage them to keep resisting the Protestant establishment's persecution of the religion, and not allow white Christians to dictate religious matters for them.[100]

As Peyotists and their supporters worked to disestablish Protestant Christianity from Indian affairs, they also sought to dismantle the church-state alliance through the weakening of state control over Native American religious matters. Here they found an unlikely source of support from members of the Oklahoma congressional delegation. Attempts at federal peyote prohibition legislation failed because of a strong pro-peyote delegation of Oklahoma congressional legislators. Particularly influential was Senator Robert Owen (D). Owen was one of the first two US senators when Oklahoma became a state. Part Cherokee on his mother's side, Owen was considered "the most powerful man in the Senate" by many, and it was generally believed that "his cooperation is indispensable in securing effective Indian legislation."[101] He did not believe peyote to be a deleterious drug, and considered it an unfortunate occurrence that the Indian Office was working to suppress the religious observances of the Peyotists.[102] Each time peyote legislation came before Congress, Senator Owen was leading the opposition. He managed to have peyote prohibition language in a 1918 Indian appropriation bill stricken in the Senate without discussion on a point of order, a move that garnered severe criticism about the actions of the Democratic party over the welfare of the Native American wards of the country.[103] In 1921, a proposed piece of legislation to restrict peyote passed the House and indications were strong that it would go through the Senate, when Senator Owen spoke against it and succeeded in getting it shelved.[104] This action prompted a response at the national conference of the Interdenominational Mission Society, which met to consider the extension of missionary work among Native Americans. The missionaries adopted a resolution severely condemning Senator R. L. Owen for his opposition to the bill, which would have prohibited the use of the peyote in Native American religious practices.[105] Though not a Peyotist, Senator Owen advocated on behalf of his Peyotist constituency that could support his own political career when Native Americans obtained citizenship status and accompanying voting rights. In responding to the discussion on peyote prohibition, Owen expressed that he knew how the people in his state felt and hinted at the significant number of potential voters in the state from the Native American community, which was sensitive to issues on peyote.[106] The Committee on Social and Religious Surveys, under the direction of G. E. E. Lindquist, alluded to the power and influence of Senator Owen when they reported that peyote bills "have been introduced in Congress again and again, but have always been defeated by some Congressman who tried to please his Indian constituents at home and cared more for their votes than to outlaw and prohibit a great evil."[107] While probably the most influential politician in opposing peyote legislation, Senator Owen was not the only Oklahoma politician to thwart federal efforts to ban the cactus.

Following the defeat of peyote legislation in 1926, Archdeacon Edward Ashley of the Episcopal Church in South Dakota commented, "The bill has been up before Congress, but Oklahoma members object to the passage because . . . they know that if this act was amended it would check a money making business in the state."[108] Quanah Parker had called upon Representative Scott Ferris (D) for help in obtaining peyote buttons in 1909 after the chief special officer, responsible for the suppression of liquor traffic on reservations, imposed a ban on bringing peyote in from Mexico and destroyed the current supply in Laredo. Ferris was able to obtain an agreement from the Office of Indian Affairs to allow the continued importation of peyote from Mexico, with a compromise on the quantity obtained and brought into the United States. In 1918, Ferris expressed a desire to appear before the congressional committee hearings to oppose the peyote bill. Because of another committee engagement, he could not personally appear at the peyote hearings but authorized the chair of that committee to cite his objection for the record.[109] Representative L. M. Gensman (R) was also a staunch supporter of the Peyotists. In a tight election in his Oklahoma district in 1922, missionaries warned Gensman that if he would not support peyote prohibition, they "would go to all the white pastors and Sunday schools in his district and use all the temperance force" they could rally to elect his opponent, Elmer Thomas. Thomas defeated Gensman in the campaign and the Protestant missionaries became emboldened to use their political power to go after Senator John Harreld (R), and Representatives Charles D. Carter (D) and James McClintic (D) to help get peyote prohibited among the Native American population.[110] Despite their limited political success in defeating a supporter of Peyotism, the church-state alliance operating in Indian affairs was still unable to obtain any significant peyote legislation. The Oklahoma political machine supporting Peyotists was too powerful in the early decades of the twentieth century, primarily because of the significant number of Native Americans residing in Oklahoma and the potential voting bloc they would represent once citizenship rights were granted to them.

Protestant missionaries and Indian Office officials wanted to eradicate the use of peyote among Native Americans in their care, but were ultimately powerless to stop the spread of Peyotism. The strong church-state alliance that had existed throughout much of the nineteenth century suddenly began to wane in the modern era as challenges to white Protestant Christianity increased and became more public in nature. The Protestant establishment experienced threats to its hegemonic status in the twentieth century that resulted in a shifting religious configuration of the nation. At the start of the new century, Protestantism was at the apex of its apparent strength and influence. However, World War I marked the end of an era, and as religious historians John Corrigan and Winthrop Hudson note, "By the time Warren G. Harding was installed in the White House, much of the contagious enthusiasm exhibited by the churches had begun to be dissipated. By 1925, the usual indices of institutional health—church attendance, Sunday school enrollment, missionary giving—showed a downward trend that was to continue for at least a decade."[111] The decline of progressive politics also affected the churches, with a shift in mood of the American people. Also hampering the Protestant advance was the para-denominational conflict over biblical interpretation and the authoritative role of scripture in Christianity, a struggle between the modernists and the fundamentalists. The Great Depression that followed the crash of 1929 did little to revive Protestant church life.[112] The failure of the Protestant establishment to gain peyote prohibition only continued to weaken its influence in federal Indian affairs.

The church-state alliance directing Indian policy shifted after the unsuccessful passage of peyote legislation, and the control over federal Indian policy became increasingly more secularized in the twentieth century. The emergence of John Collier as commissioner of Indian Affairs and his championing of Native identity and culture stopped many of the challenges against Peyotism. The failure in 1937 of the last significant piece of legislation directed exclusively at peyote meant that the politics of Peyotism were drawing to an end—at least until the white cultural appropriation of peyote in the counterculture movement of the 1960s moved peyote out of the religious realm and into the drug culture movement.

PART II

THE POLITICS OF RACIAL IDENTITY

3 FROM THE BORDERLANDS TO THE BORDERED LANDS

THE COMMERCIAL TRADE OF PEYOTE

A 1926 newspaper article reported on a complaint that had been made to the Texas attorney general by a delegation of Comanche Peyotists who arrived in Austin from Lawton, Oklahoma. The group was questioning an order they said had been issued to ban shipments of peyote into the United States. Kiyou, the spokesman for the group, said that peyote was used by the Comanches in their religious practices. He noted that shipments of peyote into the United States had been made for many years but were suddenly stopped by US customs inspector T. H. Ellis at Laredo, under directives from the Narcotics Bureau. Kiyou and his associates, Willie Ahdosy, Matt Ahdosy, Tim Koase Chony, and Irwin Perkaquanard, denied that peyote was a narcotic and insisted it was in no way "related to Mexican marijuana."[1] Although peyote was not an illegal substance in 1926, efforts had been ongoing for many years to characterize it as such. Concerns over the use of peyote in Native American religious services prompted US officials to engage in a variety of measures to stop the transnational commercial trade importing peyote into the country. The attempts to control peyote at the border also coincided with a multitude of cultural changes taking place in both the United States and Mexico, specifically in the borderlands region.

Borderlands historians such as Rachel St. John have documented the transformation of the boundary line between the United States and Mexico in the early decades of the twentieth century and narrated "how the border shifted from a line on a map to a clearly marked and policed boundary where state agents attempted to regulate who and what entered the nation."[2] The nation-states' presence on the international border expanded significantly with the emergence of the railroad and increased customs enforcement in the late nineteenth century and continued as the Mexican Revolution began in 1910.[3] In the early twentieth century, both the Mexican Revolution and World War I transformed the boundary line and the transnational communities and peoples residing in the borderlands region.[4] An increased push for the prohibition of alcohol and drugs in the United States during the early twentieth century also added the regulation of morality to the system of border control policing.[5] As the use of peyote by Native Americans in the United States became more visible to government officials and others opposed to the practice, efforts to reclassify peyote as an illegal intoxicant became more commonplace. The fact that much of the Native Americans' peyote came from Mexico fueled the impetus for further efforts to curtail the commercial trade of peyote along the US–Mexican border.

The peyote commerce was not just a concern along the borderlands of the US–Mexican international boundary line. As the Native American religion spread to the peoples of the northern plains, the concern also focused on the border between the United States and Canada. Individuals concerned about the use of peyote commented that its use had spread to Canada.[6] Noting the porous nature of the northern borderlands during the time of Prohibition, US assistant secretary of the treasury Roy A. Haynes quipped about the problem with enforcement on the Canadian border, "You cannot keep liquor from dripping through a dotted line."[7] The commercial trade of peyote that extended from the southern to the northern borderlands of the country worried Indian officials who were responsible for controlling the Native peoples throughout Indian Country, the territory that encompassed the region between the international boundaries.

Borderlands scholarship has focused on the legal, political, and social dynamics of a place where two or more entities—cultures, empires, or nations—adjoin one another and in those encounters seek to negotiate the contested geographical place and cultural space. Boundary lines played a key role in demarcating the territory under contestation, but historian Juliana Barr also reminds people to note the distinction between territory and territoriality, which encompasses both the ownership of space and its uses. Native Americans and Euro-American settlers approached the use of land on the border—designated as the "frontier"—differently. Both groups created conflicts that ultimately necessitated the need for negotiation in order to address the geopolitical concerns of coexistence, leading to the creation of reservations, or bordered lands.[8] Scholars frequently describe nineteenth-century reservations for Native Americans as instruments of colonialism, "bounded and patrolled spaces that existed within the state and territorial system of the US empire."[9] The transition from the reservation system to the allotment era (following the 1887 Dawes Act) did little to ease the forms of colonial oppression of Native peoples. Historian John Troutman writes that the Dawes Act initiated a detribalization campaign to prepare Native Americans for citizenship that was "based upon the completion of a set of specific cultural and political requirements." This policy change resulted in new forms of American colonialism, as a way to solve the "Indian problem."[10]

In spite of a promised individual homestead upon allotted lands, the allotment process continued the concept of bordered lands, with federal control over the title to an individual's allotment held in trust for a twenty-five-year period, and the promise of citizenship delayed. Federal Indian agents and superintendents continued to monitor the activity and social behaviors of the designated tribes under their jurisdiction, and, by 1913, federal competency commissions were also part of the nation-state's assimilation force acting upon Native Americans.

In addition to the coercive efforts of social control imposed upon Native Americans in the allotment process, the land loss resulting from the Dawes Act was also significant. The Office of Indian Affairs parceled the lands in such a way that, according to Troutman, "millions of additional acres of reservation lands not assigned to Native families were considered 'open' and hence available for non-Indian settlement."[11] Even in some cases where Native peoples maintained possession of their land, the federal government removed it from the direct control of Native people and managed it through a tribal trust arrangement. Commenting on the land loss through allotment, Philip Deloria states, "The story of early twentieth century land loss is without a doubt one of the vilest episodes in the long history of American colonialism."[12] The attempt to transform the identity of Peyotists in order to control their religious practice represented yet another imperialist project of the federal government in the twentieth century.

THE PEYOTE COMMERCE

Peyote is a borderlands issue by the very nature of its natural growing habitat, along the Rio Grande. The peyote that is commercially sold is the dried, flowering top of the cactus species known as *Lophophora williamsii*, native to the deserts of northeastern Mexico and areas close to the Rio Grande River in South Texas and in Trans-Pecos Texas, where the arid and rocky soils in a semiarid climate produce the optimal conditions for its growth.[13] Ethnobotanists locate the habitat of *Lophophora williamsii* specifically in the "high plateau of northern Mexico, between the basin regions of the Sierra Madre Oriental and Sierra Madre Occidental, reaching its effective southern limit in the state of San Luis Potosi." Within the United States, peyote only grows in the "south Texas borderlands, encompassing the counties of Webb, Zapata, Jim Hogg, and Starr," with small populations occurring in the Big Bend and Trans-Pecos areas, specifically Brewster County in the Big Bend region and Presidio and Val Verde Counties in western Texas.[14]

The commercial trade in peyote began with the spread of the peyote religion and the realization that the cactus does not do well in the colder climates outside of its natural growth region. Consequently, the practice of drying the tops of the plant, commonly referred to as "buttons," became important in the distribution to tribes taking up Peyotism north of peyote's natural habitat, as the dried buttons could be transported easily without losing potency.[15] Peyote trade centers developed in the borderlands, where Peyotists could come to purchase the dried peyote buttons. Areas around Los Ojuelos, Texas, were some of the earliest places where peyote began to be cultivated solely for commercial trade purposes, with other key spots located in small towns through Webb County in Texas. Among those noted for their peyote fields were Aguilares, Bruni, Encinal, Mirando City, and Torrecillas (later in the 1920s called Oilton because of oil discoveries in the area), along with Hebbronville in neighboring Jim Hogg County. Laredo served as a market and distribution point for commercial purposes.[16] Another key source of peyote came from points across the international boundary line in Mexico. Throughout the latter nineteenth and early twentieth centuries, the southern borderlands region became an important site for the peyote commerce, as Native Americans from Oklahoma helped spread the peyote religion throughout Indian Country and the demand for the product increased.

In the early days of Peyotism in the United States, representatives of the various tribes would make the trip on horseback to the borderlands region and hand-gather a sufficient quantity for their religious needs. However, the knowledge of the Native Americans' demand for peyote prompted local merchants in the lower Rio Grande Valley to gather supplies of peyote to sell to both Native Americans making the pilgrimage to south Texas and to the Peyotists who did not choose to make the journey. In the late nineteenth century, peyote became a business of such commercial importance that several large business houses in Laredo would send their representatives to Ojuelos each season to buy shipments of the product.[17] Los Ojuelos became "a stop on the Pony Express route," as it developed into an important trading center for peyote traffic along the road connecting Laredo to the west.[18] Two small stores—one operated by V. Laurel and Bro. and the other by Gayetasio [Cayetano] Ochoa—had villagers gathering peyote buttons in exchange for supplies. Laurel and Ochoa then sold the buttons to larger mercantile companies in Laredo for distribution to the Peyotists.[19] The significance of the peyote trade was such that in the little village of Los Ojuelos several families made a living by only gathering the tops of the peyote cactus for shipment to Native American tribes.[20]

Other small towns around the peyote fields in the Lower Rio Grande Valley benefited economically from the peyote commerce. Local merchants in Encinal gathered large supplies of peyote each season to ship to Native Americans in other states.[21] Smaller traders in peyote around Bruni, Hebbronville, and Torrecillas also participated in the interstate trade.[22] The local store in Torrecillas, run by J. M. Garcia and his son, operated as part of the peyote industry much like the merchants in Los Ojuelos, purchasing local supplies to sell to larger merchants in Laredo.[23] One reporter noted in the mid-twentieth century that a peyote supplier in Mirando City, Texas, shipped "hundreds of dollars' worth of peyote buttons" from the post office to Native Americans "all over the Southwest."[24] Another dependable supply of peyote from the borderlands came from Aguilares, Texas, where the Aguilares Mercantile Company emerged as an important local broker in the trade and as a supplier to the larger commercial peyote businesses located in Laredo.[25]

In the South Texas Plains, peyote fields near Eagle Pass and Spofford also contributed to the strong commercial trade.[26] The border crossings at Eagle Pass and El Paso became vital entry points for peyote to be brought into the United States from commercial enterprises in Mexico. Both cities had express companies operating out of their locales, as well as railroad lines, which contributed to a transnational trade in peyote.[27] Indian agents in Oklahoma observed that Native Americans under their supervision regularly received deliveries of peyote from individuals in Mexico, specifically from Múzquiz, a municipality of Coahuila in northeastern Mexico, and Allende, a municipality located in the Mexican state of Nuevo León.[28] Similar to what was happening in south Texas, small villages throughout northeastern Mexico opted to participate in the trade in peyote, and the commercial industry economically supported many of these small towns along the border.[29] The demand for peyote increased as the religion expanded among tribes in the United States, and its commercial importance intensified as the railroad lines helped create a strong commercial trade between the borderlands and the bordered lands of Native American reservations.[30]

The development of railroads in the borderlands region allowed for the cross-border shipment of peyote and propelled Laredo's importance as a key distribution center, with four railway lines converging in the city. The National Railroad of Mexico, the Texas Mexican Railroad, the Rio Grande and Eagle Pass Railroad,

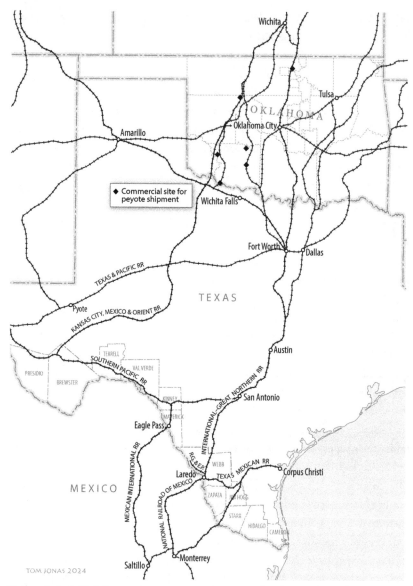

Railroads that aided the peyote commerce and connected commercial sites for peyote shipments in Oklahoma

and the International–Great Northern Railroad each had stations in Laredo dating from the 1880s that linked the borderlands of Mexico and south Texas to northern US markets.[31] The merging of the International–Great Northern with the Missouri, Kansas, and Texas railroad companies in 1881 provided service from Laredo to Denison, Texas, in order to enter Indian Territory. By 1886, the Fort Worth and Denver City Railway opened traffic to Vernon, Texas, which was about ten miles from the border of the Kiowa-Comanche reservation.[32] The National Railroad of Mexico connected Laredo and Nuevo Laredo (*Los Dos Laredos*) with Mexico City.[33] The Texas Mexican Railroad completed the link between Corpus Christi and Laredo and became important to the peyote trade, with stops through the small communities where Tejanos, known as *peyoteros*, harvested the peyote buttons to sell either directly to Peyotists or to the larger merchant companies involved in the peyote trade.[34]

For merchants, peyote sales became a very profitable business endeavor. As previously noted, many people in small villages near peyote fields throughout the southern borderlands became dependent on the peyote industry for their economic livelihood. Peyote merchants such as the Villegas family, the Wormser Brothers, and the Aguilares Mercantile Company typically bought from peyoteros and shipped the buttons in lots of one thousand or more, earning on average $2.50 for every one thousand peyote buttons gathered and dried. Often, the peyoteros took their pay in trade for food and other supplies at the merchant's store.[35] The process of harvesting peyote was laborious and time consuming; a gatherer would average about two hundred buttons a day, but it could take up to a month before the buttons were dry enough to take to the merchants.[36] The merchant houses, of course, would sell the buttons for a higher price in order to make a profit.[37] Costs to Peyotists and their distributing agents along the borders of reservations depended upon the availability of the supply and the method of shipping. The range was usually three to eight dollars for every one thousand peyote buttons, but some merchants implemented a sliding scale for bulk purchases: larger lots cost less. Early in the commercial trade, Peyotists paid on average five cents a button, but the sliding scale could decrease the cost to a penny a button.[38] Those who opposed Peyotism argued that cheaper costs only encouraged and increased consumption of the product.

As the peyote commerce grew, Laredo developed into a central supply point for the product, and was soon dubbed the headquarters of the peyote trade.[39] Regular shipments to Native Americans in Oklahoma began soon after the railroad expanded and connected the merchants of Laredo to the Peyotists in the United States. In the late nineteenth and early twentieth centuries, there were two businesses in Laredo that controlled the bulk of the commercial trade in peyote, J. Villegas & Bro. (later called the Villegas Mercantile Company and then L. Villegas & Bro.) and Wormser Brothers.[40] These businesses would often trade with peyoteros for peyote buttons to sell. These two firms supplied the majority of peyote used in religious practices by Native Americans in Oklahoma, as well as by those across the Northern Plains.[41]

The earliest, and most prominent, Laredo merchant house to become involved in the peyote industry was run by the Villegas family. A history of southwest Texas notes that the name Villegas became "identical with the interests of the border country of Texas and Mexico."[42] Joaquín Villegas and his brother Quintín were both Spaniards by birth, born in the province of Santander in northern Spain. Both migrated from Spain to Cuba in the 1860s and from there to Texas. In 1874, the brothers established themselves in Nuevo Laredo, Mexico, where they "conducted business on both sides of the river, sometimes associated, and sometimes separate."[43] Typical of binational families, the Villegas brothers lived in the two communities with two of Joaquín's children born in Mexico and two born in Texas.[44] Beatriz de la Garza frames this transnational existence as one "better understood if we remember that at the time of the settlement of this area, the Rio Grande did not divide two countries but was merely an obstacle for ranchers with lands and cattle on both sides of its banks."[45] Following the outbreak of the Mexican Revolution, Joaquín Villegas relocated his family from Nuevo Laredo to Laredo, at least partly because his eldest daughter Leonor had become a political activist writing articles criticizing Mexican president Díaz.[46]

Coinciding with the International Bridge that opened in 1889 to connect the two Laredos for pedestrians and wagons, the brothers formed the partnership of "J. Villegas & Bro.," a wholesale and export business located in Laredo that operated on both sides of the border in the *Los Dos Laredos* region. According to Alice M. Dewey's borderlands history, the store became "one of the largest wholesale grocery houses in Laredo in the early twentieth century."[47] As peyote became an important commercial product in the late nineteenth century, Joaquín Villegas discovered the value of peyote and began to carry the buttons as a wholesale product.[48] The wholesale business provided the Villegas family a great deal of social standing within both the Laredo community and abroad, and allowed both brothers to enjoy much prosperity.

The vast increase in Villegas business activities forced a reorganization and incorporation as the Villegas Mercantile Company at the start of 1903. Newspaper accounts note that the officers of the new company were "Q. Villegas, president; J. Wormser, vice-president; F. Wormser, second vice-president; Leopoldo Villegas, treasurer; and Lorenzo Villegas, secretary."[49] Of particular significance in the establishment of this organization was the inclusion of Joaquín's two sons in the family business and the adding of the Wormser brothers to the commercial venture, who would also later become involved in the commercial trade of peyote. In 1905, both Joaquín and Quintín Villegas retired altogether from the business and sold their interests to their sons, Leopoldo and Lorenzo. The younger generation carried on under the name of "L. Villegas & Bro." and continued their commercial participation in the peyote trade.[50]

The second major peyote seller in Laredo was the mercantile business Wormser Brothers. Julius and Ferdinand Wormser were German immigrants who arrived in Laredo in the early 1890s and were key members of the Jewish community of Laredo.[51] Julius Wormser began representing a large San Antonio dry goods firm in the Laredo region around 1896, but by 1899 he and his brother Ferdinand became agents and suppliers of monuments, statuary, and cemetery work for the Champion Iron Company of Kenton, Ohio.[52] As previously noted, in 1903 the Wormser brothers associated themselves with the Villegas Mercantile Company in Laredo. By 1905, they had ambitions to establish their own wholesale business and withdrew from the Villegas firm, after having learned firsthand the value of selling peyote for the religious rites of some Native Americans.[53] As peyote merchants in Laredo who obtained their supply from Los Ojuelos, Wormser Brothers supplied numerous Peyotists with the product. According to historian William Hagan, their list of customers included Quanah Parker, as "evidenced by a letter from Wormser Bros. in which they apologized for the Comanche's receipt of some spoiled peyotes and promised to replace them."[54]

Besides selling peyote buttons directly to Peyotists who made the trip to Laredo, the merchants also shipped supplies to businesses in Oklahoma that would then supply Native Americans with the product, thus contributing to a bordered lands commerce in peyote.[55] Aided by the railroads, the commercial trade in peyote also extended to communities in Oklahoma and Texas that bordered Native American reservations (see map 2). These border locales became increasingly important to the peyote trade as federal officials attempted to stop the supply to Peyotists on designated reservation lands. Traders could not sell peyote directly to Native Americans on the reservations; however, Peyotists were able to procure the item from traders across the borders of the reservation lands.[56] White merchants living alongside the bordered lands of the reservations and later allotted lands were not only able to provide Peyotists with the product for their religious practice, but to make a profit at the same time.

Several border towns in Texas and Oklahoma became important in the peyote commerce.[57] One of the earliest peyote brokers in the bordered lands around reservations was George E. Blalock of Navajoe, a town located three miles from the border of the Kiowa-Comanche reservation in Greer County (a disputed territory claimed by both the state of Texas and the United States until 1896, when the Supreme Court ruled in favor of the federal government).[58] James Mooney's early study of Peyotism revealed that Blalock had been a peyote trader in Navajoe, Oklahoma, for five years, since about 1883.[59] Indian agents also noted early on that a commercial trade in peyote was developing across the Red River by merchants and traders in Greer County.[60] Other whites living along the Red River on the Oklahoma-Texas border also got involved in the commercial business of peyote. Thomas & Rives, a wholesale and retail grocery store in Vernon, Texas, revealed in 1890 correspondence that they sold peyote buttons to the Kiowa and Comanche Peyotists. The letter indicated that the store had about five or six thousand peyote buttons on hand, and that they were not the only merchant in the area selling peyote to Native Americans.[61] As the southern border of Oklahoma Territory developed a trade network for peyote, the commercial enterprises soon expanded northward into the territory. The increased dissemination of Peyotism to tribes living further north in Oklahoma and the expansion of white settlement in the territory created more opportunities for Anglo-Americans to make a profit from the peyote religion.

The bordered-lands trade in peyote quickly spread throughout Oklahoma Territory. One newspaper reported a story about a "storekeeper near Fort Sill" who "received a large consignment of the [peyote] product from Laredo, and was sending it out in numerous lots to the Indians upon the reservation."[62] A report from a concerned Cheyenne in 1895 indicated that somewhere around Oakdale, Oklahoma Territory, the commerce in peyote was taking place.[63] His letter noted that near this Oakdale location in "Cheyenne Country near the line of this Reservation," a white man had a store where he sold peyote to Native Americans. The letter informed the Indian agent that this store kept peyote buttons on hand "by the cases in large boxes" and that the merchant offered a large case for thirty dollars. The informant also included a list of the names of Peyotists who attended a ceremony utilizing the peyote buttons purchased from this unnamed white merchant.[64] The peyote trade extended further north to Geary, Oklahoma, also along the boundary of the Cheyenne-Arapaho reservation. C. C. Brannon, a deputy special officer for Indian Affairs, wrote in 1910 that in Geary there was a "druggist selling peyote."[65] Teeter & Son had been selling peyote buttons, as well as patent medicines and bitters, to Native Americans, who often called for them and wanted to use them for sick people. Interestingly, the druggists saw "no harm to sell them as they [the Indians] could not get intoxicated on them."[66] Closer to the Kansas-Oklahoma border and in close proximity to several tribes who were practitioners of Peyotism—including the Ponca, Kaw, Tonkawa, Pawnee, Otoe-Missouria, and Osage Indians—Ponca City, Oklahoma, also became a distribution point in the peyote trade. The amount of trade in peyote was significant enough that federal Indian department representatives identified Ponca City as "the greatest peyote distributing point this side of El Paso, Texas."[67] Federal officials identified the source of peyote in northern Oklahoma as coming from a "curio merchant in Ponca City" who did "a somewhat extensive local and mail order business in this commodity, his supplies coming from Mexico and Texas."[68] The borderlands and bordered-lands commercial business in peyote provided a strong economic incentive in the cultural borderlands of the peyote industry, where only non–Native Americans profited economically from the peyote trade.

Not only did Peyotism cause concern among government officials, but the commercial trade network extending throughout Indian Country also provided cause for alarm. Those who claimed to be friends of the Native Americans feared that the peyote religion was a way for devious non–Native Americans not only to make money off the Peyotists but also to drain them of their finances once they were under the influence of peyote. US Indian officials were particularly concerned that peyote traders were targeting prosperous Native Americans.[69] Even opponents of Peyotism who were Native Americans, such as Arthur Parker, contributed to a conspiratorial borderlands plot to racialize the use of peyote by claiming that the religion was "a trick of the Mexican traders to find a market for a poison, which deceives the brain and makes these Mexican traders rich" but did not serve the Native Americans.[70] White opponents of peyote feared that its use was on the rise among Native Americans, and Indian agents reported that its use was "being taken up among the whites and soldiers" and that peyote use had become a "problem for commanders of troops on the border."[71] US federal officials deemed the peyote trade to be a threat to the morality of the nation and the American people and took steps to curtail the commercial trade. However, the ambiguous nature of peyote's legality in the early twentieth century created multiple responses to control the distribution of the product.

EFFORTS TO STOP PEYOTE AT THE BORDERS

Officials attempting to stop the peyote trade to Native Americans recognized the strong borderlands connection, both along international boundary lines with Mexico and Canada as well as state borders. The Oklahoma Territorial legislature had attempted to implement a ban on peyote by prohibiting the sale of dried peyote tops within the territorial boundaries, but they could not fully restrict the ability of

Peyotists to travel to Texas to buy peyote buttons. Unable to stop the flow into the bordered lands of the Oklahoma and Indian Territories, federal officials began to work on ways to curtail the peyote trade coming in from the borderlands of south Texas and northern Mexico.

Federal agents attempted to find their own ways to solve the "peyote problem" among Native Americans, and leading the charge was William E. "Pussyfoot" Johnson, serving as the chief special officer of the Indian Bureau to suppress liquor traffic among Native Americans.[72] Originally assigned to Indian Territory and Oklahoma Territory in 1906, Johnson had been appointed by Indian commissioner Francis E. Leupp and had the support of President Theodore Roosevelt in his work. In 1908, Johnson received a promotion to "Chief Special Officer," and his work now included the suppression of the liquor traffic on all the Native American reservations in the United States. His headquarters moved from Muskogee, Oklahoma, to Salt Lake City, Utah, with additional staff and a larger budget appropriated by Congress to aid his work on liquor prohibition.[73] Johnson began to hear about peyote in his work throughout Indian Country, and he convinced himself that the product produced intoxication in its users and was thereby subject to the act of 1897, which banned "the furnishing to an Indian or the delivery into the Indian Country, or upon an Indian allotment any article that will produce intoxication."[74] In 1909, Johnson's interpretation of the law led him to add peyote to the purview of the statute. Emboldened by his new title and the backing from the Office of Indian Affairs and the president, Johnson launched his assault on the commercial peyote trade.

Viewing the matter as a question of sobriety rather than a religious practice, in early March 1909, Johnson, who was a Presbyterian, began to search for the Native Americans' source of peyote in order to seize their supply. He enlisted the aid of Indian agents and the Indian police during raids of peyote ceremonies to obtain information about peyote suppliers and distributors and where their supplies were located.[75] Initially believing that the peyote business was not a large commercial enterprise, Johnson recognized after further investigation that an organized trade network stretched from the southern borderlands to locations adjoining reservation lands. Johnson was convinced that peyote coming into the country from Mexico somehow violated international law, and he began to consider ways to stop the traffic in peyote into the United States in order to save Native Americans from the evils of intoxication.[76]

Johnson initially tried to exert pressure on companies responsible for shipping peyote into the United States, even though there was no federal legislation in place to prohibit the importation of peyote buttons. Without any legal backing, Johnson threatened criminal prosecution of agents from the Wells Fargo Express company in 1909 if they did not cease shipping peyote from Mexico into the United States. Soon the company ordered agents to refuse the shipments of peyote coming into the country. Johnson obtained similar agreements from shipping companies operating in Laredo, Eagle Pass, and El Paso, Texas.[77] He also ordered Indian agents to confiscate any shipments that did make it onto reservations.[78] Johnson's position on the illegality of peyote came from his broad interpretation of the 1897 statute prohibiting alcohol in Indian Country and his belief about the intoxicating effects of peyote. When the Oklahoma legislature failed to get peyote added to the list of intoxicants to be banned as part of the requirement of the new state constitution, Johnson turned to the authority given to him by the Office of Indian Affairs to continue his personal crusade against peyote.

Targeting the Mexican source of peyote coming to Native Americans, Johnson initially tried to obtain a prohibitive tariff on peyote shipments from that country. Johnson's suggestion with this measure, writes anthropologist Omer Stewart, was to "couple peyotes with marijuana and hashish" as "an easy way of getting what [he] desire[d]."[79] This approach reveals the beginnings of the anti-peyote mentality pushing for federal measures to deal with the issue. It also demonstrates the willingness of federal officials to connect peyote with not only alcohol, but also with other narcotics in an era of progressive action to solve the drug epidemic in America, as will be explored more fully in the following chapter. However, Johnson's immediate focus was stopping the borderlands peyote trade to Native Americans, and the most effective way to accomplish this would be to block the source of the supply. His investigation traced a significant source of peyote coming from Laredo, Texas, specifically through the merchant houses of L. Villegas & Bro. and Wormser Brothers.[80] These two businesses soon became the targets of Chief Special Officer Johnson's battle against the peyote trade.

Johnson's most extraordinary program of action against peyote occurred in late April 1909 when he traveled to confront the peyote merchants in Laredo, Texas. Acting alone with no formal instructions from the Office of Indian Affairs, Johnson used federal monies appropriated to the Indian Office to purchase the entire supply of peyote from the Villegas and Wormser businesses.[81] He then proceeded to burn the peyote in a very public bonfire in the center of the city. He also warned the merchants that further trade in peyote would result in criminal prosecution and prison time, another threat void of official legal backing.[82] Extending his unauthorized control even further, Johnson began discussions with the Mexican consul in Laredo to attempt to negotiate an agreement to stop the peyote trade into the United States.[83] The press began to portray these pronouncements from Johnson as official public policy being made in an international war against peyote. One account wrote, "War has been declared by the Mexican and the United States government against the deadly peyote bean. The two governments will cooperate . . . to stop the sale of the bean in both countries."[84] Johnson's unilateral efforts to eliminate the peyote trade in the borderlands had far-reaching consequences for all individuals involved in the commercial enterprise.

The short-lived "ban" on peyote for Native Americans created an ever more watchful government presence on the reservation lands. Indian officials frequently reminded Peyotists that the peyote trade was being closely monitored by the government. Indian agents warned Peyotists not to go to Laredo or to Mexico to secure the item because their actions were closely watched, and they ran the risk of getting into trouble with any attempt to get peyote.[85] In Oklahoma, Rev. C. C. Brannon, a minister with the Methodist Episcopal Church and an active Republican in the state, had replaced Johnson as "the government's official booze smasher on Indian reservations."[86] Brannon shared in Johnson's belief that the regulation prohibiting alcohol in Indian Country also applied to peyote. Brannon's work battling peyote raises an interesting observation on the federal-state relationship concerning Indian policy and peyote. If Brannon seized a supply of alcohol in a locality over which the state had jurisdiction, even if inhabited by Native Americans, the seizure was brought to the state's enforcement officers. However, a seizure of peyote was destroyed in every instance because the state's prohibition law attempted no jurisdiction over that product. In effect, the policing of peyote became the domain of the federal government because Oklahoma chose not to regulate it.[87] Armed with this power given to him as an official of the US government, Brannon vigorously pursued his work to stop the peyote supply coming to Oklahoma.[88] Eventually challenges would arise concerning the legality of these actions, and a policy change on peyote would result.

The unfettered assault on the peyote trade by representatives of the Office of Indian Affairs soon came to the attention of others within the higher levels of the US government. The Wormser Brothers in Laredo started to question the ban on peyote shipments and wrote to the Secretary of the Interior to question the legality of the policy that had been implemented by Johnson.[89] Once they received clarification of the 1897 law on alcohol from the commissioner of Indian Affairs, both peyote wholesalers in Laredo resumed their commercial trade.[90] Prior to the reemergence of the large peyote merchants into the market, the supply of peyote for religious purposes began to run low, and Peyotists mobilized, contacting members of Congress for assistance in obtaining peyote buttons. In February 1910, Marcus Poco, a Comanche from Oklahoma, travelled to Mexico to obtain a supply of peyote, which was then confiscated by an agent at Eagle Pass, Texas, as Poco was crossing the Mexican border to return home. Poco promptly sent a telegram to Oklahoma congressman Scott Ferris (D), seeking his assistance in recovering the 150 pounds of peyote seized at the border. Quanah Parker (Comanche) sent an additional wire to Ferris asking for his for help in regaining the supply.[91] The Osage Peyotists also had their attorney Charles J. Kappler working to secure a supply of peyote. Johnson succumbed and began to allow Peyotists to personally travel to the southern peyote fields in the borderlands at their own expense to gather the peyote buttons for their religious practices. However, the total amount gathered could not exceed five hundred buttons.[92]

While Johnson publicly proclaimed the revision of his policy as a magnanimous gesture, the policy change reflected an economic mechanism for attempting to stop the peyote trade.[93] Johnson was aware from earlier correspondence with Indian commissioner Robert Valentine that Valentine had given permission in 1909 to Winnebago Peyotists in Nebraska and Wisconsin to acquire five hundred peyote buttons, as long as they refrained from participating in any illicit trade in peyote. Omer Stewart notes that a delegation of Winnebago Peyotists responded that a "strict compliance with the letter of the regulations ... would practically mean a prohibition," as travel expenses "to and from Texas and Mexico, for one person, including railroad fare is about $125.00 or about $5.00 a peyote," and an average quantity for a ceremony is about twenty-five peyote buttons.[94] Johnson surmised that the cost-prohibitive nature of individual pilgrimages to the borderlands would ultimately lead to the end of the Native Americans' practice in peyote. Johnson wrote to Brannon in 1910, "In return for this concession, Congressmen Ferris has promised to hold down his Indians and Attorney Kappler for the Osages has promised to hold them down to this program. It will cost about $100 for an Indian to get to Mexico and get his 500 peyotes. I hope by this proceeding that the practice will die out in a year or so."[95] However, believing that politics ruined his work in the Indian Office, Johnson left his position with Indian Affairs in 1911 to join the Anti-Saloon League of America, but the agitation against the borderlands economic trade in peyote continued throughout the early decades of the twentieth century.[96]

Coinciding with the softening of Johnson's prohibition policy in 1910 and the resumption of Peyotists obtaining supplies for their religious ceremonies, the Office of Indian Affairs requested the Treasury Department, through the Customs Office, to prohibit peyote coming in from Mexico. However, the Treasury Department claimed it had no legal basis to take such action.[97] Some success came in 1915 when the Department of Agriculture issued an order prohibiting the importation of peyote into the

United States, claiming peyote was dangerous to the American public.[98] The Post Office Appropriation Act, approved on March 3, 1917, banned the shipment of peyote through the mail, designating the product "unmailable for the reason that it is injurious and detrimental to the health, welfare, and progress of the Indians."[99] The prohibition on sending peyote through the mail echoed similar postal restrictions created by the 1873 Comstock Act, which amended the 1792 Post Office Act and made it illegal to send any obscene, lewd, and/or lascivious materials through the mail, including contraceptive devices and information. Federal efforts to eliminate the international trade in peyote came in 1924 with an executive order from President Calvin Coolidge to end the importation of peyote from Mexico.[100] In spite of these steps to restrict the Mexican peyote supply, Peyotists were still able to travel to the southern border to buy supplies, and shipping companies resumed their operations to supply peyote. Opponents of Peyotism now believed the only effective way to wipe out the commercial trade in peyote would be clear federal legislation to stop it at all borders and eliminate its interstate commerce.[101] However, the economic profits for those involved in the trade proved to be the greatest obstacle in the efforts to solve the peyote problem, for non–Native Americans profited significantly from the Native American religion.

THE RACIALIZATION OF THE PEYOTE TRADE

As significant as the narrative of attempts to prohibit the use of peyote through regulations, laws, and extralegal means is, the underlying approach was found in the rhetorical racialization of peyote. The natural growth region of the cactus in the borderlands along the Rio Grande provided a means to connect race with peyote. Anti-Peyotists sought to undermine the commercial trade by constructing a racialized identity of peyote, specifically connecting the product with Mexico. Changes in the nation-state's presence along the US–Mexico border in the early twentieth century "expanded dramatically and the border became increasingly significant as a divide between Mexicans and Americans," writes historian Rachel St. John.[102] Adjustments in customs laws and new enforcement of transborder trade regulations created a market for contraband goods obtained through smuggling.[103] In this environment of increased federal regulations and state surveillance along the international boundary, peyote's opponents began to link it to other items smuggled into the United States from Mexico. In addition to racial ideas of Mexican identity associated with peyote, anti-Peyotists called into question notions of Native American identity associated with its use. The rhetorical construction of a race- and class-based identity around peyote added further ammunition to the emerging assault on peyote.

Although peyote naturally grows on both sides of the US-Mexico border, federal officials would often connect the supply only to Mexico.[104] Their reports primarily centered on the Kiowa and Comanche, who did make pilgrimages to Mexico to obtain peyote through their informal trading networks established from their time of free travel and raids throughout the southern plains before the reservation era. The discourse of "old Mexico" became prevalent among opponents of Peyotism as they attempted to construct a narrative of a peyote problem entering the country from Mexico.[105] This characterization of a borderlands identity also extended to the distributors of peyote.

Peyote's opponents frequently identified the harvesters and brokers in the trade as "Mexican traders," though in reality most were not.[106] Johnson characterized the Villegas family business in Laredo as dealers in Mexican products, and reported that their entry into the peyote trade came when the Villegas began buying peyote buttons from "ignorant Mexicans and shipping them north to the Indians."[107] Tejano peyoteros also became "Mexicans" in the discursive characterization of the trade.[108] Though difficult to portray the German Jewish Wormser brothers as Mexicans, Johnson was able to assign them a moral characterization associated with race when he gave the following quote to a newspaper story: "The Red man is a schemer, but the bad white man who is responsible for most of his Red brother's troubles is more of a schemer and in all probability, the next move will be to smuggle into the camp of the Indians the peyote bean."[109] Johnson's insinuation of "smuggling" peyote into the United States also carried a racial connotation. Borderlands historian George Díaz notes, "People became smugglers when they sought something that states wished to regulate or deny them."[110] Yet, there was no federal legislation during this time stopping Peyotists from obtaining the product. The concept of smuggling something in to the country would only apply if the duty was not paid when it entered the United States from Mexico. The use of the term by opponents of peyote only encouraged surveillance by the state along the international border.[111] Even the use of the term to refer to the "illegal" distribution in the bordered lands of reservations in Indian Country referenced policies from the Indian office that did not directly specify peyote as an illicit substance or state laws that were not applicable on Native American lands. Attempting to racialize peyote became a way for opponents of Peyotism to convince lawmakers to prohibit the religious practice.[112]

The connection of peyote to a borderlands identity provided some small steps in the curtailment of the peyote commerce but did nothing to eliminate the large commercial industry of the product. Only federal legislation could dismantle the commercial trade in peyote, for it had spread "from the Mexican border" to "all over the Indian Country."[113] To wage a campaign against the peyote business that had become a problem in the eyes of government Indian officials and progressive reformers, a stronger racialized identity for peyote would need to be constructed, one that would find its roots in the emerging war on drugs in the United States. Race became a significant factor in transforming the sacred medicine and religious adjunct of Peyotists into a secularized and profane article of economic trade in the distribution of narcotics.

4 ANOTHER INDIAN WAR

RACE, DRUGS, AND THE WAR ON PEYOTE

Writing to a superior at the Bureau of Ethnology in 1895 about his work concerning the peyote religion, James Mooney questioned the methodology and protocol of recent scientific efforts of other individuals as part of the government's investigation of the cactus. He noted the unsystematic analysis of peyote by other government officials and gave the following advice to the Bureau of Ethnology for further study: "As [peyote] is a medical subject, and the subject of religious and governmental threats of penalties, we cannot afford to be careless in handling it."[1] Mooney's cautionary approach to the study of the peyote religion came from his own observations among Peyotists on the Kiowa-Comanche reservation in Oklahoma Territory as well as his knowledge of the reaction of officials from the Office of Indian Affairs, who would occasionally issue their own orders to suppress the perceived vice by threatening punishment in the form of "withholding of rations, annuity goods, and lease money."[2] Mooney's approach to an ethnographical study of Peyotism—in accordance with his belief in cultural relativism—was more culturally sensitive, believing and reporting the Native Americans' medicinal use of the plant and acknowledging the peyote ceremony as a religious rite.[3] Unfortunately, social reformers, both white and Native American, did not value peyote in the same way as Mooney. Convinced that the practice denigrated Native Americans and hindered their advancement into modernity, reforming activists in the Progressive Era and beyond continually sought the prohibition of peyote, though they found their efforts thwarted by the connection of the cactus to a religious practice.

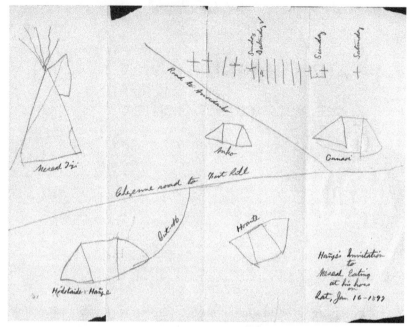

Map invitation to James Mooney requesting his presence at a peyote meeting, 1897. NAA MS2537 James Mooney Papers, Folder 8: "Ethnography, Bibliography, and Misc.," National Anthropological Archives, Smithsonian Institution, Washington, DC.

The controversy over the use of peyote as a part of Native American religious ritual coincided with a variety of Christian church-state attempts to suppress Native American religious expressions. In spite of the abandonment of the "Peace Policy" in the 1880s, attacks on Native American religions continued, notably the banishment of the sweat lodge in 1873, the prohibition of the Sun Dance and the Snake Dance, and the utilization of military force to suppress the Ghost Dance movement in 1890, resulting in the massacre at Wounded Knee. Besides spiritual traditions, officials also attempted to modify or suppress other aspects of traditional Native American culture, such as clothing, hairstyle, and language.[4] With the rapid diffusion of the peyote religion among the tribes during the reservation period, it was not long before missionaries and government officials began to view peyote as an impediment to civilization and Christianization. Cultural concerns over intoxicants, whether in the form of alcohol or other drugs, also emerged during this time. To eliminate the use of peyote and in the hope of preventing its spread among Native Americans, officials began to classify it as an intoxicant, as we saw in the previous chapter, thereby subjecting it to the prohibition standards already in place in

Indian Country. Efforts to suppress its use also corresponded to the height of the Prohibition movement among white Americans, a connection that some scholars on Peyotism have noticed.[5] What has been largely absent from the historiography on the Native American Church is the significant context of additional social reform efforts in the Progressive Era, including a shift in perspective on patent medicines and habit-forming narcotics.

Social reformers intent on prohibiting the use of peyote among Native Americans shifted their strategy and rhetoric around 1903 to transform peyote into a habit-forming narcotic and thereby turn its users into drug addicts. This transmutation of identities grounded itself in Progressive ideology and laws initiated by white social reformers to rid American culture of dangerous drugs that afflicted non–Native American populations. This change in the approach to criminalizing peyote thereby brought Native Americans into the emerging racialized war on drugs that framed laws like the Pure Food and Drug Act of 1906 and the Harrison Narcotics Acts of 1914. Since government and religious officials found it difficult to control religious practice on reservations, they decided to shift strategies and modify the identity of Peyotists, turning the religious practitioners into drug users in order to find successful ways to criminalize and outlaw the practice of using peyote. Steadfast in their sentiments regarding the evil of peyote use, reformers resorted to the tactic of dissociating peyote from its sacred status and constructing a new secular identity for the plant.

PEYOTE AND PROHIBITION: "DRY WHISKEY"

A renewed assault on drinking emerged during the latter part of the nineteenth century with efforts on the part of social reform organizations, such as the Woman's Christian Temperance Union (WCTU), and continued through the Progressive Era with groups like the Anti-Saloon League. Temperance reform became a powerful religio-social movement that advocated public remedies. In the minds of reformers, the evil of intemperance threatened the fabric of the social order.[6] Attuned to the threat alcohol posed to the physical and economic well-being of individuals and families, as well as the social and economic costs of drinking, reformers believed that "by banishing drinking the body of society would also purge itself of crime, poverty, and an irresponsible citizenry."[7] While white culture debated the issue of universal prohibition before the passage of the Eighteenth Amendment to the Constitution in 1919, prohibition had already been an integral part of Indian policy since the late nineteenth century (though liquor law infractions were frequent occurrences).

In 1892, Congress passed a comprehensive prohibition law that garnered the support of the Indian Office and organizations such as the Indian Rights Association, which extolled the measure as a moral victory in the protection of Native peoples.[8] Congress pursued further "bone-dry" legislative action in 1917 with the Post Office Appropriation Act, which prohibited the distribution of liquor advertisements and the solicitation of orders for liquor.[9]

For those wanting to drink alcohol (and those wanting to sell it), federal statutes did not provide enough deterrence, however. Despite the law, Native Americans continued to obtain alcohol in a bootleg system where excessive prices, intimidation, and violence were the norm. Large quantities of alcohol made their way into Indian Territory, and saloons cropped up along the borders of reservations, complicating the problem of enforcement in a "dry country."[10] Charles Burke, commissioner of Indian Affairs, noted that the "isolation, seclusion, and remoteness" produced by the reservation system, as well as the location of reservations with easy access to the "Canadian and Mexican borders," made the "introduction of illegal liquors easy."[11] To combat the use of alcohol among the Native American peoples, the federal government regularly appropriated funds to suppress the liquor traffic. In 1914 (coinciding with the time that the Anti-Saloon League made the decision to seek a prohibition amendment to the Constitution), Cato Sells, the commissioner of Indian Affairs before Burke, had proclaimed "whiskey to be the greatest menace to the American Indian," and had urged more money to be appropriated by Congress for the "suppression of the liquor traffic."[12]

The perceived lack of moral fortitude of Native Americans prompted religious leaders and government officials to assume a protectionist attitude in order to assist Native peoples to make "good" ethical choices, including the choice of what they purchased and consumed. The plans of the federal government for the betterment of the Native American population included limiting their access to intoxicating liquors, which they linked to the feeble efforts of Native Americans in "home improvements, stock raising, planting, cultivation and harvesting of crops, education, moral training, and all phases of Indian civilization."[13] In order to inculcate the principles of temperance among Native Americans, government officials turned to scientific instruction in government schools about the effects of alcohol on humans, as well as undertaking more drastic measures with the adult population by issuing specific orders to withhold the distribution of financial payments to those perceived to be under the influence of intoxicants.[14] In spite of some small successes in stopping the liquor traffic, the discourse of federal officials frequently lamented the inability of the government to eliminate the traffic of the liquor in Indian Territory entirely, characterizing the trade as a destructive force inhibiting the advancement of Native Americans.[15] Proponents of Indian Prohibition often used rhetoric similar to that of the general Prohibition movement of seeking a sober citizenry. Sobriety was also a necessary attribute for Native Americans in their entrance to modernity.

Running parallel to the growing anti-alcohol sentiment and Prohibition movement across the country was the increasing diffusion of the peyote religion among the southern, northern, and western Plains Indians. Viewing Peyotism as a heathenish, pagan practice of the "blanket Indians," Indian agents and missionaries became alarmed at the rapid spread of the religion among the Native groups under their charge to be civilized.[16] If reformers also wanted to get a peyote prohibition in place in Indian Territory, white officials needed to make the cactus seem as dangerous to the Native Americans as alcohol was. Nicholas O. Warner, a professor of literature, writes that alcohol has been "central to the white man's idea of the Indian, and its use has developed into an emblem of the Indian's own destruction in the face of white civilization."[17] Concern about the "drunken Indian" has long been a distorted lens enabling white Americans to create stereotypes and denounce the evils of drinking. Temperance organizations, particularly the WCTU, found the stereotype to be a powerful weapon to promote their cause, and the image dominated the writings about Native people in the temperance periodical the *Union Signal*.[18] If federal policy would define peyote as an intoxicant, too, the same imagery of the "drunken Indian" could mobilize support for extending the federal prohibition laws governing Indian Country to rid the Native Americans of their peyote. Opponents of peyote began to utilize these representations of the "drunk Indian," claiming peyote to be identical to liquor in "getting them drunk."[19]

The connection would not be difficult, as one of the first Americans to do a botanical study of the peyote plant also provided the designation that would link it to the Prohibition campaign. Dr. Valery Havard of the US Army reported on observations and collections he made in 1880–83 while stationed at several posts with expeditions charged with the exploration of west Texas. Havard wrote, "It is principally as an intoxicant that the peyote has become noted . . . If chewed it produces a sort of delirious exhilaration which has won for it the designation of 'dry whiskey.'"[20] Physiological studies on peyote began shortly after this designation of peyote as an intoxicant, where Anglo researchers described the human consumption of the plant in their planned clinical studies of peyote intoxication.[21] One of the first official governmental attempts to connect peyote to alcohol came in 1890, when Thomas J. Morgan, commissioner of Indian Affairs, declared that the peyote practice resulted "in mental, moral, and physical ruin to those who indulge in it," and "the article itself, and those who use it, are to be treated exactly as if it were alcohol or whiskey, or a compound thereof; in fact it may be classified for all practical purposes as an 'intoxicating liquor.'"[22] Echoing the rhetoric used to keep alcohol out of the mouths of Native people, the Office of Indian Affairs targeted peyote in the same way and set out to eradicate the habit among Native Americans.

Early rhetorical efforts in the fight against peyote focused on the potential harmful effects of using the plant, both to the individual Peyotist and to the larger societies—tribal and national—of which they were a part. Opponents of peyote argued it created an altered and weakened condition, both physically and mentally, like alcohol did. Reformers argued that peyote also produced a state of intoxication that resulted in deliriums and visions, and could result in death with its continued use.[23] In addition, the polemical discourse included arguments related to the negative effects intoxicants had upon the progress toward acculturation into modern society.

Native American society and potential citizenship status was already in a state of flux from the effects of the allotment policy, and non-Peyotists characterized Peyotism as a cultural barrier to becoming full American citizens. Just as alcohol abuse robbed individuals of their ability to be productive citizens committed to the principles of hard work, thrift, and a sense of morality, so, too, did peyote use diminish the Native Americans' potential for economic independence and self-sufficiency from working their allotments. The idea of promoting a strong individualized work ethic among Native Americans apart from their tribal connections and communal resources remained a key feature of government policy, whose goal was to bring the Native person into American society and eventually into American citizenship. To achieve this goal, government officials felt compelled to teach (as well as sometimes force) Native Americans to abandon old habits and customs that kept them in a state of idleness and dependent upon government monies for sustenance. Agent A. E. Woodson wrote in his annual report in 1898 concerning his efforts to compel "able-bodied Indians to labor for their own subsistence," but his correspondence reveals an underlying white assumption that justified his actions: "The prejudice manifested throughout the West toward the Indian is due largely to the fact that he is a consumer and not a producer . . . [and lives] in idleness off the labor and industry of others."[24] Progressive reformers concerned about the welfare of the race viewed self-supporting labor as the principle that would bring the Native American into the environment of competitive activity prominent in white communities and provide Native Americans economic and social emancipation from federal government protections.[25] However, reformers feared a permanent state of economic degradation resulting from the side effects of the continued use of peyote, threatening their industrial hopes for Native Americans.[26] A report on peyote included in hearings before the Oklahoma legislature in 1908 to amend a section of the revised statutes referred to peyote as "a stuff which destroys their [the Indians'] industry, force, and will power.... It is claimed that it makes a capable and industrious person worthless."[27] The racialized politics of identity encompassing labor factored into the campaign to prohibit peyote use among Native Americans.

Of particular concern to non-Peyotists was the time that Peyotists devoted to the ceremony typically referred to as a peyote meeting. The all-night ceremony during which Peyotists practiced their ritual, usually held on a Saturday, attracted the notice of Indian agents came to the public's attention through James Mooney's writing and other popular media sources. Concerned reformers often criticized the length of the meetings as an encroachment upon time that the Native Americans should devote to work. Of greater consequence were the perceived effects on the individual's physical stamina required for work on the day after attending a peyote meeting. Agents and missionaries attempted to argue that the after-effects of using peyote resulted in a weakened physical state of exhaustion that left Native Americans unable to devote the necessary amount of time to their crops, livestock, and homes.[28] Dr. E. E. Hart, government physician at the Cantonment Agency in Oklahoma, declared, "The effect on those who attend [peyote feasts] is that of general depression, followed by idleness and laziness."[29] The fear of a new cycle of economic dependency for Peyotists—at a time when the federal government pushed for the economic autonomy of Native Americans—worried many who claimed that those who used peyote were "impoverished—having nothing of their own, but living off of, and consuming what other more industrious Indians make."[30] Critics of peyote thus justified its prohibition for both physiological and sociological reasons, which led to the government suppressing other forms of Native American culture. Opponents of Peyotism viewed it as a remnant of the Indigenous past that had no place in the progressive and industrious society of the early twentieth century.

The efforts of the federal government to "Americanize" Native peoples through the boarding school process seemed to be in jeopardy from the rapid spread of the peyote religion, even though Peyotists were the minority among Native American populations. Indian agents and missionaries noticed the increasing use of peyote by students who returned to the reservations following their education at government-sponsored schools. Once back in the tribal setting, many educated Native Americans did return to some of the old customs, as well as embracing new ones, such as Peyotism. One missionary framed the situation as a waste of federal efforts and money, writing to the commissioner of Indian Affairs about peyote use,

"This [peyote] is doing more to undo what the government is accomplishing in the line of education than any other one thing; for the leaders, in many cases, are young men upon whom the government has spent hundreds of dollars to educate."[31] There was some truth to these concerns, as Peyotism was attracting a significant number of practitioners from the younger generation of returned students.[32] For progressive reformers, peyote affected the future of the entire Native American race.

Other economic fears associated with the rise of peyote use centered on the funds needed to purchase the peyote for the religious ceremonies, as well as the other costs associated with the meeting, such as food. White officials often misunderstood the significant amount of goods and gifts that were essential aspects of Native American ceremonies, often in the form of a "giveaway." While the peyote meeting had no prescribed "giveaway" component, the individual who called for and hosted the meeting was obligated to pay for the peyote buttons and to provide food for the meal at the end of the night. Gertrude Seymour reported in 1916 that the meal at the conclusion of a peyote meeting might cost fifty dollars or more.[33] The expense of the meetings worried some reformers, who viewed the use of personal funds for a ceremony that they believed promoted intoxication and potential addiction as wasteful as money spent on alcohol, and were concerned that some might even give up valuable property rights to whites in order to keep funding the peyote ceremonies. Particularly alarming was the idea of economic wastefulness, especially if the money spent by the Native Americans on peyote came from the monies provided to them by the federal government.[34] Remaining a "blanket Indian" was bad enough; becoming impoverished because of the use of peyote would be an even greater tragedy in the modern era.[35]

The racialized identities of labor combined with peyote use fueled an even greater concern for white progressives: the potential for diffusion to the white race, coming at the same time that social reformers were working to eliminate alcohol, another intoxicant that they felt was harmful to the social fabric of America. There existed an irrational fear that the presumed deleterious effects of this "dry whiskey" (such as intoxication, laziness, and irrationality) would continue to spread, not only among the Native American tribes but also into white culture, and would adversely affect the Anglo-Saxon race. Accounts of white men suspected of belonging to a "low grade" class in attendance at peyote ceremonies caught the attention of progressive reformers.[36] Attempts to document the spread of the peyote "habit" to the white population encouraged some of the prohibitionist sentiment; for example, one newspaper account noted, "Indians are not the only victims. Many white men have succumbed to the lure of the gorgeous dreams that live in the little cactus root."[37]

Internal correspondence between government officials also highlighted the potential extension of peyote use to whites, specifically noting soldiers charged with taking up the practice.[38] The evils of peyote threatened all races, and several coalitions of reformers united in their efforts to rid the entire country of peyote. At the height of the movement to rid the country of alcohol, Arthur C. Parker, president of the Society of American Indians in 1918, made the same case against peyote: "Peyote is a dangerous substitute for the whiskey that people in 'dry' states are now being denied. It is therefore a menace to the white race as well as to the Indian. Any action taken by us on this matter will be a benefit to the whole nation."[39] The logical solution to halt the expansion of peyote use seemed to be a similar prohibition movement.

As early as 1888, the Office of Indian Affairs recommended specific legislation to prohibit peyote in the "same manner that liquor traffic" among Indians was prohibited.[40] Calls to classify peyote as an "intoxicant" continued simultaneously with the calls to ban liquor.[41] The momentum for the prohibition of the "dry whiskey," considered by some to be worse than the "drink habit," was rooted in the larger movement of national Prohibition.[42] After the passage of the Eighteenth Amendment, a nationwide constitutional ban on the sale, production, importation, and transportation of alcoholic beverages, opponents of peyote continued to work to achieve similar legislative success.[43] However, although proposals for federal legislation on peyote received the support of the Woman's Christian Temperance Union, the Anti-Saloon League, the Federal Council of Churches, and other religious and secular reform groups, efforts to stop Peyotism at the federal level failed. Congress and the courts simply did not view peyote as a substitute for the Native Americans' "firewater."[44]

Problematic in the battle for peyote prohibition were arguments made by Peyotists and their supporters, as well as legal loopholes in the Prohibition law. From the introduction of peyote among the tribes of the southern plains, Native Americans categorized peyote as a medicine, which among other curative powers, possessed the strength to cure alcoholism.[45] Partly associated with sacred powers but also with an ethical way of living, the religious use of the cactus purportedly offered a means to transform the lives of Peyotists.[46] In an interesting twist of irony, ethnologist James Mooney defended the peyote religion in the 1918 congressional hearings on temperance grounds. He pointed out that "followers of the peyote rite say that the peyote does not like whiskey, and no real peyote user touches whiskey or continues to drink whiskey after he has taken up the peyote religion."[47] Mooney was aware of the Peyotists' claims that it was a cure for alcoholism. He also understood the scope of ethical obligations that came with the practice of following the "Peyote road."

Peyotism offered followers a moral code and an ethical way of living, and included teachings on how to live and act within community, which ranged from the familial level to having good relations with all of humanity.[48] Hazel Hertzberg frames the argument this way: "The peyote religion may legitimately be viewed in part as an Indian temperance movement whose anti-alcohol activities were set, as was largely the case in the temperance movement among whites, in a religious context."[49] Native Americans such as Francis LaFlesche (Omaha), who spoke to Congress in the 1918 hearings on peyote legislation, testified that the teachings of the new religion of Peyotism forbid indulgence in liquors. Though not a Peyotist, LaFlesche noted his respect for the religion because it actually saved his people from the evils that came from excessive use of alcohol, a practice introduced to Native peoples by whites who manufactured the drinks.[50] To prohibit peyote would also ban the religion and the ethical teachings, which were important to Native Americans in their liminal state of transition to modernity.

A second factor preventing a peyote prohibition also had its basis in the nature of religious practice, as well as in a loophole in the laws on alcohol prohibition. Given the repeated history of Congress making exceptions to the law when the use of wine for the religious needs of organizations and individuals was concerned, progressive reformers feared the same statutory exemptions would proscribe peyote prohibition as long as the label "intoxicant" defined the article. After Prohibition took effect on January 1, 1920, the fear was that peyote could become a legal substitute for the banned alcoholic beverages if left unregulated.[51] Peyote needed a new branding, one that would make it easier to politicize and criminalize. A new categorization—peyote as a narcotic—emerged in the popular press around 1903 and continued to strengthen as the Native American Church organized in 1918. The politics around this designation coincided with social reforms in the Progressive Era to diminish the problem of drug addiction and to professionalize both the medical and pharmaceutical professions.

A DANGEROUS NEW LABEL FOR PEYOTE

Early reports by Indian agents, missionaries, and even ethnographers like James Mooney sometimes used the rhetoric of "drug" or "narcotic" to describe peyote. Most instances of this discourse came in the form of private communications between individuals. The discursive turn that came around 1903 was the outbreak of inflammatory public references to peyote as a narcotic, often occurring in sensationalized media reports consumed by the public, in order to create a "moral panic" that might speed up congressional action.⁵² The evolving headlines of newspaper stories showcase the increasing attempts to demonize peyote, shifting from "Causing Red Skins to Get Drunk" (1908) to "Indians Laugh at Dry Laws, Sip Peyote and are Content: Drug Procured from Cactus Produces Quicker Results than Whiskey" (1919) and "Peyote Used as Drug in Indians' 'Cult of Death'" (1923).⁵³ The media construction of a new social problem of drug addiction resulting from peyote rituals contributed to "the manner in which the various newspapers sought to add to the prejudice against the use of peyote by the Indians in their religious ceremonies," in the words of James Mooney.⁵⁴ This creation of a dangerous new label for peyote—"the twin brother of alcohol, and first cousin to habit-forming drugs"—was the first step in a new direction of efforts to eradicate it through criminalization.⁵⁵

The progressive ideology of individual and social reform depended on the conversion of personal outrage into social activism, and the mobilization of public opinion in the promotion of reforms designed to improve society. Complementing this ideology was an emerging movement to control narcotics and other mind-altering substances that contributed to an individual's withdrawal from a society that valued hard work and the improvement of the common good. Thus, it was not coincidental that the national efforts to prohibit alcohol overlapped with efforts to control narcotics.⁵⁶ The strategy to frame peyote as a powerful narcotic fit into the progressive ideology that began to criminalize drugs. According to Doris Marie Provine, "Drugs are criminalized in two steps. First, the substance must be reconceptualized as dangerous.... Second, the user must be reconfigured as socially marginal and ignorant ... the kind who responds only to the stern intervention of criminal law."⁵⁷ The history of a paternalistic Indian policy already operating through the federal government fulfilled the latter requirement and made it easy to justify the protection of Native Americans against the perceived harms of peyote. Reformers believed that Native peoples, as wards of the government, needed be protected against the use of peyote and other drugs.⁵⁸

Reformers viewed Peyotists as ignorant and superstitious people who often fell victim to unscrupulous traders in the peyote traffic, and their use of peyote set them apart from educated and intelligent Native Americans.⁵⁹ The failure of the new state legislature of Oklahoma in 1908 to prohibit peyote as part of the new state statutes added further confusion to the complex politics of identity around peyote and propelled the Office of Indian Affairs to seek federal support for a national policy. Suddenly, in that same year, sensationalized news accounts appeared that proclaimed, "Uncle Sam is becoming excited over the Saturday night sprees of his Indian wards. Fearing that the former lords of this American continent are giving themselves over to the slavery of a dope habit, he has set foot on an investigation."[60] Continued escalation in the discourse of a "habit-forming drug" occurred as federal efforts to prohibit peyote stalled with the continued connection to a religious ritual.[61] Prior to the incorporation of the Native American Church, not only had peyote's classification transformed, but also the identity of Peyotists, now characterized as "peyote drug fiends."[62]

The transformation of peyote from a mere "intoxicant" to a "dangerous drug" emerged as social reformers saw federal efforts as the only means to eradicate it from Indigenous religious culture and to help all Native Americans progress into a state of civilization required for acculturation into white society. Of course, white society was also dealing with its own drug addiction problem on a national scale. Opiate addiction became a recognized societal problem in the late nineteenth century. Provine notes that "doctors turned serious attention to the extent of opiate addiction and its etiology," while muckraking journalists worked to "change the climate of opinion about the drug industry."[63] Public health officials estimated that by 1900, there were about 250,000 Americans (one in three hundred) addicted to opium, and another 200,000 who were cocaine addicts.[64] For reformers and government officials, Native Americans now joined the ranks of the drug addicts because of their use of peyote, often characterized as having the same effects as opium and cocaine.[65] Just as the federal government began to take charge of fighting drug addiction in American society, efforts to criminalize the Peyotists' use of the cactus also became federalized.

One of the first federal efforts to control the narcotic problem in America targeted the unregulated patent medicine craze, which had contributed to the widespread consumption of opiates. The sale of patent medicines—meaning that their ingredients were hidden from the public by a secret patented recipe—took shape in a variety of ways. Elixirs, pills, potions, and powders flooded the market in a consumer culture seeking remedies for diseases not yet fully understood by the medical community. The effectiveness of the secret contents was questionable.[66] The uncontrolled availability of habit-forming drugs in these products led Congress to pass the Pure Food and Drug Act in 1906, which required the accurate labeling of all ingredients in patent medicines sold to the public in interstate commerce. While the new law did not stop the sales of addictive drugs, the distribution area was limited.[67] Federal Indian officials attempted to bring peyote into the purview of the law to establish concerns over the interstate shipment of the substance.

Since the natural growth region of peyote is along the border of the Rio Grande, shipments to Peyotists in Oklahoma, the northern plains, and the western parts of the United States required interstate transportation. SAI president Arthur Parker highlighted the fact that the "drug was widely shipped throughout the Indian Country" and that the "Interstate Commerce Commission should have something to say... to inhibit the trade of this drug among Indians."[68] The Office of Indian Affairs was able to convince the Department of Agriculture to issue an order in 1915, based on the 1906 Pure Food and Drug Act, prohibiting the importation of peyote from Mexico as a source of danger to the American public, but reformers knew this was insufficient since peyote also grew in America and was available to Native Americans from interstate commerce with south Texas. They continued to fight for federal prohibition of drug use.[69] Further assistance in the cause would come from additional federal legislation on narcotics.

A second federal legislative attempt to reduce the drug addiction problem in America resulted in the passage of the Harrison Narcotic Act of 1914 and its enactment the following year. The first major national anti-narcotic law regulated the production, importation, and distribution of opiates and coca products. The original design of the law targeted record-keeping, in order to limit the number of prescriptions written and prevent addiction. However, a clause applying to doctors still allowed the distribution for professional purposes, interpreted by the courts to mean that physicians could continue to prescribe narcotics to patients in the course of normal treatment, but not for the treatment of addiction. The 1924 addition of heroin to the list of controlled drugs strengthened the Harrison Narcotic Act, and according to Peter Gahlinger, professor of medicine, "it is largely because of this act that the word 'narcotic' has come to mean any illegal drug."[70] The advent of a federal policy to criminalize illicit drugs began with the passage of this law. Opponents of peyote attempted to capitalize on the anti-narcotic sentiment and law in their battle against the sacredness of peyote in Native American religious culture.

The successful results of federal legislation in 1906 and 1914 in reforming white society from a pervasive drug culture added further impetus to the push for peyote legislation. The alteration and adulteration of peyote from a valuable medicine to an illicit drug was a necessary requirement to aid the process as Peyotists attempted to clarify its use as a medicine. Healing was the most common reason for gathering and participating in a peyote ceremony. Testimonials of the curative powers of peyote helped contribute to its rapid diffusion among the various Native American tribes. Quanah Parker embraced the peyote religion after personally experiencing the curative power of peyote in 1884, when he became seriously ill and went to a Tarahumara *curandera*, who cured him with peyote tea.[71] Parker said, "Peyote is a good medicine; it makes Indians well.... When I am sick and take white man's medicine, I do not get well; but if I take Peyote, I get well immediately."[72] Peyotists claimed their medicine would actually improve the physical condition of Native Americans—something federal Indian policy had not been able to do.[73] Progressive crusaders responded to these claims by attempting to link peyote to the patent medicine craze, outside the purview of professional physicians. The promotion of the "white man's medicine" was an important aspect of the federal civilization process that took place on the reservations as government physicians and facilities expanded, alongside reform efforts to promote sanitary conditions of living.[74] Robert Valentine, the commissioner of Indian Affairs, declared in 1890, "The only rational medical treatment comes not from among [the Indians], but that which is furnished by the Government physicians."[75] Progressive reformers touted the connection of scientific knowledge to Western medicine as a superior alternative to the superstitions of Peyotists.[76] Opponents viewed peyote use as a hindrance to the modern approach to medical care.[77] The federal government depended on the testimony of medical professionals to call into question the medicinal value of peyote, framing the debate through the cultural rhetoric of modernity versus tradition. Dr. Henry Lloyd, physician for the Uintah and Ouray Agency in Utah, contributed testimony for a report to Congress about the refusal of peyote users to submit to "rational" treatment, saying, "Indians who had learned to come to the agency physician and to employ scientific remedies under his instructions are taught by the 'Peyote chief' to take no further treatment from physicians.... Thus, the work of years in teaching the Indian to use the white man's methods of combating disease is undone."[78] Reformers perceived peyote as a rejection of both the "white man's medicine" and its "civilized" culture, which only added to peyote's new label as a dangerous drug.

The eschewing of Western medicine contributed to a sense of urgency in regulating peyote under the law of habit-forming drugs, in order to protect Peyotists from themselves. Prior to the introduction of congressional legislation focused specifically on peyote prohibition, social activists sought to manipulate and amend the current laws governing narcotics. Just two years after the passage of the Harrison Narcotic Act, Senator W. W. Thompson of Kansas introduced a bill to add peyote to the list of drugs brought within the Harrison law, but the effort to pass S.3526 failed, largely because of pro-peyote congressional representatives such as Senator Robert Owen of Oklahoma.[79] The leadership of the Society of American Indians, who supported adding peyote to the Harrison Drug Act as an amendment, also considered advocating the addition of peyote to 1917 legislation that further prohibited opium use.[80] The linkage of peyote to other narcotic substances worked to create a "moral panic," which progressive reformers hoped would stimulate federal action against this menacing substance in spite of its being cloaked in religious language.[81] However, a more insidious evil lurked behind the efforts to transform peyote into a dangerous narcotic and its users into drug addicts, as a racialized politics of identity emerged in connection to habit-forming drugs.

THE WAR ON PEYOTE

The racialization of drug use became relevant to peyote when the media began equating the cactus with opium, cocaine, and marijuana, three other drugs that incurred racial stereotypes during the Progressive Era as they became connected to specific groups of people using the drug. Although the racial connection of Native Americans and liquor is documented in the history of the prohibition of alcohol in Indian Country, little attention has been given to the racial politics of Native American identity in connection to other drugs. Race played a crucial part in the campaigns to criminalize opium, cocaine, and marijuana, and the media played a significant role in the racialized propaganda accompanying the efforts to demonize racial groups with a perceived association to a particular drug. Doris Provine writes that the "association of minorities with drug abuse" also fed the convenient fiction that racial minorities were "responsible for their own victimization."[82] Similar arguments and some of the same rhetoric accompanied the virulent campaign to eradicate peyote use in the Native American race. By identifying peyote with other racialized drugs, the federal government contributed to bringing Native Americans into the nascent war on drugs that emerged during the Progressive Era. An examination of early comparisons of peyote to other narcotics reveals the racial tensions over drug use that were prevalent in American society.

The first published reference where peyote was likened to opium occurred in 1886 from an Indian agent for the Kiowa, Comanche, and Wichita agency in Oklahoma Territory.[83] By the time of his observation, anti-Chinese sentiment in the United States had risen to high levels, prompting Congress to pass the Chinese Exclusion Act in 1882. The flood of Chinese immigration, promoted by many Americans as a way to provide manpower to help build the railroads, suddenly became a threat to the labor force following downturns in the economy, which occurred frequently in the late nineteenth century. The smoking of opium became a significant argument in the anti-Chinese movement, as the immigrants brought this cultural practice with them to America and set up opium dens in most cities where they lived. Ironically, as Peter Gahlinger observed, while Chinese immigrants "preferred to smoke opium, the rest of the country was becoming increasingly intoxicated on ingested or injected" opiates from patent medicines obtained from a variety of sources.[84] However, it was the fear of racial mixing in the opium dens that most concerned white reformers. Newspapers, for example, often portrayed opium as a "drug that Chinese men used to seduce and enslave white women."[85] The anxieties about Chinese subversion of American society produced a strong symbolic association with opium as a dangerous evil that needed eradication, along with the source of this narcotic. The foreign policy implications of the opium traffic also contributed to the push for federal legislation to restrict the drug, and in 1909 the United States convened an international meeting to discuss the opium traffic between nations.[86] To spearhead the international movement to control opium, the United States passed the Smoking Opium Exclusion Act in 1909 as a "response to the outcry against the 'filthy oriental habit' and made imports of opium illegal for any purpose except legitimate pharmaceutical use."[87] The stereotypes of the opium-purveying Chinese remained powerful in the national efforts to criminalize both the Chinese and their drug.

Anti-Peyotists hoped a racial connection between peyote and opium would bring similar legislative efforts to stop peyote use among Native Americans. Opponents of peyote worked to discredit the object's importance to the religious practice of Peyotists not only by questioning the validity of the religion, but also by making claims that Peyotism was "heathenish, bestial, and worse than opium eating."[88] After the 1918 incorporation of the Native American Church, opponents of peyote continued to reinforce a racialized connection between peyote and opium. Efforts to mischaracterize peyote's religious use appeared in newspaper stories comparing the Native Americans' use of peyote to the way "the Chinese smoke opium."[89] Federal officials questioned the granting of the NAC charter, seeing it as sanctioning the use of a habit-forming and harmful drug. Opponents claimed, "To give recognition to the Peyote Christian Church is as incongruous as it would be to recognize the Opium Christian Church."[90] Throughout the racialized war on drugs in the early twentieth century, anti-Peyotists continued to argue that "peyote was the Indian's substitute for opium."[91]

The connection of peyote to cocaine had similar racial undertones. The comparison appeared as early as 1903 and grew in prominence in public discourse throughout the rest of the decade.[92] Cocaine became a racialized drug when whites in the American South claimed that African Americans were using it in epidemic proportions. Joseph F. Spillane, a historian of alcohol and drugs, writes that by 1900, state legislatures in "Alabama, Georgia, and Tennessee had anti-cocaine bills under consideration," prompted by "fears that cocaine was giving younger Blacks a new sense of boldness."[93] Stereotypes of the cocaine-crazed African American male intent on committing crimes and causing harm to whites coincided with the "peak of lynchings, legal segregation, and voting laws all designed to remove political and social power" from Blacks.[94] The fear of "black rebellions" and African Americans stepping out of their prescribed boundaries inspired white alarm over the drug. Newspapers, state reports, and medical journals helped create a "moral panic" about Black cocaine users, highlighting crimes committed by Blacks against whites while under the influence of the narcotic. The headline of the *New York Times* on February 8, 1914, illustrated the fears and racial politics surrounding cocaine: "Negro Cocaine 'Fiends' are a New Southern Menace: Murder and Insanity Increasing among Lower Class Blacks because They Have Taken to 'Sniffing' since Deprived of Whiskey by Prohibition." Cocaine powder certainly was a cheaper alternative to alcohol, but as Peter Gahlinger observes, "Public alarm about drug abuse was not targeted at the root of the problem—the widespread use of cocaine in patent medicines and Coca-Cola—but at a scapegoat minority."[95]

Anti-Peyotists classified Peyotism as a form of drug abuse analogous to that of cocaine.[96] Early efforts to make this connection appeared in press coverage targeting the Osage use of peyote, claiming that its influence was much like cocaine.[97] Interestingly, in the comparison of peyote use by the Osage to the cocaine habits of Black Americans, one newspaper identified the Osage as the wealthiest people on earth because of the monies associated with their lands and oil.[98] The implication was that drug addiction was race-based, not class-dependent. The continued testimony of Indian agents and government officials portrayed peyote as a "narcotic which is largely used by all Indian tribes of the southwest in religious ceremonies" that was "as bad in its effects on the users as cocaine."[99] The same slippery-slope argument connecting Peyotism to organized drug use also prompted a correlation between the legal establishment of a "peyote church" and the future legitimation of a "cocaine church."[100] Newspaper stories reinforced the racialized dimensions of peyote-eating, calling it a "new dope craze," and identified peyote as a "cactus plant which grows along the Mexican border. It is known as the *Indian cocaine* and has practically the same effect as that drug."[101]

The similar racialized connection of peyote to cannabis derivatives occurred in the early twentieth century, as the effects of peyote were deemed analogous to those of "hashish," and reports linked the two terms in the context of the importation of peyote from Mexico.[102] The popular, racialized use of the term *marijuana* originated in the early 1920s after W. E. Safford, a botanist with the US Department of Agriculture, wrote, "There is a very pernicious habit-forming drug used by the lower class of Mexican in certain localities ... This is *Cannabis indica*, the hashish of the Orient, in Mexico called marihuana [*sic*]."[103] Cannabis was also an economical substitute for wood in the production of paper. To protect his interest in northwestern-forest paper mills from the competitive cannabis paper, newspaper publisher William Randolph Hearst instructed his papers to use the Mexican word *marijuana* to replace the term *cannabis* in an effort to make it sound "more foreign and menacing."[104]

Racism played an important role in the transformation of cannabis derivatives, specifically marijuana, as they moved from an ingredient in patent medicines to a recreational narcotic. The 1906 Pure Food and Drug Act required that any quantity of cannabis be marked on the label of any food or drug sold for public consumption, but the Harrison Narcotic Act of 1914 failed to garner the legislative support to add cannabis to its list of drugs. The fear of cannabis, or marijuana as it was beginning to be known, was limited in the early part of the twentieth century to areas of the country with significant populations of Mexican immigrants, who tended to use marijuana for entertainment or relaxation purposes.[105] A campaign for federal legislation prohibiting marijuana began in the mid-1920s in New Orleans, but it was not until the 1930s, when a wave of anti-Mexican sentiment swept the nation in a backlash against Mexicans as unwelcome laborers in the Great Depression, that there came a shift in federal policy dealing with marijuana.[106] Federal control came in 1937 with the passage of the Marijuana Tax Act.

Non-Peyotists also argued that peyote use produced a habit "similar in action to cannabis indica."[107] A specific borderlands racialization of peyote grew as the popular press connected the "marijuana fiends" along the Rio Grande with the "peyote fiend, also recognized by the old inhabitant of the valley country," with repeated pleas for the prohibition of both marijuana and peyote.[108] Well into the twentieth century, efforts to place peyote under the restrictions of the federal narcotics act continued to characterize peyote as the "poor man's marijuana."[109]

The justification for the legal prohibition of drugs for nonmedical purposes appeared concomitantly with social crises dividing the drug-linked racial groups and the rest of American society. The same conditions accompanied the controversy over Native American peyote use. The transition from the reservation era to the allotment era in federal Indian policy created anxieties and fears not just for Native Americans, but for white society as well. The politics of identity centered on the issue of citizenship status. Historian Tom Holm expressed that Native Americans found themselves in a state of confusion in the early years of the twentieth century, "as if whites wanted Indians to exist in a perpetual limbo of marginality, becoming neither fully Indian in a traditional sense, nor full-fledged members of the American middle class in a cultural sense."[110] Native peoples remained in a nebulous position of a limited and controlled citizenship status, or for many, no citizenship status, a situation that Arthur Parker identified as "the Indian muddle."[111] American citizenship through the Dawes Act involved a reconstruction of all the fundamental conceptions of life for some Indians. At the same time, there was a fear among whites that many Native Americans were incapable of acculturating to the "American" ways required to be a member of the body politic. Commissioner of Indian Affairs Thomas Morgan expressed the anxieties emanating from the white culture: "There are already among us tens of thousands of foreigners who have been naturalized and made citizens . . . who are in no sense qualified [for citizenship]. . . . It certainly is not desirable to add to this class of citizens any considerable number of blanket Indians who are made citizens only in name and not in fact."[112] The association of Peyotism with "blanket Indians" only added to the concern, as the use of peyote developed into a litmus test for inclusion in American society. However, as white America grappled with its own proclivities toward drug addiction in the early twentieth century, views on peyote began to change. Reformers needed to move peyote outside of the protected sphere of religion and into the secular realm, where the federal government could control its properties and its racialized users. Opponents declared war on the peyote drug.

The militaristic rhetoric in campaigns against both liquor and peyote in Indian Country echoed the expressions of military force utilized in the long history of Native American–Anglo relations. The discursive continuation into the Progressive Era in discussing cultural and social issues reflected the unequal power relations still operating. Shortly after the move to frame peyote as a habit-forming drug rather than just a mere "intoxicant," the public declaration of the war on drugs began. Newspaper headlines such as "Indian Office Makes War on Peyote Drug," "Uncle Sam Wages War on the Indian Dope," and "War on the Peyote Bean" appeared to give official notice of the government's intention to Peyotist Indians.[113] The stories that ran in newspapers also utilized the militaristic language of doing "battle" and reiterated the theme of a targeted racialized war on drugs: "Uncle Sam has entered the lists in a war of extermination against the mescal or peyote bean the Indians substitute for firewater. . . . The government has for a long time waged war against the drink evil among the Indians . . . and now there is added to the burden the drug habit."[114] Adding more urgency to controlling the use of narcotics among Native Americans was the entrance of the United States into World War I, where hundreds of Native Americans also enlisted and served as part of the US Armed Forces in the conflict.

A 1917 article expressed concern that stimulant intoxication manifested itself in "race expression as well as in the individual," describing a new level of conflict that emerged with the "problem of narcoticism" among Native American soldiers.[115]

Despite the declaration of war on the Native Americans' peyote, the continual failures of the federal government to eliminate it and to safeguard the Native American race from its perceived harmful effects sometimes forced private individuals to take up the effort. Misleading portrayals of peyote use among Native Americans included the assertion that peyote was responsible for most of the "Indian wars" in the history of US–Native American relations. A newspaper article in 1920 suggested, "Hostile Indians were often in a state of frenzied intoxication [from the use of peyote] when they committed their depredations and outrages upon white settlements. The peyote bean is now held to have been responsible for many of these bloody deeds."[116]

The cultural war on peyote by social reformers and the federal government during the Progressive Era reflected white anxieties about Native Americans entering into the twentieth century without first abandoning some of their Native identity. Arthur Parker wrote in 1916, "The future of the Indian is with the white race.... They must adjust themselves to this civilization and understand its ways, or the Indian must perish from the face of the earth." [117] Just a few months after Parker penned these assimilative sentiments, the gathering at the Sixth Conference of the Society of American Indians officially and publicly proclaimed their opposition to peyote, urging Congress to pass the Gandy bill to prohibit its commerce and use.[118] Racism played an important role in the transformation of the concerns with peyote.

Just as the media created a moral panic and a sense of urgency to take action against other habit-forming drugs associated with racial minorities, so, too, did peyote's opponents enlist the aid of the press to demonize peyote, first as an intoxicant and later as a dangerous narcotic. The stereotypical image of the "drunken Indian" turned into a portrait of a Native American drug addict, void of the rational mind necessary to fulfill the civic responsibility required for full American citizenship. The racialized war on drugs against Native Americans and other minorities conveyed the underlying assumption that non-white "Others" threatened the social fabric of the nation with their use of narcotics.

The discursive attempt to transform peyote into a dangerous drug was a means to separate it from its religious value as a medicine and a necessary adjunct for religious worship. The evocation of an interpretation that legitimized particular courses of action depended on language as the "key creator of the social worlds people experience," not as a "tool for describing an objective reality," in the words of Murray Edelman.[119] The secularization of peyote as a dangerous drug framed the assault on the religion, as evidenced in a 1914 letter from Henry Roe Cloud to his adoptive white mother Mary: "I had a talk on the Peyote matter with Lyman Abbott.... Told him to put it purely as a drug, leave out religion."[120]

The utilization of the performative power of language, however, would also become a strategy for Peyotists in their cultural and legal battle to preserve their religious right to use peyote. Through language and other forms of symbolic speech, supporters of peyote would work to transform their own identities in the cultural war over peyote. In doing so, they would re-present themselves and peyote in ways that would bring both into the modern era with a new, politico-racial and politico-religious identity.

PART III

THE POLITICS OF POLITICAL IDENTITY

5 EVADING THE "WHITE MAN'S" LAW

PEYOTISTS' USE OF THE LEGAL AND POLITICAL SYSTEMS

At a peyote meeting on Saturday night, February 9, 1907, events occurred that set in motion different tactics of resistance by Peyotists, ones they consistently utilized throughout the first half of the twentieth century in their legal struggles to maintain their religious use of the plant. Pursuant to an expanded order from Indian Bureau officials defining the agency's policy toward peyote, Indian police raided a peyote meeting near Okarche on the Cheyenne and Arapaho reservation in Oklahoma Territory, held on the property of Percy Kable, a Southern Cheyenne.[1] The Indian police was composed of Native people employed by the bureau to police their fellow tribal members on the reservation, and they were often at odds with the tribal community over the enforcement of federal Indian policies. The Indian policemen were expected to take allotments, conform to white standards of appearance by wearing the white man's attire and cutting their hair, observe the white culture's criteria for morality by practicing monogamy, and enforce the white man's laws. On that night in 1907, three of the tribal Indian police interrupted the peyote meeting and ordered it to end, placing the participants under arrest and seizing the drum and gourd used in the ceremony.[2] The Peyotists responded by sending a petition to the superintendent of the agency requesting release from arrest, and asked to be "allowed to hold similar services and worship God according to the dictates of our own conscience."[3] Three of the Indians deemed to be leaders in the peyote religion continued to face prosecution for their "crime." Although not the first or last time

Peyotists encountered the legal system, this case in 1907 marked a significant shift in the ways adherents of the peyote religion responded to the legal challenges. The utilization of the "white man's" legal and political systems to challenge the anti-peyote policies and actions of white policymakers is one of the variety of tactics used by Peyotists to preserve their religious freedom.

With the approaching application for statehood in Oklahoma Territory in 1907, concerned territorial officials feared that the Native Americans' use of peyote might become part of the criteria used in a review of the request and might result in the submission's rejection. Relying upon an 1897 territorial statute prohibiting the introduction of intoxicants such as alcohol into Indian Country, Indian agents and other reformers in Oklahoma began to reinterpret the enforcement of the law to include peyote. Prior to the admission of Oklahoma into the Union as a state, government representatives relied on the willingness of confidential informants to obtain the names of Peyotists and the force of the Indian police to make arrests. This quasi-legal practice spread to the northern plains just as the peyote religion did. However, the framework of the American legal system allowed for the continued use of peyote as religious practice and an expression of religious identity.

Not only did Peyotists take advantage of the court system to obtain short-term victories to resume their use of peyote, but they also began to organize more formally to protest both state and federal legislative attempts to ban the substance. A recognizable "peyote lobby" emerged with each push for legislation. Both Native American and white supporters of peyote went to the state and federal capitals to testify on proposed legislation, as did anti-Peyotists. The power of a peyote lobby with significant political influence in the states and Washington, DC, represented an important aspect of the pan-Indian identity related to the peyote religion. As white Protestant Christians often blurred the lines between the separation of church and state, so, too, did Peyotists, in their willingness to engage the politics of peyote and enhance their political capital while maintaining their Native American religious identity.

The use of legal and political strategies allowed Peyotists to construct their own interpretations of race and religion and to challenge those constructed by policymakers and reformers opposed to peyote. Their persistence in this strategy resulted in judicial and legislative successes to protect and preserve the peyote religion. In the first part of the twentieth century, the Native American was winning the cultural battle over peyote.

THE TRIALS AND TRIBULATIONS OF PEYOTISTS

The opposition of Indian Bureau officials to peyote began in the late nineteenth century when Indian agents first noticed the practice among Native Americans in their charge living on the reservations. As the peyote religion spread throughout the United States and attracted the attention of reformers, public pressure on the bureau developed to eliminate the practice. Superintendents and agents created their own policies to deal with the peyote problem on their assigned reservations and their own forms of punishment for the violation of such policies. Typically, the most common form of social coercion to adhere to the anti-peyote policies centered on economics and the threat from agents to withhold rations, annuity payments, and lease monies from Indians who were Peyotists. The confiscated article would also be destroyed.[4] With the impending application for statehood looming for the Oklahoma and Indian Territories in 1906, an increased concern over the Native Americans' peyote use emerged, and a change in legal punishments began.[5]

Coinciding with the Oklahoma Enabling Act, which provided for the writing of a constitution for a state formed from the merging of Indian Territory and Oklahoma Territory and which was signed on June 16, 1906, by President Theodore Roosevelt, the first mention of arrests of Peyotists in Indian Bureau correspondence appeared a few days later.[6] In a letter sent to the superintendent of the Cantonment Agency dated July 24, 1906, a report came that six Cheyenne Native Americans from his agency—Ben Buffalo, White Face Bull, Left Hand Here, Horace Little Man, Cheap, and Bob Finger—"were taken up by Superintendent Noble [at the Ponca Agency] for leading in a Mescal Bean conclave [a peyote meeting]."[7] The correspondence concerning these six individuals made no reference to subsequent prosecution, but rather focused on getting their statement about the source of supply for their peyote. The name Leonard Tyler emerged from the interrogations, and Indian officials were anxious to know how Tyler procured his peyote. Equally alarming was the information that Tyler was a graduate of the Carlisle Indian School.[8]

Leonard William Tyler (Magpie) was a full-blood Cheyenne who graduated from Carlisle in 1883 and attended Haskell Institute from 1884 to 1887, where he studied law. His allotment was near the town of Calumet, Oklahoma, but he also had a ranch near the town with cattle and horses. Besides being a successful rancher, Tyler served as an employee of the Indian Service for ten years, as an industrial teacher, a farmer, and an overseer of road works.[9] His participation in the peyote religion was later heavily documented by the Indian Bureau, who dubbed him the "great Cheyenne apostle" of Peyotism and the one responsible for introducing the religion to the Northern Cheyenne in Montana. Though Tyler denied supplying the Poncas with peyote in 1906, he admitted that he consumed and possessed the cactus tops. The bureau continued to monitor his activities as a potential peyote supplier to various tribes in Oklahoma.[10] Ironically, Tyler's obituary in 1913 ignored his Peyotist religious identity, noting instead that just months prior to his death, "he was baptized into the Reorganized Church of Jesus Christ of Latter-Day Saints."[11] In spite of his connection to Peyotism, Tyler was successfully able to avoid arrest, prosecution, and conviction as a peyote practitioner and supplier because of his statewide reputation as both a land owner and a fancy breeder and authority on stock, which was crucial to the development of Oklahoma business and industry.[12] Other Peyotists in Oklahoma would not be so fortunate.

The 1907 raid on the Cheyenne peyote meeting in Oklahoma resulted in three arrests that went to the prosecutorial stage with courtroom appearances and verdicts, but it also provided opportunities for Peyotists to participate in the American legal system and challenge attacks on their religion. Two days after the incursion on their peyote ceremony, Reuben Taylor (Istofhuts) and twelve others from the Cheyenne and Arapaho Agency drafted and signed a petition expressing their feelings about the incident and sent it to the agency superintendent. Notable in the document is the explicit expression of a hybrid religious identity that encompassed both Native and white views of religion. The Peyotists wrote, "In conducting said services, we acted as Christian Indians and did nothing which is disrespectful to the civilized Christian religion."[13] Taylor, like many other Peyotists, saw no contradiction in embracing both the "Peyote road" and the "Jesus road" and argued that the varied religious expressions did not have to be mutually exclusive. Taylor himself embraced many religious expressions throughout his life. After attending the Haskell Indian Institute, Taylor returned to Oklahoma, where he adopted the Native American religion of Peyotism in 1886 and affiliated with the Baptist expression of Christianity.[14] Interestingly, much like Leonard Tyler, later in his life Reuben Taylor also added to his religious assemblage a conversion and baptism into the Reorganized Church of Jesus Christ of Latter-Day Saints.[15]

Taylor and the other Cheyenne Peyotists who appealed to the Christian sentiments of Indian Office officials in their petition knew the likelihood of their voices being dismissed and took further legal steps to protect their right to use peyote. On the same day the Peyotists drafted their petition, they secured the services of D. K. Cunningham, a white attorney who practiced law in Kingfisher, Oklahoma, to aid their cause. Cunningham also sent a letter to Indian Bureau officials, expressing the disgrace of the ceremony participants "being told by the police that they were under arrest" and requesting that agents "instruct the Indian police not to interfere" with future peyote services.[16] Superintendent Charles Shell responded to Cunningham's request by claiming that the peyote practice was not aligned with the teachings of the Christian religion. Shell informed Cunningham that he intended to prosecute three of the ringleaders for violating the law in Oklahoma Territory.[17] Despite the plea from a white ally such as Cunningham, Oklahoma authorities followed up on Shell's request to prosecute three of the Peyotists. Reuben Taylor, Howling Wolf, and Percy Kable were charged in Kingfisher County with a violation of Section 2652 of the Oklahoma Territorial Statutes prohibiting the possession of the "Mescal Bean." Each man faced the possibility of conviction for a misdemeanor offense, punishable with a "fine ranging from $25–$200 and/or confinement in the county jail for not more than six months."[18] Like Reuben Taylor, both Howling Wolf and Percy Kable admitted to being adherents of Peyotism, claiming its use as a sacred medicine in their religious practice. However, the legal action against Howling Wolf and Kable had an added demeaning dimension to it based upon their previous experiences of interaction with the federal government.

As an active participant in the Southern Plains Wars, Howling Wolf was one of the seventy-two Cheyenne, Kiowa, Comanche, Arapaho, and Caddo Indian prisoners from the Red River War incarcerated at Fort Marion in St. Augustine, Florida, between 1875 and 1878. During his incarceration at Fort Marion, Howling Wolf, like some of the other prisoners, made drawings using available paper, but as Joyce Szabo writes, he "is the only artist known to have created drawings during the pre-reservation era, on the reservation, and at Fort Marion." Art historians like Szabo argue that Howling Wolf is "the single most important Plains artist who worked on paper during the late nineteenth century."[19] Though never imprisoned by government officials like Howling Wolf, Percy Kable also experienced a sense of derisiveness with his arrest and prosecution. Kable, who attended both Carlisle Indian School and Haskell Institute, ironically served as a member of the Indian police on the Cheyenne and Arapaho Agency from 1888 to 1903.[20] Having a great deal of experience with systems of power previously used against Native Americans, the three defendants would now utilize those systems in their efforts to vindicate themselves and their peyote practice.

The trial in the case of *Territory of Oklahoma v. Howling Wolf, Reuben Taylor, and Percy Kable* convened on February 26, 1907, in the probate court of Kingfisher County (probate courts were using special jurisdiction since gaining statehood caused the incoming courts of Oklahoma to not be fully functional until 1908).[21] The legal strategy was to challenge the rhetoric contained in the territorial statute, specifically the phrase "Mescal Bean." The defendants claimed that the substance they had at their ceremony was peyote and not mescal beans, and that the two articles were not the same thing. According to the letter of the law, the statute forbid the use of mescal beans but not peyote.[22] In preparing for the trial and hearing of this strategy from the defense, George Bowman, the county attorney, turned his attention to finding witnesses to prove that the item in question confiscated at the ceremony fell within the definition of mescal beans as applicable under the law.[23] William E. Johnson, special officer of the bureau to suppress liquor traffic among Indians, declared that though his experience with the two articles was not extensive, he knew for a fact that they were exactly the same thing.[24] Rev. Robert Hamilton, the Baptist missionary serving the reservation of the defendants, affirmed his willingness to be present at the trial. He encouraged the prosecution to convince the court that the current peyote was the same thing ingested by the Native Americans at the time the law was enacted, and *bean* was just an unfortunate word choice, both in the statute and the vernacular of Indian agents, because peyote was actually not a bean at all.[25] This approach worked, as the court found the three defendants guilty and sentenced each man to five days in jail, with a fine of twenty-five dollars plus court costs. Their attorney gave notice of appeal to the district court and put up an appeal bond of two hundred dollars per person.[26] The defense's argument was the same at the district court level—peyote and mescal beans were not the same thing, and the law did not prohibit peyote—but for the next court appearance, both sides relied heavily on the use of expert witnesses to support a scientific evaluation of peyote.

The case of *Territory of Oklahoma v. Taylor et al.* proceeded to the district court in early July 1907. In preparation, the defense enlisted the aid of James Mooney to serve as their expert witness. Mooney had been a strong supporter of Peyotism since he had begun investigating it in the 1890s (and soon would become a vocal opponent of government efforts to prohibit the cactus). The defense felt Mooney could provide credible scientific testimony that peyote and mescal beans were different in their physical properties and effects as well as their rhetorical usages.

The prosecution, on the other hand, was confident that Mooney's testimony would not hurt their case if he were subpoenaed. Even if Mooney were to minimize the evil effects of the mescal bean, government officials believed he would concur that peyote was the same as mescal beans.[27] The state, though, continued to build its own list of expert witnesses and was willing to pay for their expertise. The plaintiffs sent a peyote button to H. C. Washburn, a botanist and professor at the University of Oklahoma, to enlist his support, and secured the testimony of Dr. Charles R. Hume, the physician at the Kiowa, Comanche, and Wichita agency, as well as other employees of that agency who possessed a greater knowledge of peyote than witnesses at the first trial.[28] Government officials felt that a successful legal prosecution at the district court level would deliver a substantial blow to the traffic and use of peyote. Indian Bureau agents knew that they had caught the Peyotists with something like a button with a fuzzy center and that the Native Americans had commonly called it *mescal* but had recently changed the wording to *peyote*. Bureau officials knew the state had to prove the term *mescal bean* in the statute covered the article consumed by the Peyotists, because if they failed, they feared that the harmful effects of Peyotism would spread all over the two territories in the soon-to-be state of Oklahoma.[29]

Before the trial began on July 12, 1907, the Peyotists' attorney changed his legal strategy: Cunningham decided not to use expert witnesses. Rather, he entered a demurrer—a response that in effect pleads a motion to dismiss on the point that even if the facts alleged in the complaint were true, there is still no legal basis to continue the suit or proceedings. Cunningham submitted to Judge C. F. Irvin that the territorial statute concerning the "mescal bean" was "class legislation and that the territory had no right to enact any such law."[30] The basis for this defense came from Indian Bureau officials and their paternalistic power over the trust funds of allotted Native Americans, money that they needed to pay the legal fees for the trial. The Office of Indian Affairs in Washington, DC, received a letter of July 8, 1907, from defendant Reuben Taylor, where he indicated that he was "in need of funds to meet the expenses for his defense," and requested permission "to use his inherited lands funds for that purpose." In a response sent a few weeks after the scheduled trial date, the Office of Indian Affairs authorized Superintendent Charles Shell to issue a check for $300 to meet the necessary legal costs for Taylor's defense, drawn against his inherited Indian land funds, "of which he has $1017.72 to his credit."[31] The logic of Cunningham's argument made sense in his experience with Taylor—Native Americans were the group most likely to use peyote (or "mescal beans," as the Oklahoma government identified them) so Native Americans were also the ones most likely to be arrested and prosecuted; they were often not able to receive fair representation in the legal system because the ability to access their money was still tied to a relationship of dependency on the federal government. Therefore, the statute imposed an undue burden on these Oklahoma Peyotists.

Judge Irwin sustained the motion for dismissal and gave Indian Agency officials thirty days to make a response. Sensing that the judicial system was turning in favor of the Peyotists, Superintendent Shell decided not to use a brief furnished to him by the Office of Indian Affairs, but rather to wait on the granting of statehood and convince the new state legislature to amend the wording of the statute to include peyote. An acquittal came for Howling Wolf, Reuben Taylor, and Percy Kable because the prosecution allowed the case to lapse.[32] The willingness and determination of these Peyotists to fight the charges and the interpretation of the law used against them represented a new way of securing their cultural and legal right to use peyote. The Peyotists recognized that "whites create the institutions, oversee their operations, maintain, protect, and legitimize them, which in turn maintains their power," and then used those same social structures to achieve a racial privilege in the legal system.[33] Rather than accept the verdict and punishment from the first trial, the defendants continued to use the justice system to pursue a semantic challenge to the "white man's law" and use the rules of the colonial system to their own advantage. This in turn allowed other Peyotists to adopt the same recourse in their own trials and tribulations over the use of peyote.

Before the case of *Taylor et al.* advanced to district court, the Indian Office lionized the successful conviction of the Peyotists from the trial in probate court and encouraged agents to "take steps to prosecute all others known to have violated the [Oklahoma Territorial] statute."[34] Encouraged by this directive, Special Officer William Johnson pursued legal action against three other Cheyenne Peyotists arrested in April 1907 from a raid on a peyote meeting in Custer County at the Seger Agency.[35] The charge against John Antelope, Rufus Gilbert, and Standing Bird was the same as in the *Taylor et al.* case: a violation of Section 2652 of the Oklahoma Territorial Statutes prohibiting the possession of the "Mescal Bean." The legal defense would be the same as that in Kingfisher County—peyote and mescal beans are not the same thing, and the law does not cover the prohibition of peyote. To aid in this defense, Native Americans at the Seger Agency also contacted James Mooney, writing to him about the trouble at Clinton, Oklahoma, of using peyote. Paul Road, the author of the letter, noted that the prosecution had three witnesses lined up to prove peyote and mescal beans were the same item, and the Cheyenne defendants only had one witness to counter the state's position. Road requested that Mooney send his testimony for them to use since Mooney studied Peyotism and knew what the Native Americans were doing "in the peyote tepee."[36] Additional comments in Road's letter provided more evidence in support of Cunningham's argument that the statute was class legislation. Road indicated that the Cheyennes at Clinton were very poor people, having little money to even support their children, let alone pay for attorney fees. He pleaded with Mooney for his help. Despite their lack of strong legal representation, the testimony of the Peyotists given through an interpreter was enough to counter the expert witnesses called by the state. At the trial held in

July 1907 at Arapaho, Oklahoma, a jury found the Peyotists not guilty of violating the territorial statute.[37] The testimony that none of the Peyotists had mescal beans in their possession, but rather had peyote, was enough to convince a jury of white men that the "white man's law" had not been broken.

Native Americans in Oklahoma were not the only ones to encounter the American legal system in the practice of Peyotism. As the religion spread to the northern plains and to the western tribes, so did the desire to prosecute and punish Peyotists. By this time, the government's stance on peyote encompassed a view that the article was a dangerous intoxicant similar to a narcotic, and that federal prohibition was warranted. The Peyotists' position also evolved during this time, emphasizing the religious nature of the use of peyote. The legal arguments on both sides adapted to accommodate these contrasting positions.

The first of several court cases outside Oklahoma occurred on April 2, 1914, in Wisconsin. On March 15, a US marshal arrested Nah-qua-tah-tuck (Potawatomi), also known as Mitchell Neck, for introducing peyote on the Menominee Indian Reservation in Wisconsin. Neck had brought peyote to the house of the Neconish family, situated near the western boundary of the Menominee reservation, where they held a meeting of a religious nature. Authorities charged Neck with a violation of the Indian Prohibition Act of 1897, claiming peyote to be an intoxicant. At the trial in Milwaukee, the federal judge interpreted the 1897 law to mean a prohibition only against alcoholic beverages, and determined that the Indian Office could not legally interfere with the use and transport of peyote. The judge also considered the religious nature in the use of the peyote and acquitted Neck on the basis of the religious rights of Peyotists.[38]

As social reformers continued the national push for alcohol prohibition, government authorities continued to commit themselves to the enforcement of prohibition laws already in place in Indian Country. A South Dakota grand jury indicted William Red Nest, an Oglala Lakota residing on the Pine Ridge Reservation, on September 11, 1915, for violating the 1897 Indian Prohibition Act with his possession of peyote. Superintendent John R. Brennan identified Red Nest as one of five Oglala peyote leaders on the reservation. The case against Red Nest did not come to trial immediately, and by 1917, the US attorney dismissed the charges against him.[39] However, federal authorities continued to harass Oglala Lakota Peyotists with oppositional difficulties. On May 19, 1916, the federal government indicted Harry Black Bear for giving peyote buttons on the Pine Ridge Reservation to Jacob Black Bear, Paul Black Bear Jr., John Black Cat, and James Real Bull. The case went to trial in September in the US district court located in Deadwood, South

Dakota. R. P. Stewart, the US attorney for South Dakota, argued that peyote was an intoxicant subject to the provision of the statute prohibiting the introduction of intoxicants on a Native American reservation.[40] Attorney Thomas Sloan, a member of the Omaha tribe, an active participant in the Society of American Indians, and a Peyotist, served as an advisor to Black Bear's defense attorneys and as the primary witness for the defense in the court proceedings. Sloan testified that as one who partook of peyote "it is not an intoxicant, that its effects after long usage are not bad on the system, and that it really does have an elevating effect upon its users; that it has cured people addicted to the use of intoxicants . . . and is health producing." Sloan pointed to the level of progress made by Peyotist Indians, "who have made homes for themselves . . . and who have been uniformly successful in all of their endeavors."[41] Although a jury convicted Black Bear, the judge overruled the verdict, declaring that peyote was not an intoxicating liquor, nor a drug, and could therefore not be in the same category as other intoxicants within the meaning of the law.[42] The courts were beginning to make it clear that in order to prohibit peyote, the "white man's law" must change.

One court case from this period exemplifies both the spread of Peyotism and the progress Peyotists made in using the court system to secure their right to worship. The case of *State of Montana v. Big Sheep* in 1924 further extended the boundaries in which the Peyotists' religious identity could operate within the systems of socially constructed American identity. Big Sheep, a Crow and member of the legally organized Native American Church, faced a conviction in both state and district courts for unlawfully having peyote (a sack of fifty-six peyote buttons) in his possession at the home of Austin Stray Calf, seven miles south of Hardin, Montana, within the boundaries of the Crow Reservation. At the time of his arrest in November, the state of Montana had legislation specifically making it unlawful for a person to possess peyote. After his initial conviction, Big Sheep made an appeal, and a trial in district court convened on March 4, 1925. He based his appeal on two grounds. The first centered on the jurisdictional boundaries of state law, where Big Sheep's legal defense argued that the Montana statute lacked authority over actions taking place on the Crow Reservation, deemed to be federal land. This became the argument with which Big Sheep was able to secure the review of the issue by the Montana Supreme Court. Big Sheep also constructed his defense on his religious identity as a member in good standing in the Native American Church, where members used peyote "for sacramental purposes only in the worship of God according to their belief and interpretation of the Holy Bible, and according to the dictates of their conscience." To punish Big Sheep for his ceremonial use of peyote was to infringe on his right to freedom of religion. The previous courts overruled the religious appeals of Big Sheep, but the Montana Supreme Court considered his testimony that Peyotists in this particular chapter of the Native American Church "ground their faith upon the Fourteenth Chapter of Romans, the Fifty-Third Chapter of Isaiah, second verse, and the Second Chapter of Revelations, seventeenth verse, King James Version."[43] The Montana Supreme Court upheld the state's anti-peyote legislation but reversed the conviction of Big Sheep. In the opinion written by Justice Calloway, the court ruled on the jurisdictional issue rather than the religious argument, but the position advanced by Big Sheep demonstrated the willingness of Peyotists to locate their religious identity within the scriptural framework that was recognized in the religious system of American Christianity and protected by the legal system.

When the Wyoming legislature was considering action to prohibit peyote, two Crow Peyotists sought the advice of attorneys for possible court action to "declare that the white man, by banning the peyote plant is interfering with religious ceremonies of many Indians."[44] Barney Old Coyote, a former football star at Haskell Institute, and Holman Ceasely traveled to Sheridan, Wyoming, "to use the white man's methods to obtain their rights" by seeking the advice of attorneys as the men contemplated court action.[45]

The trials and tribulations of Peyotists in the early twentieth century demonstrated the possibility of successfully challenging white laws and policies that restricted the full expression of their religion and to advance a new political identity in American society. Similar to the legal efforts of Peyotists, other minority religious groups would also begin using the legal system to secure their religious rights, as cases in the mid-twentieth century would turn the law of religious liberty enshrined in the Free Exercise and Establishment Clauses of the Constitution into a national standard.[46] As Peyotists utilized the "white man's" legal system to gain their rights, they also organized themselves in the "white man's" political arena.

THE PEYOTE LOBBY ENTERS THE POLITICAL ARENA

As the cultural battle over peyote grew lawmakers began to consider ways to change the "white man's" laws to rid Native American society of peyote, Peyotists recognized the need to secure legal advantages for themselves in the political arena. As their religious identity expanded into the political sphere, the popular press accurately identified their organizational efforts as a "peyote lobby."

The quintessential figure representing the ability of Native Americans to utilize elements of American politics in order to achieve Native American social, economic, and political objectives is Comanche leader Quanah Parker. A devout Peyotist and polygamist, Quanah was also a successful businessman and political figure, maintaining connections and friendships with many white political leaders, including presidents. Quanah hunted with Theodore Roosevelt—the president who officially proclaimed Oklahoma a state on November 16, 1907—near his allotted homestead in southwestern Oklahoma and was a participant in the parade at Roosevelt's inauguration in 1905. In a 1910 visit to Washington, Quanah called on President William Howard Taft, and the press reported that "the Great White Father was much interested in the old chief, plied him with many questions and expressed much pleasure in the meeting." Quanah was equally pleased with the reception from Taft, expressing his approval for "Big Bill."[47] Quanah's popularity in the white imagination contributed to his ability to successfully navigate between two socially constructed racial worlds. One newspaper declared, "[Quanah Parker is the] best known Indian in the southwest [and] the most civilized of the chiefs of the blanket tribes."[48] Quanah managed to capitalize on his popularity and social capital among both Native Americans and whites. At the state and national level, he provided leadership and organization for Peyotists to oppose potential anti-peyote legislation.

While writing the proposed state constitution, the Oklahoma Constitutional Convention meeting in Guthrie considered expanding the alcohol prohibition in the new constitution to include peyote, especially given the recent failures in the judicial system to prosecute Peyotists.[49] Quanah appeared before the Committee on Sanitation and Public Health to request that officials not enact laws that would prevent Native Americans from using peyote. A reporter covering the event recorded that Quanah appeared in the city with "two of his wives and several of his head men, among whom were Ahpeahtone of the Kiowas, Apache John of the Apache, and Standing Elk of the Cheyennes." Though Quanah was the only one to address this committee, the delegation represented a pan-Indian front united in solidarity over the peyote cause. Quanah's testimony before the committee also revealed the hybridity of the cultural identity that he and other Peyotists had in mind as Oklahoma entered the Union. Quanah announced that "the new ways of the pale face were coming in. His people desired to be citizens of the new state, but hoped to be allowed to retain some of their old customs.... The most important to his mind and one that was in danger of being taken away was their right to use the mescal bean [peyote] as a medicine."[50] During his visit to Guthrie, he addressed the assembly of convention delegates and touched on the politics of identity surrounding the current state of Indian affairs. In his testimony, Quanah invoked his citizenship status as a result of the allotment process, which should have afforded him and many others equal protection under the law, and he chastised white policymakers in their current efforts to deny Native Americans the medicinal value of peyote.[51]

Quanah's efforts to stop the inclusion of a peyote prohibition in the new constitution were successful, but with increasing pressure from the Indian Office, the first state legislature began to consider amending the 1897 Indian Prohibition Act to close the legal loophole used in favor of Peyotists in the court system.[52] The bill introduced by Lieutenant Governor George Bellamy would amend a section of the revised statutes, making it a misdemeanor offense to possess peyote.[53] An earlier attempt by then-territorial senator Bellamy to ban peyote brought a small delegation of Peyotists to call on Cassius Barnes, the governor of Oklahoma Territory, asking him to veto any such legislation.[54] The 1908 bill brought an even greater gathering of Native Americans to Guthrie to oppose the legislation. Sixteen Peyotists, including Quanah Parker, registered as lobbyists in order to speak before the committees and the legislature, while many more traveled to the state capital to lend their support.[55] Delegations from several tribes organized to present a united pan-Indian Peyotist presence before the white lawmakers. Indian agency officials even became alarmed that the Peyotists had "a strong lobby at Guthrie."[56] Hailed by journalists as "one of the largest delegations of Indians ever gathered in the Oklahoma capital," reports of the protest caught the attention of the public through the expansive news coverage of Native American delegations "lobbying against the mescal bean legislation."[57]

Observers consistently identified the peyote lobby at the Oklahoma state capital as made up of "blanket Indians," the smaller tribes in the state who came to live on reservations after the establishment of Indian Territory granted land to the removed five southeast tribes (also identified in the imagined narrative of conquest as the Five Civilized Tribes). The popular imagination also portrayed blanket Indians as traditional, clinging to the customs and habits of a past that was vanishing and resisting assimilation and acculturation in the transition to a modern era. Racialized rhetoric intended for a white audience filled the stories of daily papers. One reported that about seventy-five "braves and squaws" attended the hearings before the house committee.[58] Another painted the scene at the state capital as reminiscent of the "Wild West" of the frontier converging in the modern city of the new state where many of the Native Americans who "cannot speak English" worked their way through the "crowded lobbies of the hotels with blanket[s]." The description of Guthrie as a "camp of Indians" ready to fight the peyote bill also invoked discourse taken from the Indian wars of the nineteenth century. One reporter wrote, "Guthrie could have several war dances, a couple of stomp dances, and a massacre very easily, as the material is at hand," because about one hundred of the "most famous of the vanishing type of Indians are on the grounds."[59] After the hearings ended, one editorial commentator identified "several red blanketed pilgrims in search of peyote beans still squatting on the grass in the shadow of the stately government building."[60] Most of the racial discourse reflected an astonishment at the Peyotists' ability to enter the political arena at all. Newspaper accounts revealed a white fascination with the intertribal gathering and the vivid contrasts on the floor in the state legislature where Native Americans gathered.[61]

The press also noticed the intergenerational nature of the peyote delegation, often construed as a "traditional versus progressive" tribal identity. A revelation emerged in one report that the peyote lobby "was not a bevy of tribal loafers, many of the representatives being men of affairs, college graduates, and able to fight the battle of life in any community."[62] The description of some Peyotists as graduates from good schools who spoke good English dispelled the notion that Peyotists compromised a monolithic Native American population of non-progressive people.[63] Even the Native Americans who spoke in broken English made eloquent appeals in the committee hearings when they demanded their right to follow their own religious beliefs.[64] While whites were perplexed by the mixed cultural identities of Peyotists, the peyote lobbyists were united in their political thought, having "no hesitancy in making it known that they were Democrats."[65] The seriousness of this cultural battle over peyote and the Peyotists' willingness to engage whites in the "white man's" political system became apparent in one observation of the hearings: "The white men do not seem to take the matter seriously. The red man does. When the Indian learned that it had been suggested that the bean ... was to be taken from him, he complained like the white man pleading for the firewater he drinks"—a reference to the anti-Prohibitionists in Oklahoma who opposed the "dry" Constitution.[66] While the novelty of the organized peyote lobby captivated white reporters and readers, the entrance of Peyotists into the legislative arena provided a formidable political presence in the official affairs of the state.

Indian officials were correct to fear the peyote lobby gathered in Guthrie. The organized, earnest appeals of Peyotists led the Committee on Public Health and Sanitation to move that the state legislature should not consider the measure to ban peyote. The press credited the bill's defeat to the peyote lobby who appeared before the legislature to protest against it.[67] Distressed that the state of Oklahoma failed to prevent Native Americans from using peyote, authorities in the Indian Office turned to federal regulation to transform the article into a legitimate narcotic subject. As the push for legislation moved to the federal level, the organized peyote lobby followed the struggle to Washington.

Native American leaders and white medical officials who met in Guthrie, Oklahoma, in January 1908, for a hearing to prove the difference between peyote and mescal beans. *Front Row (left to right)*: Tennyson Berry (Apache), Koday (Kiowa), Koon-Ka-Zahche Aka "Apache John" (Apache), Otto Wells (Comanche), Quanah Parker (Comanche), Ahpeatone (Kiowa), Paul George (?) (Cheyenne), and Standing Bird (Cheyenne). *2nd Row*: 1. Leonard Tyler (Cheyenne), 4. Christopher Columbus "Bud" Choate, 7. Joseph Blackbear (Cheyenne), 8. Ned Brace (Kiowa). *3rd Row*: 5. Edwin Theodore Sorrells, 6. W. H. Edley. *Back Row*: 5. William Durant. Courtesy of Oklahoma Historical Society, Oklahoma City, Frank F. Finney Sr. Collection.

The varied non-legislative proposals to restrict peyote brought Peyotists in contact with officials at the federal Indian Office and with their own congressional representatives as they sought to advocate for themselves. Many petitions and letters came to federal officials from Peyotists expressing dissatisfaction with Indian Office attempts to prohibit not only the use of peyote, but its sale and transport. Thomas Walker, a Winnebago in Nebraska, undertook a letter-writing campaign to the Indian commissioner and to his congressman, J. P. Latta, asking for a repeal of the bureau's embargo on peyote. In his correspondence with federal officials, Walker claimed an experiential religiosity with the use of peyote as both a sacred medicine and a spiritual experience.[68] Baldwin Parker (Comanche), son of Quanah

Parker, appealed to Governor Cruce of Oklahoma in a letter protesting the actions of Indian agents to restrict peyote. His letter contained an early first account from the pen of a Native American about the beneficial uses of peyote.[69] More common in their protests against action by the Indian Bureau were personal trips to the nation's capital to engage their representatives in Congress. Quanah Parker was a frequent visitor to Washington, where he presented his case that peyote was not a harmful drug.[70] Delegations of Peyotists from various tribes began to appear in Washington on a frequent basis, either personally paying the expenses for the trips or raising funds from other Peyotists to defray the costs.[71] The peyote lobby operated in DC even before proposed federal legislation emerged in Congress. The Native American presence in the nation's capital was so expansive that one newspaper story proclaimed that outside of the reservations themselves, Washington, DC, was "the greatest Indian center in the United States." Close to the government offices, hotels along Pennsylvania Avenue, which once were "aristocratic hostelries," were now filled with Native Americans who wanted to "get out among the congressmen. And there he seems to have done a nifty job of lobbying in favor of peyote."[72] Peyotists took full advantage of opportunities to take their fight for peyote directly to the people working within the white institutions of power.

As Congress considered federal peyote prohibition between 1916 and 1937, the peyote lobby continued their organized measures to defeat it. Peyotist protestors sought individual visits with congressional representatives as well as chances to voice their protests in testimony before a series of house committee hearings in 1918. Delegations of Peyotists continued to flood into Washington to maintain a strong presence and political lobby.[73] The Osage Peyotists became particularly active during this era of federal attempts at prohibition. The Osage were one of the wealthiest tribes thanks to their ownership of reservation lands, the negotiation of cash payments for their annuities, their pasture leases, and the burgeoning oil industry on their land in Oklahoma.[74] Their financial standing afforded them opportunities to take care of their interests. They successfully converted this financial capital into political capital. Newspaper coverage indicated that "whenever anything goes wrong now, a delegation of Osage invade the national capital and make things interesting on the Potomac until their wrongs are righted."[75] As Peyotists, the Osage were especially important in preventing a peyote prohibition.

After the legal incorporation of the Native American Church in November 1918, the peyote lobby became associated with this legal entity as church members, and officials mixed politics and religion out of legal necessity and political expediency.[76] The cultural battle over peyote, situated in a time of transition in modern American

The Osage peyote lobby in Washington, DC. From *Reading (PA) News-Times*, March 29, 1918, 13.

society, allowed Peyotists to secure technical experts, legal representatives, and persuasive speakers to aid their cause.[77] White reformers, Indian officials, and policymakers noticed the well-organized efforts of a peyote lobby against the antipeyote propagandists who largely acted as individuals and without organization.[78] Peyotists also took advantage of their connection with influential congressional representatives, especially the congressmen from Oklahoma. Just as the peyote lobby successfully defeated legislation in Oklahoma, they ably prevented repeated efforts to enact federal peyote prohibition legislation. A newspaper article wrote how Peyotists "were secure from an invasion of white man's law, which would deprive them of their peyote—the sacrament around which their native religion is built."[79] As the Protestant church-state alliance was in decline from the influences of secularism and pluralism, Peyotists took advantage of the opportunity to chip away at the religious hegemonic status of Protestant Christianity. Their entry into the political arena afforded Peyotists a degree of constitutional protection for their religion and caught the attention of white Americans who had been hesitant to grant citizenship status to all Native Americans.

DRESSING FOR SUCCESS IN THE "WHITE MAN'S WORLD" OF LAW AND POLITICS

Part of the success of the Peyotists was their ability to move across cultural barriers through their appearance and attire. In their adoption of what was deemed by white officials as "citizen's dress," Peyotists played upon the sartorial options of material culture to create a new political identity for themselves that displayed the hybridity of Native and white American society. The use of clothing as a form of political identity has deep roots within the American empire-building process, according to historian S. Elizabeth Bird, for "the ability to define imagery is a consequence of power."[80] Tracing the history of dress in America, Michael Zakim identified the employment of clothing by early Americans as "a symbol of colonial resistance" against the British Empire and observed how "clothing has consistently served as both material and metaphor for the social question."[81] During the nineteenth century, the mass-produced suit for men became a material marker of identification with the body politic, a "civic uniform" that helped "forge a common social life" and political identity.[82] By the late 1860s, the term "citizens' clothing" and its variations became synonymous with "the garb of a people who, though at other times part of an illiberal collective, were currently self-determining and self-owning—in a word, free."[83] The suit also became a signifier of cultural fitness for US citizenship. Indian agents repeatedly judged the willingness of Native American men to wear suits as a sign of their progress into potential citizenship status and deemed those clinging to traditional clothing as non-progressive "blanket Indians." The Indian Office even began to track the numbers of Native Americans who laid aside the "blanket of barbarism" and adopted the white man's dress, or the "garb of civilization."[84]

The liminal state of American cultural identity in the early twentieth century provided both motive and means for Peyotists to use sartorial representations to their advantage. As Stephen Kantrowitz points out in his study of the Ho-Chunk, "Clothing was as unreliable a marker of political fitness as it was of civilization."[85] Peyotists gave further evidence to this in their lobbying efforts in both Oklahoma and Washington. Newspaper reports of the blanket Indians' appearance in the cities commented on the touch of color that their Native American dress brought to the proceedings on peyote legislation. Delegations of Native Americans frequently attracted much attention because of their "blankets of varied colors," as well as their "bright shirts, and long braided hair."[86] However, coverage of the political events also noticed the monochromatic imagery of the suits worn by many in the peyote lobby. In a reference to their attire, one account noted, "The leaders are reticent men, many of them passing as plain, business representatives of the Southwest."[87] Praise for Peyotists "wearing the conventional garb of the American citizen" accompanied information on the political proceedings for white readers.[88] "Citizens' clothing" became a way to signal the hybrid identity of Native Americans in modern American society, and it helped provide a means to improve the position of those fighting to keep their Native American religion.

Visible changes in behavior, such as the adoption of the style of dress of the dominant culture, signaled to many reformers, missionaries, and Indian Office officials a willingness to change cultural norms—to assimilate into white society.[89] However, appearances can be deceiving. The photograph of Quanah Parker with three of his wives conveys this point, as his dress in "citizen's clothes" did not erase his identity as a polygamist. Among whites, Quanah's popularity as a Native American emanated more from the construction of Indianness in the American imagination. Through cultural productions emerging from Wild West shows and the nascent film industry, Native Americans performed popular ideas about Indianness for a non-Indian public willing to pay to see these images of "frontier nostalgia."[90] Native Americans both understood and used the power of representation to advance their own agendas in their performances. Philip Deloria writes that show Indians who performed Indianness gained economic and social benefits and found a sense of cultural authority accompanying their representations of Indianness for non-Indian audiences.[91] Louis Warren asserts that show Indians "shaped their performances to subvert, reinforce, or otherwise influence American ideas of Indianness."[92]

The organized peyote lobby surfaced at the same time that anthropological researchers studying Native Americans also organized and professionalized. Anthropological authority, notes anthropologist Lee Baker, "played an important political role in authenticating the genuine culture many people, white and Indian, desired to perform, protect, and police."[93] Those identified as "blanket Indians" because they chose to participate in white representations of Indianness through their attire were still able to use the image as a way to gain a legal right to practice Peyotism. Their willingness to display traditional dress in public settings fueled longstanding perceptions of Indianness in the popular imagination, and garnered publicity for the peyote lobby's visits to the white man's political power centers.

Peyotists were not the only ones to play to white representations of both white Americanness and Indianness. Indian intellectuals who formed the leadership of the

Society of American Indians (SAI) also took advantage of Anglocentric signifiers about dress and appearance to support their arguments against the use of peyote. One of the most outspoken Native American opponents from the leadership ranks of the SAI was Gertrude Simmons Bonnin, a mixed blood Yankton Dakota woman and a highly educated writer, musician, social reformer among the Utes in Utah, and political activist.[94] Her reputation as an anti-peyote campaigner put Bonnin at odds with many Peyotists and their white supporters. She often received much praise from the white public for her actions to stop the peyote religion. The SAI took a formal stance opposing peyote in 1916 just as attempts at federal legislation began, with Bonnin leading the charge and using the image of Indianness to convince policymakers and the public that peyote was harmful to Native Americans both individually and collectively.

SAI leaders knew the power of clothing and its symbolism. Shortly after the founding of the organization, which dedicated itself to the highest development of the Native race, organizers faced criticism from anthropologists and ethnologists over the purpose of the SAI. In a response in 1911, then SAI secretary Arthur Parker summarized the tensions: "The picturesque features of the Indian ceremonies and Indian social system have become idealized with them, and they fear that we are trying to 'whitemanize' the red skin."[95] Parker would later clarify the intentions of the SAI to those who held a romanticized view of Indianness. He argued that developing a hybrid identity through a change in the appearance of Native Americans was possible, for "the red skin is not of the vanishing type—he is merely changing his shirt and exchanging his war club for a seat in congress."[96] As Parker advocated for Native Americans to adopt sartorial patterns of dress that conformed to white society, he also knew the cultural potency of the white image of the Indian, and he, too, took advantage of it when it served the aims of the SAI. Deloria posits that Parker and other men in the SAI "did not hesitate to don a literary headdress in order to challenge and redirect American construction of Indianness."[97] Even Gertrude Bonnin used the Native American image when it profited her. She often appeared at public performances donning Native American attire to promote the work of the SAI among white audiences. Bonnin explained her proclivity for this strategy when asked to speak before a church group wearing Native American dress. She wrote to Parker to explain her willingness to do so: "The use of Indian dress for a drawing card is for a good cause. No doubt, there may be some who may not wholly approve of the Indian dress.... Even a clown has to dress differently from his usual citizen's suit."[98] Bonnin would use this same strategy in 1918 as hearings on the Hayden peyote prohibition bill convened in Washington.

Gertrude Bonnin in the outfit she wore to testify at the 1918 congressional hearings on peyote. From *Washington Times*, February 17, 1918, 1.

Much publicity accompanied Bonnin's appearance in the city as she prepared to testify at the hearings on the evils of peyote. Taking advantage of the media campaign on the legislative hearings, Bonnin gave an interview in the *Washington Times* accompanied by a photograph of her in Native American attire. The strategy to represent herself as a white version of Indianness backfired when ethnologist James Mooney testified at the House Committee on Indian Affairs hearings and used Bonnin's photograph to damage her credibility as a witness in the same proceedings. Mooney's expertise as an anthropologist who spent his career studying Native American cultures led him to critique Bonnin's "Indian costume." Holding a copy of the paper, Mooney made the following observation about the picture of Bonnin (who "claimed to be a Sioux woman") to members of congress: "The dress is a woman's dress from some southern tribe, as shown by the long fringes; the belt is a Navajo man's belt; the fan is a peyote man's fan, carried only by men, usually in the peyote ceremony."[99] Bonnin's Native American costume could not successfully sway the opinion of white legislators. Congress did not pass the Hayden bill to enact a federal ban on peyote.

Through their entrance into and adaptation of the "white man's" legal and political systems, Peyotists managed to thwart the eradication of the plant essential to their religious practices. Confident in the belief that they had a right to maintain their Native American religious identity, they fought to maintain cultural practices that their opponents believed were inconsistent with progress.[100] Peyotists took advantage of the legal system to expose the misunderstandings about peyote as they used semantic weaknesses in the "white man's" law to their advantage in the court systems. When policymakers attempted to close those loopholes, Peyotists organized into a successful political coalition to lobby against proposed legislation. Utilizing both external changes to their self-presentation and preservation of their traditional way of dress, Peyotists capitalized on the political power of imagery prevalent in the white systems of power to make their case for peyote in a very public way. Peyotists also turned to using the white construction of religion as another means to secure their own religious freedom.

6 "LET US KEEP OUR WORSHIP"

PEYOTISTS AND THE FIRST AMENDMENT

In 1901, Arapaho chief Niwot conveyed a plea for religious freedom to the Indian agent at the Cheyenne and Arapaho Agency: "Among white people you will find many different ways of worshipping, and many and varied beliefs . . . and they are all tolerated. . . . Why should we not be allowed to worship God in our own way? We give up our children to the schools you have built for them, and we allow you to teach them to worship God in the manner you think best. . . . We understand the way we have been taught and we want you to let us perform our religious services in the manner we believe to be right."[1] Testifying before the Oklahoma legislature in 1908, Quanah Parker echoed similar sentiments in support of the peyote religion: "[White men] have forced us to drop many of our customs. We have done so, but now let us alone in our worship. . . . We would keep the peyote."[2] The appeal to religious freedom signaled another strategy of resistance: in the wake of congressional attempts to prohibit peyote, Peyotists adopted religious rhetoric and legally organized as a church in 1918.

By advancing their claim to the First Amendment's protection of religious freedom, Peyotists also challenged the federal Indian policy that denied full citizenship rights to Native Americans (full citizenship would not come until the passage of the Indian Citizenship Act of 1924, known as the Snyder Act for Representative Homer P. Snyder (R) of New York). The push for freedom of religion—and freedom *from* the dominant culture's religion—conveyed a new, modern social identity of Native people as Americans. Important to understanding the 1918 formal institutionalization of a church representing a pan-Indian religion is the social context in which it occurred—the ending of World War I. The Native American population of the United States had contributed significantly to the war effort. Thousands of Native American men volunteered to fight on the battlefields in Europe, including many who were non-citizens who chose to serve rather than asserting this exemption right on draft registrations. Approximately twenty-five percent of the male adult Indian population served in World War I.[3] Although Congress passed a law in 1919 granting Native American veterans the right to apply for citizenship, James Olson and Raymond Wilson concluded that "in 1920 nearly 125,000 Indians (over forty percent of the Indian population) remained without the benefits and responsibilities of citizenship."[4] Interestingly, the US government valued the Indianness of many of these soldiers because of their contributions as code talkers, using their Indigenous languages in strategic military operations.[5] On the home front, Native Americans demonstrated their patriotism in the war effort by spending millions of dollars on Liberty Loan Bonds, donating to the Red Cross, and increasing the production of meat and agricultural products on Indian reservations.[6] Yet, according to correspondence with the Society of American Indians, while Native Americans "fought autocracy to make the world safe for democracy," they returned to "reservations . . . not made safe for democracy."[7] Freedom, interpreted as a right to equal citizenship, represented a concern for all Native Americans. For Peyotists who contributed to the war effort, however, the issue of freedom was particularly connected to religion.

Peyote was also connected to World War I because Native Americans used dances and peyote meetings as part of their goodbyes to those going off to serve and on the occasion of Red Cross collections.[8] Opponents of peyote, on the other hand, used the war to repeat the call for federal peyote prohibition. Believing that peyote damaged the Native race, they called upon the government to fight it as an enemy.[9]

The call for the rights of full citizenship as a response to Native American patriotism and service to America—made primarily by the Society of American Indians (SAI)—did not imply a right to full religious freedom in the use of peyote. For Peyotists, however, citizenship offered an additional claim to the full protection of First Amendment rights. Wanting to garner the full privileges of American citizenship and the religious freedom granted to Christianity, a group of Peyotists made the decision in 1918 to legally incorporate as a "church." Even after taking this step, Peyotists would still continue to do battle with the US government in order to experience the religious freedom they desired in their worship practices.

Peyotists also adopted the Western theological language of "sacrament" to describe the religious nature of their sacred medicine. This discursive shift provided them with a legal loophole to continue their use of peyote in worship. The societal acceptance of religious exceptions to alcohol prohibition allowed Peyotists to argue for their religious freedom on the basis of peyote being an essential sacrament in their religious practice. The promotion of peyote as essential and foundational to the religion became part of a preemptive strategy to defend Peyotism against the federal government's potential evocation of the dictates outlined in *Reynolds v. U.S.* (1879), a case that tested the limits of religious liberty as applied to a law that banned the Mormon religious practice of plural marriage. The court declared a law banning polygamy to be constitutional and not in violation of the Free Exercise Clause protecting religious beliefs, based on a distinction between the freedom to believe and the freedom to act. Individuals have the freedom to believe what they choose, but the practice of that belief cannot violate the laws of the nation. While laws cannot interfere with religious belief and opinions, laws can regulate some religious practices, especially those deemed non-essential to the religion. As polygamy was not foundational to Mormon beliefs in the church's earliest days, it was subject to restriction by the federal government without violating the principles of the First Amendment.[10] As in the *Reynolds* case, anti-Peyotists in the early part of the twentieth century sought to strategically define the term *religion* in a way that would fit the policies they advocated.

The emergence of the Native American Church (NAC) in 1918 coincided with the rise of the social gospel movement and fundamentalist Christianity, where new theological interpretations of "religion" emerged. Peyotism formed part of the discussion, with its opponents frequently dubbing it a "false religion," while Peyotists emphasized its ethical and moral dimensions. The transition from the nineteenth to the twentieth centuries was one of the most "fractious and transforming eras in American history," including in the world of religious belief—what Martin E. Marty describes as a "crisis in the Protestant Empire."[11] The changing American society presented challenges to the exclusivist nature of traditional Protestant religion, and the Protestant establishment sought to retain its cultural leadership by finding new ways to define religion.

PEYOTIST INDIANS ORGANIZE A CHURCH

In August 1918, Peyotists held an intertribal gathering in El Reno, Oklahoma, to discuss strategies to protect their right to use peyote. Deciding on a legal strategy of incorporation similar to other religious groups, they drafted articles of incorporation and applied for nonprofit status with the state to create the Native American

Church (NAC).[12] The state of Oklahoma formally granted legal status to the NAC on October 10, 1918. This, however, was not the first attempt at the institutional organization of their religion. Both informal and formal attempts to systematize Peyotism had occurred prior to the NAC.

Anglo observers of Indian affairs often noted the "religious meetings" associated with the use of peyote, and as early as 1906 they commented on the organization of "quasi-religious societies of mescal bean eaters."[13] As Peyotism spread beyond the borders of Oklahoma, the appearance as an organized religion also emerged in other states. One report documented that Native Americans on the Winnebago reservation in Iowa "organized a lodge of 250 members," rhetoric analogous to the emphasis placed on the importance of institutional membership in many Christian denominations.[14] During the 1914 trial of Mitchell Neck (Nah-qua-tah-tuck) in Wisconsin, testimony emerged about "a regularly organized association among the Indians called the Peyote Society, also known as the Union Church Society."[15] The "Union Church" appeared in 1909 among Peyotists, writes C. Burton Dustin, "in an attempt to accommodate white patterns of religious organizations," though it was "probably not legally incorporated" because almost nothing more is known of it.[16] In Nebraska, the emergence of the Omaha Mescal Society, claiming sixty-six members, caught the attention of Indian officials in 1912 when a delegation from the group traveled to Washington to lobby the Indian Office to lift the ban on the importation and use of peyote on reservations. By 1915, the Omaha Mescal Society was known as the "Omaha Peyote Society (later the American Indian Church Brother Association and at present the Native American Church)."[17] Though none of these early peyote organizations gained legal standing at a state or federal level, their existence indicates willingness of Peyotists to unite in a religious way just as they were doing as a political lobby.

The first legally organized Peyotist church began in 1914. Jonathan (Jack) Koshiway helped a group of Otoe Peyotists incorporate to form the Firstborn Church of Christ in Red Rock, Oklahoma. Born in Kansas in 1886 to a Sac and Fox (Thâkîwaki) father and an Otoe (Otoe-Missouria, or Jiwere Nutache) mother, Koshiway lived for many years with his father's people. By 1907, he had moved to the Otoe-Missouria reservation in Oklahoma to live among his mother's people and had married an Otoe woman.[18] It was here that Koshiway became familiar with Peyotism through Charles Whitehorn, a roadman among the Otoe Peyotists. Whitehorn made Otoe Peyotism distinctive through emphasizing Christian elements. His use of Christian symbolism was apparent in the white cross on his teepee and the additional ceremonial elements (roadmen, feathers, prayer fans, and corn husk cigarettes) that were meant to emphasize the number seven, which was associated with the days of the Creation, and, after midnight, the number twelve, in remembrance of the disciples of Christ.[19]

In deciding to form a church, Koshiway met with many white ministers to get advice on organizing. He went to H. F. Johnston, a lawyer in Perry, Oklahoma, to seek the necessary legal advice, and on December 8, 1914, the Firstborn Church of Christ incorporated under the laws of Oklahoma. Unlike the NAC, Koshiway's church did not explicitly mention peyote in its articles of incorporation, but rather acknowledged its use through a veiled reference that called for the church to "practice ceremonies, rites, customs, uses and proceedings agreeable to our present ritual."[20] Koshiway chose to emphasize the Christian syncretism of Peyotism prominent in his own religious worldviews. The statement of purpose for the church was strongly Christian. Influenced by the ethical standards of both the Mormons and the Russellites, Koshiway changed the peyote ritual, prohibiting smoking and adding the Bible as a conspicuous part of the meeting.[21] After the 1918 incorporation of the NAC, many assumed that the Firstborn Church of Christ merged into that legal entity. However, Koshiway's original church remained separate from the current chapter of the Otoe Native American Church and changed its name to the Firstborn Church of the Otoe-Missouria Tribe. It is still in existence today.[22]

While Koshiway's Firstborn Church of Christ was the first legal incorporation of the peyote religion, its emphasis on a Christian syncretism did not appeal to all Peyotists. However, the idea of a legal institutionalization of Peyotism as a means to further protect Native Americans' religious freedom was appealing and deemed necessary in the wake of federal efforts to prohibit peyote. Two years before the incorporation of the Native American Church, James Mooney reported that some of the delegates and tribes appearing before the 1916 congressional special committee were already debating the matter of "organizing their own religion, like any other church or Society, as American citizens."[23]

In his 1916 letter to Julia Prentiss, Mooney referred to the possibility of Peyotists organizing like the northwestern Indians had more than twenty years earlier, an allusion to the Indian Shaker Church. Unrelated to the American Shakers (the United Society of Believers), the movement that became the Indian Shaker Church began in 1882 in the Pacific Northwest. Religious historian Lee Irwin writes, "The tradition established by John Slocum, a Squaxin with strong ties to the Skokomish and other Southern Coast Salish peoples, assimilated many features of Christianity, both Catholic and Protestant, while also retaining indigenous elements central to Northwest Coast Native spirituality." Similar to prophets associated with the Ghost Dance movement, Slocum experienced a revelation from God that Native

Americans could achieve a medicine stronger than the shamans could if they would turn away from drinking, smoking, and gambling. His wife, Mary Slocum, reportedly experienced the "Shake" when she received the promised medicine from God. The Indian Shaker Church organized on a county level in 1892 and on a state level in 1907.[24] Indeed, after the 1918 incorporation of the NAC, Mooney advised NAC president Mack Haag to send formal greetings to the Indian Shaker Church of Washington and express solidarity with the "Shaker Indian religion, a native Indian religion which has been for many years persecuted by fine, imprisonment, and in other ways, but which has finally won the victory and is also now regularly incorporated" with hundreds of churches and thousands of members in Washington, Oregon, California, and even British Columbia.[25]

Shaker Native Americans were not the only religious minority group with whom Peyotists developed an affinity in their legal struggles for religious freedom. Another model for organization cited by Peyotists was that of the Church of Jesus Christ of Latter-day Saints, popularly identified as Mormons. As one of the most maligned groups in the history of American religion for their beliefs and practices, Mormons represented to Peyotists an example of a concession to Americanization while still retaining some of their unique religious identity in the wake of strong public opposition. Years before the incorporation of the NAC, Harry Rave (Winnebago) submitted an affidavit concerning his experience with peyote and remarked, "We must organize a church and have it run like the Mormon church."[26] Rave's statement reflected an understanding of the history of religion in America, as it recognized the transformation in social identity of a persecuted religious minority into a respectable and established social entity. By the early decades of the twentieth century, Mormonism had adapted to the hostile political climate surrounding the contentious issue of polygamy. Following the *Reynolds* decision, the Mormon Church officially renounced the practice in 1890. Religious historian Heather Curtis concluded, "By declaring that he received a revelation from Jesus Christ commanding that the church 'cease the practice and submit to the law,' LDS president Wilford Woodruff paved the way for Mormons to assert their status as loyal American citizens and as faithful Christians—a project that they embraced wholeheartedly in the years to come."[27]

Peyote's opponents had acknowledged the phenomenological connection of Peyotism to the experience of visions and revelations, even noting that some Native peoples like the Comanches viewed peyote as "an oracle, endowed with the power of revelation."[28] As Peyotism continued into the twentieth century, some began to compare the subjective phenomena associated with the Native American religion to Mormonism, especially as the experiences of Peyotist practitioners became public knowledge. The rapid spread of Peyotism invited a comparison with the growth of Mormonism, with its spirit of revelation, and the Peyotist John Wilson (who also claimed a revelation from Christ to modify the peyote ceremony) became analogous to Brigham Young, the famous prophet of the Mormon faith.[29] Mormonism provided an example for Peyotists of accommodation to the dominant Christian interpretations of religious practice while still maintaining a distinct religious identity.

The impetus for officially organizing a church devoted to the practice of Peyotism came from the desire to secure the same religious rights as afforded to white citizens. During the federal legislative battles over peyote, the pan-Indian peyote lobby in Washington decided to pursue a more permanent solution to protect the use of their sacred religious adjunct. The contentious nature of the 1918 hearings on the Hayden bill (H.R. 2614) and the public opposition to peyote by representatives of the Society of American Indians convinced Peyotists that the establishment of their own church was an effective path of resistance to further encroachments on their religious practice. After the lobbyists returned to Oklahoma following the March 1918 hearings, the press reported that Cheyenne and Arapaho Peyotists planned to gather in June at Calumet, Oklahoma, to consider organizing a "Peyote Religious Society and make incorporation like a regular white man [sic] church so they can get the government to recognize it."[30] Two months later a larger pan-Indian delegation gathered in El Reno, Oklahoma, to draft the articles of incorporation for the establishment of the Native American Church in Oklahoma.

Perhaps the most significant influence on the Peyotists' decision to incorporate as a church was ethnologist James Mooney. Working as an ethnologist for the Smithsonian, Mooney lived intermittently among the Kiowa people from 1891 to 1918, and he studied the culture of the various Native peoples residing in western Oklahoma. Just as Mooney was deeply devoted to the cause of Irish freedom, he also promoted justice and freedom for the Native American tribes of North America, witnessing firsthand the oppressive encroachment of federal policies upon Native cultural practices.[31] When Indian agents and white missionaries began their cultural assault on the peyote religion, Mooney became an expert witness in many court proceedings and legislative hearings and advocated for the use of peyote as a legitimate religious practice deserving constitutional protection.[32] Mooney's support of Peyotists would eventually put him in conflict with Indian officials, religious reformers, and anti-Peyotists who all demanded that the Bureau of Ethnology put an end to his study and support of Peyotism. Despite the risks to his professional career, Mooney continued as an adviser to Peyotists in their struggle to obtain religious freedom.

Mooney's role as an ally of Peyotism provided the impetus for Peyotists to organize themselves. Evidence suggests that Mooney was influential in the decision to legally incorporate the Native American Church, believing it to be the only valid way to ensure constitutional protection for the religion.[33] When Peyotists representing various tribes in Oklahoma met in August 1918 to discuss their options, Mooney was also present at the meeting. According to Jim Whitewolf (Kiowa-Apache), who was also there, "Mooney recommended that the Peyotists there organize, choose officers, and pick a new name.... It was Mooney who recommended the name Native American Church."[34] NAC leaders and members acknowledged that Mooney "was largely instrumental in the organization and promotion" of the church.[35] The opponents of peyote also took note of Mooney's involvement in advising and assisting the Native Americans in their organization of a peyote church.[36] Missionaries and Indian officials protested Mooney's contributions to the preservation of Peyotism and began demanding that the Bureau of Ethnology take action to stop his work in Oklahoma among the Peyotists. Feeling significant pressure from the Indian Office, the Bureau of Ethnology recalled Mooney in November 1918, citing interference with work of the Indian Service as the reason.[37] Mooney returned to Washington, confined to doing office work. His banishment from fieldwork in Oklahoma prevented him from completing his study of the peyote religion. However, until his death on December 22, 1921, Mooney continued to offer support and guidance to the leadership of the NAC in their efforts to secure the freedom to practice Peyotism.

The incorporation of the NAC was a means to preserve Native American religious identity.[38] According to the NAC charter, issued by the state of Oklahoma on October 10, 1918, the stated purpose was to "form a religious and benevolent association" in order to "foster and promote the religious belief of the several tribes of Indians in the state of Oklahoma" through the practice of peyote. Furthermore, the articles of incorporation emphasized a racialized version of their religion, calling for the organization to "cultivate a spirit of self-respect and brotherly union among the members of the Native Race of Indians." The charter established Native American religious leadership through a "General Council of the Church," consisting of elected representatives from the local churches. The General Council would then elect a president, vice-president, and secretary/treasurer to oversee the statewide organization, headquartered at El Reno, Oklahoma. The charter designated fourteen members as initial representatives to the General Council: Mack Haag (Cheyenne), Sidney White Crane (Cheyenne), Charles W. Dailey (Otoe-Missouria), George Pipestem (Otoe-Missouria), Frank Eagle (Ponca), Louis McDonald (Ponca), Wilbur

Peawa (Comanche), Mam Sookwat (Comanche), Kiowa Charley (Kiowa), Delos Lone Wolf (Kiowa), Apache Ben (Apache), Tennyson Berry (Apache), Paul Boynton (Arapaho), and Cleaver Warden (Arapaho).[39] The council elected Mack Haag to serve as president and to lead the NAC through the first phases of its organization and development as a Native American entity.

The establishment of the NAC in Oklahoma soon led other Peyotists in other parts of Indian Country to incorporate themselves as a church. The first tribal affiliation to incorporate outside of Oklahoma was the Winnebago Peyotists in Nebraska. In 1921, they received a charter from the state establishing the Peyote Church of Christ, the name reflecting the Christian hybridity of Peyotism associated with two of the charter members, Albert Hensley and Jesse Clay, who promoted the Cross Fire and Half Moon variations of the peyote ceremony discussed in chapter 1. The name followed the early example of Koshiway's church in Oklahoma, but the articles of incorporation for the Winnebago church explicitly identified peyote as a part of their religious practice. However, after some internal disagreements concerning the inclusive nature of the church identification, they amended the charter in 1922 to follow the Oklahoma model and changed the name to the Native American Church of Winnebago, Nebraska. Omaha Peyotists in Nebraska also incorporated as the Omaha Peyote Historical Society.[40]

Peyotists from the Pine Ridge Indian Reservation in South Dakota also filed for incorporation as a church in 1922. The initial church—the Native American Church of Allen County—changed its name in 1924 to the Native American Church of South Dakota, as other branches across the state soon incorporated. Eventually, there would be four NAC entities in South Dakota—two on the Pine Ridge Reservation, and one each on the Rosebud and Yankton Reservations.[41] None of the early NAC articles of incorporation in South Dakota contained the word "peyote," no doubt due to the national controversy surrounding peyote and the anti-peyote federal legislation promoted by South Dakota congressional representative Harvey L. Gandy in 1916 and 1919. Though unsuccessful in getting a federal peyote prohibition bill passed, Gandy's influence in his home state convinced the South Dakota legislature to ban peyote in 1923. However, the state law proved ineffective because the charters of the NAC branches in South Dakota did not specifically mention "peyote." Additionally, the state law did not stop Peyotism because Peyotists held their meetings on an individual's "allotment, which is held in trust by the United States government over which the state has no jurisdiction" and no federal law existed prohibiting peyote.[42] After the peyote controversy declined during John Collier's administration of Indian Affairs, the charters added the term "peyote" in the mid-1930s.[43]

Peyotists of the Bannock and Shoshone in Idaho incorporated a NAC on March 19, 1925, and Peyotists in Montana, the Crow and Northern Cheyenne, obtained a NAC charter on March 26, 1925. Although outside the parameters of this specific study of Peyotism, it is important to note the increase of the NAC throughout Indian Country in the subsequent decades. Peyotists in the following states took the necessary steps to legally incorporate as state religious organizations: Wisconsin, 1939; Iowa, 1943; New Mexico and the Four Corners area, 1945; North Dakota, 1956; California and Nevada, 1958; southern Utah, 1969; Navajo land (southern Arizona), 1966; and Washington (three separate churches in Tacoma, Colville, and Yakima), 1977. With the rapid expansion of Peyotism and its NAC organizational structure, the discussion of a federal charter began in 1923. Under President Ned Brace (Kiowa), an amendment to the Oklahoma NAC charter came in 1934 to "allow out-of-state peyote groups to affiliate." In 1944, the Oklahoma NAC name officially changed to the Native American Church of the United States. However, some Oklahoma Peyotists became dissatisfied over a national outlook for the church, preferring instead the state organization that concerned itself with Oklahoma issues affecting them. Those Peyotists interested in preserving the statewide organization of a church obtained the original 1918 charter in 1949 and continued as a state corporation. The national church reincorporated in 1950 to maintain their separate identity, though Oklahoma Peyotists continued to provide the majority of the leadership in the national organization of the NAC. When Canadian Peyotists incorporated as the NAC of Canada in 1953, the national church changed its name in 1955 to the Native American Church of North America in order to accommodate the transnational religion of Peyotism.[44]

The proliferation of NAC entities in the United States signaled a means for Peyotists to seek First Amendment protection for their religious beliefs and practices. The performative power of words became evident in the choice of Peyotists to organize and to refer to themselves as a "church." Of course, the Native American Church did not conform to the standards of religious worship denoted by the word *church* in white American culture. Incorporation as a church did not bring changes to the peyote ceremonies already practiced by Peyotists. Peyote meetings continued on Saturday nights and lasted from sunset to sunrise. The church structure mainly consisted of a tepee, and when some NAC branches began building more permanent worship structures, they built them with "conical roofs and six-walled sides to make them appear as much like a tepee as possible."[45] Of course, the religion also involved the ingestion of peyote as a religious adjunct, which became the contentious difference between religion as practiced by Native American Peyotists and

Peyote meeting in 1892 among Kiowa. Photo by James Mooney. Courtesy of Helmerich Center for American Research at Gilcrease Museum, Tulsa, Oklahoma, Oklahoma Native American Photographs Collection.

white Christians. The differences in the worship services of a church continued to be highlighted by the opponents of peyote, who noted that the use of peyote in the Native Americans' ceremonies did not have the appearance of being religious at all and should be cause for police raids.[46] However, the use of the word *church* did provide legal protection, as a majority in Congress continually defeated peyote prohibition legislation and justified the decision in terms of religious freedom. After the incorporation of the NAC, Peyotists maintained the use of peyote as a religious rite, claiming they were exempt from any law that violated the constitutional protection of religious freedom.[47] Moreover, Congress willingly agreed with their argument, as Representative L. M. Gensman (OK) acknowledged that the "Indian's Peyote religion is just as sacred to him as [the white's] religion is to him."[48]

In their adoption of the language of American religious culture, incorporation offered legal protection for the worship ceremony of the Peyotists. Organizing as a church was an effective political strategy because it had constitutional implications that legislators did not want to violate. The Native American Church became an organization whose sole purpose was defending the peyote religion, and its members dedicated themselves to the maintenance of significant political strength to protect from other attacks on their religious liberty.[49] While Peyotists maintained a Native American identity in their religious practice, their methods of obtaining protection to exercise their religion were grounded in their identity as Americans. Incorporating as a church was not the only political strategy that Peyotists used to garner their religious freedom.

PEYOTE AS A SACRAMENT

While Peyotists always considered peyote to be a sacred medicine, article 2 of the 1918 NAC charter identified peyote as a "sacrament as commonly understood and used among the adherents of this religion in the several tribes of Indians."[50] The term *sacrament* was more closely associated with Christian Eucharistic practice and sacramental theology, but its use by Peyotists became another performative aspect of their religious identity in order to achieve religious freedom. The discursive turn in the rhetoric became a way for Peyotists to reclaim the "sacred" as the religious standards of American culture attempted to secularize peyote into a "profane" narcotic subject to criminalization.

The semantic shift to "sacrament" began to be noticeable around 1908, at the same time that social reformers were attempting to transform peyote into a habit-forming drug (see chapter 4). The change also came during the time of the much-publicized state effort in Oklahoma to amend current prohibition laws to include peyote. Both Peyotists and their supporters began to use the analogy of the Christian Eucharist to translate the peyote ceremony and practice into language understandable to non-Native Americans and non-Peyotists. Joseph Springer (Iowa) testified at the 1908 Oklahoma hearings, "[We] use this medicine as the Catholic people use wine as a sacrifice," and the Peyotists' white attorney broadened the ecumenical example to claim that the ingestion of peyote at prescribed times in the ceremony was "just the same as the Baptists, Presbyterians, Methodists, and other denominations break bread and drink wine." He also utilized the word *sacrament* to convey the religious similarity for white legislators.[51] The popular press covering the 1908 hearings soon utilized the analogy to convey a religious understanding to white readers. Newspaper accounts reported that peyote was part of the Native Americans' religious services and that they wanted their rights protected. The press coverage also translated Peyotism and its ceremony into Christian language and symbolism and wrote, "Peyote is to the Indians in their communion services as bread and wine are to the white man," even claiming peyote was "as necessary as wine at the communion services of the Christian white man."[52]

Peyotists and non-Peyotists continued to use the sacramental analogy and language in the federal contestations over peyote. Transcripts of the 1918 congressional hearings on peyote legislation contain many references to peyote's use by Native Americans as being "in the same manner as wine among Christian denominations."[53] Newspaper coverage of congressional attempts to prohibit peyote also compared the peyote religious rite to Christian communion, and the idea of peyote as a sacrament became a fixture in the popular religious imagination of both Peyotists and non-Peyotists.[54] The translation of peyote into a sacred Christian religious symbol also worked its way into the rhetoric of federal officials considering potential legislation to ban the substance, where now legislators became wary of prohibiting the practice.[55] The use of the term *sacrament* with reference to the ingestion of peyote during religious ceremonies conveyed a level of respectability to the ritual by transposing a religious belief common in American society onto a Native American religious practice. Peyotists became increasingly aware of this connection when they made the decision to incorporate as a church and proclaim peyote as a sacrament.

The significance of the Eucharistic language was also evident to Peyotism's influential supporter James Mooney. As he assisted the Peyotists with their organization and charter of the NAC, no doubt he also convinced them to employ the religious language of the culture. Though not a devout practicing Catholic, Catholicism remained a part of his worldview. Mooney's sister, Mary, became a nun with the convent of the Sisters of St. Francis in Oldenburg, Indiana. Sister Mary Agnes, later Mother Mary Agnes, later founded her own Franciscan convent in Clinton, Iowa, and became the head of a convent school in Illinois.[56] James Mooney worked closely with Reverend Thomas Shahan in the Gaelic Society. Shahan, who served as domestic prelate of the Pontifical Court and rector of Catholic University, became one of Mooney's close friends. Shahan served as the godfather to Mooney's son, Brian, and confirmed all of Mooney's children into the Catholic faith. Father Shahan also instructed Mooney's wife, Ione, when she converted to Catholicism. In addition, as a founder and editor of the *Catholic Encyclopedia*, Shahan enlisted Mooney's contributions to the publication.[57] Regarding church, Mooney's wife, Ione, recalled that she never knew him to attend church on a regular basis, but he did go on special occasions and "always participated in the Catholic baptism of his children in Saint Paul's Church" because he "always seemed anxious to have his children baptized."[58] One obituary for Mooney noted that his Catholic faith had a significant impact on his life, acknowledging, "He lived and dies in the Catholic faith, of which he had a profound and affectionate knowledge, and passed away fortified with the last rites of the Holy Church."[59] Mooney's own writings and rhetoric on Peyotism led him to declare a religious right for the Peyotists since peyote was as "sacred [to them] as is the use of wine to the Christian in the sacrament of the Lord's Supper."[60] Mooney's

Catholic sensibility connecting the peyote ritual to the Eucharist constituted another reason for the NAC to declare peyote to be a sacrament.

As previously noted in chapter 4, prohibition in Indian Country had been in effect since 1892, but the national contestation over peyote also coincided with efforts to implement a nationwide alcohol prohibition, which ultimately resulted in the passage of the Eighteenth Amendment in 1919. The success of the national prohibition of alcohol was largely due to the support of white Christians. Although temperance reform action traditionally aligned itself with evangelical Protestantism, the Anti-Saloon League took unprecedented steps to identify itself as an agent of organized Christianity.[61] However, the clash of religious cultures also became evident in the prohibition movement. Robert Fuller writes, "Total abstinence from alcohol–including wine, the privileged beverage of the Bible and Christian sacraments–was thus a direct consequence of the boundary-setting behaviors at the turn of the twentieth century."[62] In the early part of the temperance movement in the nineteenth century, churches had no other choice but to serve regular wine at communion. The Christian practice regarding this sacramental element of worship changed in the 1870s, when the production of grape juice became technologically feasible. For Methodists, the "kind and quality of wine involved in Holy Communion first became an issue in Northern Methodism's lawmaking body, the General Conference, in 1860." In 1872, the General Conference recommended "the use of unfermented wine on our sacramental occasions" and reaffirmed that decision in 1876.[63] Thomas Welch, a member of Vineland Methodist Church in New Jersey, wanted to give congregations an alternative to wine. He successfully "pasteurized Concord grape juice to make unfermented sacramental wine using a process that French scientist Louis Pasteur had discovered only several years before."[64] For Methodists, the technological innovation even contributed to changes in the sacramental theological liturgy at the Lord's Table, where the sentence at the beginning of the Lord's Supper was altered to read, "Let none but the pure unfermented juice of the grape be used in administering the Lord's Supper, whenever practicable." A revision in 1916 deleted the words "whenever practicable," making grape juice the official substitute for wine in the administration of the Lord's Supper for the Methodists.[65]

Other denominations associated with the prohibition movement soon followed and switched to the use of grape juice in their Eucharistic practices.[66] However, some Christian groups considered the use of alcoholic wine to be paramount to their sacramental theology and refused to make the switch to grape juice. Chief among those Christian religious groups was the Catholic Church, which continued offering sacramental wine, not grape juice, even after passage of the Eighteenth

Amendment.[67] The crux of the matter for Catholics extended beyond a social reform issue; it was a priori a theological issue in the Sacrament of the Eucharist. In talking about the Catholic belief in transubstantiation—that is, the literal transformation of the bread and wine served at the Eucharist into the body and blood of Christ—Catholic theologians note, "The wine becomes,—it is—the actual blood of Christ. This is the most sacred part of mass. So, it is incorporated into the sacred ritual of the Church. You have to have it to have a valid sacrament."[68] In contrast, evangelical Protestants tended to view the bread and wine as symbolic in their sacramental theology, so the substitution of grape juice for wine was not a contentious theological problem. It was easier for evangelical Protestants to alter their theological beliefs to incorporate the recent technology.

Catholic and Protestant differences on the issue of prohibition also went beyond theological beliefs. Sociological factors contributed to the call for prohibition. The issue of alcohol prohibition politicized highly sensitive attitudes about the stability of the social order, as the consumption of alcohol became closely associated with newly arrived immigrants to America, who were mostly poor, uneducated, and living in the squalor of urban ghettoes.[69] Many of Irish, German, and Central European immigrants came to the United States with religious beliefs that emphasized the need for wine in the observance of the Eucharist. Temperance reformers focused on the perceived problems that Catholic and immigrant culture posed to the Christian character of the nation.[70] The drinking of alcoholic beverages among these immigrants, according to Robert Fuller, "became a symbol of their inability to assimilate into the established WASP cultural order. Religious and ethnic prejudice fueled the fire of evangelical Protestants' moral indignation at the immigrants' lifestyles."[71] The religious and sociological reasons for advocating temperance also contained an ethnocultural dimension.

The anxiety over assimilating immigrants into the American culture and way of life was also evident in the debates on granting citizenship to Native Americans, some of whom already held a limited citizenship status through the allotment process. Just as social reformers and government officials viewed alcohol as an impediment to the assimilation of immigrants into American society, they also viewed peyote as an obstacle for Native Americans. Aware of these sociological concerns, Peyotists realized that seeking First Amendment protection would require clearly identifying peyote as a religious necessity (an a priori theological conviction) in their ceremony. The federal government already provided the model for Peyotists to follow.

Statutory exemptions for the protection of religious liberty are key features of legislation, designed to balance the demands of freedom with the adaptations sometimes required by the laws of the nation. As Congress passed several pieces of legislation from 1912 to 1919 to prohibit the manufacture and sale of intoxicating beverages, Louis Fisher notes that "each time it made exception for the use of sacramental wines for religious ceremonies."[72] The Volstead Act (the National Prohibition Act of 1919) contained a statutory exemption for sacramental wine, as well as a loophole for medicinal liquor.[73] Of greater importance to Peyotists was the religious exemption to prohibition in Indian Country, which came in 1912 when the Office of Indian Affairs issued a policy change in the Indian Appropriation Act to allow the introduction and use of "wines solely for sacramental purposes under church authority" in Indian Country.[74] As peyote was typically compared to the sacramental wine used in communion, Peyotists seized upon the opportunity to use the religious exemption for sacramental wine. Interestingly, in this situation Peyotists did not deny the charge that peyote was an intoxicant like alcohol, but rather used the federal policy change to their advantage by claiming a religious exemption for peyote. The NAC articles of incorporation legally proclaimed peyote to be a sacrament administered by the authority of a "church," thus advancing the argument that the religion deserved the same constitutional protections of religious liberty afforded to others.

The use of peyote as a sacrament continued the Eucharistic analogy with a caveat that the Peyotists did not take too much of the peyote, but only enough to act as a sacred symbol in their form of communion.[75] In the few instances where peyote was identified as synonymous with the bread used in communion, a religious exemption was also in place that covered this sacramental symbol.[76] The 1917 Food and Fuel Control Act, promoting wartime protection of supplies for troops, made an "exception in the conservation of wheat by allowing the Christian churches to have wheat enough to make the host and the Hebrews to make *matzah* in order to carry on their religious ceremonies."[77] The NAC adopted the Western theological discourse of "sacrament" to take advantage of the religious exemptions given to Christian religious practices in America in order to advance their own agenda. However, as not all these Christian religious practices were acceptable to American society, Peyotists also developed an understanding and explanation of Peyotism that would preempt judicial precedents already established to judge the process of "Americanization."

The pronouncement by the Republican Party in their 1856 platform that it was the duty of Congress to prohibit in the new territories the "twin relics of barbarism—polygamy and slavery" launched a national assault on the Mormon religious practice of plural marriage. The subsequent ruling in the 1879 *Reynolds* case allowed the federal government to restrict the religious practice and identified the rationale in the distinction between belief and practice—the government cannot restrict religious beliefs, but it can control religious practices deemed harmful to society. The crux of the government's argument in *Reynolds* was that polygamy was not necessary or essential to the beliefs of the faith and that "religious liberty did not include the protection of anti-Christian action."[78] As the opponents of peyote began to characterize Peyotism as a dangerous practice, they also started to use the rhetoric associated with the calls to ban polygamy. Anti-Peyotists started calling the religious practice "the twin brother of alcohol, and first cousin to habit-forming drugs."[79] Peyotists wanted to ensure that their religious beliefs reflected the sacredness of peyote. The idea of peyote as a "sacrament" bolstered the Peyotists' claim to the protection of religious freedom by identifying it as an essential and necessary component of their religious belief.

Peyote's opponents raised the possibility of invoking the *Reynolds* decision in their efforts to prohibit peyote. George Gibbs, a missionary with the American Baptist Home Mission Society, wrote, "Just as polygamy is prohibited from Mormonism by the law, so peyote should be prohibited from Indian religion."[80] Others noted the Supreme Court had already made a distinction that "wherever there is a transgression against morals or decency, the plea of religious liberty does not prevail."[81] However, in order to meet the criteria of the belief-versus-action distinction provided in the *Reynolds* decision, opponents of peyote would need to prove that Peyotism could exist without the use of peyote. They tried to do so by arguing that peyote was a not an essential element in the religion but was only incidental to the religious ceremony.[82] Peyotists and supporters countered that peyote was indispensable, or essential, to the practice of this Native American religion.[83] A petition to Congress from Osage Peyotists claimed the same right to practice their religion as other churches that used wine in their ceremonies, because without peyote it would be "impossible for [us] to carry out [our] religion."[84] Anti-Peyotists faced a challenging task in discrediting peyote's function in the form of religious worship, so they turned to another argument that emerged from *Reynolds*—the meaning of religion as protected by the First Amendment.

RELIGION AND RELIGIOUS FREEDOM

Those opposed to Peyotism, such as commissioner of Indian Affairs Charles Burke, believed that the Native American adherents were "misled and duped into the peyote habit by agitators who use the guise of religion to promote the use of a drug."[85] Anti-Peyotists began to question the religious nature of peyote in terms of the meaning of religion. They also began to question the motives of Peyotists and their supporters in designating Peyotism as a religion. Opponents maintained that the reference to peyote as a sacrament was merely a strategy of propagandists to promote a dangerous drug and claimed that the controversy over Peyotism was "not so much the religion itself that is involved but what 'religion' is made to cover, namely, to give full license to the 'dope' habit." The same "religious feeling," many argued, could just as easily come from the use of other narcotics.[86] Critics of peyote also called into question the religious nature of the "church" implied by the organization of the Native American Church, as they charged that the Peyotists did not constitute a legitimate church organization, but merely a "collection of peyote eaters banded together in a sort of social fellowship" to enjoy the experience of intoxication "produced by consuming their religious fetish—peyote."[87] Any defense of peyote as a religious rite was, as Burke claimed, "largely fictitious, the promoters of its use having seized upon this idea in an attempt to prevent or delay prohibiting legislation," and created a fallacy for Native Americans that "they were accepting a religious practice."[88] While Peyotists claimed a constitutional right to religious freedom, peyote's opponents claimed there were no grounds for constitutional privilege for Peyotism because the use of peyote was not covered by the First Amendment.[89] In other words, anti-Peyotists considered Peyotism to be a "false religion" that did not deserve protection.

Following the promise of citizenship to Native Americans through the allotment process and after their patriotic service in World War I, Peyotists maintained the "same right to worship according to their traditions as the white man has."[90] After the formation of the NAC, James Mooney also made a comparison to the many varieties of white Christianity, and though "each claims to be the only one right and all the others wrong . . . all are allowed liberty under the Constitution."[91] More important than the structural form of religious worship was the claim of a true religious *experience* among the practitioners of Peyotism. Arthur Bonnicastle (Osage) testified to the sacredness of peyote in training one's mind to higher ideas about the worship of God. Paul Boynton (Cheyenne-Arapaho) placed the effects of peyote in the phenomenal experience of connecting with a religious and holy idea of God. While not a Peyotist, Francis La Flesche (Omaha) became thoroughly convinced that Peyotists worshipped God in their own way, and he warned Congress that they should not interfere with the peyote religion.[92] In their appeals to the Constitution, Peyotists understood the First Amendment to provide that "Congress shall make no law respecting an establishment of religion, or prohibiting the free exercise thereof." Osage Peyotists offered their own interpretation of an approach to religion and religious liberty in a letter to Congress, stating, "God is truth! Religion is one's belief as to what this truth is, and we all hold certain opinions."[93] For Peyotists, freedom of religion meant the right to use peyote in their religious worship, and as NAC president Mack Haag claimed, any friend of religious liberty should not be concerned with the "difference between faith and unbelief, nor in fact with the difference between creeds," but should be disturbed that losing religious freedom also meant a loss of the civil liberties that are valued in American society.[94]

Of significant importance to Peyotists was the belief that white society should not regulate their religious rites, particularly because they valued the Native American religious identity associated with Peyotism.[95] The peyote religion as exercised through the NAC became a way for Peyotists to retain a uniquely Native American religious identity during a time of change to their culture. Peyotists valued their hybrid identity as both Native and American, and fighting in the war abroad revealed to them the need for changes in the status of Native Americans with respect to federal Indian policy. For Peyotists, one necessary step toward change to ensure the protection of democratic rights for all people was the recognition of the NAC, and, additionally, no federal legislation prohibiting peyote. Even after incorporation in 1918 and the expansion of the church across the northern plains, Peyotists still felt persecuted by members of American Christian culture and, in particular, by the Indian Bureau and Christian officials who seemed to hold "considerable political power" over Native American affairs even in the twentieth century.[96] As the social influence of Protestant Christianity waned among whites, many Protestants looked to retain control and power over Native Americans through an unofficial church-state alliance.[97] The 1928 publication of *The Problem of Indian Administration* (more commonly called the Meriam Report) called for the continuation of government cooperation with Christian missionaries, as "the religious activities carried on by Christian missionaries are an important part of the impact of a new civilization upon Indian life," although the report did caution that "the missionaries need to have a better understanding of the Indian point of view of the Indian's religion and ethics."[98]

Even prior to the issuance of the Meriam Report, the Indian Bureau endorsed the work of Reverend G. E. E. Lindquist, a Protestant missionary who served as the director of the American Indian Survey, a study that began as part of the Interchurch World Movement and continued under the Rockefeller-funded Institute for Social and Religious Research.[99] Lindquist's work resulted in the publication of *The Red Man in the United States* (1923). In the foreword of the book, Indian commissioner Charles Burke commented, "The Indian Bureau welcomes the cooperation of the Church." The study, which reflected the views of mainstream Protestant Christianity, regarded peyote as "one of the most serious menaces to the progress of the Indian race."[100] NAC president Mack Haag was critical of Burke's leadership of the Indian Bureau and his relationship with American Protestant Christianity. He described the Indian Bureau's stance on Native American religion as one that "exceeded its own previous record of Czarism" by stifling Peyotists' "liberty of conscience," and reducing the Native American to "his wards, to the status of animals, who are denied the possession of souls."[101] Yet, despite attempts by the Indian Office to suppress the use of peyote, Congress refused to pass legislation to aid their efforts, citing the organization of a church by Peyotists as falling within the parameters of religious freedom as protected by the Constitution.[102] The Peyotists' appeal as a church to American religious values had constitutional implications that legislators did not want to overturn.

The performative power of words became evident in the Peyotists' decision to organize and to refer to themselves as a church, and to include the declaration of peyote as a sacrament in their articles of incorporation. The Peyotists' legal posture allowed them to simultaneously develop a church organization based upon a white cultural pattern and maintain the practice of their traditional religion. Adopting rhetoric from American Protestant Christian culture allowed peyote to remain a part of Native American religious identity and practice, as evidenced in a 1933 newspaper account that reported, "The Peyote church is an Indian affair.... For the first time, an Indian religion has crashed through the barriers that tribes raise to set apart their own rites and ceremonies."[103]

AFTERWORD

> We do not think Congress should pass any law to prohibit [the] Peyote religion of the Indian race to destroy that religion, as we feel we are guaranteed freedom of religious worship under the Constitution of the United States. The numerous charges and affidavits offered by different parties against our Indian religion are none of them true. We are living uprightly under the United States flag, and helping to improve the conditions of our Indian race... and to live the real civilized life.
>
> JOCK BULL BEAR (ARAPAHO)

The statements of Jock Bull Bear concerning the 1918 federal legislative attempt to prohibit peyote reflect the core debate in the cultural battle over Peyotism in the early twentieth century: could Peyotists maintain aspects of their Native culture through their religion and still be American citizens? Differing perspectives on racialized religion affected the answer to the question. The challenge for Peyotists was to overcome social constructions of both race and religion to preserve their First Amendment right to enjoy the free exercise of their religion. In his testimony before Congress, Reuben Taylor (Cheyenne) reminded lawmakers that in the history of the United States "the people came over to this country looking for free worship, and they found it... and us fellows ask why we should not have ours." Taylor and other supporters of Peyotism pushed peyote's opponents to remember not only that the Constitution established that "you cannot take a man's conscience to worship God," but also that white Christians had come to a land already inhabited by Native peoples.[1] The cultural battle over Peyotism was also a struggle over Native identity in the social context of the shift to citizenship for Native Americans.

While the early challenges to Peyotism resulted in victories for Peyotists and allowed the NAC to expand and flourish, concerns about federal policy changes still worried Peyotists. John Collier's tenure as commissioner of Indian Affairs (1933–1945) resulted in the "Indian New Deal," a new direction for US Indian policy based on Collier's own commitment to promote the revitalization of Native American life and culture. The key feature of the Indian New Deal legislation was the

Indian Reorganization Act (IRA), which passed in 1934. The intent of the bill, writes historian Colin Calloway, was to protect Native Americans "in their religion and lifestyle and represented an open admission that the Dawes Act was a mistake." The legislation provided that Native Americans who lived on reservations "be allowed to establish local self-government and tribal corporations to develop reservation resources."[2] However, in the late 1940s and the 1950s, government support for and public opinion on the reforms of the Indian New Deal shifted. As the Cold War emerged after World War II, "Americans reaffirmed their loyalty to their country and regarded with suspicion and resentment those who did not seem to fit in with mainstream society or subscribe absolutely to American values. Native Americans living on reservations, running their own governments, and maintaining their own communal lifestyles seemed an anomaly."[3] Those directing Indian policy now wanted to return to the process of Native American assimilation with the termination of the US government's relationship with Native American tribes. When Dillion Myer became commissioner of Indian Affairs in 1950, he began to implement a policy known as termination and advocated for the relocation of Native peoples.[4] These changes in Indian policy created a mood of uncertainty for members of the Native American Church about their ability to maintain their religious freedom.

In the 1950s, the international NAC improved its organizational structure to strengthen communication among its members. The NAC began to publish the *Quarterly Bulletin* to disseminate important information to Peyotists, including how and where to purchase peyote. The *Bulletin* published both the names and addresses of peyoteros, as well as the prices of peyote from the merchants. Thomas Maroukis notes that the NAC reminded members that "peyote could be legally shipped through the United States Postal Service (the 1917 ban was rescinded in 1940) and as of 1957 could be legally imported into Canada."[5] The NAC also began issuing membership cards. In case of a legal problem using peyote, the card, writes Maroukis, could be "shown to law enforcement authorities to prove membership in a bona fide American religious organization, which was entitled to use peyote for sacramental purposes."[6] The issuance of membership cards also became a way for the institutional church to have a record of individual members, an interesting change reflecting the preoccupation with church membership as a means to gauge religiosity by the Western standards of Christianity. The concern over potential legal challenges proved to be correct, as the late 1950s witnessed states attempting to assert their own religious control over Peyotists, with arrests over violation of state laws prohibiting peyote and the subsequent legal challenges in the court systems.

The 1959 arrest of Mary Attakai (Diné) in Williams, Arizona, for possession of peyote brought the first challenge to the religious liberty of Peyotists. Defended by the American Civil Liberties Union (ACLU), the arguments for acquittal focused on the free exercise of religion clause in the First Amendment. The judge in Arizona's superior court ruled the state's anti-peyote statute was unconstitutional as applied to Attakai because her use of peyote was part of her religious beliefs. The state appealed the decision to the Arizona Supreme Court, which dismissed the appeal and allowed Attakai's acquittal to stand.[7] In 1959, California passed anti-peyote legislation that was challenged with the arrest of three Diné Peyotists—Jack Woody, Leon B. Anderson, and Dan Dee Nez—in 1962 in Needles, California. The judicial system convicted the men for using and possessing peyote during a religious service, but the ACLU appealed the decision to the California Supreme Court, who reversed the conviction.[8] Texas enacted a peyote prohibition law in 1967, an act that did not include a religious exemption for the possession and use of peyote.[9] A group of Peyotists decided to test the constitutionality of the Texas law. David S. Clark (Diné) of Wind Rock, Arizona, became a participant in a test case by purchasing peyote in Laredo, Texas. When arrested, the ACLU defended Clark, and the Texas Supreme Court ruled in his favor, declaring the Texas statute unconstitutional.[10] The Texas legislature amended the 1967 law, allowing a religious exemption for Peyotists who held membership in the Native American Church and used peyote in the course of religious ceremonies. The new Texas law also added additional requirements of having peyoteros register with the state and specified that the religious exemption to possess peyote did not apply to individuals who had a Native American blood quantum of less than twenty-five percent. Texas legislators wanted the blood quantum requirement to prevent non–Native Americans from also seeking a religious exemption to use peyote.[11] Concern about the non–Native American use of peyote would present significant legal changes to the regulation and control of peyote, affecting both the NAC and the religious practice of Peyotism.

The counterculture youth movement in the 1960s and early 1970s brought heightened societal fears about drug use. "Hippies" began to visit the peyote fields of south Texas to procure peyote as a recreational drug, consumed in a non-ritualistic setting.[12] Coinciding with the white cultural appropriation of peyote use was the public demand for Congress to strengthen federal drug laws. In 1965, Congress passed the Drug Abuse Control Acts, which modified the Food, Drug, and Cosmetics Act and allowed the secretary of Health, Education, and Welfare to designate certain drugs deemed to be a stimulant, depressant, or hallucinogenic agent as controlled substances, requiring licensing for sales and distribution. Peyote was included on this list, although it came with a religious exemption for members of the Native American Church. In 1970, the Comprehensive Drug Abuse Prevention and Control Act consolidated several anti-drug laws and specifically categorized peyote as a Schedule I drug subject to controlled regulation. The federal government was finally successful in drawing peyote into the racialized war on drugs and turning the "sacred" into the "profane."

When first passed, the law did not provide a religious exemption for the use of peyote, but testimony in House hearings on the statute eventually added an exception for religious use.[13] The federal regulation of peyote now placed an added importance on membership cards for NAC adherents, and further changes to the cards were necessary to control the distribution to "members only." Additionally, the new drug law added new levels of bureaucracy and documentation for peyoteros to sell peyote buttons to members of the NAC.

In 1990, the United States Supreme Court dealt a serious blow to Peyotism by narrowing the free exercise of religion clause contained in the First Amendment. The case of *Oregon v. Smith* involved two NAC members who were fired by the Oregon Department of Education from their jobs as counselors for a rehabilitation organization for using peyote. Colin Calloway writes that in a 6–3 vote, the United States Supreme Court ruled that "state governments could prosecute people who used controlled substances as part of a religious ritual without violating their constitutional rights of religious freedom."[14] Legal scholars such as Russell Larence Barsh noted the significant change of direction in the ruling as an attempt to reassert a Protestant hegemony in Native American religious affairs by lending "support to those who argue that the United States is fundamentally a Christian nation rather than a nation based on religious freedom. It did not do this by condoning the use of Christian symbols by governing officials ... but by adopting a rule of zero tolerance for the practices of *minority* religious groups wherever they conflict with laws made by the United States' Christian *majority*."[15] In response to this ruling, Congress passed the Native American Free Exercise of Religion Act in 1994, which granted protections to Native American right to use peyote in religious ceremonies.[16]

In spite of the legal barriers created by the misclassification of peyote as a controlled substance in the late twentieth century, the Native American Church continues in its existence and religious practices today. However, new challenges to the church exist in the twenty-first century. Most significant is the limited peyote supply for religious ceremonies. Since peyote is still listed as a Schedule I narcotic, no supply can come in to the United States from Mexico. In south Texas, the growth region is now limited to four counties.[17] The most significant reason for the decreased supply of peyote buttons comes from overharvesting due to shrinking growth areas from the clearing of land for larger agribusiness enterprises and from climate change. Martin Terry, a professor of botany, says, "We are overharvesting the shrinking area of the planet that actually supports wild peyote."[18] The declining supply means that the cost for purchasing buttons for a ceremony increases. Higher prices that decrease the amount purchased does have the ability to impact the quality of the religious experience for some, but it does not stop the ceremonies.[19]

As a ritual that created misunderstanding in white culture, Peyotism has much to teach American religious history. Peyotists continue to resist the secularization of their religious practice through their continued commitment to participating in ceremonies. They honor their Native and American identities through the practice of their religion in spite of the legal obstacles placed before them. For members of the NAC who practice Peyotism, peyote is the mediator between the individual and the divine, a gift sent by Creator God to help needful human beings. The ingestion of peyote as a sacrament allows NAC participants to deal with individual and social problems. Psychologist Peter N. Jones says this comes "through a personal connection with a more powerful and knowledgeable consciousness," where NAC members "experience the holy, a transformative reorientation, courage, a moral experience of obligation, the experience of order and creativity in the world, and the mystical experience of a unity with all things."[20] There is also a communal ethos associated with the power of peyote, as the NAC connects peyote to morality in order to advance one's commitment to a holistic approach to well-being.[21] The sacrality of peyote and its ritual context serve important cultural functions among Native American peoples that promote individual and social justice systems of harmonious being and living. The history of the Native American Church offers substantial insight into the practice of religious experience through the entheogenic use of peyote, and that history reveals important strategies of resistance as Peyotists utilized the legal and political systems as Americans.

NOTES

ABBREVIATIONS

AGN-I	Archivo General de la Nación, Mexico
HCAR	Helmerich Center for American Research at Gilcrease Museum, Tulsa, Oklahoma
NAA	National Anthropological Archives, Smithsonian Institution, Suitland, Maryland
OHS	Oklahoma Historical Society Research Division, Oklahoma City
Peyote Hearings 1918	House Committee on Indian Affairs, *Prohibition of Use of Peyote among Indians*, 65th Cong., 2d sess., May 13, 1918, H. Rep. 560.
RCIA	*Annual Report of the Commissioner of Indian Affairs*. Washington, DC: Government Printing Office.
SAI Papers	Papers of the Society of American Indians

INTRODUCTION

1. Until 1890 Indian Territory encompassed reservations on most of what is now present-day Oklahoma. The geographic division of the area came after the Oklahoma Land Run of 1889, when the newly formed Oklahoma Territory was carved from Indian Territory; for the people of the Five Tribes the distinction between the two territories was more of a change in discourse than a change in locale.

2. James Mooney, "The Mescal Plant and Ceremony," *Therapeutic Gazette* 12, no. 1 (January 15, 1896): 7. Early on, there was confusion between peyote and mescal beans, with Mooney even writing in his article that traders in Indian Territory "commonly called it mescal." Peyote is a small, spineless cactus, and the stems, which grow two to three inches above ground, have a "button" or top on them. This is the part of the cactus harvested and used for the religious ritual. The common practice is to dry the buttons for storage and transport. Peyotists consume the dried buttons by chewing or swallowing, turning them into a paste with the addition of water, or making a "tea" to drink.

3. "Mescal as Medicine: Plea Made by Indian Chiefs before Committee," *Daily Ardmoreite* (Ardmore, OK), December 30, 1906, 9.

4. Quanah Parker, "Quanah Parker Delivers a Speech before the Convention," *Weekly State Democrat* (Ardmore, OK), January 3, 1907, 5.

5. "Mescal Beans to Be Investigated; Causing Red Skins to Get Drunk," *Bisbee (AZ) Daily Review*, September 1, 1908, 2; "The So-Called Mescal Button," *Oshkosh (WI) Daily Northwestern*, September 10, 1908, 4.

6. House Committee on Indian Affairs, *Prohibition of Use of Peyote among Indians*, 65th Cong., 2d sess., May 13, 1918, H. Rep. 560, 38 (hereafter cited as *Peyote Hearings 1918*), 166.

7. In the 1959 English translation of his book, *The Sacred and the Profane*, Mircea Eliade explained that "the sacred and profane are two modes of being in the world, two existential situations assumed by humans in the course of history." Mircea Eliade, *The Sacred and the Profane: The Nature of Religion*, trans. Willard R. Task (New York: Harcourt, Brace and Company, 1959), 14. The "profane 'situation,'" expands Robert C. Fuller, "is one that focuses exclusively on the material dimensions of life.... The vast majority of drug-induced states of intoxication are restricted to the profane dimension of human existence." Fuller, *Stairways to Heaven: Drugs in American Religious History* (Boulder, CO: Westview Press, 2000), 7. However, drugs "have also been intimately associated with Americans' desire to participate in the sacred" (Fuller, 9). For more on the current controversy among religious scholars over the conceptualization of "religious" and "secular," see Tyler Roberts, *Encountering Religion: Responsibility and Criticism after Secularism* (New York: Columbia University Press, 2013); Janet R. Jakobsen and Ann Pellegrini, ed., *Secularisms* (Durham, NC: Duke University Press, 2008); William E. Arnal and Russell T. McCutcheon, *The Sacred Is the Profane: The Political Nature of "Religion"* (New York: Oxford University Press, 2013).

8. Colin G. Calloway, *First Peoples: A Documentary Survey of American Indian History*, 4th ed. (Boston: Bedford/St. Martin's, 2012), 443; Hazel W. Hertzberg, *The Search for an American Indian Identity: Modern Pan-Indian Movements* (Syracuse, NY: Syracuse University Press, 1971), 31. Hertzberg elaborates on the definition: "Among American Indians the term 'progressive' had long had a special meaning. 'Progressive' Indians believed in education, hard work, and in adapting their attitudes, values, and habits of life to those of the larger American society" (31).

9. For the best example of the binary oppositional stance, see J. S. Slotkin, *The Peyote Religion: A Study in Indian-White Relations* (Glencoe, IL: The Free Press, 1956). Slotkin, an anthropologist, attempted to translate Peyotism for a white audience in order to legitimate it as a religion. Specifically, he argued that the peyote religion "is an Indian defense against consequences of White domination" and that it provided a "supernatural means of accommodation to the existing domination-subordination relation." Unlike the militant Ghost Dance program of opposition, Peyotism survived as a program of accommodation, becoming in his perspective "the Indian version of Christianity." Slotkin, *Peyote Religion*, v, 20–21, 68. For a corrective on the militancy of the Ghost Dance religion, see Louis S. Warren, *God's Red Son: The Ghost Dance Religion and the Dawn of the Twentieth Century* (New York: Basic Books, 2017).

10. Scott Richard Lyons, *X-Marks: Native Signatures of Assent* (Minneapolis: University of Minnesota Press, 2010), 172.

11. The phrase "politics of identity" emerges from the work of scholars in a variety of disciplines, including Pauline Turner Strong, an anthropologist whose work centers on both historical and contemporary representations of Native Americans and on the politics

of identity and representation. See Pauline Turner Strong, *American Indians and the American Imaginary: Cultural Representation across the Centuries* (Boulder, CO: Paradigm, 2012). See also Kwame Anthony Appiah and Henry Louis Gates Jr., eds., *Identities* (Chicago: University of Chicago Press, 1995), who address the calls for "post-essentialist" reconceptions of notions of identity. Anthony Elliott, commenting on the work of the late French historian Michel Foucault, wrote, "For Foucault, the production of identity discourses, texts, or scripts are deeply interwoven with the operation of power in society ... Identity is also, fundamentally, political." Anthony Elliott, ed., "Editor's Introduction," *Routledge Handbook of Identity Studies* (London: Routledge, 2011), xvii, xxi. Foucault's beliefs about modernity's initiative of regulating "and often criminalizing various states of mind or actions involving human bodies, all resulting in further intrusions of the state" also fit within the transformation of peyote into a narcotic to be regulated. Kent Mathewson, "Drugs, Moral Geographies, and Indigenous Peoples: Some Initial Mappings and Central Issues," in *Dangerous Harvest: Drug Plants and the Transformation of Indigenous Landscapes*, ed. Michael K. Steinberg, Joseph J. Hobbs, and Kent Mathewson (Oxford: Oxford University Press, 2004), 20.

12. For an important work on the constructed nature of human society, see Peter L. Berger and Thomas Luckmann, *The Social Construction of Reality: A Treatise in the Sociology of Knowledge* (Garden City, NY: Doubleday, 1966).

13. Barbara J. Fields, "Ideology and Race in American History," in *Region, Race, and Reconstruction: Essays in Honor of C. Vann Woodward*, ed. J. Morgan Kousser and James M. McPherson (New York: Oxford University Press, 1982), 150. Law professor Ian F. Haney-López responds by offering an interpretation that places race within the realm of social relationships. He defines race as "a vast group of people loosely bound together by historically contingent, socially significant elements of their morphology and/or ancestry" that is "subject to the macro forces of social and political struggle and the micro effects of daily decisions." Haney-López, "Social Construction of Race: Some Observations on Illusion, Fabrication and Choice," *Harvard Civil Rights–Civil Liberties Law Review* 29, no. 1 (1994): 7.

14. Ian F. Haney-López, *White by Law: The Legal Construction of Race* (New York: New York University Press, 1996), xiii.

15. Peter L. Berger, *The Sacred Canopy: Elements of a Sociological Theory of Religion* (Garden City, NY: Doubleday, 1967; New York: Anchor Books, 1990), back matter, 3. See Robert A. Orsi, *Between Heaven and Earth: The Religious Worlds People Make and the Scholars Who Study Them* (Princeton: Princeton University Press, 2005), 171.

16. See Orsi, *Between Heaven and Earth*, 171.

17. Thomas A. Tweed, "Introduction: Narrating U.S. Religious History," in *Retelling U.S. Religious History*, ed. Thomas A. Tweed (Berkeley: University of California Press, 1997), 12. See also Robert A. Orsi, *The Madonna of 115th Street: Faith and Community in Italian Harlem, 1880–1950*, 2nd ed. (New Haven, CT: Yale University Press, 2002), xix–xxiv, xl–xliv.

18. Weston La Barre, *The Peyote Cult* (New Haven: 1938; Hamden, CT: 1959; New York: 1969, 1975; Norman: University of Oklahoma Press, 1989), 72, 103. Author's emphasis.

19. See Richard Evans Schultes, "The Appeal of Peyote (*Lophophora williamsii*) as a Medicine," *American Anthropologist* 40, no. 4 (October 1938): 703–4; Slotkin, *Peyote Religion*; La Barre, *The Peyote Cult*; David F. Aberle, *The Peyote Religion Among the Navaho* (Chicago:

Aldine, 1966); Omer C. Stewart, *Peyote Religion: A History* (Norman: University of Oklahoma Press, 1987); Daniel C. Swan, *Peyote Religious Art: Symbols of Faith and Belief* (Jackson: University Press of Mississippi, 1999). A recent work on peyote and the Native American Church comes from historian Thomas C. Maroukis, who picks up where Stewart's work ended with the addition of the passage of the American Indian Religious Freedom Act and the 1990 Supreme Court decision in *Oregon v. Smith*. His work is an update of Stewart's classic 1987 study but is also a narrative history of the peyote faith, with his historical account including an analysis of religious beliefs, ceremony, and ritual, as well as art and music. In particular, Maroukis discusses the contemporary legal issues surrounding the Native American Church, and the work became a significant case study of the First Amendment right to the free expression of religion. Maroukis, *The Peyote Road: Religious Freedom and the Native American Church* (Norman: University of Oklahoma Press, 2010).

20. Philip J. Deloria, *Indians in Unexpected Places* (Lawrence: University Press of Kansas, 2004), 226.

21. bell hooks [Gloria Watkins], *Talking Back: thinking feminist, thinking black* (Boston: South End Press, 1989), 15.

22. Holly R. Baumgartner, "De-Assimilation as the Need to Tell: Native American Writers, Bakhtin, and Autobiography," in *American Indian Rhetorics of Survivance: Word Medicine, Word Magic*, ed. Ernest Stromberg (Pittsburgh: University of Pittsburgh Press, 2006), 131.

23. Hiram Price, *Report of the Commissioner of Indian Affairs for 1882* (Washington, DC: Government Printing Office, 1882), xxi (hereafter cited as *RCIA*).

24. "Letter from Indian Bureau," *Peyote Hearings 1918*.

25. For more on this debate and the suggestion of a religion as a cultural concept, see Tisa Wenger, *We Have a Religion: The 1920s Pueblo Indian Dance Controversy and American Religious Freedom* (Chapel Hill: University of North Carolina Press in association with The William P. Clements Center for Southwest Studies, Southern Methodist University, 2009), 11–16.

26. Arthur L. Greil and David G. Bromley, "Introduction," in *Defining Religion: Investigating the Boundaries between the Sacred and Secular*, ed. Arthur L. Greil and David G. Bromley (Kidlington, Oxford, UK: Elsevier Science, 2003), 5.

27. Catherine A. Brekus and W. Clark Gilpin, "Introduction," in *American Christianities: A History of Dominance and Diversity*, ed. Catherine A. Brekus and W. Clark Gilpin (Chapel Hill: University of North Carolina Press, 2011), 2–3.

28. James H. Deer to Indian Agent, October 2, 1895, Cheyenne and Arapaho Agency Records: Liquor Traffic and Peyote Use 5/27/1871–12/17/1915, Box 444, Folder 1 (CAA 50–1), Oklahoma Historical Society Research Division, Oklahoma City (hereafter cited as OHS). The confusion of peyote and mescal is addressed in footnote 2 and in subsequent chapters.

29. *Longdale (OK) Ledger*, July 27, 1906, 6.

30. G. L. Williams (superintendent of Potawatomi Agency) to Arthur Parker, June 23, 1913, 3, Reel 8—Correspondence, Papers of the Society of American Indians (hereafter cited as SAI Papers).

31. Arthur Bonnicastle statement before Board of Indian Commissioners, February 4, 1915, in *Peyote Hearings 1918*, 79.

32. Statement of James Mooney, *Peyote Hearings 1918*.

CHAPTER 1. PEYOTISM

1. "Big Animal Show in Mescal Stew," *Dallas Morning News*, June 5, 1920, 8. See also "Memorandum of Scientists, January 28, 1910, in *Peyote Hearings 1918*, 38.

2. Statement of Chester Arthur (Assiniboine) through interpreter (Gertrude Bonnin), in *Peyote Hearings 1918*, 122.

3. "Chelsea Christmas Celebration," *Wotanin Wowapi* (Poplar, MT), January 4, 2007, 3; "Military Honors at Services for Chester Arthur," *Bainville Democrat* (Bainville, MT), September 5, 1941, 1; George Edwards, ed., *The Pioneer Work of the Presbyterian Church in Montana,*, repr. from vol. 6 of the Montana State Historical Society (Helena: Independent Publishing Company, 1906), 196.

4. "Peyote," Bulletin 21, 1929, Department of the Interior, Office of Indian Affairs, Papers of Raoul Weston La Barre, Box 8, Folder: "Legal File," National Anthropological Archives, Smithsonian Institution, Suitland, MD (hereafter cited as NAA–Bureau of American Ethnology).

5. Mary N. MacDonald, "The Primitive, the Primal, and the Indigenous in the Study of Religion," *Journal of the American Academy of Religion* 79, no. 4 (December 2011): 815.

6. Western thought exhibits a disproportionate concern for the functional categorization of religion as an attempt to define meaning rather than explore the varied phenomenon of religious experience. In part, the resistance may lie in the ambiguous nature of what constitutes a religious experience and the appropriate methodological tools for study. See Clifford Geertz, *The Interpretation of Cultures* (New York: Basic Books, 1973), 90. I accept an existential approach similar to Ann Taves's "experiences deemed religious" and Dean R. Hoge and Ella I. Smith's approach advocating a definition that includes "all experiences interpreted as religiously important by the [subjects] themselves." See Ann Taves, *Religious Experience Reconsidered: A Building-Block Approach to the Study of Religion and Other Special Things* (Princeton: Princeton University Press, 2009), xiii; Dean R. Hoge and Ella I. Smith, "Normative and Non-Normative Religious Experience among High School Youth," *Sociological Analysis* 43, no. 1 (Spring 1982): 72.

7. Fuller, *Stairways to Heaven*, 11, 13.

8. William A. Richards, "Entheogens in the Study of Mystical and Archetypal Experiences," *Research in the Social Scientific Study of Religion* 13 (2003): 144; Huston Smith, *Cleansing the Doors of Perception: The Religious Significance of Entheogenic Plants and Chemicals* (New York: Jeremy P. Tarcher, 2000), xvii. Smith suggests that entheogens as "God-containing" is not without problems, whereas a word meaning "God-enabling" would be more accurate. However, he defers to using the word "entheogens" as "the appropriate word for mind-changing substances when they are taken sacramentally." Scholars encourage the shift in discourse for the word entheogen to replace the word *psychedelic*, noting the latter to be "too socio-culturally loaded from its 1960s roots to appropriately designate the revered plants and substances used in traditional rituals." Kenneth W. Tupper, "Entheogens and Existential Intelligence: The Use of Plant Teachers as Cognitive Tools," *Canadian Journal of Education* 27, no. 4 (2002): 500.

9. Fuller, *Stairways to Heaven*, 38. See also La Barre, *Peyote Cult*, 138–39; Edward F. Anderson, *Peyote: The Divine Cactus* (Tucson: University of Arizona Press, 1980).

10. Fuller, *Stairways to Heaven*, 39 (emphasis in the original); Anderson, *Peyote: The Divine Cactus*, 74–75; Josh Hanan, "Communicating with the Divine: The Role of Peyote in Native American Health and Spirituality," Paper presented at the annual meeting of the NCA 93rd Annual Convention, TBA, Chicago, IL, November 15, 2007, accessed March 12, 2011, from http://www.allacademic.com/ meta/ p188231_index.html.

11. Christopher Vecsey, *Imagine Ourselves Richly: Mythic Narratives of North American Indians* (New York: Crossroad, 1988), 173–74.

12. One member of the Native American Church noted, "Peyote is not easy to swallow: it is extremely bitter, even to experienced Peyotists, and occasionally nauseating, especially for beginners." George Morgan, "Recollections of the Peyote Road," in *Psychedelic Reflections*, ed. Lester Grinspoon and James B. Bakalar (New York: Human Sciences Press, 1983), 98–99. See also Stacy B. Schaefer, *Amanda's Blessings from the Peyote Gardens of South Texas* (Albuquerque: University of New Mexico Press, 2015), 32.

13. Thomas H. Lewis, *The Medicine Men: Oglala Sioux Ceremony and Healing* (Lincoln: University of Nebraska Press, 1990), 116; Stewart, *Peyote Religion*, 37; Fuller, *Stairways to Heaven*, 39.

14. Joseph D. Calabrese, "Reflexivity and Transformation Symbolism in the Navajo Peyote Meeting," *Ethos* 22, no. 4 (1994): 509–10.

15. Statement of Paul Boynton, in *Peyote Hearings 1918*, 183–84.

16. Calloway, *First Peoples*, 341.

17. The Society of American Indians (SAI), an organization of "progressive" Indian intellectuals formed in 1911, would also adopt the program of transforming Indians into Americans. Members described the SAI as "an organization of Indian Americans who are actively and vitally interested in the welfare and highest development of their race.... The Society of American Indians stands for the Indian American as an AMERICAN with all the rights, privileges, and duties that the name American implies." Society of American Indians to Melvil Dewey, December 5, 1911, Reel 3—Correspondence, SAI Papers.

18. Calloway, *First Peoples*, 413–15, 418.

19. Arthur C. Parker to Jean F. Morton, April 23, 1912, Reel 5, SAI Papers; "Making a White Man out of an Indian Not a Good Plan," *American Indian Magazine* 5, no. 2 (April–June 1917): 86.

20. Wenger, *We Have a Religion*, 39.

21. An exception to this is Todd M. Kerstetter, *Inspiration and Innovation: Religion in the American West* (Malden, MA: Wiley-Blackwell, 2015). John Corrigan and Winthrop S. Hudson do devote a paragraph to peyote use by Native Americans and its role in religion, but only regarding the twentieth-century controversy surrounding the Supreme Court's 1990 decision in *Oregon v. Smith* (see the conclusion to this work for more on this court ruling). Catherine Albanese gives two paragraphs to a discussion of Peyotism, but her characterization of the religion focuses on the hybrid forms of the peyote ceremony that incorporate Christian elements. See Corrigan and Hudson, *Religion in America: An Historical Account of the Development of American Religious Life*, 7th ed. (Upper Saddle River, NJ: Pearson-Prentice Hall, 2004), 433; Albanese, *America: Religions and Religion*, 4th ed. (Belmont, CA: Thomson/Wadsworth, 2007), 35.

22. James Mooney to Library of Congress, April 16, 1898, NAA MS 2537–Misc. Material Regarding Peyote, Folder "Ethnography, Bibliography, and Misc.," Records of the Bureau of American Ethnology, NAA–Bureau of American Ethnology. Mooney requested a number of books by Spanish botanists and chroniclers on the exploration of Mesoamerica that contained possible references to peyote.

23. J. M. Adovasio and G. F. Fry, "Prehistoric Psychotropic Drug Use in Northeastern Mexico and Trans-Pecos Texas," *Economic Botany* 30, no. 1 (1976): 94–96; Jan G. Bruhn, J. E. Lindgren, B. Homstedt, and J. M. Adovasio, "Peyote Alkaloids: Identification in a Prehistoric Specimen of *Lophophora* from Coahuila, Mexico," *Science* 199, no. 4336 (1978): 1437–38, in Schaefer, *Amanda's Blessings*, 31–32; Carolyn E. Boyd, "Pictographic Evidence of Peyotism in the Lower Pecos, Texas Archaic," in *The Archaeology of Rock-Art*, ed. Christopher Chippendale and Paul Tacon (Cambridge: Cambridge University Press, 1998), 227–46; Maroukis, *Peyote Road*, 14–15.

24. "Drug-Induced Religion," *Quarterly Journal of the Society of American Indians* 2, no. 2 (April–June 1914): 99; "The Drug Habit: America," *Outlook*, December 11, 1918, 574.

25. Sahagún wrote two versions of the Spanish "conquest" of Mexico; the first is Book 12 of the *General History* (1577) and the second is a revision he completed in 1585. The 1576 text is exclusively from an Indigenous, largely Tlatelolcan, viewpoint. His 1585 account added passages praising the Spanish, especially the conqueror Hernan Cortés. See Alfredo Lopez-Austin, "The Research Method of Fray Bernardino de Sahagún: The Questionnaires," in *Sixteenth-Century Mexico: The Work of Sahagún*, ed. Munro S. Edmonson (Albuquerque: University of New Mexico Press, 1974), 111–49; S. L. Cline, "Revisionist Conquest History: Sahagún's Book XII," in *The Work of Bernardino de Sahagún: Pioneer Ethnographer of Sixteenth-Century Aztec Mexico*, vol. 2, ed. Jorge Klor de Alva (Albany: State University of New York, 1988), 93–106.

26. Bernardino de Sahagún, *Historia general de las cosas de la Nueva España*, ed. Carlos María de Bustamante (Mexico City: Imprenta del ciudadano Alejandro Valdés, calle de Santo Domingo y esquina de Tacuba, 1829), 3:118, 3:214, quoted in W. E. Safford, "Narcotic Plants and Stimulants of the Ancient Americans," *Annual Report of the Board of Regents of the Smithsonian Institution, 1916* (Washington, DC: Government Printing Office, 1917), 399, 401. See also Gertrude Bonnin, "An Indian Cult and a Powerful Drug," *American Indian Magazine* 4, no. 2 (April–June 1916): 160. Problematic with Sahagún's writing is his use of the term "Chichimeca Indians," which is a pejorative "umbrella term the Spanish used to describe most of the Indigenous groups scattered through large parts of Guanajuato, Jalisco, Zacatecas, San Luis Potosí, Aguascalientes, and Durango. The Chichimeca peoples were actually composed of several distinct cultural and linguistic groups inhabiting this area," and included the Guachichiles, Guamares, Pames, Otomíes, and Purépecha (also referred to as the Tarascan Indians). See John P. Schmal, "Los Antepasados Indigenas de los Guanajuatenses: A Look into Guanajuato's Past," History of Mexico, Houston Institute for Culture, http://www.houstonculture.org/mexico/guanajuato.html.

27. Martín de la Cruz, *Libellus de medicinalibus Indorum herbism quenduidam India Collegii Sancte Crusis medicus* (1552), quoted in Alexander Dawson, "Peyote in the Colonial Imagination," in *Peyote: History, Tradition, Politics, and Conservation*, ed. Beatriz Caiuby Labate and Clancy Cavnar (Santa Barbara, CA: Greenwood, 2015), 45–46.

28. Francisco Hernández, *Francisci Hernandi, medici atque historici Philippi II, hispan et indiar: Regis, et totius novi orbis archiatri; Opera, cum edita, tum medita, ad autobiographi fidem et jusu region*, ed. Casimiro Gómez Ortega (1790), 3:70, quoted in Safford, "Narcotic Plants and Stimulants," 400–401. Various editions of Hernández's work were distributed to scientists across Europe. The 1790 edition quoted by Safford was compiled by Casimiro Gómez Ortega, based on additional material found in the Colegio Imperial de los Jesuitas de Madrid. See Simon Varey, Rafael Chabrán, and Dora B. Weiner, eds., *Searching for the Secrets of Nature: The Life and Works of Dr. Francisco Hernández* (Stanford, CA: Stanford University Press, 2000).

29. Juan de Cárdenas, *Problemas y secretos maravillosos de las Indias: Obra impresa en México, por Pedro Ocharte, en 1591, y ahora editada en facsímil* (Madrid: Ediciones Cultura Hispánica, 1945), 4, 246, quoted in Dawson, "Peyote in the Colonial Imagination," 47.

30. *Apostolicos afanes de la compañia de Jesus, escritos por un padre de la misma sagrada religion de su provincial de Mexico* (Barcelona: por Pablo Nadal Impreffor, en la calle de la Canúda, 1754), 18. In the United States, reports in the press characterized peyote as the "new agent of the devil." See "Devil in a New Dress, Our Own Peyote Bean," *El Paso (TX) Herald*, February 23, 1918, 12.

31. Safford, "Narcotic Plants and Stimulants" 402; "Devil in a New Dress," 12.

32. For more on social identities and their relationship to colonialism, see Laura A. Lewis, *Hall of Mirrors: Power, Witchcraft, and Caste in Colonial Mexico* (Durham, NC: Duke University Press, 2003); Andrew B. Fisher and Matthew D. O'Hara, eds., *Imperial Subjects: Race and Identity in Colonial Latin America* (Durham, NC: Duke University Press, 2009).

33. Irving A. Leonard, "Peyote and the Mexican Inquisition, 1620," *American Anthropologist* 44, no. 2 (April–June 1942): 324.

34. Original edict of the Holy Office from the *Archivo General de la Nación*–Ramo de Inquisición, tomo 289, Mexico City (hereafter cited as AGN-I). The Spanish and English translation is found in Leonard, "Peyote and the Mexican Inquisition," 325–26.

35. Dawson, "Peyote in the Colonial Imagination," 48–49. The Church considered Indians "potential Christians and legal 'children,'" who could "not be held legally accountable for crimes like heresy, which required the capacity to knowingly violate religious law."

36. Maroukis, *Peyote Road*, 16; Stewart, *Peyote Religion*, 20–29. The hearings occurred between 1621 and 1779. Alexander Dawson's essay in *Peyote: History, Tradition, Politics, and Conservation* contributes to the historiography with an examination of specific Inquisition hearings regarding peyote, using the Inquisitional trials as historical documents to "reveal a series of popular practices taking place outside the law." See Dawson, "Peyote in the Colonial Imagination," 50.

37. Dawson, 50.

38. Dawson, 50. He gives examples from AGN-I, vol. 341, exp. 4, 1622; AGN-I, vol. 342.10, March 1622; AGN-I, vol. 363.13, 1629; AGN-I, vol. 366, exp. 27, 1629; AGN-I, vol. 373, exp. 3, 1633; AGN-I, vol. 376, exp. 31, 1637; AGN-I, vol. 419 exp. 24, 1644; AGN-I, vol. 1328, 1716; and AGN-I, vol. 912, exp. 29, 1742.

39. Bartholome Garcia, *Manual para administrar los santos sacramentos de penitencia, eucharistia, extrema-uncion y matrimonio* (Mexico City: Imprenta de los Herederos de Doña Maria de Rivera, 1760), 15.

40. "Sacred, Also Intoxicating," *Sun* (NY), June 13, 1909, 2.

41. These include the Acaxees, Aztecs, Carrizos, Caxanes, Chichimecs, Coahuiltecans, Coras, Huichols, Opotas, Otomíes, Pimas, Tamaulipecans, Tarahumaras, Tarascans, Tepecanos, Tlaxcaltecans, and Zacatecas. See "Sacred, Also Intoxicating."

42. Maroukis, *Peyote Road*, 17.

43. Schaefer, *Amanda's Blessings*, 32. See also Stewart, *Peyote Religion*, 17–18.

44. Fuller, *Stairways to Heaven*, 39–40; Maroukis, *Peyote Road*, 18–19. For other detailed accounts of the Huichol Indians' culture and ritual peyote use, see Barbara Myerholl, *Peyote Hunt: The Sacred Journey of the Huichol Indians* (Ithaca, NY: Cornell University Press, 1974); Stacy B. Schaefer and Peter T. Furst, eds., *People of the Peyote: Huichol Indian History, Religion, and Survival* (Albuquerque: University of New Mexico Press, 1996); Peter T. Furst, *Rock Crystals and Peyote Dreams: Explorations in the Huichol Universe* (Salt Lake City: University of Utah Press, 2006).

45. Carl Lumholtz, *Unknown Mexico; A Record of Five Years' Exploration among the Tribes of the Western Sierra Madre; in the Tierra Caliente of Tepic and Jalisco; and among the Tarascos of Michoacan*, vol. 2 (New York: Charles Scribner's Sons, 1902), 359–72.

46. Maroukis, *Peyote Road*, 21.

47. Stewart, *Peyote Religion*, 30.

48. Pekka Hämäläinen, *The Comanche Empire* (New Haven, CT: Yale University Press, 2008), 142, 176, 361.

49. For example, James Mooney of the American Bureau of Ethnology claimed the Kiowa learned about peyote from the Comanche, who got it from the Mescalero Apache and Tonkawa; no doubt he based this information on Quanah Parker's (Comanche) statement that the Comanche got it from the Mescalero Apaches in Mexico. See James Mooney, in *Peyote Hearings 1918*, 70; Quanah Parker, January 21, 1908, Testimony at Oklahoma Peyote Hearings, Cheyenne and Arapaho Agency Records, Box 444, Folder 1, OHS. However, both Morris E. Opler and Omer C. Stewart claim the ethnohistorical evidence does not exist to support the Mescalero Apache as the originators of the American peyote ceremony. See Morris E. Opler, "The Influence of Aboriginal Pattern and White Contact on a Recently Introduced Ceremony, the Mescalero Peyote Rite," *Journal of American Folklore* 49, nos. 191–92 (1936): 143; Stewart, *Peyote Religion*, 48–49.

50. Stewart, *Peyote Religion*, 49–61; Swan, *Peyote Religious Art*, 4; Maroukis, *Peyote Road*, 22–23.

51. Commissioner of Indian Affairs Luke Lea set forth the doctrine in 1851 by calling for the Indians' "concentration, their domestication, and their incorporation." Reservations came to be seen as instruments for the achievement of this goal. "Although treaties were the primary mechanism for creating reservations, Congress suspended formal treaty making in 1871. Thereafter, federal reservations would be established by executive order, congressional act, or any legal combination recognized by the federal government. Before the turn of the century, 56 of 162 federal reservations were established by executive order. After 1919, however, only an act of Congress could establish reservations." Gregory Campbell, "Indian Reservations," *Dictionary of American History*, 3rd ed., vol. 4, ed. Stanley I. Kutler (New York: Charles Scribner's Sons, 2003), 297–302.

52. "The So-Called Mescal Button," *Oshkosh (WI) Daily Northwestern*, September 10, 1908, 4. It was not until the later part of the twentieth century that Indian tribes living in the eastern part of the United States adopted Peyotism. See Frank X. Tolbert, "Tolbert's Texas: Boston Indians Ordered Peyote," *Dallas Morning News*, July 7, 1966, 1.

53. *Peyote: An Abridged Compilation from the Files of the Bureau of Indian Affairs* (Washington, DC: Government Printing Office, 1922), 31.

54. J. Lee Hall, "Report of Agent for Kiowa, Comanche, and Wichita Agency, August 26, 1886," in *RCIA for 1886*, 130. The Comanche (N~~u~~m~~u~~n~~uu~~) people say "that the Creator placed his spirit on a lowly cactus they called wokweebi (WOE-KWAY-VEE). The ritual consumption of this plant brought them closer to the higher power. . . . In modern times, this cactus is known as Peyote and it is a sacrament that remains at the core of the Native American Church." Comanche National Museum and Cultural Center Facebook page, accessed January 2, 2017, https://www.facebook.com/ComancheMuseum.

55. Quanah Parker, January 21, 1908, Testimony at Oklahoma Peyote Hearings.

56. Frederick S. Barde, September 18, 1909, Frederick S. Barde Collection, Box 21 (Manuscripts: Oklahoma A&M through Mescal Bean Peyote, 1890–1916), Folder 41 (Mescal Bean Peyote), OHS.

57. Stewart, *Peyote Religion*, 58–60; Swan, *Peyote Religious Art*, 4; Maroukis, *Peyote Road*, 24.

58. Stewart, *Peyote Religion*, 80–127.

59. *Blanket Indian* referred to Indians who held to tribal culture and traditional customs. Chapter 5 will examine the term in more detail as well as analyze the implications of its use.

60. James Mooney, in *Peyote Hearings 1918*, 69.

61. Stewart, *Peyote Religion*, 148–209, 265–326; Aberle, *Peyote Religion among the Navaho*, 3.

62. Fuller, *Stairways to Heaven*, 42; Maroukis, *Peyote Road*, 25.

63. Swan, *Peyote Religious Art*, 3; Stewart, *Peyote Religion*, 40–41. Stewart posits that James Mooney's 1891 attendance at a Kiowa peyote ceremony and his description of it provides a sound basis of historical documentation as "the continued history of the peyote ceremony in the United States bears evidence to its authenticity." Stewart also provides a detailed comparative list of elements between several forms of peyote ceremonies in the United States and Mexico. See Stewart, *Peyote Religion*, 339–75.

64. "A Peculiar Plant," *Evening Sun* (Washington, DC), March 31, 1898, 13.

65. Fuller, *Stairways to Heaven*, 41–42. Fuller refers to this shift as the "Americanized" version of Peyotism. Another way to describe the shift of power from the spiritual leader to the people might be a comparison to the Protestant Reformation.

66. Maroukis, *Peyote Road*, 25; La Barre, *Peyote Cult*, 54; Hanan, "Communicating with the Divine," 14–15.

67. La Barre, *Peyote Cult*, 54.

68. Gertrude Seymour, "Peyote Worship," *The Survey* 36, no. 7 (May 13, 1916): 182; Bonnin, "An Indian Cult and a Powerful Drug," 160.

69. La Barre, *Peyote Cult*, 55; Fuller, *Stairways to Heaven*, 43.

70. Thomas W. Kavanagh, "Southern Plains Dance: Tradition and Dynamics," in *Native American Dance: Ceremonies and Social Traditions*, ed. Charlotte Heth (Washington, DC: Smithsonian Institution Press, 1992), 105. See also Clyde Ellis, *A Dancing People: Powwow*

Culture on the Southern Plains (Lawrence: University Press of Kansas, 2013), 13. Similar arguments can also be made for Native peoples in other regions of the country.

71. Ellis, *A Dancing People*, 14.

72. For example, the year before Indian agents noticed the peyote practice, the report from the Cheyenne and Arapaho Agency included an observation about their "medicine dance," or more accurately, the Sun Dance. The agent noted a number of men who "gash their arms and legs, and pierce holes in their chests, pass ropes through the holes and suspend themselves from the center of [a pole] until their struggling tears the flesh loose.... They dance night and day without food or water until exhausted.... Such evidence of devotion in the performance of duty is worthy of a better religion." See D. B. Dyer, "Report of Agent for Cheyenne and Arapaho Agency, July 22, 1885," in *RCIA for 1885*, 79.

73. La Barre, *Peyote Cult*, 55; Carl Lumholtz, "Tarahumari Dances and Plant-Worship," *Scribner's Magazine* 16, no. 4 (October 1894): 455; Lumholtz, *Unknown Mexico*, 155–57; Stewart, *Peyote Religion*, 32.

74. James Mooney, in *Peyote Hearings 1918*, 74; "Eat 'Dry Whiskey,'" *Dakota Farmer's Leader* (Canton, SD), October 1, 1915, 3.

75. Mooney, "The Mescal Plant and Ceremony," 7; "Mescal Buttons to be Investigated; Causing Red Skins to Get Drunk," *Bisbee (AZ) Daily Review*, September 1, 1908, 2.

76. Swan, *Peyote Religious Art*, 24.

77. Fuller, *Stairways to Heaven*, 42.

78. James Mooney, ca. 1897, NAA MS 1930–Notes Used on Peyote, James Mooney Papers, NAA–Bureau of American Ethnology. Mooney's notes from a Kiowa-Comanche ceremony are also summarized in La Barre, *Peyote Cult*, 43–53; Stewart, *Peyote Religion*, 36–39; and Swan, *Peyote Religious Art*, 24–30.

79. James Mooney, "In Kiowa Camps," Papers and Addresses Delivered at the January Meeting of the Mississippi Valley Historical Association, January 18, 1910, *Proceedings of the Mississippi Valley Historical Association for the Year 1909–1910*, vol. 3 (Cedar Rapids, IA: Torch Press, 1911), 49.

80. James Mooney, ca. 1897, NAA MS 1930–Notes Used on Peyote.

81. James Mooney, in *Peyote Hearings 1918*, 70, 72; Swan, *Peyote Religious Art*, 23; Maroukis, *Peyote Road*, 25; Schaefer, *Amanda's Blessings*, 34.

82. Maroukis, *Peyote Road*, 30; Stewart, *Peyote Religion*, 91; Swan, *Peyote Religious Art*, 30.

83. Stewart, *Peyote Religion*, 93.

84. Dr. F. G. Ellis, "The Mescal Intoxicant," *Indian School Journal* (March 1909): 32; Rev. W. C. Roe, in *Peyote Hearings 1918*, 44; James Mooney, in *Peyote Hearings 1918*, 89.

85. Robert D. Hall, "The Peyote Question: Conference of Friends of the Indians," *American Indian Magazine* 6, no. 2 (Summer 1918): 69; Paul Radin, "The Winnebago Tribe," *Bureau of American Ethnology Annual Report* 37 (1915–1916): 395–97; Stewart, *Peyote Religion*, 152.

86. "Drug-Induced Religion," 101; Radin, "The Winnebago Tribe," 395–97; Stewart, *Peyote Religion*, 152.

87. "Drug-Induced Religion," 101.

88. Stewart, *Peyote Religion*, 93.

89. Willard Hughes Rollings, *Unaffected by the Gospel, Osage Resistance to the Christian Invasion (1673–1906): A Cultural Victory* (Albuquerque: University of New Mexico Press, 2004), 185.

90. Anderson, *Peyote: The Divine Cactus*, 66–69.

91. James Mooney to Bureau of American Ethnology, 1921, Box 1, Folder "Letters," James Mooney Papers, NAA–Bureau of American Ethnology; "Sacramental Service Native Indian Church," *Calumet (OK) Chieftain*, April 17, 1919, 1.

92. Justin Gage, *We Do Not Want the Gates Closed between Us: Native Networks and the Spread of the Ghost Dance* (Norman: University of Oklahoma Press, 2020). See also Warren, *God's Red Son*.

93. Mary C. Collins, "Address in Proceedings of the Board of Indian Commissioners of the Nineteenth Lake Mohonk Indian Conference, October 16, 1901," in *RCIA for 1901*, 807; Bonnin, "An Indian Cult and a Powerful Drug," 161; *Thirty-Third Annual Report of the Bureau of American Ethnology to the Secretary of the Smithsonian Institution, 1911–1912* (Washington, DC: Government Printing Office, 1919), 104–5.

94. Robert G. Valentine, *RCIA for 1909*, 13; "Getting Drunk on Cactus," *The Farmer* (Bridgeport, CT), May 17, 1916, 12; "Mescal, A Menace to the Indians," in *Peyote Hearings 1918*.

95. Jock Bull Bear (Arapaho), in *Peyote Hearings 1918*, 106; Arthur Bonnicastle (Osage), in *Peyote Hearings 1918*, 80; Fred Lookout (Osage), in *Peyote Hearings 1918*, 149.

96. Fuller, *Stairways to Heaven*, 57.

97. William James, *Varieties of Religious Experience: A Study in Human Nature*, Centenary Edition (New York: Routledge, 2002), 301.

98. James, *Varieties of Religious Experience*, 327–28.

99. Dr. Harvey W. Wiley, "Peyote," *American Indian Magazine* 7, no. 1 (Spring 1919): 38; Jacob Reid, in *Peyote Hearings 1918*, 87.

100. "Peyote," Bulletin 21, 1929.

101. Stansberry Hagar to Herbert Welch, August 25, 1923, Reel 7, SAI Papers; "The Many Methods of Worship," *Oklahoma State Register* (Guthrie, OK), January 23, 1908.

102. Fuller, *Stairways to Heaven*, 11.

103. Bill Kte'pi, "Introduction," in *Handbook to Life in America*, vol. 5: *The Age of Reform, 1890 to 1920*, ed. Rodney P. Carlisle (New York: Facts on File, Infobase, 2009), 1.

104. Charles Burke, *RCIA for 1921*, 37.

105. Aberle, *Peyote Religion among the Navaho*, 7, 352.

CHAPTER 2. THE PUSH FOR PEYOTE LEGISLATION

1. Paul Boynton, January 21, 1908, Testimony at Oklahoma Peyote Hearings, Cheyenne and Arapaho Agency Records, Box 444, Folder 1, OHS. See also Dennis Wiedman, "Upholding Indigenous Freedoms of Religion and Medicine: Peyotists at the 1906–1908 Oklahoma Constitutional Convention and First Legislature," *American Indian Quarterly* 36, no. 2 (Spring 2012): 215–46.

2. Justin Gage, "Continuing the Movement," We Do Not Want the Gates Closed between Us, 2022, https://nativeamericannetworks.com/continuingthemovement/.

3. *Peyote: An Abridged Compilation*, 12.

4. Wenger, *We Have a Religion*, 4.

5. Arthur Parker to Jean E. Morton, April 23, 1912, Reel 5—Correspondence, SAI Papers.

6. John D. C. Atkins, *RCIA for 1885*, vii–viii; *RCIA for 1892*, 6; *RCIA for 1906*, 29–30.

7. *RCIA for 1885*, v–vi.

8. *Peyote: An Abridged Compilation*, 8, 14.

9. Bruce Kinney (superintendent of Missions, American Baptist Home Mission Society) to Robert Valentine (commissioner of Indian Affairs), September 29, 1909, Cheyenne and Arapaho Agency Records, Box 444, Folder 2, Item 70–71, OHS.

10. *RCIA for 1885*, iv; *RCIA for 1891*, 7; *RCIA for 1901*, 805; *RCIA for 1909*, 21.

11. "Methods to Help the Indians: Mission Workers in Oklahoma Talk about Plans," *Oklahoma State Capital* (Guthrie, OK), October 2, 1898; *RCIA for 1891*, 6.

12. *RCIA for 1921*, 37.

13. "Making a White Man out of an Indian Not a Good Plan," *American Indian Magazine* 5, no. 2 (April–June 1917): 85.

14. Arthur C. Parker, "The Editor's Viewpoint: The Functions of the Society of American Indians," *American Indian Magazine* 4, no. 1 (January–March 1916): 8. Parker served as both the executive secretary of the SAI (1911–1915) and later its president (1916–1918).

15. "Annual Convention of the Society of American Indians," *The Indian Leader* 20, no. 8 (October 1916): 15.

16. Robert Fuller, "Cosmology," in *Religion in American History*, ed. Amanda Porterfield and John Corrigan (West Sussex, UK: Wiley-Blackwell, 2010), 208–9.

17. Corrigan and Hudson, *Religion in America*, 276.

18. Kathryn Lofton, "Cosmology," in Porterfield and Corrigan, *Religion in American History*, 270–71, 274.

19. Lofton, "Cosmology," 274; Corrigan and Hudson, *Religion in America*, 279–90; Martin E. Marty, *Modern American Religion*, vol. 1: *The Irony of It All, 1893–1919* (Chicago: University of Chicago Press, 1986), 32–43. The extent of the popular interest stimulated by the new biblical studies of higher criticism was indicated by "the reception that was given in 1881 to the English Revised Version of the New Testament, which incorporated the results of scholarly analysis of the text. The *Chicago Times* and the *Chicago Tribune* both printed the entire text, and 200,000 copies of the revised New Testament were sold in New York within less than a week." Corrigan and Hudson, *Religion in America*, 279.

20. Peter W. Williams, "Community," in Porterfield and Corrigan, *Religion in American History*, 286. Emphasis added.

21. See Jennifer Graber, *The Gods of Indian Country: Religion and the Struggle for the American West* (New York: Oxford University Press, 2018).

22. Russel Lawrence Barsh, "Progressive-Era Bureaucrats and the Unity of Twentieth-Century Indian Policy," *American Indian Quarterly* 15, no. 1 (Winter 1991): 2; Scott Richard Lyons, *X-Marks*, 80. For an introduction to scientific race theories, especially in the American context, see Reginald Horsman, *Race and Manifest Destiny: The Origins of American Racial Anglo-Saxonism* (Cambridge, MA: Harvard University Press, 1981).

23. David Wallace Adams, *Education for Extinction: American Indians and the Boarding School Experience, 1875–1928* (Lawrence: University Press of Kansas, 1995), 14. Interestingly,

during Lewis Henry Morgan's career, he wanted and actively pursued an appointment as commissioner of Indian Affairs but was denied the opportunity by President Ulysses Grant. For more about Morgan's life, see Daniel Noah Moses, *The Promise of Progress: The Life and Work of Lewis Henry Morgan* (Columbia: University of Missouri Press, 2009).

24. An Act to Provide for the Allotment of Lands in Severalty to Indians on the Various Reservations, and to Extend the Protection of the Laws of the United States and the Territories over the Indians, and for Other Purposes, *U.S. Statutes at Large* 24 (1887): 388–91, §6.

25. Alan Trachtenberg, *Shades of Hiawatha: Staging Indians, Making Americans, 1880–1930* (New York: Hill and Wang, 2004), 39.

26. "Report of the Indian Inspector for Indian Territory, October 7, 1905," in *RCIA for 1905*, 18.

27. *RCIA for 1903*, 2.

28. Lee D. Baker, *Anthropology and the Racial Politics of Culture* (Durham, NC: Duke University Press, 2010), 7. Baker continues, "Although some privileges were afforded to those responsible individuals who acted white, actual rights afforded white people never followed even the most sincere attempts to perform respectability."

29. Clyde Ellis, "American Indians and Christianity," *Encyclopedia of Oklahoma History and Culture*, Oklahoma Historical Society, 2009, www.okhistory.org/publications/enc/entry?entry=AM011.

30. *RCIA for 1869*, 10.

31. Marty, *Modern American Religion*, 97.

32. Wenger, *We Have a Religion*, 19–20.

33. *RCIA for 1909*, 21.

34. Rev. J. J. Methvin, "Report of Missionary at Anadarko, August 29, 1892," in *RCIA for 1892*, 390.

35. E. E. White, "Report of Agent for Kiowa, Comanche, and Wichita Agency, August 18, 1888," in *RCIA for 1888*, 99.

36. In 1878 (20 U.S. Stat. 86), Congress authorized payments for Indian police to assist agents in maintaining order on reservations; the Court of Indian Offenses followed in 1883, with Native judges in charge of the reservation courts. The first Court of Indian Offenses in the area that was to become the State of Oklahoma was originally established prior to statehood in Indian Territory in 1886. The original Court of Indian Offenses was created to provide law enforcement for the Kiowa, Comanche, and Apache (KCA) reservation. See "History–Court of Indian Offenses," US Department of the Interior, Indian Affairs, https://www.bia.gov/regional-offices/southern-plains/court-indian-offenses. The purpose of the court was to prosecute violators of the Code of Indian Offenses, which prohibited traditional ceremonial activities throughout Indian Country, notably traditional customs, dances, and plural marriages. See Hiram Price, *Rules Governing the Court of Indian Offenses* (March 30, 1883), https://commons.und.edu//indigenous-gov-docs/131/. For more on the Court of Indian Offenses, see Laurence Armand French, *Policing American Indians: A Unique Chapter in American Jurisprudence* (Boca Raton, FL: CRC Press, 2016). Agent White's order, which was extended to other agencies, called for the Court of Indian Offenses to "consider the use, sale, exchange, gift, or introduction" of peyote as a "misdemeanor punishable under Section 9 of the 'Rules governing the Court of

Indian Offenses.'" Thomas Jefferson Morgan to S. L. Patrick, July 31, 1890, Sac and Fox and Shawnee Agency Records, Box 613, Folder SFSA 35–1, OHS.

37. I use his first name throughout this work in order to distinguish him from Arthur Parker, the executive secretary of the Society of American Indians. I will use the last name to designate Arthur Parker. For more on Quanah Parker, see chapter 5. See also Zoe A. Tilghman, *Quanah: The Eagle of the Comanches* (Oklahoma City: Harlow, 1938); Paul Foreman, *Quanah the Serpent Eagle* (Flagstaff, AZ: Northland Press, 1983); Troxey Kemper, *Comanche Warbonnet: A Story of Quanah Parker* (Tsaile, AZ: Navajo Community College Press, 1991); William T. Hagan, *Quanah Parker: Comanche Chief* (Norman: University of Oklahoma Press, 1993); Bill Neeley, *The Last Comanche Chief: The Life and Times of Quanah Parker* (New York: Castle Books, 2007); Cynthia Kay Rhodes, *Between Two Worlds: The Legend of Quanah Parker* (New York: Eloquent Books, 2009); S. C. Gwyne, *Empire of the Summer Moon: Quanah Parker and the Rise and Fall of the Comanches, the Most Powerful Indian Tribe in American History* (New York: Scribner, 2010).

38. "Indian Law Enforcement History," Bureau of Indian Affairs Law Enforcement Services, 13, http://web.archive.org/web/20000226013721/bialaw.fedworld.gov/history/index.htm. See also William T. Hagan, *Indian Police and Judges* (New Haven, CT: Yale University Press, 1966), 135–39.

39. Stewart, *Peyote Religion*, 133.

40. *RCIA for 1915*, 446.

41. Rev. B. F. Gassaway to W. A. Jones, April 16, 1903, Record Group 75, Letters Received, no. 33469, National Archives, Washington, DC.

42. Rev. W. C. Roe (missionary, Reformed Church of America), September 18, 1909, Frederick S. Barde Collection, Manuscripts, Box 21, Folder 41, OHS; "The Deadliest of Drugs," *Arizona Republican* (Phoenix, AZ), June 21, 1918, 4.

43. Rev. W. C. Roe, in *Peyote Hearings 1918*, 45.

44. "The Ravages of Peyote," *Thirty-Fourth Annual Report of the Indian Rights Association*, December 14, 1916, in *Peyote Hearings 1918*, 20; "Owen is Flayed by the Missionaries; His Stand on the Peyote Bean Opens Door to Indians to Become Inebriates," *Oklahoma Weekly Leader* (Guthrie, OK), October 27, 1921, 4; "Oklahoma Indians Again on Warpath," *Lubbock (TX) Morning Avalanche*, February 23, 1927, 7; "Faith of Oklahoma Indians Requires Use of Narcotics," *Salt Lake (UT) Tribune*, June 17, 1934, 10; "Peyote Stirs Up Discussion; Head of Baptist Mission Criticizes Collier for Not Halting Rites," *Daily Ardmoreite* (Ardmore, OK), October 19, 1934, 1.

45. Rev. Dr. E. E. Higley (Methodist missionary) "Make War on Use of Peyote," *Sunday Tulsa (OK) Daily World*, April 17, 1921; *Peyote: An Abridged Compilation*, 14; "Peyote Sacrament Draws the Indians," *Dallas Morning News*, January 8, 1923, 4.

46. Rev. T. J. Davis (Baptist missionary to Cheyenne Indians) to Rev. Bruce Kinney (secretary, Baptist Home Mission Society), December 14, 1918, Peyote Papers, Folder 30, Item 3827.2021, Helmerich Center for American Research at Gilcrease Museum, Tulsa, OK (hereafter HCAR).

47. Rev. F. L. King to Rev. Bruce Kinney, September 28, 1918, Peyote Papers, Folder 10, Item 3827.2002.1, HCAR.

48. Delos Lone Wolf (Kiowa), "How to Solve the Indian Problem," *American Indian Magazine* 4, no. 3 (July–September 1916): 258; Thomas Sloan (Omaha), "Statement at Board of Indian Commissioners Peyote Hearing, February 4, 1915," in *Peyote Hearings 1918*, 83.

49. Rev. Bruce Kinney (secretary, Baptist home Mission Society) to Rev. Isaac McCoy (Baptist missionary), Peyote Papers, Folder 23, Item 3827.2015.1, HCAR.

50. "Oklahoma Indians Again on Warpath," 7.

51. When ethnologist James Mooney first wrote about the peyote ceremony, he mistakenly referred to peyote as mescal. Mooney's early writings contributed to the confusion regarding the botanical classification, which had further social implications. Thomas Maroukis writes, "Part of the misunderstanding concerning the danger of Peyote was its confusion with the mescal bean. In the late nineteenth century, Peyote tops were referred to as mescal beans.... The mescal bean plant produces pods that contain red beans that are highly hallucinogenic and potentially dangerous.... In his later writings, Mooney corrected himself and said Peyote is mistakenly known as mescal. Nevertheless, the confusion lived on as some scholars continued to misuse the word *mescal* until the issue was fully clarified by ethnobotanist Richard Evans Schultes in the 1930s." Maroukis, *Peyote Road*, 6–7. The botanical classification for the mescal bean is *Sophora secundiflora*, also called *frijolillo* or carol bean, and peyote is *Lophophora williamsii*. See Stewart, *Peyote Religion*, 136.

52. Maroukis, *Peyote Road*, 32.

53. "Red Men Win Fight," *Daily Ardmoreite* (Ardmore, OK), January 28, 1908, 1; "Red Men Victors in Peyote Fight," *Lawton (OK) Constitution-Democrat*, January 30, 1908, 8.

54. "Must Have Their Bean," *Searchlight* (Guthrie, OK), January 24, 1908, 9.

55. Rev. H. L. Price to Conference of Indian Agents and Missionaries to the Cheyennes and Arapahos, March 7, 1911, Cheyenne and Arapaho Agency Records, Box 444, Folder 2, OHS.

56. Superintendent of Cheyenne and Arapaho Agency to commissioner of Indian Affairs, December 23, 1914, Cheyenne and Arapaho Agency Records, Box 444, Folder 3, OHS; William E. Johnson to Charles E. Shell, September 4, 1907, Cheyenne and Arapaho Agency Records, Box 444, Folder 1, OHS; E. B. Merritt to W. W. Scott, April 13, 1918, Cheyenne and Arapaho Agency Records, Box 444, Folder 4, OHS.

57. W. C. Kohlenberg to Willis Dunn, April 1, 1911, Cheyenne and Arapaho Agency Records, Box 444, Folder 2, OHS; G. H. Hawks to Walter F. Dickens, March 18, 1911, Cheyenne and Arapaho Agency Records, Box 444, Folder 2, OHS.

58. "Vote Adopted by the Board of Indian Commissioners at Its Annual Meeting," March 6–7, 1912, Reel 8, SAI Papers. The creation of the Board of Indian Commissioners was part of Grant's "Peace Policy" initiative to solve the Indian problem. Established on April 10, 1869, the Board of Indian Commissioners consisted of ten members selected by the president to serve in a voluntary capacity. It remained an all-Protestant body until 1902, when Theodore Roosevelt appointed two Catholics to fill vacancies on the board. See R. Pierce Beaver, "The Churches and President Grant's Peace Policy," *Journal of Church and State* 4, no. 2 (November 1962): 176–77; Henry E. Fritz, "The Last Hurrah of Christian Humanitarian Indian Reform: The Board of Indian Commissioners, 1909–1918," *Western History Quarterly* 16, no. 2 (April 1985): 147–162.

59. Stewart, *Peyote Religion*, 213.
60. Stewart, 215.
61. Stewart, 217.
62. "Resolutions," *Indian's Friend* 29, no. 3 (January 1917): 7; Stewart, *Peyote Religion*, 217.
63. "Third National Indian Student Conference," *The Native American* (Phoenix Indian School, AZ) 17, no. 17 (October 28, 1916): 307; "Indian Progress," *Indian's Friend* 29, no. 2 (November 1916): 6.
64. Arthur Parker to Oliver Lamere, September 24, 1913, Reel 4—Correspondence, SAI Papers.
65. Arthur Parker to Rides A White Hipped Horse, December 12, 1913, Reel 6—Correspondence, SAI Papers.
66. K. Tsianina Lomawaima, "The Society of American Indians," *Oxford Research Encyclopedia of American History*, http://americanhistory.oxfordre.com/view/10.1093/acrefore/9780199329175.001.0001/acrefore-9780199329175-e-31.
67. Thomas C. Maroukis, "The Peyote Controversy and the Demise of the Society of American Indians," *Studies in American Indian Literatures* 25, no. 2/*American Indian Quarterly* 37, no. 3 (Summer 2013): 163.
68. Arthur C. Parker to Charles Dagenett, December 4, 1911, Reel 2, SAI Papers.
69. Arthur C. Parker to Charles Dagenett, December 22, 1911, Reel 2, SAI Papers.
70. Thomas C. Moffett to Arthur C. Parker, April 8, 1916, Reel 5, SAI Papers.
71. "Society of American Indians," *Indian's Friend* 29, no. 2 (November 1916): 4.
72. Arthur C. Parker to S. M. Brosius, June 16, 1913, Reel 1, SAI Papers.
73. Stewart, *Peyote Religion*, 221; Statement of Richard H. Pratt, *Peyote Hearings 1918*, 147.
74. Stewart, *Peyote Religion*, 226–27, 238.
75. Stewart, 227–29; "Use of Peyote by Indians is Now Increasing," *Evening Republican* (Mitchell, SD), February 10, 1926, 6.
76. James Mooney to Joseph B. Thoburn, October 26, 1920, Joseph Thoburn Collection, Box 31, Folder 7, Item PE1, OHS.
77. Seymour, "Peyote Worship," 184.
78. David J. Wishart, "Indian Agents," *Encyclopedia of the Great Plains*, University of Nebraska-Lincoln, 2011, http://plainshumanities.unl.edu/encyclopedia/doc/egp.pg.032. Wishart adds, "In the United States, the post of Indian agent was abolished in 1908 by commissioner of Indian Affairs Francis Leupp. Thereafter, doctors and teachers, officially called superintendents, took over the agents' duties. Leupp believed that they would be more successful in promoting assimilation."
79. Henry E. Fritz, "The Making of Grant's 'Peace Policy,'" *Chronicles of Oklahoma* 37, no. 4 (1959): 413. Fritz elaborates, "Appointments for the office of Indian Agent were approved by the President and then confirmed in the Senate. Senate approval was usually given a candidate who had been recommended through political channels in the state or territory in which he sought assignment. There was no competition in the purchase of supplies at the agencies since a single contractor or firm was given a monopoly of the trade."
80. "Must Have Their Bean," 9.

81. Testimony of Otto Wells (Comanche) in report of Lt. Gov. George Bellamy, February 25, 1908, Sac and Fox and Shawnee Agency Records, Box 613, Folder SFSA 35–1, Item 20–21, OHS.

82. Jock Bull Bear (Arapaho), *Peyote Hearings 1918*, 105; *Peyote: An Abridged Compilation*, 33. Charges of economic harm to Peyotist Indians came from sources such as S. M. Brosius of the Indian Rights Association, who claimed advocates of peyote "seek to influence the most thrifty Indians; and once under their control, liberal contributions for the parent organization follow.... It is alleged that secret agents visit this reservation [Uintah and Ouray] for the purpose of introducing the use of the drug, and derive financial contributions from their victims." Statement of S. M. Brosius, *Peyote Hearings 1918*, 20.

83. Seymour, "Peyote Worship," 184.

84. Statement of Francis La Flesche (Omaha), *Peyote Hearings 1918*, 114.

85. Rev. Lyman Abbott, "The Menace of Peyote," *American Indian Magazine* 5, no. 2 (April–June 1917): 135.

86. Statement of Francis La Flesche (Omaha), *Peyote Hearings 1918*, 114.

87. J. W. Hadley to unknown recipient, September 15, 1913, NAA MS 2537—Misc. Material Regarding Peyote, NAA—Bureau of American Ethnology.

88. Cato Sells, *RCIA for 1918*, 24, 31.

89. "Religious Persecution," in *General Report of the President of the Native American Church*, Oklahoma, June 8, 1925, Joseph Thoburn Collection, Manuscripts, Box 23, Folder 1, OHS.

90. Citizenship Certificate, James Mooney [Sr.], August 2, 1859, James Mooney Papers, Box 1, Folder "Biographical Materials," NAA–Bureau of American Ethnology; John Swanton, "James Mooney," *American Anthropologist* 24, no. 2 (April–June 1922): 209. James Mooney Jr. was born in 1861 after his parents had become naturalized American citizens. For a complete biography of Mooney, see Moses, *Indian Man*.

91. Ely M. Janis, "The Irish National Land League in the United States and Ireland: Nationalism, Gender, and Ethnicity in the Gilded Age" (PhD diss., Boston College, 2008).

92. Swanton, "James Mooney," 210; Thomas Shahan to James Mooney, September 15, n.d., James Mooney Papers, Box 1, Folder: "Letters," NAA–Bureau of American Ethnology; Thomas Shahan to James Mooney, "Personal," September 15, n.d., James Mooney Papers, Box 1, Folder: "Letters," NAA–Bureau of American Ethnology. For more on Mooney's writings about Irish culture, see "The Gaelic Factor in the World's Population," "The Gaelic Language of Ireland," and "Clan Origin (notes concerning Ireland)," James Mooney Papers, Box 1, Folder: "Articles and Talks," NAA–Bureau of American Ethnology.

93. John C. Knowles to James Mooney, May 11, 1914, James Mooney Papers, Box 1, Folder: "Letters," NAA–Bureau of American Ethnology.

94. James Mooney, ca. 1918, NAA MS 2537–Misc. Material Regarding Peyote, NAA–Bureau of American Ethnology.

95. Bruce Kinney to Matthew Sniffen, August 21, 1918, Peyote Papers, Folder 4, Item 3827.1996b, HCAR.

96. T. J. Davis to unknown recipient, January 29, 1919, Reel 9, SAI Papers.

97. Matthew Sniffen to Bruce Kinney, September 9, 1918, Peyote Papers, Folder 5, Item 3827.1999, HCAR.

98. C. V. Stinchecum to Bruce Kinney, November 21, 1918, Peyote Papers, Folder 24, Item 3827.2012, HCAR.

99. James Mooney to Joseph B. Thoburn, June 16, 1921, Joseph Thoburn Collection, Box 3, Folder 1, OHS.

100. James Mooney to Mack Haag, October 25, 1920, Joseph Thoburn Collection, Box 31, Folder 7, OHS.

101. Sherman Coolidge, M. J. Kenshaw, and Charles Dagenett to Arthur C. Parker, February 21, 1914, Reel 2, SAI Papers.

102. Senator Robert L. Owen, October 20, 1921, "Con: The Senate Discusses Legislation to Suppress the Use of Peyote," *Congressional Digest* 1, no. 5 (February 1922): 13.

103. "State News Notes," *Anadarko (OK) American-Democrat*, April 5, 1918, 2; "Neglecting the Indian," *Enid (OK) Events*, April 11, 1918, 8.

104. "Owen is Flayed by the Missionaries," 4; "History of Legislation Prohibiting the Use of Peyote," *Congressional Digest* (February 1922): 12.

105. "Owen Condemned on Peyote Stand," *Muskogee (OK) Daily Phoenix and Times*, October 27, 1921, 4.

106. Owen, "Con: The Senate Discusses Legislation," 13.

107. "Peyote Used as Drug in Indians' 'Cult of Death,'" *Bridgeport (CT) Telegram*, February 9, 1923, 8.

108. "Use of Peyote by Indians is Now Increasing," 6.

109. Statement of Representative John Tillman, *Peyote Hearings 1918*, 164.

110. A missionary to the Cheyenne and Arapaho to Rodney W. Roundy, January 16, 1923, Peyote Papers, Folder 58, Item 3827.2066, HCAR.

111. Corrigan and Hudson, *Religion in America*, 369.

112. Corrigan and Hudson, 373–74, 381–82.

CHAPTER 3. FROM THE BORDERLANDS TO THE BORDERED LANDS

1. "Indians Plead with Moody Not to Put a Ban on Plant Used in Rites," *Dallas Morning News*, January 7, 1926, 12.

2. Rachel St. John, *Line in the Sand: A History of the Western US-Mexico Border* (Princeton, NJ: Princeton University Press, 2011), 2. For recent US-Mexico borderlands histories focusing on the national period, see Juan Mora-Torres, *The Making of the Mexican Border: The State, Capitalism, and Society in Nuevo León, 1848–1910* (Austin: University of Texas Press, 2001); Benjamin H. Johnson, *Revolution in Texas: How a Forgotten Rebellion and Its Bloody Suppression Turned Mexicans into Americans* (New Haven, CT: Yale University Press, 2003); John Nieto-Phillips, *The Language of Blood: The Making of Spanish-American Identity in New Mexico, 1880s–1930s* (Albuquerque: University of New Mexico Press, 2004); Samuel Truett and Elliott Young, eds., *Continental Crossroads: Remapping US-Mexico Borderlands History* (Durham, NC: Duke University Press, 2004); Elliott Young, *Catarion Garza's Revolution on the Texas-Mexico Border* (Durham, NC: Duke University Press, 2004); David Romo, *Ringside Seat to a Revolution: An Underground Cultural History of El Paso and Juárez, 1893–1923* (El Paso: Cinco Puntos Press, 2005); Samuel Truett, *Fugitive Landscapes: The Forgotten History*

of the US-Mexico Borderlands (New Haven, CT: Yale University Press, 2006); Eric V. Meeks, *Border Citizens: The Making of Indians, Mexicans, and Anglos in Arizona* (Austin: University of Texas Press, 2007); Katherine Benton-Cohen, *Borderline Americans: Racial Division and Labor War in the Arizona Borderlands* (Cambridge, MA: Harvard University Press, 2009); Kelly Lytle Hernández, *Migra: A History of the US Border Patrol* (Berkeley: University of California Press, 2010); Anthony Mora, *Border Dilemmas: Racial and National Uncertainties in New Mexico, 1848–1912* (Durham, NC: Duke University Press, 2011); Miguel Antonio Levario, *Militarizing the Border: When Mexicans Became the Enemy* (College Station: Texas A&M University Press, 2012); George T. Díaz, *Border Contraband: A History of Smuggling across the Rio Grande* (Austin: University of Texas Press, 2015).

 3. St. John, *Line in the Sand*, 96–97. The *zona libre*, a "twenty-kilometer-wide strip adjacent to the boundary line," was created in 1884 and became a free trade zone in which American goods could be imported into Mexico duty free. The zona libre ended on July 1, 1905, when Mexican president Porfirio Díaz abolished it, hoping to "make the border less dependent on imports and to promote agricultural and industrial development" (St. John, 97). The goal of customs officers was to monitor, restrict, and tax goods through designated points of entry.

 4. Díaz, *Border Contraband*, 66. Díaz writes, "Between the years of the onset of the Mexican Revolution and the First World War, the US Customs Service on the border transformed from primarily being a revenue-collecting agency to being a national security force" (66). See also St. John, *Line in the Sand*, 96, 138.

 5. St. John, *Line in the Sand*, 150; Díaz, *Border Contraband*, 89–110.

 6. *Peyote: An Abridged Compilation*, 12; Robert D. Hall, "The Peyote Question: Conference of Friends of the Indians," *American Indian Magazine* 6, no. 2 (Summer 1918): 68. See also James Mooney to Bureau of American Ethnology, 1921, Box 6, Folder "Letters," James Mooney Papers, NAA–Bureau of American Ethnology; "A worker for the good of the American Indian" to Congressmen McClintic and Carter and Senator Harreld, January 16, 1923, Peyote Papers, Folder 59, Item 3827.2067, HCAR.

 7. Roy A. Haynes, *Prohibition Inside Out* (New York: Doubleday, 1923), 87. For more on the emerging scholarship about the Canadian-American borderlands, see Lauren McKinsey and Victor Konrad, *Borderlands Reflections: The United States and Canada* (Orono: University of Maine, 1989); Robert Lecker, ed., *Borderlands: Essays in Canadian-American Relations* (Toronto: ECW Press, 1991); Victor Konrad, "The Borderlands of the United States and Canada in the Context of North American Development," *International Journal of Canadian Studies* 4 (Fall 1991): 77–95; W. H. New, *Borderlands: How We Talk about Canada* (Vancouver: University of British Columbia Press, 1998); Erika Lee, "Enforcing the Borders: Chinese Exclusion along the US Borders with Canada and Mexico, 1882–1924," *Journal of American History* 89, no. 1 (2002): 54–86; John J. Bukowczyk, Nora Faires, David R. Smith, and Randy William Widdis, eds., *Permeable Border: The Great Lakes Basin as Transnational Region, 1650–1990* (Pittsburg: University of Pittsburgh Press, 2005); Sterling Evans, ed., *The Borderlands of the American and Canadian Wests: Essays on Regional History of the Forty-Ninth Parallel* (Lincoln: University of Nebraska Press, 2006); Benjamin Johnson and Andrew R. Graybill, eds., *Bridging National Borders in North America: Transnational and Comparative Histories* (Durham, NC: Duke University Press, 2010).

8. Juliana Barr, "Geographies of Power: Mapping Indian Borders in the 'Borderlands' of the Early Southwest," *William and Mary Quarterly* 68, no. 1 (January 2011): 10. For other works on Indigenous borderlands history, see Juliana Barr, *Peace Came in the Form of a Woman: Indians and Spaniards in the Texas Borderlands* (Chapel Hill: University of North Carolina Press, 2007); Ned Blackhawk, *Violence over the Land: Indians and Empires in the Early American West* (Cambridge, MA: Harvard University Press, 2008); Kathleen DuVal, *The Native Ground: Indians and Colonists in the Heart of the Continent* (Philadelphia: University of Pennsylvania Press, 2007); Richard White, *The Middle Ground: Indians, Empires, and Republics in the Great Lakes Region, 1650–1815* (New York: Cambridge University Press, 1991); Eva Marie Garroutte, *Real Indians: Identity and the Survival of Native America* (Berkeley: University of California Press, 2003).

9. Philip Deloria, "From Nation to Neighborhood," *The Cultural Turn in US History: Past, Present, and Future*, ed. James W. Cook, Lawrence B. Glickman, and Michael O'Malley (Chicago: University of Chicago Press, 2008), 359.

10. John W. Troutman, *Indian Blues: American Indians and the Politics of Music, 1879–1934* (Norman: University of Oklahoma Press, 2009), 6–7. See also Calloway, *First Peoples*, 414–23.

11. Troutman, *Indian Blues*, 7. Studies of land loss under the Dawes Act reveal that Indian landholdings shrank from 138 million acres in 1887 to 52 million in 1934, when the policy was repealed. See Janet McDonnell, *The Dispossession of the American Indian, 1887–1934* (Bloomington: Indiana University Press, 1991).

12. Deloria, *Indians in Unexpected Places*, 151.

13. Martin Terry, Keeper Trout, Bennie Williams, Teodoso Herrera, and Norma Fowler, "Limitations to Natural Production of *LophophoraWilliamsii* (Cactaceae) I. Regrowth and Survivorship in Two Years Post Harvest in a South Texas Population," *Journal of the Botanical Research Institute of Texas* 5, no. 2 (2011): 662. See also "Drug-Induced Religion," *Quarterly Journal of the Society of American Indians* 2, no. 2 (April–June 1914): 100; "Getting Drunk on Cactus," *The Farmer* (Bridgeport, CT), May 17, 1916, 12. A second species of peyote cactus is *Lophophora diffusa*, which comes from a "more southern population that occurs in the dry central area of the state of Querétaro" in Mexico. It differs in appearance from the *Lophophora williamsii*, the "commonly known peyote cactus that is so widely used by Native Americans." Anderson, *Peyote: The Divine Cactus*, 159.

14. Servando Z. Hinojosa, "Human-Peyote Interaction in South Texas," *Culture & Agriculture* 22, no. 1 (Spring 2000): 29.

15. Schaefer, *Amanda's Blessings*, 36–37. See also George Morgan, "Man, Plant, and Religion: Peyote Trade on the Mustang Plains of Texas" (Ph.D. diss., University of Colorado, 1976); George Morgan, "Hispano-Indian Trade of an Indian Ceremonial Plant, Peyote (*Lophophora williamsii*) on the Mustang Plains of Texas," *Journal of Ethnopharmacology* 9 (1983): 319–21; George R. Morgan and Omer C. Stewart, "Peyote Trade in South Texas," *Southwestern Historical Quarterly* 87, no. 3 (1984): 270–96.

16. Lisa D. Barnett, "Policing Peyote Country in the Early Twentieth Century," in *Border Policing: A History of Enforcement and Evasion in North America*, ed. Holly M. Karibo and George T. Díaz (Austin: University of Texas Press, 2020), 149. See also Morgan, "Man, Plant, and Religion," 81–82; Schaefer, *Amanda's Blessings*, 30, 38–39.

17. "Trade in 'Jag' Beans Ends," *Yakima (WA) Herald*, June 16, 1909, 2.

18. Schaefer, *Amanda's Blessings*, 22.

19. William E. Johnson, 1909, in "History, Use, and Effects of Peyote in Two Installments–Article I," *Indian School Journal* 7, no. 7 (May 1912): 240, Record Group 75: Records of the Bureau of Indian Affairs, 1793—1999, Series: The Indian School Journal, 1904—1926, National Archives at Fort Worth, TX; James Mooney to W. H. Holmes, November 25, 1903, Records of the Bureau of American Ethnology, Series 1, Box 109, Folder: "1903," NAA–Bureau of American Ethnology; *Laredo (TX) Times*, May 2, 1909.

20. "Indians Pleading for Sacred Bean," *Fort Worth (TX) Star-Telegram*, August 1, 1909, 10; "Winnebagos Seek Removal of Government Embargo on Peyote," *Fort Worth (TX) Star-Telegram*, August 1, 1909, 10; Johnson, "History, Use, and Effects of Peyote," 240; William E. Johnson, special officer for Indian Affairs overseeing the suppression of the liquor traffic among Indians, claimed the gathering of peyote for commercial enterprises in Los Ojuelos represented "almost the entire occupation of the people of this village." See William E. Johnson to unknown recipient, April 10, 1918, Reel 9—Correspondence, SAI Papers. For more about the Cardenas family and their participation in the peyote trade in Los Ojuelos (and later Mirando City), see Schaefer, *Amanda's Blessings*.

21. "A Strange Booze Bean Grows in Texas," *Coconino (AZ) Sun*, August 13, 1920, 3; "The Peyote Bean is a Powerful Stimulant with Terrible Effects," *Helena (MT) Daily Independent*, November 11, 1923, 18.

22. "Limit Indians: May Gather Peyote but Only in Certain Quantities," *Fort Worth (TX) Star-Telegram*, April 30, 1910, 5; "Texas-Mexican Ry," *San Antonio (TX) Express*, May 14, 1913, 16; "Osage Indians Travel De Luxe in Autos to Gather Peyote," *San Antonio (TX) Express*, November 28, 1924, 7; "Oklahoma Indians Gathering Peyote," *Dallas Morning News*, August 2, 1925, 12.

23. Johnson, "History, Use, and Effects of Peyote," 240. Unlike Laurel and Ochoa in Los Ojuelos, who sold to both the Villegas firm and Wormser Brothers in Laredo, Garcia had made a contract to market his supply of peyote exclusively to Wormser Brothers.

24. Frank X. Tolbert, "Tolbert's Texas: Boston Indians Ordered Peyote," *Dallas Morning News*, July 7, 1966, 1.

25. Henry Larson to W. W. Scott, April 24, 1915, Cheyenne and Arapaho Agency Records, Box 444, Folder 3, OHS; *Peyote: An Abridged Compilation*, 4; Stewart, *Peyote Religion*, 229; Schaefer, *Amanda's Blessings*, 39.

26. Charles E. Shell to Express Agent, April 23, 1909, Cheyenne and Arapaho Agency Records, Box 444, Folder 2, OHS; William E. Johnson to Charles E. Shell, May 4, 1909, Cheyenne and Arapaho Agency Records, Box 444, Folder 2, OHS.

27. Johnson to Shell, May 4, 1909; A. T. Payne (superintendent of Wells Fargo & Company Express, OKC) to Charles E. Shell, May 10, 1909, Cheyenne and Arapaho Agency Records, Box 444, Folder 2, OHS.

28. Johnson, "History, Use, and Effects of Peyote," 240; William E. Johnson to unknown recipient, April 10, 1918; "Indians Gather Weed for Sacramental Use," *San Antonio (TX) Express*, September 24, 1924, 5; "Gather Peyote Beans for Rites," *Kingston (NY) Daily Freeman*, November 6, 1924, 12; "Gather Peyote Beans," *Checotah (OK) Times*, November 14, 1924, 2.

Johnson identified the shipments coming from Múzquiz to the Indians as being shipped in the name of Ramon Galon, and the peyote shipments from Allende made by the Garza brothers. See Johnson Shell, May 4, 1909. Johnson also noted, "About twenty-five miles northwest of Múzquiz is the Mexican reservation of the Kickapoo Indians." Johnson, "History, Use, and Effects of Peyote," 240. The Mexican Kickapoos "use peyote, not ceremoniously but for medicinal purposes. They also gather large quantities to sell to the Oklahoma Kickapoos and other Indians who practice the peyote cult." Felipe A. Latorre and Dolores L. Latorre, *The Mexican Kickapoo Indians* (New York: Dover, 1976), 97–98.

29. *Peyote: An Abridged Compilation*, 6; "Drug-Induced Religion," 100.

30. "A Strange Booze Bean Grows in Texas," 3; "Getting Drunk on Cactus," 12.

31. Beatriz de la Garza, *A Law for the Lion: A Tale of Crime and Injustice in the Borderlands* (Austin: University of Texas Press, 2003), 2; Díaz, *Border Contraband*, 39. See also John A. Adams Jr., *Conflict, and Commerce on the Rio Grande: Laredo, 1755–1955* (College Station: Texas A&M Press, 2008).

32. Stewart, *Peyote Religion*, 61.

33. Borderlands historian George Díaz writes, "With the arrival of the railroad in the late 1880s the twin communities grew immensely in population and importance, and by 1893 los dos Laredo had each become the greatest inland ports of their respective countries, earning them their titles as 'gateway' cities." Díaz, *Border Contraband*, 9.

34. Morgan and Stewart define the difference: "The peyote traders of Laredo were essentially middlemen rather than *peyoteros*. *Peyoteros* traditionally harvest and dry their peyote. Laredo merchants and shippers obtained their supply from traders and *peyoteros*." See Morgan and Stewart, "Peyote Trade in South Texas," 276.

35. *Laredo (TX) Times*, May 5, 1909; "Indians Pleading for Sacred Bean," 10; "Plea for Bean is Being Made," *Paducah (KY) Evening Sun*, August 9, 1909, 3; Johnson, "History, Use, and Effects of Peyote," 240; Johnson to unknown recipient, April 10, 1918; Stewart, *Peyote Religion*, 6.

36. Stewart, *Peyote Religion*, 6. Peyote buttons are harvested by cutting the tops off the flowering cactus, not by pulling the cactus out of the ground by the roots, which destroys the cactus and prevents future buttons from being harvested.

37. "Drug-Induced Religion," 100.

38. Robert Valentine, *RCIA for 1911*, 33; *Anaconda (MT) Standard*, September 1, 1912; "Drug-Induced Religion," 100; *Peyote Hearings 1918*, 15; Arthur Bonnicastle (Osage), February 4, *Peyote Hearings 1918*, 80; Johnson to unknown recipient, April 10, 1918; *Peyote: An Abridged Compilation*, 6. Some ambitious peyote entrepreneurs were able to charge more for each peyote button, especially in the early days of the trade in the bordered lands around the reservations. For example, Mooney recorded that George E. Blalock paid five dollars for one thousand buttons and sold them to the Native Americans for twenty-five cents each. See James Mooney, Notebook, NAA MS 1887–Misc. Notes of James Mooney, 1889, Folder 1: "Peyote," NAA–Bureau of American Ethnology.

39. *Galveston (TX) Daily News*, August 15, 1909; "Won't Even Let Poor Indians Chew the Joyous Bean," *Spokane (WA) Press*, May 17, 1909, 5; Rev. William H. Ketchum to Secretary of Interior, March 9, 1911, in *Peyote Hearings 1918*, 43.

40. Barnett, "Policing Peyote Country," 150.

41. *Peyote: An Abridged Compilation*, 5–6; *Laredo Times*, May 2, 1909; *Indian School Journal* (May 1912).

42. *A Twentieth Century History of Southwest Texas*, vol. 2 (Chicago: Lewis, 1907), 83. Ethnologist James Mooney recorded the commercial supply of peyote coming from J. Villegas & Bro. in his official field notes from 1889. See Mooney, Notebook.

43. *Twentieth Century History of Southwest Texas*, 83; de la Garza, *A Law for the Lion*, 45; Bessie Lindheim, "Leonor Villegas Magnon and the Mexican Revolution," in *The Story of Laredo (Volumes 10–18)*, ed. Stan Green (Laredo, TX: Border Studies, 1991), 107. Newspaper advertisements and stories in the *Laredo (TX) Times* recorded their business and civic ventures in Laredo. Quintín served as a dealer in family groceries, grain, hay, flour, etc. from 1884 until 1888, when Joaquín purchased his grocery business and subsequently advertised himself as "Joaquín Villegas, wholesale and retail grocer" in Laredo. A story from August 2, 1886, noted the participation of Quintín Villegas at a Laredo citizens' meeting, presenting a resolution promoting the "American dollar as the basis of all business transactions in Laredo with Mexican dollars to be taken at their value on the date of payment." *Laredo (TX) Times*, October 10, 1884; August 2, 1886; April 7, 1888; April 30, 1888; May 9, 1888; May 18, 1888.

44. Leopoldo was born in Corpus Christi, Texas; Leonor in Nuevo Laredo, Mexico; Lorenzo in Cuatrociénagas, Mexico; and Lina in San Antonio, Texas. See Lindheim, "Leonor Villegas Magnon," 107.

45. De la Garza, *A Law for the Lion*, 3, 46; Lindheim, "Leonor Villegas Magnon," 107.

46. For more on Leonor Villegas de Magnón and her life as a social activist, see *Handbook of Texas Online*, s.v. "Villegas De Magnon, Leonor," by Nancy Baker Jones, last updated January 15, 2017, http://www.tshaonline.org/handbook/online/articles/fvi19.

47. Alicia M. Dewey, *Pesos and Dollars: Entrepreneurs in the Texas-Mexico Borderlands, 1880–1940* (College Station: Texas A&M University Press, 2014), 36; *Twentieth Century History of Southwest Texas*, 83; Lindheim, "Leonor Villegas Magnon," 107. Until 1889, barges, ferries, and small flat boats or skiffs carried people and goods across the border. The "first bridge, a railroad span, across the Río Bravo was erected in 1881" to promote tourist travel by rail and connect goods carried by the National Railroad of Mexico to the Texas Mexican Railroad. This concession by Mexican president Porfirio Díaz created an international route by rail. See Daniel D. Arreola, *Postcards from the Río Bravo Border: Picturing the Place, Placing the Picture, 1900s-1950s* (Austin: University of Texas Press, 2013). The international pedestrian bridge, built in 1889, initiated a port of entry between the two countries that was less expensive to traverse and thus allowed a binational culture to flourish.

48. *Laredo (TX) Times*, May 2, 1909.

49. "Big Business Change," *Brownsville (TX) Daily Herald*, November 18, 1902.

50. De la Garza, *A Law for the Lion*, 46; *Twentieth Century History of Southwest Texas*, 83; Johnson, "History, Use, and Effects of Peyote," 240.

Leopoldo also became active in politics as part of the "Independent Club, or Old Party (Partido Viejo) as it was called in Laredo and Webb counties. Until it collapsed in 1978, it was one of the strongest political machines in South Texas. With headquarters on Jarvis Plaza in downtown Laredo, the Independent Club consisted of elected officials in the city, county, and schools, as well as businessmen, lawyers, and citizens who were economically dependent under the *patrón* system. Besides controlling all city and county offices, the club endorsed state and national candidates with pledges that Webb County would vote as a block. In the beginning the club also raised the necessary funds to run various campaigns by assessing each member a monthly fee . . . By 1900 the Independent was firmly entrenched in the community." Leopoldo Villegas served as mayor of Laredo from 1920–1926 due in large part to the political machine. *Handbook of Texas Online*, s.v. "Independent Club," by Elena Holloway, accessed January 26, 2017, http://www.tshaonline.org/handbook/online/articles/wmiqt.

51. *Encyclopedia of Southern Jewish Communities*, Goldring-Woldenberg Institute of Southern Jewish Life, s.v. "Laredo, Texas," accessed June 28, 2024, http://www.isjl.org/texas-laredo-encyclopedia.html; Stanley C. Green, *A History of Laredo's Jewish Community* (Laredo: Webb County Heritage Foundation, 1992), 4.

52. *Brownsville (TX) Daily Herald*, August 28, 1896, 3; June 15, 1897, 3; October 24, 1899, 2; January 6, 1900, 2.

53. Johnson, "History, Use, and Effects of Peyote," 240. The *Brownsville (TX) Daily Herald* reported on January 17, 1905, that Julius Wormser of Laredo had purchased property in the city. The article identified him as "a member of the firm of Villegas Bros., wholesale grocers at Laredo," and commented that his intent was to come to Brownsville "and open a like business in his newly acquired property." However, less than a month later (on February 2), the *Brownsville (TX) Daily Herald* reported that the property acquired by Wormser was going to be rented as a hotel and restaurant. Given the references to peyote and the Wormser business, it seems that that the Wormser Brothers company chose to operate out of Laredo instead of Brownsville.

54. Hagan, *Quanah Parker, Comanche Chief*, 117.

55. James Mooney, *Peyote Hearings 1918*, 70.

56. W. D. Myers, "Report of Agent for Kiowa, Comanche, and Wichita Agency," in *RCIA for 1889*, 191. For more information about the efforts to curtail peyote use on reservation lands, see chapter 4.

57. *Peyote Hearings 1918*, 15.

58. The town of Navajoe was founded in 1896 and located "about ten miles east and three miles north of Altus," within the disputed area claimed by the state of Texas and Oklahoma Territory. The territorial dispute was resolved by a Supreme Court ruling the same year (*US v. Texas*) that decided that Greer County was not a part of Texas. This was "followed by a special act of Congress attaching the region to Oklahoma Territory." When the town's founders applied for the establishment of a post office under the name Navajo, the "Post Office Department insisted an adding an *e* to the name to avoid possible confusion with another Navajo post office in Arizona so it was officially recorded as *Navajoe*." Edward Everett Dale, "Old Navajoe," *Chronicles of Oklahoma* 24, no. 2 (1946): 128, 130, 141.

59. Mooney, Notebook; Mooney, *Peyote Hearings 1918*, 85.

60. Myers, "Report of Agent for Kiowa, Comanche, and Wichita Agency," 191; Charles F. Ashley, "Report of Agent for Cheyenne and Arapaho Agency," in *RCIA for 1890*, 180.

61. Thomas & Rives Wholesale and Retail Grocers to Mr. Adams (agent), September 6, 1890, Kiowa Agency Records, Box 454, Folder KA50–5, Item 146, OHS.

62. "Trade in 'Jag' Beans End," 2.

63. Oakdale was renamed Mountain View on October 9, 1900. See *Encyclopedia of Oklahoma History and Culture*, s.v. "Mountain View," by Ethel Crisp Taylor, last updated March 25, 2024, www.okhistory.org/publications/enc/entry?entry=MO028.

64. James H. Deer (Cheyenne) to Indian Agent, October 2, 1895, Cheyenne and Arapaho Agency Records, Box 444, Folder 1, Item 42–44, OHS.

65. C. C. Brannon to M. Russell, February 12, 1910, Record Group 75, File: "Education-Liquor 66110–1910," National Archives, Washington, DC; Stewart, *Peyote Religion*, 143.

66. Teeter & Son to Indian Agent, May 14, 1904, Cheyenne and Arapaho Agency Records, Box 444, Folder 1, Item 73, OHS.

67. "Make War on Use of Peyote," *Sunday Tulsa (OK) Daily World*, April 17, 1921, 5.

68. *Peyote: An Abridged Compilation*, 33.

69. "Indian Woman in Capital to Fight Growing Use of Peyote Drug by Indians," *Washington Times*, February 17, 1918, 9; Statement of S. M. Brosius, *Peyote Hearings 1918*, 17, 19; "The Ravages of Peyote," Thirty-Fourth Annual Report of the IRA, December 14, 1916, in *Peyote Hearings 1918*, 20; Hall, "The Peyote Question," 68.

70. Arthur Parker to George Masquequa, October 31, 1914, Reel 4—Correspondence, SAI Papers.

71. E. B. Merritt to W. W. Scott, April 13, 1918, Cheyenne and Arapaho Agency Records, Box 445, Folder 4, Item 167, OHS; "Devil in a New Dress, Our Own Peyote Bean," *El Paso (TX) Herald*, February 23, 1918, 12.

72. Various explanations of Johnson's moniker have been given, but "it is generally believed he was so nicknamed from the way he sneaked up on law violators" with "cat-like stealth." "W. E. 'Pussyfoot' Johnson, Noted Liquor Foe, Dies," *Chicago Tribune*, February 3, 1945, 12; F. A. MacKenzie, *"Pussyfoot" Johnson—Crusader—Reformer—A Man among Men* (New York: Fleming H. Revell, 1920), 81–101.

73. MacKenzie, *"Pussyfoot" Johnson*, 67–68, 104–6; Charles E. Shell to Rev. Bruce Kinney, September 30, 1909, Cheyenne and Arapaho Agency Records, Box 444, Folder 2, Item 73, OHS.

74. Johnson to Shell, May 4, 1909.

75. Johnson to Shell, March 6, 1907, Cheyenne and Arapaho Agency Records, Box 444, Folder 1, OHS.

76. Shell to Express Agent, April 23, 1909.

77. Johnson to Shell, May 4, 1909. See also Barnett, "Policing Peyote Country," 153.

78. Johnson to Shell, May 4, 1909.

79. Stewart, *Peyote Religion*, 139.

80. *Laredo (TX) Times*, May 2, 1909; William E. Johnson to Gertrude Bonnin, April 10, 1918, Reel 9—Correspondence, SAI Papers.

81. "Johnson estimated that he bought nearly 200,000 peyote buttons, using $443 of federal money appropriated to the Indian Office to purchase the peyote." Barnett, "Policing Peyote Country in the Early Twentieth Century," 154.

82. "Mescal Beans Seized," *Galveston (TX) Daily News*, April 28, 1909, 7.

83. Barnett, "Policing Peyote Country" 154.

84. "Governments War on Deadly Bean," *La Crosse (WI) Tribune*, August 21, 1909, 1.

85. Charles E. Shell to Lesly Red Leaf, September 1, 1909, Cheyenne and Arapaho Agency Records, Box 444, Folder 2, Item 64, OHS; Charles E. Shell to Ed Butler, September 1, 1909, Cheyenne and Arapaho Agency Records, Box 444, Folder 2, Item 63, OHS.

86. "War on Peyote Bean: Booze Smasher Brannon Takes up Fight Against Mexican Drug Used by Indians," *Sapulpa (OK) Evening Light*, April 12, 1910, 3.

87. "War on the Peyote Bean," *Guthrie (OK) Daily Leader*, April 13, 1910, 3; *Lawton (OK) Constitution-Democrat*, April 14, 1910. Brannon served the Interior Department out of Pawhuska, OK.

88. "Peyote Beans Seized," *Inola (OK) Register*, February 24, 1910; *Adair County (OK) Sentinel*, February 25, 1910.

89. William E. Johnson, documents relating to a campaign for the suppression of peyote, Peyote Correspondence, File: 2989–1908–126, Record Group 75, National Archives, Washington, DC; Stewart, *Peyote Religion*, 140.

90. Barnett, "Policing Peyote Country," 155.

91. *Muskogee (OK) Times-Democrat*, February 12, 1910.

92. "Laredo is Indians' Mecca," *San Antonio (TX) Daily Express*, March 9, 1910; *Laredo (TX) Times*, March 13, 1910; F. H. Abbott to William B. Freer, September 16, 1910, Cheyenne and Arapaho Agency Records, Box 444, Folder 2, Item 166, OHS; "A Strange Booze Bean Grows in Texas," 3.

93. "Laredo is Indians' Mecca."

94. Stewart, *Peyote Religion*, 145.

95. William E. Johnson to C. C. Brannon, 1910, documents relating to a campaign for the suppression of peyote, Peyote Correspondence, File: 2989–1908–126, Record Group 75, National Archives, Washington, DC; Stewart, *Peyote Religion*, 143–45.

96. Johnson to Bonnin, April 10, 1918; Maroukis, *Peyote Road*, 40.

97. Maroukis, *Peyote Road*, 49.

98. Cato Sells, "Report of the Commissioner of Indian Affairs," in *RCIA for 1915*, 15; E. B. Merritt to Willis E. Dunn, May 14, 1915, Cheyenne and Arapaho Agency Records, Box 444, Folder 3, Item 324, OHS; Maroukis, *Peyote Road*, 49.

99. Cato Sells to Superintendents, March 29, 1917, Circular No. 1286: "Bone-Dry Legislation," Kiowa Agency Records, Box 454, Folder KA50-6, Item 198-99, OHS; "Peyote Causing Trouble; Barred from US Mails," *Rock Island (IL) Argus*, March 7, 1919, 2; "Refuse S.D. Indians Charter for a Church," *Sioux City (IA) Journal*, November 28, 1922, 5.

100. Rupert N. Richardson, "A Comanche Peyote Festival," *Lubbock (TX) Morning Avalanche*, October 7, 1928, 5; Virgil N. Lott, "Some Confessions of a Peyote Smoker," *Dallas Morning News*, November 15, 1931, 7.

101. *Peyote Hearings 1918*, 17.

102. St. John, *Line in the Sand*, 4.

103. St. John, *Line in the Sand*, 101; Díaz, *Border Contraband*, 1–2.

104. J. Lee Hall, "Report of Agent for Kiowa, Comanche, and Wichita Agency," August 26, 1886, in *RCIA for 1886*, 130; E. B. White, "Report of Agent for Kiowa, Comanche, and Wichita Agency," August 18, 1888, in *RCIA for 1888*, 98; Louis Meeker to Department of Interior,

December 28, 1896, NAA MC 2537–Misc. Material Regarding Peyote, Folder: "Meeker, Louis L.," NAA–Bureau of American Ethnology.

105. Kiowa Indians to John Blackmon, January 10, 1907, Kiowa Agency Records, Box 454, Folder KA50-6, Item 27, OHS; Payne to Shell, May 10, 1909; Robert Valentine, *RCIA for 1911*, 33; Superintendent of Cheyenne and Arapaho Agency to commissioner of Indian Affairs, December 23, 1914, Cheyenne and Arapaho Agency Records, Box 444, Folder 3, OHS; Cato Sells, *RCIA for 1915*, 15; Cato Sells, *RCIA for 1916*, 62; "Ravages of Peyote," in *Peyote Hearings 1918*, 20.

106. Parker to Masquequa, October 31, 1914; "Drug-Induced Religion," 100.

107. Johnson, "History, Use, and Effects of Peyote," 239; Johnson to Bonnin, April 10, 1918.

108. "Trade in 'Jag' Beans Ends," 2; *Brownsville (TX) Daily Herald*, August 20, 1909; "A Strange Booze Bean Grows in Texas," 3; "Non-Alcoholic Intoxicant," *New York Times*, June 13, 1920.

109. *Laredo (TX) Times*, May 9, 1909.

110. Díaz, *Border Contraband*, 1.

111. Barnett, "Policing Peyote Country," 156–57.

112. "Beans May Be Sold," *Fort Worth (TX) Star-Telegram*, December 24, 1906, 7; *Sun* (NY), June 13, 1909; *Anaconda (MT) Standard*, July 11, 1909; *Hays (KS) Free Press*, January 29, 1920; "Peyote Menace Gains Headway," *Evening Republican* (Mitchell, SD), February 5, 1925, 12.

113. "Prohibition of Peyote," *Chattanooga (TN) News*, September 10, 1920, 4.

CHAPTER 4. ANOTHER INDIAN WAR

1. James Mooney to W. J. McGee, November 6, 1895, Box 109 [James Mooney], Folder "1895," Series 1 Correspondence—Letters Received 1888–1906, Records of the Bureau of American Ethnology, NAA–Bureau of American Ethnology. William John McGee was the ethnologist-in-charge of the Bureau of American Ethnology from 1893 to 1903. See *The McGee Memorial Meeting of the Washington Academy of Sciences held at the Carnegie Institution, Washington, D.C., December 5, 1913* (Baltimore: Williams & Wilkins, 1916), 65.

2. E. E. White, "Report of Agent for Kiowa, Comanche, and Wichita Agency, August 18, 1888," in *RCIA for 1888*, 99. Mooney attended his first peyote ceremony during the summer of 1891, while working on the Kiowa-Comanche reservation.

3. James Mooney, "The Mescal Plant and Ceremony," 7. L. G. Moses, in his biography of Mooney, wrote, "Mooney's support of the Peyote religion signified his recognition that culture should never be defined in the singular. Regardless of his own tastes and preferences in the matter, Indian cultures were no less civilized than white cultures, only different." Moses, *The Indian Man: A Biography of James Mooney* (Urbana: University of Illinois Press, 1984), 234.

4. Historian Hazel Hertzberg describes the new direction for public policy: "The Indian alone was to be melted and was to come out white, in culture if not in color. The name, which the reformers gave to this process, of which the Dawes Act and the allotment policy were both instrument and symbol, was significant. They called it the 'vanishing policy.'" Hertzberg, *Search for an American Indian Identity*, 22.

5. Maroukis, *Peyote Road*, 105; Wenger, *We Have a Religion*, 140, 153–54; Stewart, *Peyote Religion*, 130–47.

6. Many scholars have written about the rise of the Prohibition movement in America. See Thomas R. Pegram, *Battling Demon Rum: The Struggle for a Dry America, 1800–1933* (Chicago: Ivan R. Dee, 1998); K. Austin Kerr, *Organized for Prohibition: A New History of the Anti-Saloon League* (New Haven: Yale University Press, 1985); Ruth Bordin, *Woman and Temperance: The Quest for Power and Liberty, 1873–1900* (Philadelphia: Temple University Press, 1981); Garrett Peck, *The Prohibition Hangover: Alcohol in America from Demon Rum to Cult Cabernet* (New Brunswick, NJ: Rutgers University Press, 2009); James E. Klein, *Grappling with Demon Rum: The Cultural Struggle over Liquor in Early Oklahoma* (Norman: University of Oklahoma Press, 2008).

7. Albanese, *America: Religions and Religion*, 262.

8. Francis Paul Prucha, *American Indian Policy in Crisis: Christian Reformers and the Indian, 1865–1900* (Norman: University of Oklahoma Press, 1976), 222. For other works devoted to the issue of alcohol and federal Indian policy, see William E. Unrau, *White Man's Wicked Water: The Alcohol Trade and Prohibition in Indian Country, 1802–1892* (Lawrence: University Press of Kansas, 1996); Jill E. Martin, "'The Greatest Evil': Interpretations of Indian Prohibition Laws, 1832–1953," *Great Plains Quarterly* 23, no. 1 (Winter 2003): 35–53.

9. Cato Sells to Superintendents, Circular No. 1286 (Bone-Dry Legislation), March 29, 1917, Kiowa Agency Records, Box 454, Folder KA50–6, Item 198, OHS.

10. Thomas Jefferson Morgan, *RCIA for 1891*, 74; Cato Sells, *RCIA for 1918*, 75.

11. Charles Henry Burke, *RCIA for 1924*, 21.

12. Cato Sells to All Employees in the Indian Service, March 25, 1914, Kiowa Agency Records, Box 454, Folder KA50–6, Item 56, OHS. The opening paragraph concerning the "curse of whiskey" was printed on individual cards, and copies were sent to four of the Indian schools for distribution. See Kiowa Agency Records, Box 454, Folder KA50–6, Item 57, OHS.

13. Hubert Work, "Bureau of Indian Affairs: The Poverty of the Indian Service," in *RCIA for 1927*, 19.

14. Cato Sells, *RCIA for 1915*, 13–14. Sells's order specifically targeted the Osages, but he soon expanded it to include payments to the Kiowa, Sac and Fox, Cheyenne, Arapaho, Pawnee, and other Indians. He reported in 1918 that he had successful used "this legal weapon" by withholding the "payment of more than one million dollars from the Osages in Oklahoma" until sobriety "among these Indians was so noticeable." Sells, *RCIA for 1918*, 75.

15. Sells, *RCIA for 1915*, 12.

16. Bruce Kinney to Robert G. Valentine, September 29, 1909, Cheyenne and Arapaho Agency Records, Box 444, Folder 2, Item 70–71, OHS.

17. Nicholas O. Warner, "Images of Drinking in 'Women Singing,' *Ceremony*, and *Houses Made of Dawn*," *MELUS* 11, no. 4, Literature of the Southwest (Winter 1984): 15. See also Jerrold Levy and Stephen Kunitz, *Indian Drinking* (New York: John Wiley & Sons, 1974); Joy Leland, *The Firewater Myths* (New Brunswick, NJ: Rutgers University Press, 1976); Roy Harvey Pearce, *Savagism and Civilization: A Study of the Indians and the American Mind* (Baltimore: Johns Hopkins University Press, 1965).

18. Izumi Ishii, *Bad Fruits of the Civilized Tree: Alcohol and the Sovereignty of the Cherokee Nation* (Lincoln: University of Nebraska Press, 2008), 156.

19. Henry A. Larson, "The Indian and His Liquor Problem," *American Indian Magazine* 4, no. 3 (July–September 1916): 235.

20. Valery Havard, "Report on the Flora of Western and Southern Texas," *Proceedings of the United States National Museum* 8, no. 29 (September 23, 1885): 449, 521.

21. Early peyote studies included J. R. Briggs, "Muscale Buttons—Physiological Action—A Mexican Fruit with Possible Medicinal Virtues," *Druggists' Bulletin* 1, no. 5 (May 1887): 78; D. W. Prentiss and F. P. Morgan, "Anhalonium Lewinii (Mescal Buttons): A Study of the Drug, with Especial Reference to Its Physiological Action upon Man, with Report of Experiments," *Therapeutic Gazette* 11, no. 9 (September 16, 1895): 577–85; S. W. Mitchell, "Remarks on the Effects of Anhelonium Lewinii (the Mescal Button)," *British Medical Journal* 2 (December 5, 1896): 1625–29; Havelock Ellis, "Mescal: A New Artificial Paradise," in *Annual Report of the Board of Regents of the Smithsonian Institution* (Washington, DC: US Government Printing Office, 1897), 537–48. James Mooney also reported his experiences of ingesting peyote after participating in the Indian religious ceremony in 1891.

22. Thomas J. Morgan to S. L. Patrick, July 31, 1890, Sac and Fox and Shawnee Agency Records, Box 613, Folder SFSA 35–1, Item 86, OHS.

23. White, "Report of Agent," 98; William J. Pollock, "Report of Agent for Osage Agency, August 16, 1899," in *RCIA for 1899*, 297; Robert G. Valentine, *RCIA for 1909*, 14; Cato Sells, *RCIA for 1914*, 42. Valentine even argued that the effects of peyote indulgence lasted longer than those of alcohol, and he warned against the persistent use of peyote.

24. A. E. Woodson, "Report of Agent for Cheyenne and Arapaho Agency, August 31, 1898," in *RCIA for 1898*, 235.

25. Francis E. Leupp, *RCIA for 1908*, 27; Robert G. Valentine, *RCIA for 1911*, 6. Other Indian commissioners also commented on the racialized politics of identity around labor, with specific references to African Americans and Chinese laborers who did not depend upon the government for rations and monies, but had learned the "industrial necessity of making their own living." William A. Jones, *RCIA for 1903*, 3; Leupp, *RCIA for 1906*, 4; Charles H. Burke, *RCIA for 1923*, 20.

26. Seymour, "Peyote Worship," 183; *Peyote Hearings 1918*, 17.

27. "Peyote," February 29, 1908, Sac and Fox and Shawnee Agency Records, Box 613, Folder SFSA 35–1, Item 40, OHS.

28. J. W. Lyans to Major W. L. Walker, August 29, 1898, Cheyenne and Arapaho Agency Records, Box 444, Folder 1, Item 49–52, OHS; Valentine, *RCIA for 1911*, 33; "Editorial Column," *Red Lake (MN) News*, March 15, 1916; National Indian Association, "Peyote," *Indian's Friend* 29, no. 1 (September 1916): 6; "Indian Woman in Capital to Fight Growing Use of Peyote Drug by Indians," *Washington Times*, February 17, 1918, 9; "Peyote–Its Prohibition," *Congressional Digest* 1, no. 5 (February 1922), 17.

29. Office of Indian Affairs Bulletin 21, *Peyote* (1923), Cheyenne and Arapaho Agency Records, Box 445, Folder 5, Item 268, OHS.

30. Kiowa Indians to John A. Blackmon, January 10, 1907, Kiowa Agency Records, Box 454, Folder, KA50–6, Item 27, OHS.

31. Kinney to Valentine, September 29, 1909.

32. *RCIA for 1903*, 275; *RCIA for 1906*, 302–3; *RCIA for 1912*, 43; "An American Indian Cult," *American Indian Magazine* 4, no. 2 (April–June 1916): 160; Indian Rights Association Report, in *Peyote Hearings 1918*, 16; Seymour, "Peyote Worship," 184; Robert D. Hall, "The Peyote Question: Conference of Friends of the Indians," *American Indian Magazine* 6, no. 2 (Summer 1918): 67–68.

33. Seymour, "Peyote Worship," 182. See also "The Use and Effects of Peyote, Article II," *Indian School Journal* (Chilocco Indian School), June 1912, 291, Record Group 75, National Archives and Records Administration–Fort Worth.

34. Gertrude Bonnin to Arthur Parker, January 12, 1917, p. 3, Reel 1—Correspondence, SAI Papers; *RCIA for 1904*, 290; *RCIA for 1906*, 322; "War on the Peyote Bean," *Guthrie (OK) Daily Leader*, April 13, 1910, 3; "The Case Against the 'Peyote,'" *Outlook*, May 24, 1916, 162; *Peyote: An Abridged Compilation*, 30.

35. "The Use and Effects of Peyote, Article II," 291.

36. "Drug-Induced Religion," *Quarterly Journal of the Society of American Indians* 2, no. 2 (April–June 1914): 100.

37. "Devil in a New Dress, Our Own Peyote Bean," *El Paso (TX) Herald*, February 23, 1918, 12. See also "National Convention of W.C.T.U.," *Freeport (IL) Daily Journal-Standard*, January 9, 1918, 8; Merritt, "Peyote–Its Prohibition," 16.

38. E. B. Merritt to W. W. Scott, April 13, 1918, Cheyenne and Arapaho Agency Records, Box 445, Folder 4, Item 167, OHS.

39. Parker, "The Peyote Question," 69.

40. White, *RCIA for 1918*, 99.

41. Cato Sells, *RCIA for 1913*, 14.

42. Gertrude Bonnin, *Peyote Hearings 1918*, 24; Herbert Welsh, *Peyote—An Insidious Evil* (Philadelphia: Indian Rights Association, 1918), 1.

43. Harvey W. Wiley, "Peyote," *American Indian Magazine* 7, no. 1 (Spring 1919): 37.

44. "Use of Mescal Spreading in U.S.," *El Paso (TX) Herald* (weekend edition), June 12–13, 1920, 7; "Non-Alcoholic Intoxicant," *New York Times*, June 13, 1920. For a chronological account of the varied legislative proposals against peyote, see chapter 2.

45. Mooney, "The Mescal Plant and Ceremony," 9. Mooney and others noted that peyote was particularly helpful in the relief of consumptive diseases, which was one reason why peyote attracted returned students from the East. See also Louis Meeker to Secretary of the Department of the Interior, December 28, 1896, p. 3, NAA MC 2537–Misc. Material Regarding Peyote, Folder: "Meeker, Louis L.," NAA–Bureau of American Ethnology.

46. J. M. Lee, "Report of Agent for Cheyenne and Arapaho Agency, August 31, 1886," in *RCIA for 1886*, 119; H. M. Noble, "Report of Superintendent of Ponca School (Ponca and Tonkawa), August 4, 1906," in *RCIA for 1906*, 321; "Drug-Induced Religion," 104; "Peyote Protected by the Courts," *American Indian Magazine* 4, no. 4 (October–December 1916): 346.

47. James Mooney, *Peyote Hearings 1918*, 60–147; Hertzberg, *Search for an American Indian Identity*, 266. Recent work by Dr. Joseph Calabrese also shows a connection between peyote use and a decrease in rates of alcoholism among Native American peoples. He claims, "Peyote's omniscience and omnipresence continues to function outside rituals, helping

to keep NAC members from committing moral infringements like consuming alcohol." Joseph D. Calabrese, "Spiritual Healing and Human Development in the Native American Church: Toward a Cultural Psychiatry of Peyote," *Psychoanalytic Review* 84, no. 2 (April 1997): 239. See also Joseph D. Calabrese, "The Supreme Court versus Peyote: Consciousness Alteration, Cultural Psychiatry, and the Dilemma of Contemporary Subcultures," *Anthropology of Consciousness* 12, no. 2 (2001): 4–19.

48. Maroukis, *Peyote Road*, 87.

49. Hertzberg, *Search for an American Indian Identity*, 241.

50. Francis LaFlesche, "The Lobby Discusses Legislation to Suppress the Use of Peyote," *Congressional Digest* 1, no. 5 (February 1922): 15.

51. "The Peyote Evil," in *Fortieth Annual Report of the Board of Directors of the Indian Rights Association* (Philadelphia: Indian Rights Association, 1922), 38.

52. Doris Marie Provine, *Unequal under the Law: Race in the War on Drugs* (Chicago: University of Chicago Press, 2007), 8; Clayton J. Mosher and Scott Akins, *Drugs and Drug Policy: The Control of Consciousness Alteration* (Thousand Oaks, CA: Sage Publications, 2007), 2–3.

53. "Mescal Beans to Be Investigated; Causing Red Skins to Get Drunk," *Bisbee (AZ) Daily Review*, September 1, 1908, 2; "Indians Laugh at Dry Laws, Sip Peyote and Are Content," *Evening Public Ledger* (Philadelphia, PA), October 13, 1919, 8; "Peyote Used as Drug in Indian 'Cult of Death,'" *New York Times*, January 14, 1923, 3.

54. James Mooney, Misc. Notes, n.d., p.1, NAA MS 2537–Misc. Material Regarding Peyote, Folder: "Legislation and Agitation," NAA–Bureau of American Ethnology. Murray Edelman writes about the "spectacle constituted by news reporting" that "continuously constructs and reconstructs social problems, crises, enemies, and leaders and so creates a succession of threats and reassurances." He notes that the problems enter into discourse and into "existence as reinforcements of ideologies, not simply because they are there or because they are important for wellbeing" but rather because they contribute to the division and categorization of people and become a means of determining inclusion and exclusion from certain aspects of societal functions. Edelman applies the epistemological principle of construction to "political developments as creations of the publics concerned with them." Edelman, *Constructing the Political Spectacle* (Chicago: University of Chicago Press, 1988), 1–2, 12–18.

55. Bonnin, *Peyote Hearings 1918*, 24.

56. Provine, *Unequal under the Law*, 63.

57. Provine, 63.

58. Carl Hayden, "The House Discusses Legislation to Suppress the Use of Peyote," *Congressional Digest* 1, no. 5 (February 1922): 14. The same rhetoric appeared in earlier debates on the Gandy legislation introduced in Congress. In its coverage on the Gandy bill, one magazine reported, "The Indians of the West, recognized as wards of our Nation, are suffering under an appalling and continuing calamity." "The President, Congress, and the War," *Outlook*, April 11, 1917, 644.

59. Gertrude and Raymond Bonnin to S. M. Brosius, October 12, 1916, in *Peyote Hearings 1918*, 13–14; "Peyote," *Red Lake (MN) News*, November 1, 1918.

60. "The So-Called Mescal Button," *Oshkosh (WI) Daily Northwestern*, September 10, 1908, 4. The story also ran in varied versions in other newspapers in the West. See *Bisbee*

(AZ) Daily Review, September 1, 1908, 2; *Daily Arizona Silver Belt* (Globe, AZ), September 6, 1908, 6; *The Oasis* (Arizola, AZ), September 5, 1908.

61. *Evening Review* (East Liverpool, OH), June 24, 1915, 4.

62. *Peyote Hearings 1918*, 15; Ruper N. Richardson, "A Comanche Peyote Festival," *Lubbock (TX) Morning Avalanche*, October 7, 1928, 5.

63. Provine, *Unequal under the Law*, 66–67.

64. Peter M. Gahlinger, *Illegal Drugs: A Complete Guide to Their History, Chemistry, Use, and Abuse* (New York: Plume 2004), 58; David F. Musto, *American Disease: Origins of Narcotic Control* (New Haven, CT: Yale University Press, 1973), 5.

65. J. Lee Hall, *RCIA for 1886*, 130; Myers, *RCIA for 1889*, 191; O. A. Mitscher, *RCIA for 1900*; *RCIA for 1903*, 471; Valentine, in *RCIA for 1909*, 13; "Dead Indian is Raising Beans," *Oklahoma State Capital* (Guthrie, OK), June 1, 1907, 5; *New State Tribune* (Muskogee, OK), January 23, 1908; *Syracuse Herald*, July 3, 1913; Lyman Abbott, "The Menace of Peyote," *American Indian Magazine* 5, no. 2 (April–June 1917): 134–35; Matthew K. Sniffen to Warren Moorehead, June 5, 1923, Reel 5—Correspondence, SAI Papers.

66. Gahlinger, *Illegal Drugs*, 27; Musto, *American Disease*, 2–3.

67. Gahlinger, *Illegal Drugs*, 43; Musto, *American Disease*, 216; Provine, *Unequal under the Law*, 67.

68. Arthur C. Parker to Franklin E. Lane, May 6, 1913, Reel 4—Correspondence, SAI Papers; S. C. Snylin to Arthur C. Parker, May 24, 1913, 1, Reel 8—Correspondence, SAI Papers.

69. "Government Has Broken Up Sale of Liquor to Indians," *Times-Democrat* (Lima, OH), January 11, 1916, 8; Merritt, "Peyote–Its Prohibition," 16.

70. Gahlinger, *Illegal Drugs*, 59–60; Mosher and Akins, *Drugs and Drug Policy*, 202.

71. Gahlinger, *Illegal Drugs*, 402; Stewart, *Peyote Religion*, 72; La Barre, *Peyote Cult*, 85.

72. "Will Ask Congress to Spare Peyote," *Fort Worth (TX) Star-Telegram*, October 10, 1909, 12.

73. Speech by Roley McIntosh, February 29, 1908, Sac and Fox and Shawnee Agency Records, Box 613, Folder SFSA 35–1, Item 12, OHS.

74. Hiram Price, *RCIA for 1882*, xlviii; John Oberly, *RCIA for 1888*, xxix; Charles E. Adams, "Report of Agent for Kiowa, Comanche, and Wichita Agency, August 20, 1891," *RCIA for 1891*, 350; J. P. Woolsey, "Report of Agent for Ponca, Pawness, Otoe, and Oakland Agency, August 15, 1894," *RCIA for 1894*, 247; A. E. Woodson, "Report of Agent for Cheyenne and Arapaho Agency, October 4, 1899," *RCIA for 1899*, 284; Valentine, *RCIA for 1909*, 2; Cato Sells, *RCIA for 1915*, 16–17; Cato Sells, *RCIA for 1917*, 20–21.

75. Thomas J. Morgan, *RCIA for 1890*, xix.

76. Robert Valentine, *RCIA for 1910*, 9–10; Sells, *RCIA for 1915*, 16; Charles Burke, *RCIA for 1921*, 9–10.

77. "Report on the Investigation of Kiowa Indian Agency," in *RCIA for 1903: Indian Affairs*, 471.

78. *Peyote Hearings 1918*, 12.

79. Gertrude Bonnin, "An Indian Cult and a Powerful Drug," *American Indian Magazine* 4, no. 2 (April–June 1916): 162; "The Case Against the 'Peyote,'" 162; Stewart, *Peyote Religion*, 217.

80. Gertrude Bonnin to Arthur C. Parker, June 13, 1917, Reel 1—Correspondence, SAI Papers. Bonnin reported that S. M. Brosius "found a Senate bill (S.2046) introduced by Senator Phelan of California; 'An act to prohibit the importation and use of opium for other than medical purposes.' Mr. Brosius thinks this bill can be amended so as to include 'Peyote and Mescal and their derivatives.'"

81. Mary C. Collins, "The Religious Nature of the Indian," *American Indian Magazine* 6, no. 2 (Summer 1918): 91.

82. Provine, *Unequal under the Law*, 32.

83. Hall, *RCIA for 1886*, 119. See also O. A. Mitscher, "Report of Agent for Osage Agency," in *RCIA for 1900: Indian Affairs*, 339; "Report on the Investigation of Kiowa Indian Agency," in *RCIA for 1903*, 471.

84. Gahlinger, *Illegal Drugs*, 27.

85. Provine, *Unequal under the Law*, 71.

86. Musto, *American Disease*, 3–4; Gahlinger, *Illegal Drugs*, 29. A subsequent meeting in 1912 produced an international agreement requiring countries to control their narcotics trade.

87. Gahlinger, *Illegal Drugs*, 58.

88. "Indians Get Crazy Drunk on Mescal and Peyote," *Stroud (OK) Democrat*, January 12, 1912, 1. See also "Want to Use Mescal Bean," *Dallas Morning News*, August 6, 1905, 11; *Red Rock (OK) Opinion*, February 7, 1906, 4; "Would Bar Drug; Chemist Talks of Deadly Effects of Peyote," *Carney (OK) Enterprise*, June 30, 1916; Report of Harmon Harms, *Peyote Hearings 1918*, 36.

89. "Peyote," *Mohave County Miner and Our Mineral Wealth* (Kingman, AZ), January 28, 1921, 4.

90. *Peyote: An Abridged Compilation*, 11.

91. "Gather Peyote Beans for Rites," *Kingston (NY) Daily Freeman*, November 6, 1924, 12; "Gather Peyote," *Checotah (OK) Times*, November 14, 1924, 2.

92. "Want Mescal," *New State Tribune* (Muskogee, OK), January 23, 1908, 1. See also Valentine, *RCIA for 1909*, 13; *Syracuse Herald* (NY), July 13, 1913; William E. Johnson to unknown, April 10, 1918, enclosure with letter from Gertrude Bonnin to Richard H. Pratt, January 29, 1919, Reel 9, SAI Papers; Sniffen to Moorehead, June 5, 1923.

93. Joseph F. Spillane, *Cocaine: From Medical Marvel to Modern Menace in the United States, 1884–1920* (Baltimore: Johns Hopkins University Press, 2000), 94–104.

94. Musto, *American Disease*, 7; Gahlinger, *Illegal Drugs*, 41.

95. Gahlinger, *Illegal Drugs*, 41. The *New York Times* article supports his argument, giving absolutely no mention of popular cocaine use among whites in consumer products and patent medicines.

96. William E. Johnson, note on petition to Congress, 1907, Cheyenne and Arapaho Agency Records, Box 444, Folder 1, Item 244, OHS; "Pleading for Sacred Bean," *Fort Worth (TX) Star-Telegram*, August 1, 1909; "War on the Peyote Bean," 3; Bonnin to Brosius, October 12, 1916, 13–14; Statement of Dr. Lyman F. Keblar, *Peyote Hearings 1918*, 56; *Lawton (OK) Constitution-Democrat*, April 14, 1919, 3.

97. "Use Mescal Bean," *Manchester (OK Territory) Journal*, June 5, 1903, 2; "How the Mescal Bean Acts on Indians," *Guthrie (OK Territory) Daily Leader*, July 22, 1903.

98. "How the Mescal Bean Acts on Indians."

99. "Mescal Beans Convict Them," *Oklahoma State Register* (Guthrie, OK), March 14, 1907.

100. Testimony of Dr. Harvey W. Wiley, *Peyote Hearings 1918*, 26.

101. "Peyote Eating New Drug Craze," *Evening Star* (Washington, DC), June 19, 1922, 4. Author's emphasis.

102. "Want Mescal," 1. See also Valentine, *RCIA for 1909*, 13; Lyman Abbott, "The Menace of Peyote," *American Indian Magazine* 5, no. 2 (April–June 1917): 134. A specific reference to "marijuana" is found in "The Peyote Evil," *Indian Rights Association*, 1922, 39. Cannabis is an extraordinarily globalized plant, and has a variety of identifications all around the world. This is one of the reasons the drug has so many names. As an intoxicant, cannabis often went by the name of "hashish" or "Indian hemp," and later emerged in popular discourse as "marijuana." See Dale H. Gieringer, "The Origins of Cannabis Prohibition in California," *Contemporary Drug Problems*, Federal Legal Publications, 1999, 2.

103. Typed memorandum, W. E. Safford, "Narcotics and Intoxicants Used by American Indians," May 10, 1921, quoted in Musto, *American Disease*, 330.

104. Gahlinger, *Illegal Drugs*, 61.

105. Musto, *American Disease*, 219.

106. Provine, *Unequal under the Law*, 82–85; Gahlinger, *Illegal Drugs*, 62.

107. Jacob Reid to Edward Ayer, March 19, 1916, in *Peyote Hearings 1918*, 127.

108. "Bad Liquor Sold across Rio Grande," *Dallas Morning News*, October 3, 1924, 8.

109. "Senators Holdum Powow, Keepum Hands Off Peyote," *Dallas Morning News*, April 16, 1957, 11. The headline is indicative of the racialized portrayal of peyote as a uniquely Indian drug. And, unlike the attempts to eliminate class-based distinctions from the peyote and cocaine connection, the comparison of peyote and marijuana users contained both class and racial dimensions.

110. Tom Holm, *The Great Confusion in Indian Affairs: Native Americans and Whites in the Progressive Era* (Austin: University of Texas Press, 2005), 152.

111. Arthur C. Parker to E. M. Wistar, December 9, 1912, Reel 7—Correspondence, SAI Papers.

112. Thomas Jefferson Morgan, *RCIA for 1892*, 6–7.

113. "Indian Office Makes War on Peyote Drug," *Dallas Morning News*, August 15, 1909; "Uncle Sam Wages War on the Indian Dope," *Galveston (TX) Daily News*, August 15, 1909; "War on the Peyote Bean," 3.

114. "Great Battle by Uncle Sam to Free Indians from Subtle Slavery of the Mescal Bean," *Washington Post*, April 28, 1912, 8.

115. Jeanette Marks, "Narcoticism and the War," *North American Review* 206, no. 743 (December 1917): 879.

116. "A Strange Booze Bean Grows in Texas," *Coconino (AZ) Sun*, August 13, 1920, 3.

117. Arthur C. Parker, "The Editor's Viewpoint: The Functions of the Society of American Indians," *American Indian Magazine* 4, no. 1 (January–March 1916): 8.

118. "Annual Convention of the Society of American Indians," *The Indian Leader* 20, no. 8 (October 1916): 15.

119. Edelman, *Constructing the Political Spectacle*, 103–4.

120. Henry Roe Cloud to Mary Roe, April 18, 1914, Reel 9—Part II, Series 1, Papers of the SAI in Other Repositories, SAI Papers.

CHAPTER 5. EVADING THE "WHITE MAN'S" LAW

1. Thomas Jefferson Morgan to S. L. Patrick, July 31, 1890, Sac and Fox and Shawnee Agency Records, Box 613, Folder SFSA 35–1, Item 111, OHS. The order from Indian commissioner Morgan extended an 1888 order from the Indian agent at the Kiowa, Comanche, and Wichita Agency to Indian agents on other reservations, and directed them to use the Indian Police in efforts to "stamp out the evil practice" of using peyote. See chapter 2 for more information concerning the 1888 order and its expanded implementation in 1890.

2. "Indian Law Enforcement History," Bureau of Indian Affairs Law Enforcement Services, 11, http://web.archive.org/web/20000226013721/bialaw.fedworld.gov/history/index.htm. The system of Indian police began in 1874 with John Clum, the Apache agent at San Carlos in southwestern Arizona. In 1878, Congress adopted legislation to expand the model to other Indian agencies to combat "evil practices" occurring on reservations. See Hagan, *Indian Police and Judges*.

3. Petition from Peyotist Indians to Charles E. Shell, February 11, 1907, Cheyenne and Arapaho Agency Records, Box 444, Folder 1, Item 145, OHS.

4. See chapter 4 for more about these practices.

5. The impetus for Oklahoma statehood actually began after the Land Run of 1889, when white settlers moved into the Unassigned Lands (Oklahoma District). The "Organic Act of 1890 established a territorial government for Oklahoma Territory and defined the boundaries of Oklahoma Territory and Indian Territory comprising present Oklahoma. The law also called for the election of a non-voting delegate from Oklahoma Territory to the U.S. House of Representatives." A statehood movement continued to garner popularity and support among white settlers. See Linda D. Wilson, "Statehood Movement," *Encyclopedia of Oklahoma History and Culture*, www.okhistory.org/publications/enc/entry?entry=ST025.

6. Wilson, "Statehood Movement."

7. Established in 1902, the Cantonment Agency came from the Cheyenne and Arapaho Agency, along with the Seger Agency and the Red Moon Agency. They merged back into the Cheyenne and Arapaho Agency in 1927.

8. Ralph S. Connell to Byron E. White, July 24, 1906, Cheyenne and Arapaho Agency Records, Box 444, Folder 1, Item 102, OHS; Ralph S. Connell to G. W. H. Stouch, July 28, 1906, Cheyenne and Arapaho Agency Records, Box 444, Folder 1, Item 104, OHS.

9. Leonard William Tyler (Magpie) Student File, National Archives and Records Administration, RG 75, Series 1327, Box 127, Folder 5045, Carlisle Indian School Digital Resource Center, Archives & Special Collections, Waidner-Spahr Library, Dickinson College (Carlisle, PA), http://carlisleindian.dickinson.edu/student_files/leonard-william-tyler-magpie-student-file.

10. Donald J. Berthrong, *The Cheyenne and Arapaho Ordeal: Reservation and Agency Life in the Indian Territory, 1875–1907* (Norman: University of Oklahoma Press, 1976), 316–17; Stewart, *Peyote Religion*, 105.

11. "Obituary," *Calumet (OK) Chieftain*, May 2, 1913, 1.

12. "Leonard Tyler, Stock Raiser," *El Reno (OK) Daily American*, May 20, 1909, 19. The article on Leonard Tyler also noted that he was "one of the large land owners" in Oklahoma and "has met with phenomenal success" in farming and stockbreeding ventures. Tyler possessed "620 acres of the finest land in Oklahoma," and he "is well versed in the [stockbreeding] business and has ample facilities to raise the very best." The "stockbreeding industry in Oklahoma is still in its infancy" but "will become one of the most important activities in the State." Tyler's acculturation to white living also extended to his residence, as his wealth permitted an addition to his house "consisting of kitchen, bed room, pantry, and bath room." "Rural News," *Calumet (OK) Chieftain*, May 21, 1909, 5.

13. Petition, February 11, 1907.

14. Reuben Taylor, in *Peyote Hearings 1918*, 192; *Baptist Home Mission Monthly* 19, no. 9 (September 1897): 331; Stewart, *Peyote Religion*, 104.

15. "Missionary Converts Hundreds of Indians," *Evening Record* (Ellensburg, WA), December 22, 1926, 7.

16. D. K. Cunningham to Charles E. Shell, February 11, 1907, Cheyenne and Arapaho Agency Records, Box 444, Folder 1, Item 142–43, OHS.

17. Charles E. Shell to D. K. Cunningham, February 12, 1907, Cheyenne and Arapaho Agency Records, Box 444, Folder 1, OHS; Berthrong, *Cheyenne and Arapaho Ordeal*, 318.

18. William E. Johnson to Charles E. Shell, February 19, 1907, Cheyenne and Arapaho Agency Records, Box 444, Folder 1, Item 159, OHS. The statute read: "That it shall be unlawful for any person to introduce on any Indian reservation or Indian allotment situated within this territory or to have in possession, barter, sell, give, or otherwise dispose of, any 'Mescal Bean,' or the product of any such drug, to any allotted Indian in this territory: *Provided,* That nothing in this Act shall prevent its use by any physician authorized under existing laws to practice his profession in this Territory." *Territory of Oklahoma Session Laws of 1899 Passed at the Fifth Regular Session of the Legislative Assembly of the Territory of Oklahoma* (Guthrie: State Capital Printing, 1899), 122–23.

19. Joyce M. Szabo, "Howling Wolf," *Encyclopedia of the Great Plains*, ed. David J. Wishart, University of Nebraska-Lincoln, 2011, http://plainshumanities.unl.edu/encyclopedia/doc/egp.art.035. For more on Howling Wolf and his art, see Karen Daniels Petersen, *Howling Wolf: A Cheyenne Warrior's Graphic Interpretation of His People* (Palo Alto, CA: American West, 1968); Joyce M. Szabo, *Howling Wolf and the History of Ledger Art* (Albuquerque: University of New Mexico Press, 1994).

20. John Oberly, *RCIA for 1888*, 90; Daniel Browning, *RCIA for 1896*, 555; William Jones, *RCIA for 1897*, 515; William Jones, *RCIA for 1902*, 709; William Jones, *RCIA for 1903*, 592. Kable received ten dollars a month as an agency police officer, but his main occupation was farming, primarily growing corn on his thirty acres of land. See Percy E. Kable Student File, National Archives and Records Administration, RG 75, Series 1327, Box 7, Folder 318, Carlisle Indian School Digital Resource Center, Archives & Special Collections, Waidner-Spahr Library, Dickinson College (Carlisle, PA), http://carlisleindian.dickinson.edu/student_files/percy-e-kable-student-file.

21. Austin Vance (editor-in-chief of *American Indian Law Review* and former OU law student, now an attorney), in discussion with the author, October 1, 2016. Vance notes several

other cases not related to probate that were in the probate courts in Oklahoma in 1907, namely St. Louis & S. F. R. Co. v. Bradfield, 88 P. 1050 (Okla. 1907) and Higgins v. St., 92 P. 153 (Okla. 1907), which addressed negligence and property law respectively. He also observes that the "area of jurisdiction of probate courts around statehood has not been explored in-depth."

22. "Mescal Beans Convict Them," *Oklahoma State Register* (Guthrie, OK), March 14, 1907.

23. George L. Bowman to Charles E. Shell, February 13, 1907, Cheyenne and Arapaho Agency Records, Box 444, Folder 1, Item 153, OHS; George L. Bowman to Charles E. Shell, February 15, 1907, Cheyenne and Arapaho Agency Records, Box 444, Folder 1, Item 154, OHS.

24. Johnson to Shell, February 19, 1907.

25. Rev. Robert Hamilton to Charles E. Shell, February 20, 1907, Cheyenne and Arapaho Agency Records, Box 444, Folder 1, Item 161, OHS.

26. "Mescal Beans Convict Them"; Charles E. Shell to J. P. Blackmon, July 7, 1907, Kiowa Agency Records, Box 454, Folder KA50-6, Item 60, OHS. Omer Stewart writes that the appeal bond "was secured by John W. Block and three Cheyenne peyotists, John Red Wolf, Clark Starr, and Leonard Tyler." Stewart, *Peyote Religion*, 135.

27. William E. Johnson to Charles E. Shell, April 29, 1907, Cheyenne and Arapaho Agency Records, Box 444, Folder 1, Item 185, OHS.

28. Johnson to Shell, April 29, 1907; Berthrong, *Cheyenne and Arapaho Ordeal*, 322–23.

29. Shell to Blackmon, July 7, 1907.

30. Berthrong, *Cheyenne and Arapaho Ordeal*, 323; Petition of Indian Agents and Superintendents to 60th Congress of the US, 1907, Cheyenne and Arapaho Agency Records, Box 444, Folder 1, Item 244, OHS. "Class legislation" is a term "applied to statutory enactments which divide the people or subjects of legislation into classes, with reference either to the grant of privileges or the imposition of burdens, upon an arbitrary, unjust, or invidious principle of division." Class legislation violates equal protection, guaranteed through the Fourteenth Amendment to the US Constitution. See *Black's Law Dictionary Free Online Legal Dictionary*, 2nd ed., http://thelawdictionary.org/class-legislation/.

31. C. F. Larrabee to Charles E. Shell, July 23, 1907, Cheyenne and Arapaho Agency Records, Box 444, Folder 1, Item 220, OHS.

32. Berthrong, *Cheyenne and Arapaho Ordeal*, 323.

33. John D. Foster, *White Race Discourse: Preserving Racial Privilege in a Post-Racial Society* (Lanham, MD: Lexington Books, 2013), 5.

34. C. F. Larrabee to Charles E. Shell, May 10, 1907, Cheyenne and Arapaho Agency Records, Box 444, Folder 1, Item 195, OHS.

35. Stewart, *Peyote Religion*, 135–36.

36. Paul M. Road to James Mooney, May 20, 1907, NAA MS 2537—Misc. Material Regarding Peyote, Folder: "Legislation and Agitation," NAA–Bureau of American Ethnology. Stewart identified the author of the letter as "Paul Mouse," who also served as the interpreter for the Native Americans at the trial. Perhaps this identification comes from the use of his middle initial, but his signature on the original document reads "Paul M. Road." See Stewart, *Peyote Religion*, 136.

37. "Waging a Fight against Mescal," *Shawnee (OK) News*, July 30, 1907, 6; "Indians Acquitted," *Shawnee (OK) News*, July 30, 1907, 7.

38. William E. Safford, "An Aztec Narcotic," *Journal of Heredity* 6, no. 7 (July 1915): 306; *Peyote Hearings 1918*, 138; Stewart, *Peyote Religion*, 215.

39. Stewart, *Peyote Religion*, 176, 215.

40. Paul B. Steinmetz, *Pipe, Bible, and Peyote Among the Oglala Lakota: A Study in Religious Identity* (Syracuse, NY: Syracuse University Press, 1998), 89–90; Stewart, *Peyote Religion*, 176–77, 215.

41. "Peyote Protected by the Courts," *American Indian Magazine* 4, no. 4 (October–December 1916): 346.

42. *American Indian Magazine* (October–December 1916): 345–46; Stewart, *Peyote Religion*, 215.

43. *State v. Big Sheep*, 75 Mont. 219, 243 P. 1067 (1926); "Indian Wages Unusual Fight," *Ogden (UT) Standard Examiner*, September 23, 1925, 3; Karel Kurst-Swanger, *Worship and Sin: An Exploration of Religion-Related Crime in the United States* (New York: Lang, 2008), 114; Stephen V. Beyer, *Singing to the Plants: A Guide to Mestizo Shamanism in the Upper Amazon* (Albuquerque: University of New Mexico Press, 2010), 356–57.

44. "Mexican Stole for Sweetie, Wants Trial Delayed to Learn English," *Punxsutawney (PA) Spirit*, April 5, 1929, 8.

45. "Indians Protest Law against Use of 'Church Chew,'" *Salt Lake (UT) Tribune*, March 17, 1929, 11.

46. "The Free Exercise Clause was incorporated against the states in *Cantwell v. Connecticut*, 310 U.S. 296 (1940), and the Establishment Clause was incorporated in *Everson v. Board of Education*, 330 U.S. 1 (1947). *Cantwell* and *Everson* marked the beginning of modern First Amendment jurisprudence due to the importance of holding the states and the federal government to the same legal standard." Leslie C. Griffin, "Religion and the Courts, 1790–1947," unpublished paper, University of Houston Law Center, https://www.law.uh.edu/faculty/lgriffin/recent-writings/RelCourts.pdf.

47. *Claremore (OK) Messenger*, June 17, 1910, 1.

48. "Mescal Bean and Peyote: Strong Pleas Made by Indians that Peyote Stay," *Daily Ardmoreite* (Ardmore, OK), January 26, 1908, 1.

49. The Oklahoma Enabling Act of 1906 included several requirements for the Oklahoma Constitution, including the "prohibition of the manufacture, sale, barter, or gift of liquor for 21 years after statehood." See Danny M. Adkison, "Oklahoma Constitution," *Encyclopedia of Oklahoma History and Culture*, www.okhistory.org/publications/enc/entry?entry=OK036.

50. "Old Indian Warrior Begs for Privilege," *Oklahoma State Register* (Guthrie, OK), December 20, 1906, 2.

51. "Quanah Parker Delivers a Speech before the Convention," *Weekly State Democrat* (Lawton, OK), January 3, 1907, 5.

52. "Beans May Be Sold," *Fort Worth (TX) Star-Telegram*, December 24, 1906, 7; "Special Officer Johnson Does Not Meet with Success in Case against Indians," *Weekly Examiner* (Bartlesville, Indian Territory), August 3, 1907, 2.

53. Memorandum by George Bellamy, "Speeches Made on the Subject of the Mescal Bean or Peoti," February 25, 1908, Sac and Fox and Shawnee Agency Records, Box 613, Folder SFSA 35–1, Item 187, OHS.

54. "Delegation of Indians See the Governor to Secure Veto of Mescal Bean Bill," *Guthrie (OK Territory) Daily Leader*, March 9, 1899, 4. The delegation consisted of Black Coyote (Arapaho), Little Raven (Arapaho), Yellow Bear (Cheyenne), and Three Fingers (Cheyenne).

55. A. Frank Ross to Charles F. Shell, January 14, 1908, Cheyenne and Arapaho Agency Records, Box 444, Folder 1, Item 255, OHS; "Protest by Indians," *Evening News* (Ada, OK), January 22, 1908, 1; "Quanah Parker to Lobby," *Lawton (OK) Constitution-Democrat*, January 23, 1908, 6; Stewart, *Peyote Religion*, 138.

56. J. B. Rounds to "Dear Brother," January 7, 1908, Cheyenne and Arapaho Agency Records, Box 444, Folder 1, OHS.

57. "Indians Make Plea for 'Personal Liberty': Don't Want Lid on Mescal Bean,", *El Reno (OK) Daily American*, January 21, 1908, 1; "House Hears Mescal Story," *Oklahoma State Capital* (Guthrie, OK), January 23, 1908, 3; *Oklahoma Weekly Leader* (Guthrie, OK), January 23, 1908, 5; "Indians Want to Be Heard," *Searchlight* (Guthrie, OK), January 24, 1908, 1; "Plead for Mescal Bean: Forty Blanketed Warriors Invade Oklahoma Senate," *Tahlequah (OK) Arrow*, January 25, 1908.

58. "House Hears Mescal Story," 3.

59. "Indians Want to Be Protected: Gather in Guthrie to Fight Mescal Bean and Peyote Bill," *Weekly Times-Journal* (Oklahoma City, OK), January 24, 1908, 4.

60. Matt Duhr, "Chips from the Oklahoma Law Factory," *Oklahoma State Capital* (Guthrie, OK), January 29, 1908, 2.

61. "Indians and the Bean," *Checotah (OK) Enquirer*, January 24, 1908.

62. "Indians Want to Be Heard," 1.

63. "They Want Their Beans," *Searchlight* (Guthrie, OK), January 24, 1908, 14; *El Reno (OK) Daily American*, January 21, 1908, 1.

64. *Oklahoma State Register* (Guthrie, Oklahoma), January 23, 1908; *Oklahoma State Capital* (Guthrie, Oklahoma), January 23, 1908, 3; *El Reno (OK) Daily American*, January 21, 1908, 1; *Searchlight* (Guthrie, OK), January 24, 1908, 1, 14; "Plead for Mescal Bean."

65. "Protest by Indians," 1. Quanah Parker commented, "We know the democratic party does right by the rich and poor, and we know the republican party does right by the rich" (1).

66. *Oklahoma State Register* (Guthrie, OK), January 23, 1908.

67. "Redmen Victors in Peyote Fight," *Oklahoma State Register* (Guthrie, OK), January 30, 1908; Duhr, "Chips from the Oklahoma Law Factory," 2; "Legislative Doings," *Quinlan (OK) Mirror*, February 6, 1908, 2; "Many Odd Bills are Introduced in Legislature," *Oklahoma State Capital* (Guthrie, OK), February 26, 1908, 3.

68. "Indians Pleading for Sacred Bean," *Fort Worth (TX) Star-Telegram*, August 1, 1909, 10.

69. "Protest from Parker, the Comanche: Son of Dead Indian Chieftain Writes Letter to Governor on Peyote Bean Agitation," *Oklahoma State Register* (Guthrie, OK), April 13, 1911, 3.

70. "Indians Want Their Bean; Quanah Parker to Tell President It Is Not Intoxicating," *Enid (OK) Daily Eagle*, September 27, 1909; "Big Chief Parker to Washington," *Oklahoma Democrat* (Altus, OK), September 30, 1909; *Claremore (OK) Messenger*, June 17, 1910, 1.

71. "Won't Give Approval," *Lawton (OK) Constitution-Democrat*, December 7, 1911, 3; "Ban is Placed on the Sun Dance and Peyote Bean among Cheyennes," *Guthrie (OK) Daily Star*, June 29, 1912, 4.

72. "Poor Lo Can Now Continue His Spree on Peyote Bean," *Lawton (OK) Constitution-Democrat*, July 17, 1913.

73. "Make War on the Use of Peyote," *Sunday Tulsa (OK) Daily World*, April 17, 1921, 5; W. W. Scott to Cato Sells, March 27, 1918, Cheyenne and Arapaho Agency Records, Box 444, Folder 1, Item 160, OHS; E. B. Merritt to W. W. Scott, April 13, 1918, Cheyenne and Arapaho Agency Records, Box 444, Folder 1, Item 167, OHS; *Peyote Hearings 1918*, 20.

74. In 1870, the Osage ratified the Drum Creek Treaty, which provided for the sale of remaining Osage lands in Kansas with the proceeds used to relocate the tribe to Indian Territory. The government purchased the Osage lands in Kansas for $1.25 an acre, and under the "peace" administration of President Ulysses Grant negotiated a compromise with the Cherokee Nation for the Osage to purchase surplus land in northern Oklahoma for seventy cents an acre, allowing the Osage a clear title to the land. The Osage maintained a surplus of over one million dollars from this land deal, and in 1879 they gained an agreement from the commissioner of Indian Affairs for payment of their annuities in cash, distributed to individual Osage Indians four times a year. In 1882, the Osage began to lease 350,000 acres of their pastures to white farmers and ranchers for four cents an acre, bringing in another fourteen thousand dollars a year, also distributed to individuals. This grazing lease money continued to increase each year, making the "Osage a prosperous people with the prosperity divided equally." In 1896, the Osage would grant a ten-year lease to Edwin Foster, and his lease would lead to the discovery of oil on Osage land. See Rollings, *Unaffected by the Gospel*, 167, 175–76, 179, 182.

75. "Puritanism in Extreme," *Tulsa (OK) Daily World*, February 22, 1919; "Osages Plead for Their Sacred Herb," *Tulsa (OK) Daily World*, February 24, 1919; *Bismarck (ND) Tribune*, March 7, 1919, 1.

76. "Tama Indians Ask to Retain Use of Peyote in Church," *Waterloo (IA) Evening Courier*, February 24, 1925, 9; "Indians Win Bean Fight," *San Antonio (TX) Light*, February 20, 1927; "Indians Hauling Pyote for Rites," *Lubbock (TX) Morning Avalanche*, January 26, 1928, 10; "Indian Tribes Will Ask Congress to Authorize Use of Peyote Cactus," *Wichita Daily Times* (Wichita Falls, TX), March 2, 1930, 4.

77. "Oklahoma Indians Again on Warpath," *Lubbock (TX) Morning Avalanche*, February 23, 1927, 7.

78. "Peyote," Bulletin 21, Department of the Interior, Office of Indian Affairs, 1929, 4, Papers of Raoul Weston La Barre, Box 8—Peyote Studies Printed and Processed Material, Folder: "Legal File," NAA–Bureau of American Ethnology.

79. "Indians May Still Chew Peyote Bean," *Amarillo (TX) Globe*, April 15, 1927, 9.

80. S. Elizabeth Bird, "Introduction: Constructing the Indian, 1830s–1990s," in *Dressing in Feathers: The Construction of the Indian in American Popular Culture*, ed. S. Elizabeth Bird (Boulder, CO: Westview Press, 1996), 6. See also Scott, *X-Marks*, 61.

81. Michael Zakim, *Ready-Made Democracy: A History of Men's Dress in the American Republic, 1760–1860* (Chicago: University of Chicago Press, 2003), 1. Karen Halttunen also studied fashion in the antebellum period as part of the "sentimental ideal of social conduct" among the middle class. She, too, identifies dress as a powerful political expression that shapes social relations. See Halttunen, *Confidence Men and Painted Women: A Study of Middle-Class Culture in America, 1830–1870* (New Haven: Yale University Press, 1982).

82. Zakim, *Ready-Made Democracy*, 125–26.

83. Stephen Kantrowitz, "'Citizen's Clothing': Reconstruction, Ho-Chunk Persistence, and the Politics of Dress," in *Civil War Wests: Testing the Limits of the United States*, ed. Adam Arenson and Andrew Graybill (Berkeley: University of California Press, 2015), 248.

84. References contained in the *Report of the Commissioner of Indian Affairs* for various years are numerous. For the years covering this study, see specifically: P. B. Hunt, 1880, 72–73; L. J. Miles, 1880, 76; J. H. Seger, 1881, 71; P. B. Hunt, 1881, 78; P. B. Hunt, 1882, 65, 68; W. H. Roble, 1884, 90; L. J. Miles, 1884, 79; John D. C. Atkins, 1885, iv, x; D. B. Dyer, 1885, 75; P. B. Hunt, 1885, 84, 87; L. J. Miles, 1885, 89; J. Lee Hall, 1886, 127; G. D. Williams, 1887, 74; A. F. Standing, 1887, 85–86; A. D. Williams, 1888, 90; A. E. Woodson, 1893, 244; A. E. Woodson, 1895, 246; J. P. Woolsey, 1896, 264; Frank D. Baldwin, 1897, 232; A. E. Woodson, 1897, 226; Thomas Jefferson Morgan, 1898, 8; A. E. Woodson, 1898, 233; Martin J. Bentley, 1899, 292; William J. Pollock, 1899, 294; O. A. Mitscher, 1900, 339; Lauretta E. Ballew, 1901, 325; William A. Jones, 1902, 14; George W. H. Stouch, 1902, 281; John H. Seger, 1903, 255–56; O. A. Mitscher, 1903, 271; William A. Jones, 1904, 24–25; George W. H. Stouch, 1904, 288; Horace B. Durant, 1905, 203; George W. H. Stouch, 1905, 295.

85. Kantrowitz, "'Citizen's Clothing,'" 245.

86. "Indians Make Plea for 'Personal Liberty,'" 1; "Poor Lo Can Now Continue His Spree"; "Puritanism in Extreme"; "Osages Plead for Their Sacred Herb."

87. "Indians Want to Be Heard," 1.

88. "Indians Want to Be Protected," 4.

89. Kenneth L. Karst, "Paths to Belonging: The Constitution and Cultural Identity," in *Critical White Studies: Looking behind the Mirror*, ed. Richard Delgado and Jean Stefancic (Philadelphia: Temple University Press, 1997), 410.

90. Ellis, *A Dancing People*, 62.

91. Deloria, *Indians in Unexpected Places*, 79.

92. Louis S. Warren, *Buffalo Bill's America: William Cody and the Wild West Show* (New York: Alfred A. Knopf, 2005), 191.

93. Baker, *Anthropology and the Racial Politics of Culture*, 15.

94. *American Indian Magazine* 4, no. 3 (July–September 1916): 268; "Our Sioux Secretary," *American Indian Magazine* 5, no. 4 (October–December 1917): 268–69. For biographical works on Bonnin, see Tadeusz Lewandowski, *Red Bird, Red Power: The Life and Legacy of Zitkala-Ša* (Norman: University of Oklahoma Press, 2016); William Willard, "Zitkala-Ša: A Woman Who Would Be Heard," *Wicazo Sa Review* 1, no. 1 (Spring 1985): 11–16; David L. Johnson and Raymond Wilson, "Gertrude Simmons Bonnin, 1876–1938: 'Americanize the First American,'" *American Indian Quarterly* 12, no. 1 (Winter 1988): 27–40; P. Jane Hafen, "Zitkala-Ša: Sentimentality and Sovereignty," *Wicazo Sa Review* 12, no. 2 (Autumn 1997): 31–41; Carl Carpenter, "Detecting Indianness: Gertrude Bonnin's Investigation of Native American Identity," *Wicazo Sa Review* 20, no. 1 (Spring 2005): 139–59; Julianne Newmark, "Pluralism, Place, and Gertrude Bonnin's Counternativism from Utah to Washington, D.C.," *American Indian Quarterly* 36, no. 3 (Summer 2012): 318–47.

95. Arthur Parker to Charles Dagenett, December 22, 1911, Reel 2—Correspondence, SAI Papers.

96. Arthur Parker to Charles E. Miller et al. ("Dear Fellow American"), April 2, 1912, Reel 5—Correspondence, SAI Papers.

97. Deloria, *Playing Indian*, 124.

98. Gertrude Bonnin to Arthur Parker, March 2, 1917, Reel 1—Correspondence, SAI Papers.

99. James Mooney, *Peyote Hearings 1918*, 63.

100. Arthur Parker, "Problems of Race Assimilation in America," *American Indian Magazine* 4, no. 4 (October–December 1916): 295.

CHAPTER 6. "LET US KEEP OUR WORSHIP"

1. Lefthand (Niwot) quoted in George W. H. Stouch, "Report of Indian Agent for Cheyenne and Arapaho Agency, September 12, 1901," in *RCIA for 1901*, 316.

2. Quanah Parker, "Mescal Bean and Peyote," *Daily Ardmoreite* (Ardmore, OK), January 26, 1908, 1.

3. Cato Sells to Henry M. Tidwell, February 4, 1918, Reel 6—Correspondence, SAI Papers. Estimates range from 5,000 to 12,500 men who served in the military during the war, the broad spectrum perhaps indicative of the categorization of Indians as either full-bloods or mixed-bloods, or the delineation between combative and non-combative service roles. See Thomas A. Britten, *American Indians in World War I: At Home and at War* (Albuquerque: University of New Mexico Press, 1997), 84; Arthur Parker to James W. Wadsworth Jr., January 24, 1918, Reel 7—Correspondence, SAI Papers; "Resolutions Passed," *American Indian Magazine* 6, no. 2 (Summer 1918): 97; "Indian Society is Welcomed to City," *American Indian Magazine* 6, no. 3 (Autumn 1918): 118; Cato Sells, *RCIA for 1919*, 13. Equally significant to take into account is the non-citizen Indian population of the United States in the same period. At the start of World War I, there were "approximately 304,640 Indians by blood in the United States. Of this number, 166,311 [were] citizens and 138,329 [were] still without the privileges of citizenship. Nearly one-half the Indians of the United States [were] not its citizens." Gabe E. Parker, "The Great End: American Citizenship for the Indian," *Quarterly Journal of the Society of American Indians* 2, no. 1 (January–March 1914): 60–61.

4. James S. Olson and Raymond Wilson, *Native Americans in the Twentieth Century* (Provo, UT: Brigham Young University Press, 1984), 84. Citizenship status did not guarantee voting rights for Indians. States possessed the power to determine voter eligibility, and "states such as New Mexico and Arizona kept erecting voting barriers and did not allow most of their Native Americans to vote until after WWII." Olson and Wilson, 86.

5. Granted, the majority of code talkers in World War I were Choctaw, members of one of the tribes originally from the southeast United States who were designated as "civilized." However, Department of Defense records indicate that there were also Cherokee and Comanche individuals included in this operation. See Gary Robinson, *The Language of Victory: American Indian Code Talkers of World War I and World War II* (Bloomington, IL: iUniverse, 2014), 42; Denise Winterman, "World War One: The Original Code Talkers," *BBC News Magazine*, May 19, 2014, http://www.bbc.com/news/magazine-26963624.

6. Sells to Tidwell, February 4, 1918. Thomas Britten notes, "By the war's end, Native Americans had purchased over 25 million dollars worth of Liberty bonds, a per capita

investment of about 75 dollars [for every Native American man, woman, and child]." See Britten, *American Indians in World War I*, 133.

7. James I. Irving to Arthur Parker, January 14, 1920, Reel 4—Correspondence, SAI Papers.

8. James Mooney to Dr. J. Walter Fewkes, August 21, 1918, Box 200, Folder "James Mooney, 1916–1934," Series 1—Correspondence—Letters Received 1909–1949, NAA–Bureau of American Ethnology.

9. "Indian Woman in Capital to Fight Growing Use of Peyote Drug by Indians," *Washington Times*, February 17, 1918, 9. See also "The President, Congress, and the War," *Outlook*, April 11, 1917, 644.

10. Todd M. Gillett, "The Absolution of Reynolds: The Constitutionality of Religious Polygamy," *William & Mary Bill of Rights Journal* 8, no. 2 (2000): 504–5.

11. Lofton, "Cosmology," 270–72. See also Martin E. Marty, *Pilgrims in Their Own Land* (Boston: Little, Brown, 1984); George M. Marsden, *Religion and American Culture* (Orlando: Harcourt Brace Jovanovich, 1990), 168–69.

12. Maroukis, *Peyote Road*, 3–4.

13. "How the Mescal Bean Acts on Indians," *Guthrie (OK) Daily Leader*, July 22, 1903; H. M. Noble, "Report of Superintendent of Ponca School (Ponca and Tonkawa), August 4, 1906," *RCIA for 1906*, 321.

14. "The Mescal Bean and Its Effects," *Guthrie (OK) Daily Leader*, May 3, 1906.

15. Safford, "An Aztec Narcotic," 306–8; *Report of the Thirty-Second Annual Lake Mohonk Conference of the Indian and Other Dependent Peoples, October 14–16, 1914* (Lake Mohonk, NY: Lake Mohonk Conference, 1914), 66; Stewart, *Peyote Religion*, 223.

16. C. Burton Dustin, *Peyotism and New Mexico* (Santa Fe: Vergara, 1960), 9: "Peyote Studies, 1958–1963," in La Barre, *Peyote Cult*, 217; Stewart, *Peyote Religion*, 223.

17. Benson Tong, "Allotment, Alcohol, and the Omahas," *Great Plains Quarterly* (Winter 1997): 28.

18. Kenneth N. Hopkins, "Peyotism and the Otoe-Missouria Indians of Oklahoma," *Oklahoma State Historical Review* 3 (Spring 1982): 9; La Barre, *Peyote Cult*, 167. "Sac and Fox" is actually a term merging the names of two peoples: "Sac" (Sauk), or Thâkîwaki, and "Fox," or Meskwâki. The names were mistakenly combined by the US government during treaty negotiations in 1804. "Although historically associated and closely related by language and culture, the two peoples have always remained geographically and politically distinct. The Meskwâki have resided on the Meskwâki Settlement in central Iowa since 1856, and the Thâkîwaki have been in central Oklahoma since the 1870s. The contemporary Sac and Fox population in Oklahoma claim to be predominately of Thâkîwaki descent and typically refer to themselves as both 'Sac and Fox' and Sauk, and to their heritage language as Sauk." *Oklahoma Indian Country Guide: One State, Many Nations* (Oklahoma City: Oklahoma Tourism & Recreation Department, n.d.), 54, 47–48.

19. Hopkins, "Peyotism and the Otoe-Missouria Indians of Oklahoma," 9. See also James H. Howard, "An Oto-Omaha Peyote Ritual," *Southwestern Journal of Anthropology* 12, no. 4 (Winter 1956): 432–36.

20. "Articles of Incorporation, The Firstborn Church of Christ, Red Rock, Oklahoma," December 8, 1914, Oklahoma Secretary of State; Stewart, *Peyote Religion*, 223–24; Maroukis, *Peyote Road*, 48.

21. Hopkins, "Peyotism and the Otoe-Missouria Indians of Oklahoma," 10; La Barre, *Peyote Cult*, 117–18.

22. See obituaries of members of the church found in the *Ponca City (OK) News*.

23. James Mooney to Julia Bent Prentiss, July 29, 1916, Peyote Papers, Folder 1, Item 3827.1992a, HCAR.

24. Lee Irwin, *Coming Down from Above: Prophecy, Resistance, and Renewal in Native American Religions* (Norman: University of Oklahoma Press, 2008), 267–77, 408–10; Slotkin, *Peyote Religion*, 58. See also Holm, *The Great Confusion in Indian Affairs*, 42. Although Peyotists expressed a religious camaraderie with the Indian Shaker Church, the two religions seem to have competed with one another for adherents: "Where Shakerism thrives, peyote is not popular." *Peyote: An Abridged Compilation*, 12.

25. James Mooney to Mack Haag, October 25, 1920, Joseph Thoburn Collection, Box 31, Folder 7, Item CH-3, OHS.

26. Seymour, "Peyote Worship," 182. Also printed in *The Red Man* (Carlisle Indian School, PA) 8, no. 10 (June 1916): 344.

27. Heather D. Curtis, "Community," in Porterfield and Corrigan, *Religion in American History*, 224. For more on the Americanization of Mormonism, see also Albanese, *America: Religions and Religion*, 159–60; Williams, "Community," 298.

28. E. E. White, "Report of Agent for Kiowa, Comanche, and Wichita Agency, August 18, 1888," in *RCIA for 1888*, 98. For more on the subject of peyote producing visions, see Frederick S. Barde, September 18, 1909, Frederick S. Barde Collection, Box 21, Folder 41, Item 1982.089, 3, OHS; James Mooney, January 18, 1910, Address to Nebraska State Historical Society, Box 1 [James Mooney], Folder "Articles and Speeches," NAA–Bureau of American Ethnology; Memorandum of Scientists, January 28, 1910, in *Peyote Hearings 1918*, 38; Statement of Mr. Snyder, *Peyote Hearings 1918*, 17.

29. "America's Strangest Religion—For Red Men Only," *Butte (MT) Standard*, April 16, 1933. For more on John Wilson's changes to the peyote ceremony, see chapter 1.

30. "Indian Corner: Items and Stories in Indian English," *Geary (OK) Times*, May 30, 1918, 5; "Indians Would Keep Peyote Bean to Be Used as Church Sacrament," *Oklahoma State Register* (Guthrie, OK), May 29, 1919, 5.

31. "Obituary of Mr. James Mooney," 1921, James Mooney Papers, Box 1, Folder: "Biographical Material," NAA–Bureau of American Ethnology; John Swanton, "James Mooney," 210; Alicia Mooney to Bill Colby, January 22, 1977, James Mooney Papers, Box 1, Folder: "Files on Mooney and Use of the Mooney Material," NAA–Bureau of American Ethnology; Carl Sweezy quoted in Althea Bass, *The Arapaho Way: A Memoir of an Indian Boyhood* (New York: Clarkson Potter, 1966), 62, James Mooney Papers, Box 1, Folder: "Printed Materials Concerning Mooney," NAA–Bureau of American Ethnology.

32. James Mooney, "Eating the Mescal," 1892, American Press Association, NAA MS 1887 (Notes of James Mooney), Folder 3, NAA–Bureau of American Ethnology; DOJ attorney

Peyton to James Mooney, April 24, 1914, Records of the Bureau of American Ethnology, Series 1—Correspondence, Box 200, Folder: "James Mooney, 1903–1916," NAA–Bureau of American Ethnology; Mooney to Fewkes, August 21, 1918; James Mooney, 1918, NAA MS 2537–Misc. Material Regarding Peyote, Folder: "Legislation and Agitation," NAA–Bureau of American Ethnology; Statement of James Mooney, *Peyote Hearings 1918*, 89; James Mooney to Joseph Thoburn, October 26, 1920, Joseph Thoburn Collection, Box 31, Folder 7, Item CH-3, OHS; James Mooney to Bureau of American Ethnology, 1921, James Mooney Papers, Box 1, Folder: "Letters," NAA–Bureau of American Ethnology.

33. T. J. Davis to Bruce Kinney, September 17, 1918, Peyote Papers, Folder 6, Item 3827.2000, HCAR. See also Maroukis, *Peyote Road*, 56; Slotkin, *Peyote Religion*, 58; La Barre, *Peyote Religion*, 169; Aberle, *Peyote Religion among the Navaho*, 19; Hertzberger, *Search for an American Indian Identity*, 277; Wenger, *We Have a Religion*, 139; Moses, *Indian Man*, 207; William Willard, "The First Amendment, Anglo-Conformity, and American Indian Religious Movements," *Wicazo Sa Review* 7, no. 1 (Spring 1991): 26–30; Baker, *Anthropology and the Racial Politics of Culture*, 20, 66.

34. Jim Whitewolf, *The Life of a Kiowa-Apache Indian*, ed. Charles S. Brant (New York: Dover, 1969), 130; quoted in Maroukis, *Peyote Road*, 56.

35. "Resolution Adopted by the Native American Church of Clinton, Okla. on the Death of the Hon. James Mooney," 1921–22, James Mooney Papers, Box 1, Folder: "Biographical Materials," NAA–Bureau of American Ethnology. Also in Joseph Thoburn Collection, Box 23, Folder 1, OHS.

36. Bruce Kinney to Gertrude Bonnin, November 22, 1918, Peyote Papers, Folder 25, Item 3827.2017, HCAR; C. V. Stinchecum to commissioner of Indian Affairs, February 17, 1919, Cheyenne and Arapaho Agency Records, Box 445, Folder 5, Item 21, OHS; Superintendent of the Cheyenne and Arapaho Agency to commissioner of Indian Affairs, March 6, 1919, Cheyenne and Arapaho Agency Records, Box 445, Folder 5, Item 32, OHS.

37. C. V. Stinchecum to Bruce Kinney, November 21, 1918, Peyote Papers, Folder 24, Item 3827.2012, HCAR; W. W. Scott to C. V. Stinchecum, November 23, 1918, Cheyenne and Arapaho Agency Records, Box 445, Folder 4, Item 229, OHS. Later information revealed the missionary's complaints against Mooney's support of Peyotism to be the real reason for his recall from the field. See Robert Owen to Cato Sells, February 21, 1921, Joseph Thoburn Collection, Box 31, Folder 7, Item PE-1, OHS. Mooney also later wrote that he was not alone in his support of Peyotism but that he had been "singled out for the sacrifice." James Mooney to Joseph B. Thoburn, June 16, 1921, Joseph Thoburn Collection, Box 3, Folder 1, Item 86.01.276.B, OHS.

38. Mack Haag to Joseph Thoburn, December 15, 1920, Joseph Thoburn Collection, Box 31, Folder 7, OHS.

39. "Articles of Incorporation for the Native American Church of Oklahoma," October 10, 1918, Cheyenne and Arapaho Agency Records, Box 445, Folder Native American Church, Item 226a-c, OHS.

40. Stewart, *Peyote Religion*, 230; Hertzberger, *Search for an American Indian Identity*, 277; Maroukis, *Peyote Road*, 124.

41. "Refuse South Dakota Indians Charter for a Church," *Sioux City (IA) Journal*, November 28, 1922, 5; "Would Close Four Indian Churches for Use of Peyote," *Evening Republican*

(Mitchell, SD), February 4, 1925, 1; "Peyote Menace Gains Headway," *Evening Republican* (Mitchell, SD), February 5, 1925, 12; Stewart, *Peyote Religion*, 230; Maroukis, *Peyote Road*, 124.

42. "Use of Peyote by Indians Is Now Increasing," *Evening Republican* (Mitchell, SD), February 10, 1926, 6.

43. Maroukis, *Peyote Road*, 125.

44. Maroukis, *Peyote Road*, 146–48, 151; Stewart, *Peyote Religion*, 239–43, 257, 286, 292, 311–12, 320–21.

45. *Miami (OK) News-Record*, January 8, 1933, 6; "Indians Would Keep Peyote Bean," 5; "Summary of Peyote Questionnaire," in *Peyote: An Abridged Compilation*, 32–33.

46. "Indians Register Kick over Prohibition, Must Have Their Peyote," *Washington Herald*, February 8, 1919, 6.

47. "Make War on the Use of Peyote," *Tulsa (OK) Daily World*, April 17, 1921.

48. Representative L. M. Gensman (OK), "The House Discusses Legislation to Suppress the Use of Peyote," *Congressional Digest* 1, no. 5 (February 1922): 14.

49. Cleaver Warden, "Minutes of the 6th Annual Conference of the Native American Church, Oklahoma," June 8, 1925, Joseph Thoburn Collection, Box 23, Folder 1, OHS; Mack Haag, *General Report of the President of the Native American Church, Oklahoma*, June 8, 1925, Joseph Thoburn Collection, Box 23, Folder 1, OHS.

50. "Articles of Incorporation for the Native American Church of Oklahoma," October 10, 1918.

51. Testimony of Chief Joseph Springer, February 25, 1908, in "Report of George Bellamy," Sac and Fox and Shawnee Agency Records: Liquor Traffic, Peyote, Mescal Use, Box 613, Folder SFSA 35–1, Item 38, OHS; Testimony of D. K. Cunningham, February 25, 1908, in "Report of George Bellamy," Sac and Fox and Shawnee Agency Records: Liquor Traffic, Peyote, Mescal Use, Box 613, Folder SFSA 35–1, Item 22–23, OHS.

52. "Indians Want to Be Protected: Gather in Guthrie to Fight Mescal Bean and Peyote Bill," *Weekly Times-Journal* (Oklahoma City, OK), January 24, 1908, 4; "They Want Their Beans," *Searchlight* (Guthrie, OK), January 24, 1908, 14; "Want Mescal," *New State Tribune* (Muskogee, OK), January 23, 1908, 1; "The Many Methods of Worship," *Oklahoma State Register* (Guthrie, OK), January 23, 1908.

53. *Peyote Hearings 1918*, 111, 113–14, 122, 161.

54. "Puritanism in Extremes," *Tulsa (OK) Daily World*, February 22, 1919, 4; "Osages Plead for Their Sacred Herb," *Tulsa (OK) Daily World*, February 24, 1919, 2; "Ban on Peyote Bean Beverage Hard on Indian," *Daily Ardmoreite* (Ardmore, OK), July 17, 1922, 8; "Indians Still May Chew the Peyote Bean," *Escanaba (MI) Daily Press*, May 4, 1927, 2; "A Comanche Peyote Festival," *Lubbock (TX) Morning Avalanche*, October 7, 1928, 5; "Faith of Oklahoma Indians Requires Use of Narcotics," *Salt Lake (UT) Tribune*, June 17, 1934; "Indian School at Santa Fe is Criticized," *Santa Fe New Mexican*, August 21, 1936, 4.

55. *Thirty-Third Annual Report of the Bureau of American Ethnology to the Secretary of the Smithsonian Institution, 1911–1912* (Washington, DC: Government Printing Office, 1919), 104–5; "Peyote–Its Prohibition," *Congressional Digest* 1, no. 5 (February 1922): 17; Senator J. W. Harreld to T. J. Davis, January 19, 1923, Peyote Papers, Folder 61, Item 3827.2068, HCAR; Elmer Thomas, "A Bill Re-Establishing Narcotic Farms," 71st Cong. 2nd sess., S. 3367, (1929–1930),

in Papers of Raoul Weston La Barre, Box 8, Folder: "Legal File," NAA–Bureau of American Ethnology. The Thomas bill provided an exemption for "peyote for sacramental purposes."

56. Moses, *Indian Man*, 4; Alicia Mooney to Bill Colby, January 22, 1977.

57. Moses, *Indian Man*, 168; "Obituary of Mr. James Mooney."

58. Alicia Mooney to Bill Colby, January 22, 1977.

59. "Obituary of Mr. James Mooney."

60. James Mooney, 1918, NAA MS 2537—Misc. Material Regarding Peyote; James Mooney to Bureau of American Ethnology, 1921.

61. Pegram, *Battling Demon Rum*, 114. The ASL even advertised itself as "the church in action against the saloon." Pegram, 115.

62. Fuller, *Stairways to Heaven*, 104.

63. Jennifer L. Woodruff Tait, *The Poisoned Chalice: Eucharistic Grape Juice and Common-Sense Realism in Victorian Methodism* (Tuscaloosa: University of Alabama Press, 2011), 12–13.

64. Peck, *Prohibition Hangover*, 180.

65. Tait, *Poisoned Chalice*, 13.

66. Even Christian groups like the Mormons, who had used wine as a sacrament, adopted a total ban on alcoholic beverages in 1900. See Fuller, *Stairways to Heaven*, 108–14.

67. Though not for Eucharistic purposes, Jews also defended their need for kosher sacramental wine to be used in their home-centered weekly Sabbath rituals. See Marni Davis, *Jews and Booze: Becoming American in the Age of Prohibition* (New York: New York University Press, 2012). Not all Catholics agreed on the issue of alcohol prohibition. There was an abstinence society within the Catholic Church (the Catholic Total Abstinence Union, organized in 1871 by Father Theobald Mathew of Ireland), but it was a short-lived movement. See Peck, *Prohibition Hangover*, 181.

68. Peck, *Prohibition Hangover*, 181–82.

69. Fuller, *Stairways to Heaven*, 104.

70. Tait, *Poisoned Chalice*, 63. See also Davis, *Jews and Booze*, 160–62, regarding the anti-Semitic views related to Jews and alcohol.

71. Fuller, *Stairways to Heaven*, 104.

72. Louis Fisher, "Statutory Exemptions for Religious Freedom," *Journal of Church and State* 44, no. 2 (Spring 2002): 291, 300.

73. Daniel Okrent, *Last Call: The Rise and Fall of Prohibition* (New York: Scribner, 2010), 182–95; John F. Quinn, "Father Mathew's Disciples: American Catholic Support for Temperance, 1840–1920," *Church History* 65, no. 4 (December 1996), 639; David T. Courtwright, *Forces of Habit: Drugs and the Making of the Modern World* (Cambridge, MA: Harvard University Press, 2001), 187. Okrent also identifies another loophole in prohibition law for farmers who fermented their own cider and "fruit juices." His book examines the exploitation of the loopholes in prohibition law by fake clergymen, as well as numerous doctors, dentists, and even veterinarians who wrote prescriptions for remedies containing significant quantities of alcohol.

74. F. Habbott to superintendents, Circular No. 690 (Introduction of Wines for Sacramental Purposes), September 14, 1912, Cheyenne and Arapaho Agency Records, Box 444, Folder 3, Item 88, OHS.

75. "Protest by Indians," *Evening News* (Ada, OK), January 22, 1908; "The Many Methods of Worship."

76. "Indians Want to Be Protected," 4; "The Peyote Cult," *Dallas Morning News*, February 18, 1918, 2.

77. Statement of Charles J. Kappler, *Peyote Hearings 1918*, 160.

78. Sarah Barringer Gordon, *The Mormon Question: Polygamy and Constitutional Conflict in Nineteenth-Century America* (Chapel Hill: University of North Carolina Press, 2002), 71.

79. Gertrude Bonnin, *Peyote Hearings 1918*, 24.

80. George Gibbs to Arthur Parker, July 2, 1918, Reel 3—Correspondence, SAI Papers.

81. "The Peyote Question: Conference of the Friends of the Indians," *American Indian Magazine* 6, no. 2 (Summer 1918): 71. See also Rev. H. H. Clause, in "Peyote," 1929, Bulletin 21, Department of the Interior, Office of Indian Affairs, Papers of Raoul Weston La Barre, Box 8, Folder: "Legal File," NAA–Bureau of American Ethnology.

82. "Peyote," 1929, NAA–Bureau of American Ethnology. See also "Non-Alcoholic Intoxicant," *New York Times*, June 13, 1920, where Representative Gandy argued, "Peyote would have to be the religion itself if it is to be sacred under that clause of the Constitution which guarantees freedom of religious worship."

83. "Chaff from Assembly's Legal Grind," *Billings (MT) Gazette*, January 27, 1929, 6. See also Statement of Mr. Tillman, *Peyote Hearings 1918*, 89, 122; Statement of Charles J. Kappler, *Peyote Hearings 1918*, 160; "Indian Woman in Capital," 9; "Ban on Peyote Bean Beverage Hard on Indian," 8; "Oklahoma Indians Again on Warpath," *Lubbock (TX) Morning Avalanche*, February 23, 1927, 7; "A Comanche Peyote Festival," 5.

84. Fred Lookout, Eves Tallchief, Edgar McCarthy, and Arthur Bonnicastle, representing Blackdog and Clermont Lodges to the Senate and House Committees on Indian Affairs, in *Peyote Hearings 1918*, 161–62.

85. Charles Burke, "Refuse S.D. Indians Charter for a Church," *Sioux City (IA) Journal*, November 28, 1922, 5. See also Bonnin, *Peyote Hearings 1918*, 21; Mary C. Collins, "The Religious Nature of the Indian," *American Indian Magazine* 6, no. 2 (Summer 1918): 91.

86. Unknown writer to Warren K. Moorehead, May 28, 1923, Reel 5—Correspondence, SAI Papers; Matthew K. Sniffen to Warren K. Moorehead, June 5, 1923, Reel 5—Correspondence, SAI Papers; Arthur Parker to Henry Roman Nose, June 16, 1915, Reel 6—Correspondence, SAI Papers. See also Jacob Reid to Edward Ayer, March 19, 1916, in *Peyote Hearings 1918*, 139; "Non-Alcoholic Intoxicant"; "Peyote–Its Prohibition," 14, 17.

87. *Peyote: An Abridged Compilation*, 25. See also Charles Eastman, *Peyote Hearings 1918*, 139.

88. Charles H. Burke, *RCIA for 1922*, 20. See also Hall, "The Peyote Question," 69; "A worker for the good of the American Indian" to Congressmen McClintic and Carter and Senator Harreld, January 16, 1923, Peyote Papers, Folder 59, Item 3827.2067, HCAR; "Peyote," 1929, NAA–Bureau of American Ethnology.

89. *Peyote: An Abridged Compilation*, 25.

90. "Puritanism in Extremes," 4.

91. Mooney to Haag, October 25, 1920.

92. Arthur Bonnicastle to Board of Indian Commissioners, February 4, 1915, in *Peyote Hearings 1918*, 80; Statement of Paul Boynton, *Peyote Hearings 1918*, 181; Statement of Francis La Flesche, *Peyote Hearings 1918*, 81.

93. Osage Indians to Charles Carter, February 7, 1918, in *Peyote Hearings 1918*, 160–61.

94. Haag, "Religious Persecution," in *General Report of the President of the Native American Church, Oklahoma.*

95. Statement of William E. Safford, *Peyote Hearings 1918*, 188–89; Bear, "Peyote–Its Prohibition," 16; Lone Wolf, "Peyote–Its Prohibition," 16; "America's Strangest Religion."

96. Haag, "Religious Persecution," in *General Report of the President of the Native American Church, Oklahoma.*

97. Martin Marty points to the decline in Protestant Christianity's influence in 1924, with the "chance that an Irish Catholic might become a Presidential nominee, and in 1928 New York Governor Alfred E. Smith, a Catholic, was nominated." Additionally, the 1920s found Protestants fighting against each other in the conflict between fundamentalism and modernism. Martin E. Marty, *Righteous Empire: The Protestant Experience in America* (New York: The Dial Press, 1970), 212, 215.

98. *The Problem of Indian Administration: Report of a Survey Made at the Request of Honorable Hubert Work, Secretary of the Interior, and Submitted to Him, February 21, 1928* (Baltimore, MD: Johns Hopkins Press, 1928), 812, 817, 845–46.

99. David W. Daily, "About G. E. E. Lindquist," G. E. E. Lindquist Native American Photographs, the Burke Library Archives (Columbia University Libraries) at Union Theological Seminary, New York, https://lindquist.cul.columbia.edu/about_gee_lindquist. For more on Lindquist and his connection with the Indian Bureau, see David W. Daily, *Battle for the BIA: G. E. E. Lindquist and the Missionary Crusade against John Collier* (Tucson: University of Arizona Press, 2004).

100. G. E. E. Lindquist, *The Red Man in the United States: An Intimate Study of the Social, Economic and Religious Life of the American Indian*, with a foreword by Charles Burke (New York: George H. Doran, 1923), vi, 69.

101. Haag, "Religious Persecution," in *General Report of the President of the Native American Church, Oklahoma.* The situation with the Office of Indian Affairs improved when John Collier became commissioner in 1933.

102. "The Peyote Question," 71.

103. "America's Strangest Religion."

CONCLUSION

Epigraph: Jock Bull Bear (Arapaho), *Peyote Hearings 1918*, 106.

1. Statement of Reuben Taylor (Cheyenne), *Peyote Hearings 1918*, 193.
2. Calloway, *First Peoples*, 488.
3. Calloway, 495.
4. Calloway, 496. Myer was the "former head of the War Relocation Authority that had taken thousands of Japanese Americans from the West Coast and put them in internment camps during World War II." Calloway, 496.
5. Maroukis, *Peyote Road*, 185.

6. Maroukis, 185.

7. Maroukis, 187.

8. Maroukis, 189.

9. "Nine Indians Plead for Peyote Supply," *Dallas Morning News*, November 30, 1967, 9; "No Legal Way to Get Peyote, Indians Told," *Dallas Morning News*, December 1, 1967, 5; Maroukis, *Peyote Road*, 192.

10. *Dallas Morning News*, March 21, 1968, 18; Schaefer, *Amanda's Blessings*, 118.

11. Maroukis, *Peyote Road*, 192–93.

12. "Mirando City Is Scene for the Peyote Rites," *Dallas Morning News*, September 2, 1972, 15; "Peyote Country Folks Seem to Avoid Addiction," *Dallas Morning News*, February 19, 1973, 27.

13. Maroukis, *Peyote Road*, 193–94.

14. Calloway, *First Peoples*, 570.

15. Russel Lawrence Barsh, "The Supreme Court, Peyote, and Minority Religions: Zero Tolerance," *Wicazo Sa Review* 7, no. 2 (Autumn 1991): 49. Barsh summarized: "Smith was an Indian drug and alcohol abuse counselor in Portland, Oregon, who was fired because of his religious use of Peyote, and subsequently denied benefits by the State of Oregon. Under Oregon law, the denial of benefits was lawful only if Smith had been fired."

16. Calloway, *First Peoples*, 571.

17. Figure 1.8 in Swan, *Peyote Religious Art*.

18. Alvaro Céspedes, "In the Only State Where Selling Peyote Is Legal, the Cactus Is Threatened and Still Controversial," *Texas Standard*, November 13, 2018, https://www.texasstandard.org/stories/in-the-only-state-where-selling-peyote-is-legal-the-cactus-is-threatened-and-still-controversial/.

19. Elsie Whitehorn (an Otoe who is a Firstborn Church Peyotist and a Peyotist in the Otoe-Missouria chapter of the Native American Church), conversation with the author at the Otoe-Missouria tribal complex, Red Rock, OK, April 25, 2023.

20. Peter N. Jones, "The American Indian Church and Its Sacramental Use of Peyote: A Review for Professionals in the Mental-Health Arena," *Mental Health, Religion & Culture* 8, no. 4 (December 2005): 284, 287.

21. Fuller, *Stairways to Heaven*, 192.

BIBLIOGRAPHY

ARCHIVAL COLLECTIONS

Helmerich Center for American Research at Gilcrease Museum, Tulsa, Oklahoma
    Peyote Papers
National Anthropological Archives, Smithsonian Institution, Suitland, Maryland
    NAA MS 2537–Misc. Material Regarding Peyote
    Papers of James Mooney
    Papers of Raoul West La Barre
    Records of the Bureau of American Ethnology
National Archives and Records Administration, Fort Worth, Texas
    Records of the Bureau of Indian Affairs, 1793–1999, Department of the Interior, Office of Indian Affairs, Ponca Agency, 11/1/1870–1919, Record Group 75
    Records of US Customs Service, Abstracts of Duties, Del Rio and Laredo, TX, Record Group 36
    Records of US Customs Service, Imported Merchandise, Laredo, TX, Record Group 36
    Records of US Customs Service, Impost Books for Laredo, TX, Record Group 36
    Records of US Customs Service, Imported Merchandise, Laredo, TX, Record Group 36
    Records of US Customs Service, Letters Sent from Del Rio, Eagle Pass, and Laredo, TX, Record Group 36
National Archives and Records Administration, Washington, DC
    Correspondence of the Chief Special Officer Relating to Peyote, 1908–1918, RG: 75
Oklahoma Historical Society Research Division, Oklahoma City, Oklahoma
    Cheyenne and Arapaho Agency Records
    Frederick S. Barde Collection
    Joseph Thoburn Collection
    Kiowa Agency Records
    Sac and Fox and Shawnee Agency Records
Smithsonian Institution, Washington, DC
    Personnel Records, 1892–1952, SIA 05–123
United States National Museum, Division of Plants Records, Record Unit 221
Society of American Indian papers, 1906–1946, microfilm
University of Oklahoma Western History Collections, Norman, Oklahoma
    Doris Duke Collection
    Indian Pioneer Papers

DIGITAL ARCHIVES

Amon Carter Museum, Fort Worth, Texas, Online Projects (http://www.cartermuseum.org/learn/online-projects).
 Erwin E. Smith Collection
 Texas Bird's-Eye Views
Archivo General de la Nación, Mexico (http://www.gob.mx/agn).
HathiTrust Digital Library (https://www.hathitrust.org/).
The History Collection, University of Wisconsin–Madison Libraries, (https://uwdc.library.wisc.edu/collections/History/).
G. E. E. Lindquist Native American Photographs, Burke Library Archives at Union Theological Seminary, Columbia University, New York City, NY (https://lindquist.cul.columbia.edu/).
National Archives and Records Administration, Fort Worth, Texas
 Records of the Bureau of Indian Affairs, 1793–1999, Series: The Indian School Journal, 1904–1926, Record Group 75
Student Files. Carlisle Indian School Digital Resource Center, Archives & Special Collections, Waidner-Spahr Library, Dickinson College, Carlisle, PA (http://carlisleindian.dickinson.edu/student_files).
World Digital Library, Library of Congress with the support of the United Nations Educational, Scientific, and Cultural Organization, (https://www.wdl.org/en/).

NEWSPAPERS AND MAGAZINES

Abilene (TX) Daily Reporter
Adair County (OK) Sentinel
Albuquerque (NM) Morning Journal
Amarillo (TX) Globe
American Indian Magazine (published by the Society of American Indians)
Anaconda (MT) Standard
Anadarko (OK) American-Democrat
Arizona Republican (Phoenix, AZ)
Atlanta Constitution
Bainville (MT) Democrat
Baptist Home Mission Monthly (NY)
Beckley Raleigh Register (WV)
Billings (MT) Gazette
Bisbee (AZ) Daily Review
Bismarck (ND) Tribune
Brazil (IN) Daily Times
Bridgeport (CT) Telegram
Brownsville (TX) Daily Herald
Butte (MT) Standard
Calumet (OK) Chieftain

Carney (OK) Enterprise
Chattanooga (TN) News
Checotah (OK) Enquirer
Checotah (OK) Times
Chicago Tribune
Citizen (Berea, KY)
Claremore (OK) Messenger
Coconino (AZ) Sun
Congressional Digest
Daily Ardmoreite (Ardmore, OK)
Daily Arizona Silver Belt (Globe, AZ)
Daily Capital Journal (Salem, OR)
Dakota Farmer's Leader (Canton, SD)
Dallas Morning News
Denver (CO) News
El Paso (TX) Herald
El Reno (OK) Daily American
El Reno (OK) Daily Democrat
Enid (OK) Daily Eagle
Enid (OK) Events
Escanaba (MI) Daily Press
Evening News (Ada, OK)
Evening Public Ledger (Philadelphia, PA)
Evening Record (Ellensburg, WA)
Evening Republican (Mitchell, SD)
Evening Review (East Liverpool, OH)
Evening Star (Washington, DC)
Farmer (Bridgeport, CT)
Fort Worth (TX) Star-Telegram
Freeport (IL) Daily Journal-Standard
Galveston (TX) Daily News
Geary (OK) Times
Guthrie (Oklahoma Territory) Daily Leader
Guthrie (OK) Daily Star
Hays (KS) Free Press
Helena (MT) Daily Independent
Indian Leader (published by Haskell Institute, Lawrence, KS)
Indian School Journal (published by Chilocco Indian Agricultural School, Chilocco, OK)
Indian's Friend (published by the National Indian Association, Philadelphia, PA)
Indiana State Journal (Indianapolis, IN)
Inola (OK) Register
Journal of the American Medical Association
Kingston (NY) Daily Freeman

BIBLIOGRAPHY

Kokomo (IN) Tribune
La Crosse (WI) Tribune
Laredo (TX) Times
Lawton (OK) Constitution-Democrat
Lexington (OK) Leader
Lubbock (TX) Morning Avalanche
Manchester (Oklahoma Territory) Journal
Miami (OK) News-Record
Mohave County Miner and Our Mineral Wealth (Kingman, AZ)
Muskogee (OK) Times-Democrat
Native American (published by the Phoenix Indian School, AZ)
New State Tribune (Muskogee, OK)
New York Times
Oasis (Arizola, AZ)
Ogden (UT) Standard Examiner
Oklahoma City Daily Pointer
Oklahoma Democrat (Altus, OK)
Oklahoma State Capital (Guthrie, OK)
Oklahoma State Register (Guthrie, OK)
Oklahoma Weekly Leader (Guthrie, OK)
Oshkosh (WI) Daily Northwestern
Outlook (New York City, NY)
Paducah (KY) Evening Sun
Ponca City (OK) News
Puck Magazine
Pulaski (VA) Southwest Times
Punxsutawney (PA) Spirit
Quarterly Journal of the Society of American Indians
Quinlan (OK) Mirror
Red Lake (MN) News
Red Man (published by Carlisle Indian School, PA)
Red Rock (OK) Opinion
Rock Island (IL) Argus
Saints' Herald (published by the Reorganized Church of Jesus Christ of Latter-Day Saints, Independence, MO)
Salt Lake (UT) Tribune
San Antonio (TX) Express
San Antonio (TX) Light
Santa Fe New Mexican
Sapulpa (OK) Evening Light
Searchlight (Guthrie, OK)
Shawnee (OK) News

Sioux City (IA) Journal
Spokane (WA) Press
Stroud (OK) Democrat
Sun (New York City, NY)
Syracuse (NY) Herald
Tahlequah (OK) Arrow
Times-Democrat (Lima, OH)
Tulsa (OK) Daily World
Union Signal (published by WCTU)
Washington Herald
Washington Post
Washington Times
Waterloo (IA) Evening Courier
Weekly Examiner (Bartlesville, Indian Territory)
Weekly State Democrat (Lawton, OK)
Weekly Times-Journal (Guthrie, OK)
Weekly Times-Journal (Oklahoma City, OK)
Wichita Daily Times (Wichita Falls, TX)
Wotanin Wowapi (Poplar, MT)
Yakima (WA) Herald

PUBLISHED PRIMARY SOURCES

Abbott, Lyman. "The Menace of Peyote." *American Indian Magazine* 5, no. 2 (April–June 1917): 134–36.

American Periodicals. "Marvels of the Mescal Buttons: The Strange Indian Cactus." *Globe-Democrat* (St. Louis). In *Current Literature (1888–1912)* 20, no. 1 (July–December 1896): 47.

Andreae, Percy. *The Prohibition Movement in Its Broader Bearings upon Our Social, Commercial, and Religious Liberties.* Chicago: Felix Mendelsohn, 1915.

Annual Reports of the Bureau of American Ethnology to the Secretary of the Smithsonian Institution. Washington, DC: Government Printing Office, 1880–1931.

Annual Reports of the Commissioner of Indian Affairs. Washington, DC: Government Printing Office, 1880–1937.

Apostolicos afanes de la compañia de Jesus, escritos por un padre de la misma sagrada religion de su provincial de Mexico. Barcelona: por Pablo Nadal Impreffor, en la calle de la Canúda, 1754.

"Articles of Incorporation, The Firstborn Church of Christ, Red Rock, Oklahoma." Oklahoma Secretary of State, December 8, 1914.

"Articles of Incorporation, Native American Church of Oklahoma." Oklahoma Secretary of State, October 10, 1918.

Bonnin, Gertrude. "An Indian Cult and a Powerful Drug." *American Indian Magazine* 4, no. 2 (April–June 1916): 160–63.

Briggs, J. R. "Muscale Buttons—Physiological Action—A Mexican Fruit with Possible Medicinal Virtues." *The Druggists' Bulletin* 1, no. 5 (May 1887): 78.

Cárdenas, Juan de. *Problemas y secretos maravillosos de las Indias: Obra impresa en México, por Pedro Ocharte, en 1591, y ahora editada en facsímil.* 1591. Reprint, Madrid: Ediciones Cultura Hispánica, 1945.

Collins, Mary C. "The Religious Nature of the Indian." *American Indian Magazine* 6, no. 2 (Summer 1918): 89–92.

Cruz, Martín de la. *Libellus de medicinalibus indorum herbis: Manuscrito Azteca de 1552: versión española con estudios y comentarios por diversos autores.* Mexico: Instituto Mexicano del Seguro Social, 1964.

Edwards, George, ed. *The Pioneer Work of the Presbyterian Church in Montana.* Reprinted from volume 6 of the Montana State Historical Society. Helena: Independent Publishing Company, 1906.

Ellis, Havelock. "Mescal: A New Artificial Paradise." In *Annual Report of the Board of Regents of the Smithsonian Institution,* 537–48. Washington, DC: US Government Printing Office, 1897.

Garcia, Bartholome. *Manual para administrar los santos sacramentos de penitencia, eucharistia, extrema-uncion y matrimonio.* Mexico City: Imprenta de los Herederos de Doña Maria de Rivera, 1760.

Hall, Robert D. "The Peyote Question: Conference of Friends of the Indians." *American Indian Magazine* 6, no. 2 (Summer 1918): 67–74.

Havard, Valery. "Report on the Flora of Western and Southern Texas." *Proceedings of the United States National Museum* 8, no. 29 (September 23, 1885): 449–553.

Haynes, Roy A. *Prohibition Inside Out.* New York: Doubleday, 1923.

Hernández, Francisco. *Francisci Hernandi, medici atque historici Philippi II, hispan et indiar: Regis, et totius novi orbis archiatri; Opera, cum edita, tum medita, ad autobiographi fidem et jusu region.* Edited by Casimiro Gómez Ortega. Madrid, 1790.

House Committee on Indian Affairs. *Prohibition of Use of Peyote Among Indians.* 65th Cong., 2nd sess., May 13, 1918, H.R. Rep. 560.

Larson, Henry A. "The Indian and His Liquor Problem." *American Indian Magazine* 4, no. 3 (July–September 1916): 234–36.

Lindquist, G. E. E. *The Red Man in the United States: An Intimate Study of the Social, Economic and Religious Life of the American Indian.* Foreword by Charles Burke. New York: George H. Doran, 1923.

Lone Wolf, Delos. "How to Solve the Indian Problem." *American Indian Magazine* 4, no. 3 (July–September 1916): 257–58.

Lumholtz, Carl. "Tarahumari Dances and Plant-Worship." *Scribner's Magazine* 16, no. 4 (October 1894): 451–56.

———. *Unknown Mexico: A Record of Five Years' Exploration among the Tribes of the Western Sierra Madre; in the Tierra Caliente of Tepic and Jalisco; and among the Tarascos of Michoacan.* Vol 2. New York: Charles Scribner's Sons, 1902.

Marks, Jeanette. "Narcoticism and the War." *North American Review* 206, no. 743 (December 1917): 879–84.

McGee Memorial Meeting of the Washington Academy of Sciences Held at the Carnegie Institution, Washington, D.C., December 5, 1913. Baltimore: Williams & Wilkins, 1916.

McKenzie, Fayette Avery. "The American Indian of Today and Tomorrow." *The Journal of Race Development* 3, no. 2 (October 1912): 135–55.

———. "The Assimilation of the American Indian." *American Journal of Sociology* 19, no. 6 (May 1914): 761–72.

———. *"Pussyfoot" Johnson—Crusader—Reformer—A Man among Men*. New York: Fleming H. Revell, 1920.

Mitchell, S. W. "Remarks on the Effects of Anhelonium Lewinii (the Mescal Button)." *British Medical Journal* 2 (December 5, 1896): 1625–29.

Mooney, James. "A Kiowa Mescal Rattle." *American Anthropologist* 5, no. 1 (January 1892): 64–66.

———. "In Kiowa Camps." Papers and Addresses Delivered at the January Meeting of the Mississippi Valley Historical Association, January 18, 1910. In *Proceedings of the Mississippi Valley Historical Association for the Year 1909–1910*, vol. 3, 43–57. Cedar Rapids, IA: Torch Press, 1911.

———. "The Mescal Plant and Ceremony." *Therapeutic Gazette* 12, no. 1 (January 15, 1896): 7–11.

Parker, Arthur C. "The Editor's Viewpoint: The Functions of the Society of American Indians." *American Indian Magazine* 4, no. 1 (January–March 1916): 8–14.

———. "Problems of Race Assimilation in America." *American Indian Magazine* 4, no. 4 (October–December 1916): 285–304.

———. "The Social Elements of the Indian Problem." *American Journal of Sociology* 22, no. 2 (September 1916): 252–67.

Parker, Gabe E. "The Great End: American Citizenship for the Indian." *Quarterly Journal of the Society of American Indians* 2, no. 1 (January–March 1914): 60–61.

Peyote: An Abridged Compilation from the Files of the Bureau of Indian Affairs. Washington, DC: Government Printing Office, 1922.

"The Peyote Evil." In *Fortieth Annual Report of the Board of Directors of the Indian Rights Association*. Philadelphia: Indian Rights Association, 1922.

Prentiss, D. W., and F. P. Morgan. "Anhalonium Lewinii (Mescal Buttons): A Study of the Drug, with Especial Reference to Its Physiological Action upon Man, with Report of Experiments." *The Therapeutic Gazette* 11, no. 9 (September 16, 1895): 577–85.

The Problem of Indian Administration: Report of a Survey Made at the Request of Honorable Hubert Work, Secretary of the Interior, and Submitted to Him, February 21, 1928 (The Meriam Report). Baltimore, MD: Johns Hopkins Press, 1928.

Radin, Paul. "The Winnebago Tribe." *Bureau of American Ethnology Annual Report* 37 (1915–1916): 395–97.

Report of the Thirty-Second Annual Lake Mohonk Conference of the Indian and Other Dependent Peoples, October 14th, 15th, and 16th, 1914. Lake Mohonk Conference, 1914.

Safford, William E. "An Aztec Narcotic." *Journal of Heredity* 6, no. 7 (July 1915): 291–311.

———. "Narcotic Plants and Stimulants of the Ancient Americans." In *Annual Report of the Board of Regents of the Smithsonian Institution, 1916*. Washington, DC: Government Printing Office, 1917.

Sahagún, Bernardino de. *Historia general de las cosas de la Nueva España, El dozeno libro: tracta de como los españoles conquistaron a la ciudad de Mexico.* Edited by Carlos María de Bustamante. 1577. Reprint, Mexico City: Imprenta del ciudadano Alejandro Valdés, calle de Santo Domingo y esquina de Tacuba, 1829.

Science News Letter. "For Red Men Only." June 17, 1933, 374–75, 382.

———. "Peyote Button Induces Religious Fervor." September 20, 1930, 188.

Seymour, Gertrude. "Peyote Worship: An Indian Cult and a Powerful Drug." *The Survey* 36, no. 7 (May 13, 1916): 181–84.

Slosson, Preston William. *The Great Crusade and After, 1914–1928.* New York: Macmillan, 1935.

State v. Big Sheep. 75 Mont. 219, 243 P. 1067 (1926).

Swanton, John. "James Mooney." *American Anthropologist* 24, no. 2 (April–June 1922): 209–14.

Territory of Oklahoma Session Laws of 1899 Passed at the Fifth Regular Session of the Legislative Assembly of the Territory of Oklahoma. Guthrie, OK: State Capital Printing, 1899.

Twentieth Century History of Southwest Texas. Vol. 2. Chicago: Lewis, 1907.

United States Congress. House. *Peyote Hearings before a Subcommittee of the Committee on Indian Affairs of the House of Representatives on H.R. 2614.* 2 vol. 65th Cong., 2nd sess. Washington, DC: Government Printing Office, 1918.

United States Statutes at Large 24:388–91; 27:260; 29:506.

Welsh, Herbert. *Peyote—An Insidious Evil.* Philadelphia: Indian Rights Association, 1918.

Wiley, Harvey W. "Peyote." *American Indian Magazine* 7, no. 1 (Spring 1919): 37–42.

Wright, Hamilton. *Report on the International Opium Commission and on the Opium Problem as Seen within the United States and Its Possessions.* 61st Cong., 2nd sess., February 21, 1910, S. Doc. 377.

BOOKS AND ARTICLES

Aberle, David F. *The Peyote Religion among the Navaho.* Chicago: Aldine, 1966.

Adams, David Wallace. *Education for Extinction: American Indians and the Boarding School Experience, 1875–1928.* Lawrence: University Press of Kansas, 1995.

Adams, John A., Jr. *Conflict and Commerce on the Rio Grande: Laredo, 1755–1955.* College Station: Texas A&M Press, 2008.

Adkison, Danny M. "Oklahoma Constitution." In *Encyclopedia of Oklahoma History and Culture.* www.okhistory.org.

Adovasio, J. M., and G. F. Fry. "Prehistoric Psychotropic Drug Use in Northeastern Mexico and Trans-Pecos Texas." *Economic Botany* 30, no. 1 (1976): 94–96.

Ahlstrom, Sydney E. *A Religious History of the American People.* New Haven, CT: Yale University Press, 1972.

Akers, Brian P. "Peyote and Peyotism." Master's thesis, Western Michigan University, 1986.

Albanese, Catherine. *America: Religions and Religion.* 4th ed. Belmont, CA: Thomson/Wadsworth, 2007.

Alcoff, Linda Martin. *The Future of Whiteness.* Cambridge: Polity Press, 2015.

Allen, Chadwick. "Introduction: Locating the Society of American Indians." *Studies in American Indian Literature* 25, no. 2/*American Indian Quarterly* 37, no. 3 (Summer 2013): 3–22.

Allen, Theodore. *The Invention of the White Race*. Vol. 1, *Racial Oppression and Social Control*. New York: Verso Books, 1994.
Anderson, Edward F. *Peyote: The Divine Cactus*. Tucson: University of Arizona Press, 1980.
Appiah, Kwame Anthony, and Henry Louis Gates Jr., eds. *Identities*. Chicago: University of Chicago Press, 1995.
Arnal, William E., and Russell T. McCutcheon. *The Sacred Is the Profane: The Political Nature of "Religion."* New York: Oxford University Press, 2013.
Arreola, Daniel D. *Postcards from the Río Bravo Border: Picturing the Place, Placing the Picture, 1900s–1950s*. Austin: University of Texas Press, 2013.
Baird, Robert. "Going Indian: Discovery, Adoption, and Renaming toward a 'True American,' from *Deerslayer* to *Dances with Wolves*." In Bird, *Dressing in Feathers*, 195–209.
Baker, Lee D. *Anthropology and the Racial Politics of Culture*. Durham, NC: Duke University Press, 2010.
Bannon, John Thomas, Jr. "The Legality of the Religious Use of Peyote by the Native American Church: A Commentary on the Free Exercise, Equal Protection, and Establishment Issues Raised by the Peyote Way Church of God Case." *American Indian Law Review* 22, no. 2 (1997/1998): 475–507.
Barkan, Elliott R., Rudolph J. Vecoli, Richard D. Alba, and Oliver Zunz. "Race, Religion, and Nationality in American Society: A Model of Ethnicity; From Contact to Assimilation (with Comment, with Response)." *Journal of American Ethnic History* 14, no. 2 (Winter 1995): 38–101.
Barnett, Lisa D. "Policing Peyote Country in the Early Twentieth Century." In *Border Policing: A History of Enforcement and Evasion in North America*, edited by Holly M. Karibo and George T. Díaz, 147–62. Austin: University of Texas Press, 2020.
Barr, Juliana. "Geographies of Power: Mapping Indian Borders in the 'Borderlands' of the Early Southwest." *William and Mary Quarterly* 68, no. 1 (January 2011): 5–46.
———. *Peace Came in the Form of a Woman: Indians and Spaniards in the Texas Borderlands*. Chapel Hill: University of North Carolina Press, 2007.
Barrett, James R., and David Roediger. "How White People Became White." In Delgado and Stefancic, *Critical White Studies*, 402–6.
Barsh, Russel Lawrence. "Progressive-Era Bureaucrats and the Unity of Twentieth-Century Indian Policy." *American Indian Quarterly* 15, no. 1 (Winter 1991): 1–17.
———. "The Supreme Court, Peyote, and Minority Religions: Zero Tolerance." *Wicazo Sa Review* 7, no. 2 (Autumn 1991): 49–52.
Bass, Althea. *The Arapaho Way: A Memoir of an Indian Boyhood*. New York: Clarkson Potter, 1966.
———. "James Mooney in Oklahoma." *Chronicles of Oklahoma* 32, no. 2 (1954): 246–62.
Baumgartner, Holly R. "De-Assimilation as the Need to Tell: Native American Writers, Bakhtin, and Autobiography." In *American Indian Rhetorics of Survivance: Word Medicine, Word Magic*, edited by Ernest Stromberg, 131–47. Pittsburgh: University of Pittsburgh Press, 2006.
Beaver, R. Pierce. "The Churches and President Grant's Peace Policy." *Journal of Church and State* 4, no. 2 (November 1962): 174–90.

Bee, Robert L. "Peyotism in North American Indian Groups." *Transactions of the Kansas Academy of Science* 68, no. 1 (Spring 1965): 13–61.
———. "Potawatomi Peyotism: The Influence of Traditional Patterns." *Southwestern Journal of Anthropology* 22, no. 2 (Summer 1966): 194–205.
Benton-Cohen, Katherine. *Borderline Americans: Racial Division and Labor War in the Arizona Borderlands*. Cambridge, MA: Harvard University Press, 2009.
Berg, S. Carol. "Arthur C. Parker and the Society of the American Indian, 1911–1916." *New York History* 81, no. 2 (April 2000): 237–46.
Berger, Peter L. *The Sacred Canopy: Elements of a Sociological Theory of Religion*. Garden City, NY: Doubleday, 1967. Reprint, New York: Archer Books, 1990.
Berger, Peter L., and Thomas Luckmann. *The Social Construction of Reality: A Treatise in the Sociology of Knowledge*. Garden City, NY: Doubleday, 1966.
Berkhofer, Robert F., Jr. *The White Man's Indian: Images of the American Indian from Columbus to the Present*. New York: Knopf, 1978.
Berthrong, Donald J. *The Cheyenne and Arapaho Ordeal: Reservation and Agency Life in the Indian Territory, 1875–1907*. Norman: University of Oklahoma Press, 1976.
Beyer, Stephen V. *Singing to the Plants: A Guide to Mestizo Shamanism in the Upper Amazon*. Albuquerque: University of New Mexico Press, 2010.
Bird, S. Elizabeth, ed. *Dressing in Feathers: The Construction of the Indian in American Popular Culture*. Boulder, CO: Westview Press, 1996.
———. "Introduction: Constructing the Indian, 1830s–1990s." In Bird, *Dressing in Feathers*, 1–12.
Birt, Robert E. "The Bad Faith of Whiteness." In Yancy, *What White Looks Like*, 55–64.
Black, Jason Edward. *American Indians and the Rhetoric of Removal and Allotment*. Jackson: University Press of Mississippi, 2015.
———. "Native Resistive Rhetoric and the Decolonization of American Indian Removal Discourse." *Quarterly Journal of Speech* 95, no. 1 (February 2009): 66–88.
Blackhawk, Ned. *Violence over the Land: Indians and Empires in the Early American West*. Cambridge, MA: Harvard University Press, 2008.
"Blalock Mexico Colony–People." The Blalock Mexico Project, 2010, http://blalockmexicocolony.org/bmc/people/colonists_pages/blalock_george.html.
Bonnie, Richard J., and Charles H. Whitehead II. *The Marihuana Conviction: History of Marihuana Prohibition in the United States*. Charlottesville: University of Virginia Press, 1974.
Bordin, Ruth. *Woman and Temperance: The Quest for Power and Liberty, 1873–1900*. Philadelphia: Temple University Press, 1981.
Boyd, Carolyn E. "Pictographic Evidence of Peyotism in the Lower Pecos, Texas Archaic." In *The Archaeology of Rock-Art*, edited by Christopher Chippendale and Paul Tacon, 227–46. Cambridge: Cambridge University Press, 1998.
Brant, Charles S. "Peyotism among the Kiowa-Apache and Neighboring Tribes." *Southwestern Journal of Anthropology* 6, no. 2 (Summer 1950): 212–22.
Brekus, Catherine A., and W. Clark Gilpin. "Introduction." In *American Christianities: A History of Dominance and Diversity*, edited by Catherine A. Brekus and W. Clark Gilpin, 1–24. Chapel Hill: University of North Carolina Press, 2011.

Brito, Silvester John. "The Development and Change of the Peyote Ceremony through Time and Space." PhD diss., Indiana University, 1975.

Britten, Thomas A. *American Indians in World War I: At Home and at War*. Albuquerque: University of New Mexico Press, 1997.

Brown, Linda Joyce. *The Literature of Immigration and Racial Formation: Becoming White, Becoming Other, Becoming American in the Late Progressive Era*. New York: Routledge, 2004.

Bruhn, Jan G., J. E. Lindgren, B. Homstedt, and J. M. Adovasio. "Peyote Alkaloids: Identification in a Prehistoric Specimen of *Lophophora* from Coahuila, Mexico." *Science* 199, no. 4336 (1978): 1437–38.

Bukowczyk, John J., Nora Faires, David R. Smith, and Randy William Widdis, eds. *Permeable Border: The Great Lakes Basin as Transnational Region, 1650–1990*. Pittsburg: University of Pittsburgh Press, 2005.

Butler, Judith. *Gender Trouble: Feminism and the Subversion of Identity*. New York: Routledge, 1990. Reprint, 1999.

Calabrese, Joseph D. "Reflexivity and Transformation Symbolism in the Navajo Peyote Meeting." *Ethos* 22, no. 4 (1994): 494–527.

———. "Spiritual Healing and Human Development in the Native American Church: Toward a Cultural Psychiatry of Peyote." *Psychoanalytic Review* 84, no. 2 (April 1997): 235–55.

———. "The Supreme Court versus Peyote: Consciousness Alteration, Cultural Psychiatry, and the Dilemma of Contemporary Subcultures." *Anthropology of Consciousness* 12, no. 2 (2001): 4–19.

Calloway, Colin G. *First Peoples: A Documentary Survey of American Indian History*. 4th ed. Boston: Bedford/St. Martin's, 2012.

Campbell, Gregory. "Indian Reservations." In *Dictionary of American History*, 3rd ed., vol. 4, edited by Stanley I. Kutle, 297–302. New York: Charles Scribner's Sons, 2003.

Carey, Elaine, and Andrae M. Marak, eds. *Smugglers, Brothels, and Twine: Historical Perspectives on Contraband and Vice in North America's Borderlands*. Tucson: University of Arizona Press, 2011.

Carpenter, Carl. "Detecting Indianness: Gertrude Bonnin's Investigation of Native American Identity." *Wicazo Sa Review* 20, no. 1 (Spring 2005): 139–59.

Catches, Vincent. "Native American Church: The Half-Moon Way." *Wicazo Sa Review* 7, no. 1 (Spring 1991): 17–24.

Chambers, John Whiteclay II. *The Tyranny of Change: America in the Progressive Era, 1900–1917*. New York: St. Martin's Press, 1980.

Chaney, Colt. "Quanah Parker and Comanche Culture: Divided Loyalties." Master's thesis, Southwestern Oklahoma State University, 2012.

Clark, David Anthony Tyeeme. "Representing Indians: Indigenous Fugitives and the Society of American Indians in the Making of Common Culture." PhD diss., University of Kansas, 2004.

"Class Legislation." In *Black's Law Dictionary Free Online Legal Dictionary*. 2nd ed. http://thelawdictionary.org/class-legislation/.

Cline, S. L. "Revisionist Conquest History: Sahagún's Book XII." In *The Work of Bernardino de Sahagún: Pioneer Ethnographer of Sixteenth-Century Aztec Mexico*, vol. 2, edited by Jorge Klor de Alva, 93–106. Albany: State University of New York, 1988.

Cohen, Bronwen J. "Nativism and Western Myth: The Influence of Nativist Ideas on the American Self-Image." *Journal of American Studies* 8, no. 1 (April 1974): 23–39.

Collier, John. "The Peyote Cult." *Science* 115, no. 2992 (May 2, 1952): 503–4.

Comanche National Museum and Cultural Center Facebook page. https://www.facebook.com/ComancheMuseum.

Córdova, James M. "Drinking the Fifth Cup: Notes on the Drunken Indian Image in Colonial Mexico." *Word and Image: A Journal of Verbal and Visual Enquiry* 31, no. 1 (January–March 2015): 189–218.

Corrigan, John, and Winthrop S. Hudson. *Religion in America: An Historical Account of the Development of American Religious Life*. 7th ed. Upper Saddle River, NJ: Pearson-Prentice Hall, 2004.

Courtwright, David T. *Dark Paradise: A History of Opiate Addiction in America*. Cambridge, MA: Harvard University Press, 2001.

———. *Forces of Habit: Drugs and the Making of the Modern World*. Cambridge, MA: Harvard University Press, 2011.

Curtis, Heather D. "Community." In Porterfield and Corrigan, *Religion in American History*, 210–28.

Daily, David W. "About G. E. E. Lindquist." In G. E. E. Lindquist Native American Photographs, the Burke Library Archives at Union Theological Seminary, Columbia University, New York. https://lindquist.cul.columbia.edu/about_gee_lindquist.

———. *Battle for the BIA: G. E. E. Lindquist and the Missionary Crusade Against John Collier*. Tucson: University of Arizona Press, 2004.

Dale, Edward Everett. "Old Navajoe." *Chronicles of Oklahoma* 24, no. 2 (1946): 128–45.

Davis, Marni. *Jews and Booze: Becoming American in the Age of Prohibition*. New York: New York University Press, 2012.

Dawson, Alexander S. "Peyote in the Colonial Imagination." In Labate and Cavnar, *Peyote*, 43–62.

———. *The Peyote Effect: From the Inquisition to the War on Drugs*. Oakland: University of California Press, 2018.

Delgado, Richard, and Jean Stefancic, eds. *Critical White Studies: Looking behind the Mirror*. Philadelphia: Temple University Press, 1997.

Deloria, Philip J. "From Nation to Neighborhood." In *The Cultural Turn in US History: Past, Present, and Future*, edited by James W. Cook, Lawrence B. Glickman, and Michael O'Malley, 343–82. Chicago: University of Chicago Press, 2008.

———. *Indians in Unexpected Places*. Lawrence: University Press of Kansas, 2004.

———. *Playing Indian*. New Haven, CT: Yale University Press, 1998.

———. "Playing Indian: Otherness and Authenticity in the Assumption of American Indian Identity." PhD diss., Yale University, 1994.

Deloria, Vine, Jr., and Clifford M. Lytle. *The Nations Within: The Past and Future of American Indian Sovereignty*. New York: Pantheon Books, 1984.

Dewey, Alicia M. *Pesos and Dollars: Entrepreneurs in the Texas-Mexico Borderlands, 1880–1940.* College Station: Texas A&M University Press, 2014.

Díaz, George T. *Border Contraband: A History of Smuggling across the Rio Grande.* Austin: University of Texas Press, 2015.

Dominguez, Susan Rose. "The Gertrude Bonnin Story: From Yankton Destiny into American History, 1804–1928." PhD diss., Michigan State University, 2005.

Douglas, Mary. *Purity and Danger: An Analysis of Concepts of Pollution and Taboo.* New York: Frederick A. Praeger, 1966.

Driscoll, Christopher M. *White Lies: Race and Uncertainty in the Twilight of American Religion.* New York: Routledge, 2016.

Dubuisson, Daniel. *The Western Construction of Religion: Myths, Knowledge, and Ideology.* Baltimore, MD: Johns Hopkins University Press, 2003.

Duran, Bonnie. "Indigenous versus Colonial Discourse: Alcohol and American Indian Identity." In Bird, *Dressing in Feathers*, 111–28.

Duster, Troy. *The Legislation of Morality.* New York: Free Press, 1970.

Dustin, C. Burton. *Peyotism and New Mexico.* Santa Fe: Vergara, 1960.

DuVal, Kathleen. *The Native Ground: Indians and Colonists in the Heart of the Continent.* Philadelphia: University of Pennsylvania Press, 2007.

Edelman, Murray. *Constructing the Political Spectacle.* Chicago: University of Chicago Press, 1988.

Eliade, Mircea. *The Sacred and the Profane.* Translated by Willard R. Task. New York: Harcourt, Brace, 1959.

Elliott, Anthony. "Editor's Introduction." *Routledge Handbook of Identity Studies.* London: Routledge, 2011.

Ellis, Clyde. *A Dancing People: Powwow Culture on the Southern Plains.* Lawrence: University Press of Kansas, 2013.

———. "American Indians and Christianity." In *The Encyclopedia of Oklahoma History and Culture.* www.okhistory.org.

Emmons, David M. *Beyond the American Pale: The Irish in the West, 1845–1910.* Norman: University of Oklahoma Press, 2010.

Encyclopedia of Southern Jewish Communities. Goldring-Woldenberg Institute of Southern Jewish Life, 2014. http://www.isjl.org/texas-laredo-encyclopedia.html.

Epps, Garrett. *Peyote vs. the State: Religious Freedom on Trial.* Norman: University of Oklahoma Press, 2009.

Evans, Sterling, ed. *The Borderlands of the American and Canadian Wests: Essays on Regional History of the Forty-Ninth Parallel.* Lincoln: University of Nebraska Press, 2006.

Feeney, Kevin. "Peyote, Conservation, and Indian Rights in the United States." In Labate and Cavnar, *Peyote*, 105–28.

Fields, Barbara J. "Ideology and Race in American History." In *Region, Race, and Reconstruction: Essays in Honor of C. Vann Woodward*, edited by J. Morgan Kousser and James M. McPherson, 143–77. New York: Oxford University Press, 1982.

Fields, Karen E., and Barbara J. Fields. *Racecraft: The Soul of Inequality in American Life.* New York: Verso, 2012.

Fisher, Andrew B., and Matthew D. O'Hara, ed. *Imperial Subjects: Race and Identity in Colonial Latin America*. Durham, NC: Duke University Press, 2009.

Fisher, Louis. "Statutory Exemptions for Religious Freedom." *Journal of Church and State* 44, no. 2 (Spring 2002): 291–316.

Foreman, Paul. *Quanah the Serpent Eagle*. Flagstaff, AZ: Northland Press, 1983.

Forren, John P. "State and Federal Legal Protections for Peyote Use in the United States." In Labate and Cavnar, *Peyote*, 85–104.

Foster, John D. *White Race Discourse: Preserving Racial Privilege in a Post-Racial Society*. Lanham, MD: Lexington Books, 2013.

Foster, Morris W. *Being Comanche: A Social History of an American Indian Community*. Tucson: University of Arizona Press, 1991.

Foucault, Michel. *The Birth of the Clinic: An Archaeology of Medical Perception*. New York: Pantheon, 1973.

———. *Discipline and Punish: The Birth of the Prison*. New York: Random House, 1977.

———. *The History of Sexuality*. Vol. 1, *An Introduction*. New York: Random House, 1978.

———. *Madness and Civilization: A History of Insanity in the Age of Reason*. New York: Random House, 1965.

Frankenberg, Ruth. *White Women, Race Matters: The Social Construction of Whiteness*. Minneapolis: University of Minnesota Press, 1993.

Franklin, Jimmie Lewis. *Born Sober: Prohibition in Oklahoma, 1907–1959*. Norman: University of Oklahoma Press, 1971.

French, Laurence Armand. *Policing American Indians: A Unique Chapter in American Jurisprudence*. Boca Raton, FL: CRC Press, 2016.

———. "Psychoactive Agents and Native American Spirituality: Past and Present." *Contemporary Justice Review* 11, no. 2 (June 2008): 155–63.

Fritz, Henry E. "The Last Hurrah of Christian Humanitarian Indian Reform: The Board of Indian Commissioners, 1909–1918." *Western History Quarterly* 16, no. 2 (April 1985): 147–62.

———. "The Making of Grant's 'Peace Policy.'" *The Chronicles of Oklahoma* 37, no. 4 (1959): 411–32.

Fuller, Robert C. "Cosmology." In Porterfield and Corrigan, *Religion in American History*, 190–209.

———. *Stairways to Heaven: Drugs in American Religious History*. Boulder, CO: Westview Press, 2000.

Furnish, Patricia Lee. "'Aboriginally Yours': The Society of American Indians and U.S. Citizenship, 1890–1924." PhD diss., University of Oklahoma, 2005.

Furst, Peter T. *Rock Crystals and Peyote Dreams: Explorations in the Huichol Universe*. Salt Lake City: University of Utah Press, 2006.

Gage, Justin. *We Do Not Want the Gates Closed between Us: Native Networks and the Spread of the Ghost Dance*. Norman: University of Oklahoma Press, 2020.

Gahlinger, Peter M. *Illegal Drugs: A Complete Guide to Their History, Chemistry, Use, and Abuse*. New York: Plume, 2004.

Garrett, David. "Vine of the Dead: Reviving Equal Protection Rites for Religious Drug Use." *American Indian Law Review* 31, no. 1 (2006/2007): 143–62.

Garrity, John F. "Jesus, Peyote, and the Holy People: Alcohol Abuse and the Ethos of Power in Navajo Healing." *Medical Anthropology Quarterly* 14, no. 4 (December 2000): 521–42.

Garroutte, Eva Marie. *Real Indians: Identity and the Survival of Native America*. Berkeley: University of California Press, 2003.

Garza, Beatriz de la. *A Law for the Lion: A Tale of Crime and Injustice in the Borderlands*. Austin: University of Texas Press, 2003.

Gates, E. Nathaniel., ed. *Racial Classification and History*. Critical Race Theory: Essays on the Social Construction and Reproduction of "Race." New York: Garland, 1997.

Geertz, Clifford. *The Interpretation of Cultures*. New York: Basic Books, 1973.

Gerteis, Joseph, and Alyssa Goolsby. "Nationalism in America: The Case of the Populist Movement." *Theory and Society* 34, no. 2 (April 2005): 197–225.

Gieringer, Dale H. "The Origins of Cannabis Prohibition in California." In *Contemporary Drug Problems*, 2–36. New York: Federal Legal Publications, 1999.

Gillett, Todd M. "The Absolution of Reynolds: The Constitutionality of Religious Polygamy." *William and Mary Bill of Rights Journal* 8, no. 2 (2000): 497–534.

Goldschmidt, Henry. "Introduction: Race, Nation, and Religion." In *Race, Nation, and Religion in the Americas*, edited by Henry Goldschmidt and Elizabeth McAlister, 3–31. New York: Oxford University Press, 2004.

Goode, Erich, and Nachman Ben-Yehuda. "Moral Panics: Culture, Politics, and Social Construction." *Annual Review of Sociology* 20 (1994): 149–71.

———. *Moral Panics: The Social Construction of Deviance*. 2nd ed. Cambridge, MA: Wiley-Blackwell, 2009.

Gordon, Sarah Barringer. *The Mormon Question: Polygamy and Constitutional Conflict in Nineteenth-Century America*. Chapel Hill: University of North Carolina Press, 2002.

Grant, Ted. "Meet Ted Grant, Vice-Chairman of the Otoe-Missouria Tribe." August 22, 2014. The National Museum of the American Indian [blog]. http://blog.nmai.si.edu/main/2014/08/meet-native-america-ted-grant.html.

Green, Rayna Green. "The Tribe Called Wannabee: Playing Indian in America and Europe." *Folklore* 99, no. 1 (1988): 30–55.

Green, Stanley C. *A History of Laredo's Jewish Community*. Laredo: Webb County Heritage Foundation, 1992.

Greil, Arthur L., and David G. Bromley, eds. *Defining Religion: Investigating the Boundaries Between the Sacred and the Secular*. Kidlington, Oxford, UK: Elsevier Science, 2003.

———. "Introduction." In Greil and Bromley, *Defining Religion*, 3–17.

Grob, Charles S. "Psychiatric Research with Hallucinogens: What Have We Learned?" *The Heffter Review of Psychedelic Research* 1 (1998): 8–20.

Gusfield, Joseph R. *Symbolic Crusade: Status Politics and the American Temperance Movement*. Urbana: University of Illinois Press, 1963.

Gusinde, Martin. *Der Peyote-Kult, Entstehung und Verbreitung*. Vienna, Austria: Druck der Missionsdruckerei St Gabriel, 1939.

Gwyne, S. C. *Empire of the Summer Moon: Quanah Parker and the Rise and Fall of the Comanches, the Most Powerful Indian Tribe in American History*. New York: Scribner, 2010.

Hafen, P. Jane. "'Help Indians Help Themselves': Gertrude Bonnin, the SAI, and the NCAI." *Studies in American Indian Literature* 25, no. 2 (2013): 199–218.
———. "Zitkala-Ša: Sentimentality and Sovereignty." *Wicazo Sa Review* 12, no. 2 (Autumn 1997): 31–41.
Hagan, William T. *Indian Police and Judges.* New Haven, CT: Yale University Press, 1966.
———. *Quanah Parker, Comanche Chief.* Norman: University of Oklahoma Press, 1993.
Hale, Grace Elizabeth. *Making Whiteness: The Culture of Segregation in the South, 1890–1940.* New York: Pantheon Books, 1998.
Halttunen, Karen. *Confidence Men and Painted Women: A Study of Middle-Class Culture in America, 1830–1870.* New Haven, CT: Yale University Press, 1982.
Hämäläinen, Pekka. *The Comanche Empire.* New Haven, CT: Yale University Press, 2008.
Hamill, James. *Going Indian.* Urbana: University of Illinois Press, 2006.
Hampton, Carol McDonald. "American Indian Religion under Assault: Opposition to the Peyote Faith." PhD diss., University of Oklahoma, 1984.
Hanan, Josh. "Communicating with the Divine: The Role of Peyote in Native American Health and Spirituality." Paper presented at the annual meeting of the NCA 93rd Annual Convention, TBA, Chicago, IL, November 15, 2007. Accessed March 12, 2011. http://www.allacademic.com/meta/p188231_index.html.
Haney-López, Ian F. "Social Construction of Race: Some Observations on Illusion, Fabrication, and Choice." *Harvard Civil Rights–Civil Liberties Law Review* 29, no. 1 (1994): 1–62.
———. *White by Law: The Legal Construction of Race.* New York: New York University Press, 1996.
Hanson, Jeffery R. "Ethnicity and the Looking Glass: The Dialectics of National Indian Identity." *American Indian Quarterly* 21, no. 2 (Spring 1997): 195–208.
Harris, Cheryl I. "Whiteness as Property." *Harvard Law Review* 106, no. 8 (June 1993): 1707–91.
Hartigan, John, Jr. *Odd Tribes: Toward a Cultural Analysis of White People.* Durham, NC: Duke University Press, 2005.
Hatch, Nathan O. *The Democratization of American Christianity.* New Haven, CT: Yale University Press, 1989.
Hayes, Alden. "Peyote Cult on the Goshiute Reservation at Deep Creek, Utah." *New Mexico Anthropologist* 4, no. 2 (April–June 1940): 34–36.
Hayward, Clarissa Rile. *How Americans Make Race: Stories, Institutions, Spaces.* New York: Cambridge University Press, 2013.
Headley, Clevis. "Delegitimizing the Normativity of 'Whiteness': A Critical Africana Philosophical Study of the Metaphoricity of 'Whiteness.'" In Yancy, *What White Looks Like,* 87–106.
Herbrechtsmeier, William. "The Burden of the Axial Age: Transcendentalism in Religion as a Function of Empire." In Greil and Bromley, *Defining Religion,* 109–26.
Hernández, Kelly Lytle. *Migra: A History of the US Border Patrol.* Berkeley: University of California Press, 2010.
Hertzberg, Hazel W. *The Search for an American Indian Identity: Modern Pan-Indian Movements.* Syracuse: Syracuse University Press, 1971.

Hinojosa, Servando Z. "Human-Peyote Interaction in South Texas." *Culture & Agriculture* 22, no. 1 (Spring 2000): 29–36.

"History–Court of Indian Offenses." US Department of the Interior, Indian Affairs. https://www.bia.gov/WhoWeAre/RegionalOffices/SouthernPlains/WeAre/ciospr/index.htm.

Hoge, Dean R., and Ella I Smith. "Normative and Non-Normative Religious Experience among High School Youth." *Sociological Analysis* 43, no. 1 (Spring 1982): 69–82.

Holloway, Elena. "Independent Club." *Handbook of Texas Online*. http://www.tshaonline.org/handbook/online/articles/wmiqt.

Holm, Tom. *The Great Confusion in Indian Affairs: Native Americans and Whites in the Progressive Era*. Austin: University of Texas Press, 2005.

hooks, bell [Gloria Watkins]. *Talking Back: thinking feminist, thinking black*. Boston: South End Press, 1989.

Hopkins, Dwight N. *Being Human: Race, Culture, and Religion*. Minneapolis: Fortress Press, 2005.

Hopkins, Kenneth N. "Peyotism and the Otoe-Missouria Indians of Oklahoma." *Oklahoma State Historical Review* 3 (Spring 1982): 1–28.

Horsman, Reginald. *Race and Manifest Destiny: The Origins of American Racial Anglo-Saxonism*. Cambridge, MA: Harvard University Press, 1981.

Howard, James H. "An Oto-Omaha Peyote Ritual." *Southwestern Journal of Anthropology* 12, no. 4 (Winter 1956): 432–36.

Hoxie, Frederick E. "Exploring a Cultural Borderland: Native American Journeys of Discovery in the Early Twentieth Century." *The Journal of American History* 79, no. 3 (December 1992): 969–95.

Hughey, Michael W. "Americanism and Its Discontents: Protestantism, Nativism, and Political Heresy in America." *International Journal of Politics* 5, no. 4 (Summer 1992): 533–53.

Huhndorf, Shari M. *Going Native: Indians in the American Cultural Imagination*. Ithaca, NY: Cornell University Press, 2001.

Hultkrantz, Åke. *Belief and Worship in Native North America*. Syracuse: Syracuse University Press, 1981.

Ignatiev, Noel. *How the Irish Became White*. New York: Routledge, 1995.

"Indian Law Enforcement History." Bureau of Indian Affairs Law Enforcement Services, 13. http://web.archive.org/web/20000226013721/bialaw.fedworld.gov/history/index.htm.

Irwin, Lee. *Coming Down from Above: Prophecy, Resistance, and Renewal in Native American Religions*. Norman: University of Oklahoma Press, 2008.

———. "Freedom, Law, and Prophecy: A Brief History of Native American Religious Resistance." *American Indian Quarterly* 21, no. 1 (Winter 1997): 35–55.

Ishii, Izumi. *Bad Fruits of the Civilized Tree: Alcohol and the Sovereignty of the Cherokee Nation*. Lincoln: University of Nebraska Press, 2008.

Jakobsen, Janet R., and Ann Pellegrini, eds. *Secularisms*. Durham, NC: Duke University Press, 2008.

James, William. *Varieties of Religious Experience: A Study in Human Nature*. Centenary Edition. New York: Routledge, 2002.

Janis, Ely M. "The Irish National Land League in the United States and Ireland: Nationalism, Gender, and Ethnicity in the Gilded Age." PhD diss., Boston College, 2008.

Johnson, Benjamin H. *Revolution in Texas: How a Forgotten Rebellion and Its Bloody Suppression Turned Mexicans into Americans.* New Haven, CT: Yale University Press, 2003.

Johnson, Benjamin, and Andrew R. Graybill, eds. *Bridging National Borders in North America: Transnational and Comparative Histories.* Durham, NC: Duke University Press, 2010.

Johnson, David L., and Raymond Wilson. "Gertrude Simmons Bonnin, 1876–1938: 'Americanize the First American.'" *American Indian Quarterly* 12, no. 1 (Winter 1988): 27–40.

Jones, Nancy Baker. "Villegas De Magnon, Leonor." *Handbook of Texas Online*. http://www.tshaonline.org/handbook/online/articles/fvi19.

Jones, Peter N. "The American Indian Church and Its Sacramental Use of Peyote: A Review for Professionals in the Mental-Health Arena." *Mental Health, Religion & Culture* 8, no. 4 (December 2005): 277–90.

———. "The Native American Church, Peyote, and Health: Expanding Consciousness for Healing Purposes." *Contemporary Justice Review* 10, no. 4 (December 2007): 411–25.

Kantrowitz, Stephen. "'Citizen's Clothing': Reconstruction, Ho-Chunk Persistence, and the Politics of Dress." In *Civil War Wests: Testing the Limits of the United States*, edited by Adam Arenson and Andrew Graybill, 242–64. Berkeley: University of California Press, 2015.

Karst, Kenneth L. "Paths to Belonging: The Constitution and Cultural Identity." In Delgado and Stefancic, *Critical White Studies*, 407–13.

Kavanagh, Thomas W. "Southern Plains Dance: Tradition and Dynamics." In *Native American Dance: Ceremonies and Social Traditions*, edited by Charlotte Heth, 105–24. Washington, DC: Smithsonian Institution Press, 1992.

Kelsey, George D. *Racism and the Christian Understanding of Man.* New York: Charles Scribner's Sons, 1965.

Kemper, Troxey. *Comanche Warbonnet: A Story of Quanah Parker.* Tsaile, AZ: Navajo Community College Press, 1991.

Kerr, K. Austin. *Organized for Prohibition: A New History of the Anti-Saloon League.* New Haven, CT: Yale University Press, 1985.

Kerstetter, Todd M. *Inspiration and Innovation: Religion in the American West.* Malden, MA: Wiley-Blackwell, 2015.

Klein, James E. *Grappling with Demon Rum: The Cultural Struggle over Liquor in Early Oklahoma.* Norman: University of Oklahoma Press, 2008.

Konrad, Victor. "The Borderlands of the United States and Canada in the Context of North American Development." *International Journal of Canadian Studies* 4 (Fall 1991): 77–95.

Kracht, Benjamin R. *Religious Revitalization among the Kiowas: The Ghost Dance, Peyote, and Christianity.* Lincoln: University of Nebraska Press, 2018.

Kte'pi, Bill. "Introduction." In *Handbook to Life in America.* Vol. 5, *The Age of Reform, 1890 to 1920*, edited by Rodney P. Carlisle, 1–16. New York: Facts on File, Infobase, 2009.

Kurst-Swanger, Karel. *Worship and Sin: An Exploration of Religion-Related Crime in the United States.* New York: Lang, 2008.

La Barre, Weston. "Kiowa Folk Sciences." *Journal of American Folklore* 60, no. 236 (April–June 1947): 105–14.

———. "Materials for a History of Studies of Crisis Cults: A Bibliographic Essay." *Current Anthropology* 12, no. 1 (1971): 3–44.
———. *The Peyote Cult*. Hamden, CT: Shoe String Press, 1959.
———. "Primitive Psychotherapy in Native American Cultures: Peyotism and Confession." *The Journal of Abnormal and Social Psychology* 42, no. 3 (1947): 294–309.
———. "Twenty Years of Peyote Studies." *Current Anthropology* 1, no. 1 (January 1960): 45–60.
La Barre, Weston, David P. McAllester, J. S. Slotkin, Omer C. Stewart, and Sol Tax. "Statement on Peyote." *Science* 114, no. 2970 (November 30, 1951): 582–83.
Labate, Beatriz Caiuby, and Clancy Cavnar, eds. *Peyote: History, Tradition, Politics, and Conservation*. Santa Barbara, CA: Greenwood, 2015.
La Farge, Oliver. "Defining Peyote as a Narcotic." *American Anthropologist* 62, no. 4 (August 1960): 687–98.
LaGrand, James B. "The Changing 'Jesus Road': Protestants Reappraise American Indian Missions in the 1920s and 1930s." *The Western Historical Quarterly* 27, no. 4 (Winter 1996): 479–504.
Lake, Randall A. "Between Myth and History: Enacting Time in Native American Protest Rhetoric." *The Quarterly Journal of Speech* 77, no. 2 (May 1991): 123–51.
Latorre, Felipe A., and Dolores L. Latorre. *The Mexican Kickapoo Indians*. New York: Dover 1976.
Lecker, Robert, ed. *Borderlands: Essays in Canadian-American Relations*. Toronto: ECW Press, 1991.
Lee, Daniel B. "A Great Racial Commission: Religion and the Construction of White America." In *Race, Nation, and Religion in the Americas*, edited by Henry Goldschmidt and Elizabeth McAlister, 85–110. New York: Oxford University Press, 2004.
Lee, Erika. "Enforcing the Borders: Chinese Exclusion along the US Borders with Canada and Mexico, 1882–1924." *Journal of American History* 89, no. 1 (2002): 54–86.
Leland, Joy. *The Firewater Myths*. New Brunswick, NJ: Rutgers University Press, 1976.
Leonard, Irving A. "Peyote and the Mexican Inquisition, 1620." *American Anthropologist* 44, no. 2 (April–June 1942): 324–26.
Levario, Miguel Antonio. *Militarizing the Border: When Mexicans Became the Enemy*. College Station: Texas A&M University Press, 2012.
Levy, Jerrold, and Stephen Kunitz. *Indian Drinking*. New York: John Wiley & Sons, 1974.
Lewandowski, Tadeusz. *Red Bird, Red Power: The Life and Legacy of Zitkala-Ša*. Norman: University of Oklahoma Press, 2016.
Lewis, Laura A. *Hall of Mirrors: Power, Witchcraft, and Caste in Colonial Mexico*. Durham, NC: Duke University Press, 2003.
Lewis, Thomas H. *The Medicine Men: Oglala Sioux Ceremony and Healing*. Lincoln: University of Nebraska Press, 1990.
Lindheim, Bessie. "Leonor Villegas Magnon and the Mexican Revolution." In *The Story of Laredo (Volumes 10–18)*, edited by Stan Green, 100–120. Laredo, TX: Border Studies, 1991.
Linton, Ralph. "The Comanche Sun Dance." *American Anthropologist* 37, no. 3 (July–September 1935): 420–28.
———. "Nativistic Movements." *American Anthropologist* 45, no. 2 (1943): 230–41.

Lippy, Charles. "Politics." In Porterfield and Corrigan, *Religion in American History*, 249–65.
Lipsitz, George. *The Possessive Investment in Whiteness: How White People Profit from Identity Politics*. Philadelphia: Temple University Press, 2006.
Lisa, Laurie. "The Life Story of Zitkala-Ša/Gertrude Simmons Bonnin: Writing and Creating a Public Image." PhD diss., Arizona State University, 1996.
Lofton, Kathryn. "Cosmology." In Porterfield and Corrigan, *Religion in American History*, 266–84.
Lomawaima, K. Tsianina. "The Mutuality of *Citizenship* and *Sovereignty*: The Society of American Indians and the Battle to Inherit America." *Studies in American Indian Literature* 25, no. 2/*American Indian Quarterly* 37, no. 3 (Summer 2013): 333–51.
———. "The Society of American Indians." In *Oxford Research Encyclopedia of American History*. http://americanhistory.oxfordre.com/view/10.1093/acrefore/9780199329175.001.0001/acrefore-9780199329175-e-31.
Lopez-Austin, Alfredo. "The Research Method of Fray Bernardino de Sahagún: The Questionnaires." In *Sixteenth-Century Mexico: The Work of Sahagún*, edited by Munro S. Edmonson, 111–49. Albuquerque: University of New Mexico Press, 1974.
Lynch, Gordon, ed. *Between Sacred and Profane: Researching Religion and Popular Culture*. New York: I.B. Tauris, 2007.
Lyons, Scott Richard. *X-Marks: Native Signatures of Assent*. Minneapolis: University of Minnesota Press, 2010.
MacDonald, Mary N. "The Primitive, the Primal, and the Indigenous in the Study of Religion." *Journal of the American Academy of Religion* 79, no. 4 (December 2011): 814–26.
Madsen, Deborah L. "Introduction: Contemporary Discourses on 'Indianness.'" In *Native Authenticity: Transnational Perspectives on Native American Literary Studies*, edited by Deborah L. Madsen, 1–18. Albany: State University of New York Press, 2010.
Mahoney, Martha R. "The Social Construction of Whiteness." In Delgado and Stefancic, *Critical White Studies*, 330–33.
Maroukis, Thomas C. "The Peyote Controversy and the Demise of the Society of American Indians." *Studies in American Indian Literatures* 25, no. 2/*American Indian Quarterly* 37, no. 3 (Summer 2013): 161–80.
———. *The Peyote Road: Religious Freedom and the Native American Church*. Norman: University of Oklahoma Press, 2010.
Marsden, George M. *Religion and American Culture*. Orlando: Harcourt Brace Jovanovich, 1990.
Marston, Sallie A. "Adopted Citizens: Discourse and the Production of Meaning among Nineteenth Century American Urban Immigrants." *Transactions of the Institute of British Geographers* 14, no. 4 (1989): 435–45.
Martin, Jill E. "'The Greatest Evil': Interpretations of Indian Prohibition Laws, 1832–1953." *Great Plains Quarterly* 23, no. 1 (Winter 2003): 35–53.
Marty, Martin E. *Modern American Religion*. Vol. 1, *The Irony of It All, 1893–1919*. Chicago: University of Chicago Press, 1997.
———. *Pilgrims in Their Own Land*. Boston: Little, Brown, 1984.

———. *Righteous Empire: The Protestant Experience in America*. New York: The Dial Press, 1970.
Mathewson, Kent. "Drugs, Moral Geographies, and Indigenous Peoples: Some Initial Mappings and Central Issues." In *Dangerous Harvest: Drug Plants and the Transformation of Indigenous Landscapes*, edited by Michael K. Steinberg, Joseph J. Hobbs, and Kent Mathewson, 11–23. Oxford: Oxford University Press, 2004.
McCutcheon, Russell T. "The Category 'Religion' and the Politics of Tolerance." In Greil and Bromley, *Defining Religion*, 139–62.
McDonnell, Janet. *The Dispossession of the American Indian, 1887–1934*. Bloomington: Indiana University Press, 1991.
McGuire, Meredith B. "Contested Meanings and Definitional Boundaries: Historicizing the Sociology of Religion." In Greil and Bromley, *Defining Religion*, 127–38.
McKenna, Terence. *Food of the Gods: A Search for the Original Tree of Knowledge; A Radical History of Plants, Drugs, and Human Evolution*. New York: Bantam Books, 1992.
McKinsey, Lauren, and Victor Konrad. *Borderlands Reflections: The United States and Canada*. Orono: University of Maine, 1989.
McNickle, D'Arcy. "Peyote and the Indian." *Scientific Monthly* 57, no. 3 (September 1943): 220–29.
Mechling, Jay. "'Playing Indian' and the Search for Authenticity in Modern White America." In *Prospects: An Annual of American Cultural Studies*, vol. 5, edited by Jack Salzman, 17–33. New York: Burt Franklin, 1980.
Meeks, Eric V. *Border Citizens: The Making of Indians, Mexicans, and Anglos in Arizona*. Austin: University of Texas Press, 2007.
Moore, Stephen T. *Bootleggers and Borders: The Paradox of Prohibition on a Canada-US Borderland*. Lincoln: University of Nebraska Press, 2014.
Mora, Anthony. *Border Dilemmas: Racial and National Uncertainties in New Mexico, 1848–1912*. Durham, NC: Duke University Press, 2011.
Mora-Torres, Juan. *The Making of the Mexican Border: The State, Capitalism, and Society in Nuevo León, 1848–1910*. Austin: University of Texas Press, 2001.
Morgan, George. "Hispano-Indian Trade of an Indian Ceremonial Plant, Peyote (*Lophophora williamsii*) on the Mustang Plains of Texas." *Journal of Ethnopharmacology* 9 (1983): 319–21.
———. "Man, Plant, and Religion: Peyote Trade on the Mustang Plains of Texas." PhD diss., University of Colorado, 1976.
———. "Recollections of the Peyote Road." In *Psychedelic Reflections*, edited by Lester Grinspoon and James B. Bakalar, 91–95. New York: Human Sciences Press, 1983.
Morgan, George R., and Omer C. Stewart, "Peyote Trade in South Texas." *Southwestern Historical Quarterly* 87, no. 3 (1984): 270–96.
Morgan, H. Wayne. *Drugs in America: A Social History, 1800–1880*. Syracuse, NY: Syracuse University Press, 1981.
Moses, Daniel Noah. *The Promise of Progress: The Life and Work of Lewis Henry Morgan*. Columbia: University of Missouri Press, 2009.
Moses, L. G. *The Indian Man: A Biography of James Mooney*. Urbana: University of Illinois Press, 1984.

Mosher, Clayton J., and Scott Atkins. *Drugs and Drug Policy: The Control of Consciousness Alteration*. Thousand Oaks, CA: Sage Publications, 2007.

Musto, David F. *The American Disease: Origins of Narcotic Control*. New Haven, CT: Yale University Press, 1973.

Myerholl, Barbara. *Peyote Hunt: The Sacred Journey of the Huichol Indians*. Ithaca, NY: Cornell University Press, 1974.

Naum, Magdalena. "Re-Emerging Frontiers: Postcolonial Theory and Historical Archaeology of the Borderlands." *Journal of Archaeological Method and Theory* 17, no. 2 (June 2010): 101–31.

Naylor, Celia E. "'Playing Indian'? The Selection of Radmilla Cody as Miss Navajo Nation, 1997–1998." In *Crossing Waters, Crossing Worlds: The African Diaspora in Indian Country*, edited by Tiya Miles and Sharon P. Holland, 145–63. Durham, NC: Duke University Press, 2006.

Neeley, Bill. *The Last Comanche Chief: The Life and Times of Quanah Parker*. New York: Castle Books, 2007.

Neuman, Lisa K. *Indian Play: Indigenous Identities at Bacone College*. Lincoln: University of Nebraska Press, 2013.

New, W. H. *Borderlands: How We Talk About Canada*. Vancouver: University of British Columbia Press, 1998.

Newmark, Julianne. "Pluralism, Place, and Gertrude Bonnin's Counternativism from Utah to Washington, D.C." *American Indian Quarterly* 36, no. 3 (Summer 2012): 318–47.

Nieto-Phillips, John. *The Language of Blood: The Making of Spanish-American Identity in New Mexico, 1880s–1930s*. Albuquerque: University of New Mexico Press, 2004.

Norris, Ada Mahasti. "Zitkala-Ša and National Indian Pedagogy: Storytelling, Activism, and the Project of Assimilation." PhD diss., Duke University, 2003.

Nye, Edgar Wilson. *Bill Nye's History of the United States*. Philadelphia: J.B. Lippincott, 1894.

Oklahoma Indian Country Guide: One State, Many Nations. Oklahoma City: Oklahoma Tourism & Recreation Department.

Okrent, Daniel. *Last Call: The Rise and Fall of Prohibition*. New York: Scribner, 2010.

Olson, James, and Heather Olson Beal. *The Ethnic Dimension in American History*. 4th ed. Oxford: Wiley-Blackwell, 2010.

Olson, James S., and Raymond Wilson. *Native Americans in the Twentieth Century*. Provo, UT: Brigham Young University Press, 1984.

Omni, Michael, and Howard Winant. *Racial Formation in the United States*. 2nd ed. New York: Routledge, 2004.

Opler, Marvin K. "Fact and Fancy in Ute Peyotism." *American Anthropologist* 44, no. 1 (January–March 1942): 151–59.

Opler, Morris E. "The Influence of Aboriginal Pattern and White Contact on a Recently Introduced Ceremony, the Mescalero Peyote Rite." *Journal of American Folklore* 49 (1936): 143–66.

Orsi, Robert A. *Between Heaven and Earth: The Religious Worlds People Make and the Scholars Who Study Them*. Princeton: Princeton University Press, 2005.

———. *The Madonna of 115th Street: Faith and Community in Italian Harlem, 1880–1950*. 2nd ed. New Haven, CT: Yale University Press, 2002.

Outlaw, Lucious T., Jr. "Rehabilitate Racial Whiteness?" In Yancy, *What White Looks Like*, 159–71.

Pastorello, Karen. *The Progressives: Activism and Reform in American Society, 1893–1917*. New York: Wiley Blackwell, 2014.

Pearce, Roy Harvey. *Savagism and Civilization: A Study of the Indians and the American Mind*. Baltimore: Johns Hopkins University Press, 1965.

Peck, Garrett. *The Prohibition Hangover: Alcohol in America from Demon Rum to Cult Cabernet*. New Brunswick, NJ: Rutgers University Press, 2009.

Pegram, Thomas R. *Battling Demon Rum: The Struggle for a Dry America, 1800–1933*. Chicago: Ivan R. Dee, 1998.

Perkinson, James W. *White Theology: Outing Supremacy in Modernity*. New York: Palgrave Macmillan, 2004.

Petersen, Karen Daniels. *Howling Wolf: A Cheyenne Warrior's Graphic Interpretation of His People*. Palo Alto, CA: American West, 1968.

Porterfield, Amanda, and John Corrigan, eds. *Religion in American History*. West Sussex, UK: Wiley-Blackwell, 2010.

Porter, Joy. "Progressivism and Native American Self-Expression in the Late Nineteenth and Early Twentieth Century." In *Native Diasporas: Indigenous Identities and Settler Colonialism in the Americas*, edited by Gregory D. Smithers and Brooke N. Newman, 273–95. Lincoln: University of Nebraska Press, 2014.

Provine, Doris Marie. *Unequal under the Law: Race in the War on Drugs*. Chicago: University of Chicago Press, 2007.

Prucha, Francis Paul. *American Indian Policy in Crisis: Christian Reformers and the Indian, 1865–1900*. Norman: University of Oklahoma Press, 1976.

Prue, Robert E. "King Alcohol to Chief Peyote: A Grounded Theory Investigation of the Supportive Factors of the Native American Church for Drug and Alcohol Abuse Recovery." PhD diss., University of Kansas, 2008.

Quinn, John F. "Father Mathew's Disciples: American Catholic Support for Temperance, 1840–1920." *Church History* 65, no. 4 (December 1996): 624–40.

Rhodes, Cynthia Kay. *Between Two Worlds: The Legend of Quanah Parker*. New York: Eloquent Books, 2009.

Richards, William A. "Entheogens in the Study of Mystical and Archetypal Experiences." *Research in the Social Scientific Study of Religion* 13 (2003): 143–55.

———. "Entheogens in the Study of Religious Experiences: Current Status." *Journal of Religion and Health* 44, no. 4 (Winter 2005): 377–89.

Roberts, Tyler. *Encountering Religion: Responsibility and Criticism after Secularism*. New York: Columbia University Press, 2013.

Robertson, Sarah E. "Native Sacrament: Peyote Identity and the Law, 1890–2004." Master's thesis, Southern Methodist University, 2011.

Robinson, Gary. *The Language of Victory: American Indian Code Talkers of World War I and World War II*. Bloomington, IL: iUniverse, 2014.

Rodríguez, Rubén Rosario. *Racism and God-Talk: A Latino/a Perspective.* New York: New York University Press, 2008.

Roediger, David R. "Irish-American Workers and White Racial Formation in the Antebellum United States." In *Racial Classification and History,* Critical Race Theory: Essays on the Social Construction and Reproduction of "Race," edited by Nathaniel E. Gates, 247–77. New York: Garland, 1997.

———. *Towards the Abolition of Whiteness: Essays on Race, Politics, and Working Class History.* New York: Verso Books, 1994.

Rollings, Willard Hughes. *Unaffected by the Gospel: Osage Resistance to the Christian Invasion (1673–1906); A Cultural Victory.* Albuquerque: University of New Mexico Press, 2004.

Romo, David. *Ringside Seat to a Revolution: An Underground Cultural History of El Paso and Juárez, 1893–1923.* El Paso: Cinco Puntos Press, 2005.

Rosenthal, Nicolas G. *Reimagining Indian Country: Native American Migration and Identity in Twentieth-Century Los Angeles.* Chapel Hill: University of North Carolina Press, 2012.

———. "Representing Indians: Native American Actors on Hollywood's Frontier." *The Western Historical Quarterly* 36, no. 3 (Autumn 2005): 329–52.

Rowlodge, Jess. Interview, April 16, 1968. Doris Duke Collection, T-239, Western History Collections, University of Oklahoma, Norman, Oklahoma.

Ruether, Rosemary Radford. "Is Christ White? Racism and Christology." In *Christology and Whiteness: What Would Jesus Do?,* edited by George Yancy, 101–13. New York: Routledge, 2012.

Schaefer, Stacy B. *Amanda's Blessings from the Peyote Gardens of South Texas.* Albuquerque: University of New Mexico Press, 2015.

Schaefer, Stacy B., and Peter T. Furst, eds. *People of the Peyote: Huichol Indian History, Religion, and Survival.* Albuquerque: University of New Mexico Press, 1996.

Schmal, John P. "Los Antepasados Indigenas de los Guanajuatenses: A Look into Guanajuato's Past." History of Mexico. Houston Institute for Culture. http://www.houstonculture.org/mexico/guanajuato.html.

Shonle, Ruth. "Peyote, the Giver of Visions." *American Anthropologist* 27, no. 1 (January–March 1925): 53–75.

Slotkin, J. S. *The Peyote Religion: A Study in Indian-White Relations.* Glencoe, IL: Free Press, 1956.

Smith, Huston. *Cleansing the Doors of Perception: The Religious Significance of Entheogenic Plants and Chemicals.* New York: Jeremy P. Tarcher, 2000.

Smith, Huston, and Reuben Snake, eds. *One Nation under God: The Triumph of the Native American Church.* Santa Fe: Clear Light, 1996.

Smith, Rogers M. "The 'American Creed' and American Identity: The Limits of Liberal Citizenship in the United States." *The Western Political Quarterly* 41, no. 2 (June 1988): 225–51.

Smithers, Gregory D. "The Soul of Unity: The Quarterly Journal of the Society of American Indians, 1913–1915." *Studies in American Indian Literature* 25, no. 2/*American Indian Quarterly* 37, no. 3 (Summer 2013): 263–89.

Soni, Varun. "Peyote, Christianity, and Constitutional Law: Toward an Antisubordination Jurisprudence." In Labate and Cavnar, *Peyote,* 63–83.

Southern, David W. *The Progressive Era and Race: Reaction and Reform, 1900–1917.* Wheeling, IL: Harlan Davidson, 2005.

Spickard, James V. "Cultural Context and the Definition of Religion: Seeing with Confucian Eyes." In Greil and Bromley, *Defining Religion,* 189–99.

Spillane, Joseph F. *Cocaine. From Medical Marvel to Modern Menace in the United States, 1884–1920.* Baltimore: Johns Hopkins University Press, 2000.

St. John, Rachel. *Line in the Sand: A History of the Western US-Mexico Border.* Princeton: Princeton University Press, 2011.

Steinmetz, Paul B. *Pipe, Bible, and Peyote Among the Oglala Lakota: A Study in Religious Identity.* Syracuse, NY: Syracuse University Press, 1998.

Stewart, Omer C. "Anthropological Theory and History of Peyotism." *Ethnohistory* 26, no. 3 (Summer 1979): 277–81.

———. *Peyote Religion: A History.* Norman: University of Oklahoma Press, 1987.

———. "Peyotism in Montana." *Montana: The Magazine of Western History* 33, no. 2 (Spring 1983): 2–15.

———. "The Southern Ute Peyote Cult." *American Anthropologist* 43, no. 2 (April–June 1941): 303–8.

Stromberg, Ernest. "Resistance and Mediation: The Rhetoric of Irony in Indian Boarding School Narratives by Francis La Flesche and Zitkala-Sa." In *American Indian Rhetorics of Survivance: Word Medicine, Word Magic,* edited by Ernest Stromberg, 95–109. Pittsburgh: University of Pittsburgh Press, 2006.

Strong, Pauline Turner. *American Indians and the American Imagination: Cultural Representation across the Centuries.* Boulder, CO: Paradigm, 2012.

Swan, Daniel C. *Peyote Religious Art: Symbols of Faith and Belief.* Jackson: University Press of Mississippi, 1999.

Swatos, William H., Jr. "Differentiating Experiences: The Virtue of Substantive Definitions." In Greil and Bromley, *Defining Religion,* 39–53.

Szabo, Joyce M. "Howling Wolf." In *Encyclopedia of the Great Plains,* edited by David J. Wishart. University of Nebraska-Lincoln. 2011. http://plainshumanities.unl.edu/encyclopedia/doc/egp.art.035.

———. *Howling Wolf and the History of Ledger Art.* Albuquerque: University of New Mexico Press, 1994.

Tait, Jennifer L. Woodruff. *The Poisoned Chalice: Eucharistic Grape Juice and Common-Sense Realism in Victorian Methodism.* Tuscaloosa: University of Alabama Press, 2011.

Taves, Ann. *Religious Experience Reconsidered: A Building-Block Approach to the Study of Religion and Other Special Things.* Princeton: Princeton University Press, 2009.

Taylor, Ethel Crisp. "Mountain View." In *Encyclopedia of Oklahoma History and Culture.* www.okhistory.org.

Taylor, Paul C. "Silence and Sympathy: Dewey's Whiteness." In Yancy, *What White Looks Like,* 227–41.

Terry, Martin, Keeper Trout, Bennie Williams, Teodoso Herrera, and Norma Fowler. "Limitations to Natural Production of *LophophoraWilliamsii* (Cactaceae) I. Regrowth and Survivorship in Two Years Post Harvest in a South Texas Population." *Journal of the Botanical Research Institute of Texas* 5, no. 2 (2011): 661–75.

Tilghman, Zoe A. *Quanah: The Eagle of the Comanches.* Oklahoma City: Harlow, 1938.

Tong, Benson. "Allotment, Alcohol, and the Omahas." *Great Plains Quarterly* 17, no. 1 (Winter 1997): 19–33.

Trachtenberg, Alan. *Shades of Hiawatha: Staging Indians, Making Americans, 1880–1930.* New York: Hill and Wang, 2004.

Trennert, Robert A., Jr. *The Phoenix Indian School: Forced Assimilation in Arizona, 1891–1935.* Norman: University of Oklahoma Press, 1988.

Troutman, John W. *Indian Blues: American Indians and the Politics of Music, 1879–1934.* Norman: University of Oklahoma Press, 2009.

Truett, Samuel. *Fugitive Landscapes: The Forgotten History of the US-Mexico Borderlands.* New Haven, CT: Yale University Press, 2006.

Truett, Samuel, and Elliott Young, eds. *Continental Crossroads: Remapping US-Mexico Borderlands History.* Durham, NC: Duke University Press, 2004.

Tupper, Kenneth W. "Entheogens and Existential Intelligence: The Use of Plant Teachers as Cognitive Tools." *Canadian Journal of Education* 27, no. 4 (2002): 499–516.

Tweed, Thomas A. "Introduction: Narrating U.S. Religious History." In *Retelling U.S. Religious History*, edited by Thomas A. Tweed, 1–23. Berkeley: University of California Press, 1997.

Unrau, William E. *White Man's Wicked Water: The Alcohol Trade and Prohibition in Indian Country, 1802–1892.* Lawrence: University Press of Kansas, 1996.

Varey, Simon, Rafael Chabrán, and Dora B. Weiner, eds. *Searching for the Secrets of Nature: The Life and Works of Dr. Francisco Hernández.* Stanford, CA: Stanford University Press, 2000.

Vecsey, Christopher. *Imagine Ourselves Richly: Mythic Narratives of North American Indians.* New York: Crossroad, 1988.

Voget, Fred W. "The American Indian in Transition: Reformation and Accommodation." *American Anthropologist* 58, no. 2 (April 1956): 249–63.

Wagner, Roland M. "Pattern and Process in Ritual Syncretism: The Case of Peyotism among the Navajo." *Journal of Anthropological Research* 31, no. 2 (Summer 1975): 162–81.

Wallace, Anthony F. C. "Revitalization Movements." *American Anthropologist* 58, no. 2 (1956): 264–81.

Warner, Nicholas O. "Images of Drinking in 'Women Singing,' *Ceremony*, and *Houses Made of Dawn*." *MELUS* 11, no. 4, Literature of the Southwest (Winter 1984): 15–30.

Warren, Louis S. *Buffalo Bill's America: William Cody and the Wild West Show.* New York: Alfred A. Knopf, 2005.

———. *God's Red Son: The Ghost Dance Religion and the Making of Modern America.* New York: Basic Books, 2017.

Weisiger, Marsha. *Dreaming of Sheep in Navajo Country.* Seattle: University of Washington Press, 2009.

Welch, Deborah Sue. "Zitkala-Ša: An American Indian Leader, 1876–1938." PhD diss., University of Wyoming, 1985.

Wenger, Tisa. Review of *The Peyote Road: Religious Freedom and the Native American Church*, by Thomas C. Maroukis. *Pacific Historical Review* 80, no. 3 (August 2011): 475–76.

———. *We Have a Religion: The 1920s Pueblo Indian Dance Controversy and American Religious Freedom*. Chapel Hill: University of North Carolina Press, 2009.

Wishart, David J. "Indian Agents." *Encyclopedia of the Great Plains*. University of Nebraska-Lincoln, 2011. http://plainshumanities.unl.edu/encyclopedia/doc/egp.pg.032.

White, Richard. *The Middle Ground: Indians, Empires, and Republics in the Great Lakes Region, 1650–1815*. New York: Cambridge University Press, 1991.

Whitewolf, Jim. *The Life of a Kiowa-Apache Indian*. Edited by Charles S. Brant. New York: Dover, 1969.

Wiedman, Dennis. "Upholding Indigenous Freedoms of Religion and Medicine: Peyotists at the 1906–1908 Oklahoma Constitutional Convention and First Legislature." *American Indian Quarterly* 36, no. 2 (Spring 2012): 215–46.

Willard, William. "The First Amendment, Anglo-Conformity, and American Indian Religious Movements." *Wicazo Sa Review* 7, no. 1 (Spring 1991): 26–30.

———. "Zitkala-Ša: A Woman Who Would be Heard." *Wicazo Sa Review* 1, no. 1 (Spring 1985): 11–16.

Williams, Peter W. "Community." In Porterfield and Corrigan, *Religion in American History*, 285–301.

Wilson, Linda D. "Statehood Movement." In *Encyclopedia of Oklahoma History and Culture*. www.okhistory.org.

Winterman, Denise. "World War One: The Original Code Talkers." *BBC News Magazine*, May 19, 2014. http://www.bbc.com/news/magazine-26963624.

Wishar, David J. "Indian Agents." In *Encyclopedia of the Great Plains*. University of Nebraska-Lincoln, 2011. http://plainshumanities.unl.edu/encyclopedia/doc/egp.pg.032.

Yancy, George. "Introduction: Framing the Problem." In *Christology and Whiteness: What Would Jesus Do?*, edited by George Yancy, 1–18. New York: Routledge, 2012.

———, ed. *What White Looks Like: African-American Philosophers on the Whiteness Question*. New York: Routledge, 2004.

Young, Elliott. *Catarion Garza's Revolution on the Texas-Mexico Border*. Durham, NC: Duke University Press, 2004.

Young, Robert. *White Mythologies: Writing History and the West*. New York: Routledge, 1990.

Zakim, Michael. *Ready-Made Democracy: A History of Men's Dress in the American Republic, 1760–1860*. Chicago: University of Chicago Press, 2003.

INDEX

Abbott, Lyman, 56, 101
Absentee Shawnee (indigenous tribe), 28
Ahdosy, Matt, 63
Ahdosy, Willie, 46, 63
Ahpeahtone (also Apiatan), 46, 116, 119
Alabama, 96
alcohol (also liquor), 2, 6, 32, 49, 64, 74–76, 82–87, 89–91, 95–97, 99, 106, 113–14, 116, 118, 129, 140–143; 18th Amendment, 83–84, 89, 140–41; bootleg system, 84; chief special officer to suppress on reservations, 59, 72, 74–76, 110, 112; intoxicant (also intoxication), 49, 64, 72, 74–75, 82, 84–86, 88–91, 100, 106, 113–14, 142, 144; harms, 83, 85–86, 88, 90; liquor laws, 8, 49, 74, 76, 83–84, 89, 142; prohibition, 7, 49, 64, 74, 82–85, 89–91, 95, 97, 113, 116, 118, 129, 138, 140–42; prohibition on Native American reservations, 74–76, 82–85, 95, 106, 113, 140; religious exemption, 90, 129, 141–142, 200n67, 200n73; sobriety, 74–75; temperance, 49, 59, 83, 85, 89–90, 140–41; trade, 84–85, 89; whiskey, 84, 86, 89, 91, 97; wine, 90, 138–40, 142–43
America (also American), 2–11, 16, 19–20, 22–25, 29, 34, 36–37, 39–45, 47, 50–52, 57, 60, 64–65, 72–73, 75, 78, 83–87, 91–93, 95–100, 106, 113–15, 120, 122–24, 127–29, 131–33, 136—39, 141–42, 145–48, 151

American Baptist Home Mission Society (also American Baptist Missionary Society), 47, 57, 143
American Civil Liberties Union (also ACLU), 149
American Indian Survey, 145
American West, 19, 25–26, 28, 43, 123
Anderson, Leon B. 149
annuities, 51, 55, 120, 193n
Antelope, John, 112
anthropology (also anthropologist), 6–8, 20, 23–25, 29–30, 44–45, 47–48, 54, 123–24
Anti-Saloon League of America, 77, 83–84, 89, 140
Apache (indigenous tribe), 24, 26, 119, 134–35
Apache Ben, 135
Apache John (also Koon-Ka-Zahche), 116, 119
Arapaho (indigenous tribe, also Southern Arapaho), 28, 38, 47, 109, 127, 133, 135, 144, 147
Arizona, 53–54, 136, 149
Arthur, Chester Y., 15
Ashley, Edward, 59
Ashurst, Henry F., 53
atheism, 42
Atkins, John D. C., 39
Attakai, Mary, 149
automobiles, 25

Barnes, Cassius, 117
Bellamy, Edward, 42

233

Bellamy, George, 117
Berry, Tennyson, 119, 135
Bible, 15–16, 42–43, 60, 114–15, 131, 140, 165n; biblical interpretation, 16, 43, 60; inerrancy, 16; higher criticism studies, 43, 165n19; modernism v. fundamentalism, 43, 60; in peyote ceremony, 33, 114–15, 131; scriptural authority, 42–43, 60
Big Moon ceremony, 32–33, 48
Big Sheep, 114–15
Big Trees, Mrs., 11
Black Bear, Harry, 113–14
Black Bear, Jacob, 113
Black Bear, Paul Jr., 113
Black Cat, John, 113
Black Dog II, 33
Blackbear, Joseph, 119
Blalock, George E., 72
"blanket" tribes (also "blanket Indian"), 28, 51, 85, 88, 99, 116–18, 122–23
Board of Home Missions for the Presbyterian Church, 52
boarding schools, 19, 41, 84, 87, 118
Bonnicastle, Arthur, 11, 144
Bonnin, Gertrude Simmons (also Zitkala-Ša), 2, 15, 53, 124–26
borderlands (also border), 8, 20, 23, 60, 63–67, 69–70, 73–79, 98; bordered lands (*See* reservations); policing, 64, 78–79; smuggling, 78–79; state borders, 73, 129
botany (also botanist), 16, 65, 85, 97, 110, 151
Bowleg, Mrs. Billie, 11
Bowman, George, 110
Boynton, Paul, 18, 38, 39, 135, 144
Brace, Ned, 119, 136
Brannon, C. C., 72, 76–77
Brennan, John R., 113
Buffalo, Ben, 107
Bull Bear, Jock, 147

Bureau of American Ethnology, 53, 81, 133–34
Burke, Charles, 40, 84, 143–46

Caddo (indigenous tribe), 24, 28, 32, 46, 109
California, 132, 136, 149
Calloway, Llewellyn L., 115
Canada, 64, 73, 84, 132, 136, 148
cannabis. *See* marijuana
Cantonment Agency, 87, 107, 188n7
Cárdenas, Juan de, 21
Carlisle school, 38, 107, 109
Carrizo (indigenous tribe), 24
Carter, Charles D., 59
Catholic Church, 21–24, 40, 42–43, 56–57, 131, 138–41, 200n67; catechism, 22; Franciscan, 21, 139; immigration, 42–43, 57; Inquisition, 22, 160n36; nuns, 139, tension with Protestants, 57, transubstantiation, 141
Ceasely, Holman, 115
Champion Iron Company, 71
Chavez, Dennis, 53
Cheap, 107
Cherokee (indigenous tribe), 28, 58
Cheyenne (indigenous tribe, also Southern Cheyenne), 11, 28, 47, 72, 105, 107–9, 112, 116, 119, 133–34, 144, 147
Cheyenne and Arapaho Agency, 58, 72, 105, 108–9, 127
Chichimeca people, 21, 159n26
Chickasaw (indigenous tribe), 28
Chinese Exclusion Act, 95
Chippewa (indigenous tribe, also Ojibwe), 28, 33
Chiwat, 26
Choate, Christopher Columbus "Bud," 119
Choctaw (indigenous tribe), 28
Chony, Tim Koase, 63
Christian (also Christianity), 2–3, 10, 16, 19, 21, 26, 34–41, 43–50, 52–54, 56, 58, 60, 82, 96, 106, 108–9, 115, 121,

128–33, 135, 137–48, 150; Christian Native Americans, 2, 15–16, 33, 108; elements to peyote ceremony, 8, 26, 32–33, 108, 130–31, 135; Eucharist (also communion and Lord's Supper), 138–42; evangelical, 16, 39, 42, 140–41; evangelism (also conversion), 40, 44, 46–48, 54, 82; hegemony, 10, 39, 41–43, 45, 54, 60, 121, 129, 150; institutional organization, 129–31, 140, 146, 148; "Jesus Road," 108; minister, 45, 47, 49, 76, 131; money, 55; white (also whiteness), 10, 36, 38–39, 42, 44–45, 50, 52–54, 56, 58–60, 106, 137, 144–45, 147
Christian Science, 42
Christian Socialism, 42
church, 5, 9, 16, 37, 39–41, 45, 47–49, 54–55, 60, 96–97, 106, 120, 124, 127–46, 148; authority, 142; church-state alliance, 39–41, 43, 45, 48, 54–56, 58–60, 82, 106, 121, 145
Church of Jesus Christ of Latter-Day Saints. *See* Mormon
Citizen Potawatomi (indigenous tribe, also Potawatomi), 28, 32, 113
citizenship (also citizen), 1, 5, 37, 39–41, 43–45, 47, 50–52, 56, 60. 65, 85–86, 98–99, 116, 122–23, 127, 131, 133, 141, 144, 147, 195n; American citizen, 3, 19, 36–37, 39, 45, 57, 86, 99–100, 123, 128, 131–32, 147; Christian citizen (also Christian citizenship), 10, 36, 40, 44, 48; "citizen's clothes," 50; Indian Citizenship Act of 1924, 127; requirements for Native Americans, 39, 44–45, 65, 86, 99–100, 116, 122, 144; status for Native Americans, 1–2, 4, 9, 41, 43–44, 52, 60, 65, 86, 98–99, 116, 122, 127–28, 141, 144–45, 147, 195n3, 195n4
civilize (also civilization), 2, 20, 25, 30, 36, 39–41, 44–46, 53, 82, 84–85, 92, 94, 100, 108, 116–17, 122, 145, 147; barbarism (also savagery), 44, 57, 122, 142; heathen, 36, 40, 45, 53, 85, 96
Clark, David S., 149
Clay, Jesse, 135
clothing (also sartorial), 105, 118, 122–26; attire, 105, 118, 122–24; "citizen's dress," 122–24; hair, 105; Native American dress, 124–26; political identity, 122, 126; suit, 122–23; "white man's dress," 122, 124, 126
cocaine, 2, 8–9, 92, 95–97; association with Blacks in the South, 9. 96–97; state anti-cocaine legislation, 96
Cold War, 148
Collier, John, 60, 135, 147
colonialism, 10, 22, 45, 48, 64–65, 112, 117
Colorado, 28, 54
Comanche (indigenous tribe), 11, 20, 24, 26, 29, 32, 38, 46, 55, 63, 71–72, 76–77, 79, 109, 116, 119, 132, 135, 162n54
Committee on Social and Religious Surveys, 59
Comstock Act, 78
Congress (also congressional), 2, 4, 9–11, 15, 18, 28, 35–36, 40–41, 47, 49, 52–54, 58–59, 74, 76, 79, 83–84, 89–92, 94–95, 100, 106, 118–20, 124, 126, 128, 131, 137, 139, 142–47, 149–50; congressional testimony, 35, 38, 56–57, 94, 97, 106, 147, 150; policymakers, 34, 39–40, 44, 106, 117, 121, 147; representatives, 4, 40, 53, 59, 66, 94, 119–20, 135, 138
Coolidge, Calvin, 78
Cora (indigenous tribe), 23
court cases, 113–14, 129; *Oregon v. Smith*, 150, 203n15; *Reynolds v. US*, 129, 132, 142–43; *State of Montana v. Big Sheep*, 114; *Territory of Oklahoma v. Howling Wolf, Reuben Taylor, and Percy Kable*, 109–10; 112
Court of Indian Offenses, 19, 46, 166n36
Cross Fire ceremony, 33, 48, 135
Crow (indigenous tribe), 114–15, 136

Cruce, Lee, 120
Cruz, Martin de la, 21
Cuba, 70
Cunningham, D. K., 108–9, 111–12
curandera, 93
Curtis, Charles, 53
customs enforcement, 63–64, 77–78

Daily, Charles W., 46, 134
Dakota (indigenous tribe), 28, 33, 124; Nakota, 28, 33; Yankton, 124
dance (also dancing), 23, 29–30, 36, 117, 128
Davis, T. J., 47
Dee Nez, Dan, 149
Deer, James, 11
Delaware (indigenous tribe), 28, 32
Democratic party, 58
denomination (also denominational), 20, 26, 38–40, 43, 45, 47, 130, 138–40; Baptist, 45, 47, 108, 110, 138; Episcopal, 59; Methodist (also Methodist Episcopal Church), 76, 138, 140; Methodist Episcopal Church South, 46, Presbyterian, 15, 38, 52, 74, 138; Reformed Church of America, 47; United Evangelical Church, 49
Díaz, Porfirio, 70
Do-Kish, Mrs., 11
drugs (also narcotics), 2–4, 6, 8, 16, 40, 48, 50, 58, 60, 63–64, 72, 75, 80–83, 90–101, 113–14, 118, 120, 138, 143–44, 149–50; abuse, 95, 97; addict, 83, 90, 92–93, 95, 99–100; Drug Abuse Control Act, 149; Food, Drug, and Cosmetic Act, 4, 149; Controlled Substance Act, 4, 150; controlled substances, 93, 98, 149–50; habit-forming, 2, 83, 91–92, 95–97, 100, 138, 144; harms, 91, 96; illicit, 93, 96; medicine, 94, 132; Narcotics Bureau, 63; pharmaceutical, 90. 96; recreational, 98, 149; Schedule I, 4, 150
"drunken Indian" stereotype, 85, 100

"dry" whiskey, 83, 85, 88–89
Durant, William, 119

Eagle, Frank, 134
Eddy, Mary Baker, 42
Edge, Stanley, 46
Edley, W. H., 119
education, 11, 40, 43–45, 50, 84, 87–88, 150
Ellis, T. H., 63
entheogen, 16–17, 151, 157n8
ethnology (also ethnologist), 1, 3, 11, 20, 23, 28–29, 36, 53, 56–58, 81, 89–90, 124–25, 133
evolution, 43–44

Federal Council of Churches, 89
federal government (also US government), 4, 44, 46, 49–51, 54–55, 58, 63–65, 71–74, 76, 78–85, 87, 89, 91–92, 94–95, 99–100, 106, 109–11, 113, 118, 128–29, 133, 135, 141–43, 145, 148, 150; courts, 72, 89, 93, 113, 129, 143, 150; Customs Office, 77, 172n4; Department of Agriculture, 77, 93, 97; Department of Interior,57, 76; Interstate Commerce Commission, 93; legislation, 49, 78–79, 83–84, 89, 92–93, 96, 98, 106, 118, 145; Treasure Department, 64, 77; US Attorney, 113–14; US Marshal, 113
federal Indian policy, 7, 10, 19, 25, 39, 40, 43, 45, 51, 55–56, 65, 76, 79, 82–84, 86, 91, 94, 98, 105, 111, 116, 127, 133, 135, 145, 147–48; allotment (also Dawes Act), 7–8, 10, 19, 34, 39, 43–45, 54, 65, 71, 86, 98–99, 105, 107, 111, 116, 135, 141, 144, 148, 173n11, 180n4; Christianization, 40, competency commissions (also Burke Act), 39, 65; economic dependency, 87, 111; federal-state relationship, 76; Grant's peace policy, 40, 82; Indian agents, 11, 18, 30, 46, 48–49, 55, 65, 67, 72, 74–76, 85–87, 90,

95, 97, 106–7, 110–12, 120, 122, 127, 133, 169n78, 169n79; Indian Citizenship Act, 39; Indian New Deal, 147–48; Indian problem, 25, 44, 51, 55, 65; land loss from Dawes Act, 65, 173n11; relocation, 148; reservation system, 8, 10, 18–19, 25, 30, 43, 45–46, 49, 65, 79, 82, 84, 98, 161n51; termination policy, 148; trust funds, 54, 65, 111, 135; wards of federal government, 39–40, 56, 58, 91, 146, 184n58
Ferris, Scott, 59, 77
Finger, Bob, 107
Firstborn Church of Christ, 130–31, 135; incorporation, 131; Otoe-Missouria tribe, 131
Florida, 109
"friends," 2, 49–50, 73
Food and Fuel Control Act of 1917, 142
Fort Marion, 109
Fort Peck Indian Reservation, 11
Fox of Iowa (indigenous tribe), 28

Gaapiatan, 31
Gaelic Society, 57, 139
Gandy, Harry L., 15, 50, 53, 135
Garcia, Bartholome, 22
Garcia, J. M., 67
Gassaway, B. F., 46
Gensman, L. M., 59, 137
George, Paul, 119
Georgia, 96
Ghost Dance (also Wounded Knee), 7, 20, 26, 34, 38, 82, 131
Gibbs, George, 143
Gilbert, Rufus, 112
giveaway, 19, 88
Gosiute (indigenous tribe, also Goshute), 28, 33
Great Depression, 60, 98
Greer County, 72, 177n58
Griffin, Mrs. Paul (also former Mrs. Deer), 11

Haag, Mack, 132, 134–35, 145–46
Hadley, J. W., 56
Hagar, Stansberry, 36
Half Moon ceremony, 32, 135
Hall, J. Lee, 26
Hall, Robert D. 49
Hamilton, Robert, 110
Harding, Warren G. 60
Harreld, John, 59
Harrison Narcotics Act, 83, 93–94, 98
Hart, E. E., 87
Haskell Institute, 107–9, 115
Havard, Valery, 85
Hayden, Carl, 53
Haynes, Roy A., 64
Hearst, William Randolph, 98
Hensley, Albert, 33, 135
Hensley, George, 42
Hernández de Toledo, Francisco, 21, 160n28
heroin, 93
Ho-Chunk (indigenous tribe), 122
Howling Wolf, 109, 112
Huichols (indigenous tribe, also Wixáritari), 23, 29
Hume, Charles R., 110

Idaho, 54, 136
identity, 2–4, 7–8, 25, 36, 42, 60, 78–80, 83, 87–88, 91–92, 95, 98, 100–1, 108, 114–16, 118, 122–24, 126–27, 132–34, 136–38, 145–47, 154–55n11; American, 2,4,9,19, 25, 36–37, 39–41, 44, 98, 114, 122, 127, 138, 145; class-based, 78; construction of, 3, 9, 78–80, 83, 95, 114, 122–24m 154–55n11; cultural, 42, 79, 116, 118, 122, 145; hybrid cultural, 4, 37, 101, 108, 116, 122–24, 145; Native American, 2–4, 8–9, 18–19, 30, 32, 39, 44, 60, 78, 98, 100, 106, 122–23; Native American religious identity, 106, 126, 134, 137, 145–46; political, 9, 36, 39, 44, 91, 101, 103, 106, 115–17, 122;

identity (*continued*)
   racial, 8, 19, 36–37, 41, 56, 60, 78–80, 87–88, 95, 101; religious, 8–9, 18, 32, 37, 40–41, 56, 83, 101, 106, 108, 114–15, 132–33, 137–38; social, 3–4, 37, 78, 101, 132
Illinois, 139
immigrant (also immigration), 3–4, 7, 42–43, 45, 56–57, 71, 79, 95, 98, 141
Indiana, 57, 139
Indian Country, 4, 8, 10, 15, 40, 43–46, 64, 66, 73–76, 70–80, 83, 85, 93, 95, 106, 113, 135–36, 140, 142
Indian police, 46, 74, 105–9, 188n1
Indian Rights Association, 36, 50, 84
Indian Reorganization Act, 148
Indian Service, 107
Indian Shaker Church, 131–32, 197n24
Indian wars, 100, 117
Ingersoll, Robert G., 42
Inquisition. *See* Catholic Church
Institute for Social and Religious Research, 145
Interchurch World Movement, 145
Interdenominational Mission Society, 58
Iowa (indigenous tribe), 28, 138
Iowa, 28, 52, 54, 130, 136, 139
Iowa Tribe of Kansas (indigenous tribe), 28
Ireland, 57, 133
Irvin, C. F., 111

James, William, 35
Jehovah's Witnesses, 42
Jews (also Jewish), 42–43, 71, 79, 142, 200n67
Johnson, William E. "Pussyfoot," 74–77, 79, 110, 112, 178n72
Johnston, Henry S., 131
Jones, William, 44

Kable, Percy, 105, 109, 112
Kansas, 28, 42, 50, 53–54, 72, 94, 130

Kappler, Charles J. 77
Karankawa (indigenous tribe), 24
Kaw (indigenous tribe), 28, 53, 73
Kickapoo (indigenous tribe), 28, 32, 175n28
Kickapoo Tribe in Kansas (indigenous tribe) 28
King, F. L., 47
Kinney, Bruce, 57
Kiowa (indigenous tribe), 6, 20, 24, 26, 29, 31–32, 46, 72, 79, 109, 116, 119, 134–37
Kiowa Charley, 135
Kiowa-Comanche reservation, 11, 26, 46, 69, 81
Kiowa, Comanche, and Wichita Agency, 46, 95, 110–11
Kiyou, 63
Koday, 119
Koshiway, Jonathan "Jack," 130–31, 135

La Flesche, Francis, 52–53, 56, 90, 144
Lake Mohonk Conference of the Friends of the Indian. *See* "friends"
Lakota (indigenous tribe), 20, 28, 33, 113
Lamere, Oliver, 52
Land League, 57
Laredo, Texas. *See* Texas
Latta, J. P., 119
Laurel, V., 66–67
law, 8, 10, 38, 46, 48–49, 53–54, 74, 76, 78–79, 83–85, 89–94, 97, 105–17, 122, 129, 132, 137, 142–43, 147, 149; demurrer, 111; enforcement, 113; equal protection, 116–17; judicial interpretation, 113, 129; jurisdiction, 114, 129; police, 108, 148; "white man's" law, 105–6, 112–15, 121, 126
Leavitt, Scott, 53
Left Hand Here, 107
legal system, 4–5, 9, 48, 64, 73, 105–6, 108–17, 123, 126, 129–33, 135, 137, 142, 146, 148–51; affidavit, 132, 147; arrest, 105–9, 111–14, 148–49; attorney, 52, 63, 77, 108, 110–12, 114–15, 131, 138;

conviction, 108–10, 112, 114–15, 149; costs, 111–12; court system, 106, 108–15, 117, 126, 133, 148; district court, 110–14; expert witnesses, 110–12, 114, 125, 133; federal judge, 113–15; grand jury, 113; incarceration, 109–10; language in statutes, 48, 110–13, 135, 141; legality of peyote, 73, 75, 149; prosecution, 105, 107–9, 111, 113, 116, 150; punishment, 109–10, 112–14; race, 112; state and probate courts, 54, 109, 112–14, 149, 189–90n21; trial, 107, 109–13, 115, 130
Leupp, Francis E., 2, 74
Lewis, Sinclair, 42
Lindquist, G. E. E., 59, 145
Lipan Apache (indigenous tribe), 24, 26
liquor. *See* alcohol
Little Man, Horace, 107
Lone Wolf, Delos, 46, 135
Louisiana, 98
Lumholtz, Carl, 23

mara'akame, 23
marijuana (also cannabis), 2, 8–9, 63, 75, 95, 97–98, 187n102; association with Mexicans, 9. 63, 97–98, 187n109; Marijuana Tax Act, 98
McClintic, James, 59
McDonald, Louis, 134
media, 87, 90–91, 95, 97–98, 100, 116–18, 120–23, 125–26, 133, 138, 184n54; newspaper, 2, 11, 63, 70, 72, 79, 88, 91, 96–99, 116–18, 120–22, 125, 138–39, 146; journalist, 92, 116–17
medical (also medicine), 90, 92–94, 97; disease, 94; doctors (also physicians), 21, 29, 87, 92–94; prescriptions, 93; Western medicine, 94
Menominee (indigenous tribe), 28, 22, 113
Meriam Report, 145
mescal (also mescal beans), 11, 38, 45, 48, 49, 52, 99, 107, 109–13, 116–17, 119, 130, 153n2, 168n51

Mescalero Apache (indigenous tribe), 24
Methvin, J. J., 46
Mexico, 8, 19, 21–26, 28–30, 36, 40, 48, 59, 63–64, 66–67, 69–70, 73–80, 84, 93, 97–98, 150; border with US, 8, 17, 24–26, 30, 63–64, 66–67, 73–74, 77–80, 84, 97, 172n3; indigenous peoples, 18, 20–21, 23–24; Mexican identity, 78, 98; Mexican Revolution, 24, 64, 70; Nuevo Laredo, 69–70; peyote growth region, 65–66, 78; transborder trade with US, 78–79, 93, 97; US–Mexican War, 24
Michelson, Truman, 53
Minnesota, 28
missionary (also missionaries), 21, 30, 36, 39–41, 43–49, 52–60, 82, 85, 87, 90, 110, 123, 133–34, 143, 145
mixed-blood, 28, 124
Mni-Sda Presbyterian Church (also Chelsea Church), 15
modernity, 3, 19, 25, 34, 39, 42, 45, 50, 60, 87, 117, 120, 123, 127
Moffett, Thomas C. 52
Montana, 28, 53–54, 108, 114–15, 136
Mooney, Ione, 139
Mooney, James, 1, 11, 20, 28, 30–31, 53–54, 56–58, 72, 81–82, 87, 89–91, 110, 112, 125–26, 131–34, 137, 139, 144
Mooney, Mary (also Sister Mary Agnes and Mother Mary Agnes), 139
morality, 45, 56, 64, 73, 79, 86, 105, 129, 131, 143
moral panic, 90, 94, 97, 100
Morgan, Lewis Henry, 43–44, 166n23
Morgan, Thomas Jefferson, 45, 85, 99
Morman (also Church of Jesus Christ of Latter-Day Saints), 47, 129, 131–33, 142–43; opposition to, 132, 143; Reorganized Church of Jesus Christ of Latter-Day Saints, 108
Muscogee (Creek) (indigenous tribe), 28
Myer, Dillion, 148

narcotics. *See* drugs
nation (also nation-state), 21–22, 25–26, 39–40, 43, 47, 60, 63–65, 78–79, 89, 96, 98, 100, 120, 129, 141–42, 150
National Indian Association, 50
National Indian Student Conference, 50
Native American (also historical term "Indian"), 1–4, 10–11, 16–18, 20, 23–26, 28–30, 34, 36–40, 43–48, 50–51, 53–60, 63–67, 69, 71–79, 81–100, 105–120, 122, 124–39, 141, 143–51; assimilation, 8, 19, 34, 36, 39, 45, 51, 65, 81–82, 86–87, 92, 99–100, 105, 117, 123, 141, 148; blood quantum, 149; clothing, 82, 117, 122–23; culture, 56–57, 60, 82, 86–87, 92–93, 99–100, 116–17, 122–24, 126–28, 133, 144–48, 151; economics, 86–87, 97, 112, 190n30; hair, 82, 123; identity, 4, 19–20, 39, 50, 60, 78, 91, 95, 100, 106, 115–18, 123–24, 126, 137, 145, 147; language, 82, 117–18, 128; image and performance of Indianness, 123–26; pan–Indian, 9, 34, 106, 116–17, 127, 130, 133–34
Native American Church (NAC), 3–5, 10–11, 16, 34, 41, 47, 53, 58, 83, 90, 92, 96, 114–15, 120, 129–40, 142, 144–51; charter, 135–36, 138; incorporation, 9–10, 20, 41, 53, 92, 96, 114,120, 127–37, 139, 142, 144–46; membership cards, 148–50; national church, 136; Native American Church of North America, 136, 148; *Quarterly Bulletin*, 148; structure and leadership, 134–37, 139, 145–46, 148
Native American Free Exercise of Religion Act, 150
Navajo (indigenous tribe), 28, 33, 126, 136, 149
Navajo V-way ceremony, 33
Nebraska, 28, 77, 119, 130, 135
Neck, Mitchell (also Nah-qua-tah-tuck), 113, 130
Neconish family, 113

Nevada, 54, 136
Newberne, Robert E., 40
New Mexico, 28, 53–54, 136
New Spain, 21
Niwot, 127
Noble, H. M., 107
North Dakota, 28, 54, 136
Northern Arapaho (indigenous tribe), 28.
Northern Cheyenne (indigenous tribe), 28, 108, 136
Northern Paiute (indigenous tribe) 28

Ochoa, Gayetasio, 66–67
Office of Indian Affairs (also Bureau of Indian Affairs), 10, 19, 26, 30, 34–36, 39, 45–46, 48–49, 53, 55–60, 64–65, 73–77, 79, 81, 84, 86–87, 89, 91, 93, 99, 105, 107–8, 111–13, 117–20, 122–23, 130, 134–35, 142, 145–46; Board of Indian Commissioners, 49, 168n58; Commissioner of Indian Affairs, 30, 39–40, 44–46, 55–56, 60, 74, 76–77, 84–85, 87, 94, 99, 119, 135, 143, 145, 147–48; confidential informants, 106; government physicians, 87, 94, 110; Indian Appropriation Act, 142; Indian officials, 34, 53, 64, 73, 76, 79–80, 82, 85, 92, 105–9, 111, 113, 117–19, 121, 123, 130, 133–34
Ohio, 71
Oklahoma, 19, 24–26, 28–29, 34, 38, 41, 47, 49, 53, 55, 57–60, 63, 66–67, 69, 71–77, 87, 91–92, 94, 106–9, 111–13, 116–22, 129–331, 133–36, 138, 188n5; Calumet, Okla., 107, 133; congressional delegation, 58–59, 121; El Reno, Okla., 49, 129, 133–34; Indian Territory, 1, 8, 18–19, 25, 28, 69, 74, 84–85, 107, 111, 117, 153n1; Kingfisher, Okla., 108–9; Oklahoma Territory, 1, 8, 18–19, 45, 48, 56, 72–74, 81, 95, 105–7, 109, 111–13, 117, 153n1, 177n58; politics, 42, 59, 121; Ponca City, Okla., 11, 72; Red Rock,

Okla., 130; state capital, 117–18; state constitution, 1, 75, 107, 116–18, 191n49; state legislature, 26, 38, 55, 75, 91, 112, 117–18, 127; statehood, 106–7, 111, 116, 188n5

Old Coyote, Barney, 115

Omaha (indigenous tribe), 28, 32, 52, 56, 90, 114, 135, 144

Omaha Peyote Historical Society, 135

opium (also opiates), 2, 8–9, 92–96; addiction, 92; association with Chinese, 9, 95–96

Oregon, 132, 150

Osage (indigenous tribe), 28, 32–33, 55, 72, 77, 97, 120–21, 143–44, 181n14, 193n74

Otoe-Missouria (indigenous tribe), 28, 46, 72, 130, 134

Owen, Robert, 58–59, 94

pagan, 21, 36, 40, 47–48, 52, 85

Parker, Arthur, 41, 50, 52–53, 73, 89, 93, 99–100, 124

Parker, Baldwin, 119

Parker, Quanah, 1, 26, 32, 46, 59, 71, 77, 93, 116–17, 119–20, 123, 127

Pasteur, Louis, 140

patent medicine, 72, 83, 92, 94, 96–98

Pawnee (indigenous tribe), 28, 72

Peawa, Wilbur, 134–35

Perkaquanard, Irwin, 63

Pe-wo, 46

peyote, 1—7, 21–22, 24, 29, 32, 39–42, 45–47, 49–50, 52–60, 63–67, 70–71, 73–83, 85–101, 105–20, 124–35, 137–40, 142–51, 153n2; buttons, 17–18, 20, 26, 31–32, 59, 66–67, 69–74, 76–77, 79, 88, 99–100, 107, 110–11, 113–14, 118, 150–51, 153n2, 175n36; cactus, 1, 5–6, 17–18, 23, 35, 48, 59, 65–67, 78, 81, 85, 88–89, 91–92, 95, 97, 105, 108, 110, 115, 126, 153n2; costs, 69, 72, 77, 88, 151; cultural appropriation by whites, 60, 149; cure for alcoholism, 89–90, 114, 183–84n 47; diffusion and spread among tribes, 7–8, 19, 24–26, 72, 83, 85, 87, 93, 106–7, 113–14, 133, 161n49, 162n52; ethics (also Peyote Road), 89–90, 108, 129, 144; evil, 21–22, 40, 45, 59, 83, 89, 110, 125; Grandfather Peyote, 5, 32; growth region, 65–66, 78–79, 92, 150; healing powers, 93–94, 183n45; imagined and constructed harms, 73–76, 78–79, 83, 85–97, 100, 124, 128, 138, 143, 146, 170n82; importation from Mexico, 59, 63–64, 67, 74–78, 93, 130, 150; intoxication, 74–75, 85–87, 89–92, 99–100, 113–14, 142, 144; link to alcohol, 75–76, 82, 85–87, 89–91, 99–100, 138, 142–43; link to drugs, 58, 60, 75–76, 80, 82–83, 90–101, 113, 118, 120, 138, 143–44, 149–50, 187n102, 187n109; mescal confusion, 11, 48–49, 52, 107, 109–13, 116–17, 119, 130, 153n2, 168n51; new Native American religion, 29, 34, 36, 39, 56, 90, 108, 143; peyote fields, 67, 69, 77, 149; peyote prohibition, 59–60, 63, 76–78, 81–83, 85, 87–90, 92–93, 98, 100, 106–7, 110, 112, 115–20, 126, 131, 135, 137, 143, 145, 147; peyote religion, 2–4, 6, 8–9, 11, 18–19, 25, 34, 36, 40, 56, 66–67, 73, 78, 81–82, 85, 87, 89–93, 100, 105–8, 113, 121, 123–24, 130–34, 136–38, 144, 147; peyote organizations, 130–31, 133; pilgrimages, 77–79; racialized identity, 78–80, 95–100; religious use, 2–5, 18, 33–34, 37, 41–42, 63, 70–72, 76–77, 80–82, 89, 92, 96, 100, 105–7, 109, 111, 113, 126, 129, 143, 146, 149; right to use, 112–13, 116, 123, 126, 129, 133, 137, 144–45, 149; sacred medicine, 1, 4, 18, 21, 33–34, 80–81, 83, 89, 93, 133, 138, 143; spread to whites, 88–89, 149; use by returned students, 87–88; war on peyote, 76, 81, 83, 91, 95, 99–101, 137, 140

242 INDEX

peyote, ceremonies (also meetings), 30, 31, 74, 77, 81, 87–88, 91–93, 97, 105, 107–10, 112–15, 126, 128, 130–31, 133, 135–41, 143, 145–46, 149–51; all night ceremony, 30–31, 46, 87; altar, 30, 32–33; burning cedar, 31; Christian elements, 32–33; circle, 30–31; costs, 88; drums, 29, 31, 105; fire, 29, 31; food, 29, 31, 88; frequency, 30; healing, 93, 114; numbers, 29, 131; prayers, 29–31; roadman, 29, 31, 130; Saturday night, 87, 91, 136; singing songs, 29–33; tobacco (also smoking), 29, 32–33, 130–31; rattles, 29, 31, 105; teepee, 30–33, 112, 130, 136

peyote, commercial trade, 63–80, 91–93, 97, 100, 119, 130, 148–50; Aguilares Mercantile Company, 67, 69climate change, 151; economic benefits, 66–67, 69, 71, 73, 78; harvesting, 69, 79, 151, 175n36; interstate trade, 67, 71–72, 78, 92–93, 149; mercantile companies, 67, 69–70; merchants (also business houses), 66–67, 69–72, 75–76, 79, 148; *peyoteros*, 69–70, 79, 148–50, 175n34; prices, 148, 151, 175n38; shipments, 66–69, 71, 74–76, 78, 92–93, 119, 148; supply, 150–151; Teeter & Son, 72; Thomas & Rives, 72; trade centers, 66, 73; traders, 71–74, 76, 79, 91; transnational trade with Mexico, 67, 75–79, 93, 97, 148; V. Laurel and Bro., 66; Villegas family businesses (also J. Villegas & Bro., Villegas Mercantile, L. Villegas & Bro.), 69–71, 75, 79, 176n43; Wormser Brothers, 69–71, 75–76

peyote, opposition to, 2, 8, 34–36, 39–40, 46, 49–50, 52–54, 60, 63–64, 69, 71, 73–83, 85–87, 89–94, 96–101, 105–21, 124–25, 128–35, 137–41, 143–150; 1897 Oklahoma territorial statute, 106, 109–13, 117, 138, 189n18; 1908 Oklahoma legislation, 117–18, 138; 1918 hearings, 11, 15, 18, 47, 57, 59, 89, 90120, 124–25, 133, 138–39; ban from Mexico, 59, 63, 74, 76–77, 93; criminalize, 36, 40, 49, 63–64, 83, 90–94, 150; executive order, 78; Gandy bill, 50, 52–53, 100; federal legislative efforts, 2, 4, 8,–9, 34, 36, 38, 40–41, 49–50, 53, 56, 58–59, 78, 89, 91, 94, 98, 116, 120–22, 124–25, 127–29, 131, 133, 135, 137–39, 143–45, 147, 150; failed legislative efforts, 41, 46, 53–54, 58, 60, 75, 89, 91, 94, 100, 121, 126, 137, 146; federal officials, 71, 74, 76–77, 86, 89, 92, 106–7, 113–15, 117–19, 133, 139, 141, 146; Hayden bill, 53, 124, 126, 133; medical professionals, 94; Montana law, 114–15; Native American opposition, 8, 15, 41, 50, 52–53, 73, 89, 93–94, 100, 124, 133; non-Native opposition, 8, 15, 21–22, 34–36, 41, 49–50, 53, 73–74, 81–83, 86, 89–, 107, 115, 133, 135; Oklahoma peyote hearings, 55, 87, 117, 127, 138; Oklahoma territorial legislature, 48–49, 73, 75, 106, 112, 117; orders from Indian Office officials, 46, 81, 105, 107, 113, 118–20, 130, 146; Post Office Appropriation Act, 78; prohibition efforts for peyote, 2, 4, 9, 34, 41, 48–50, 52–54, 56, 58–60, 73–74, 77–79, 81, 83, 87–89, 92–94, 98, 106, 113, 115, 126–28, 131, 138–39, 143, 145–47; prohibitive tariff, 75; religious opposition, 21–22, 36–37, 40, 45, 47, 49, 50, 653, 56, 60, 89–90; state legislative efforts,34, 49, 54–55, 87, 91, 106, 114–15, 118; state prohibition laws, 76, 87, 89, 91, 110, 112, 114–17, 135, 138, 148–49; withhold rations and annuities, 78, 107

peyote, resistance strategies, 2–4, 9, 20, 49, 53–54, 58, 105–6, 109–21, 127, 129–31, 133, 135–39, 141–43, 145–46, 151; appeal to religious freedom, 127, 129, 136–39, 141, 143, 145–46; clothing, 122–123; essential to worship, 129, 138–39, 141, 143; incorporate as church, 129–31, 133–38, 146; legal system and courts,

106, 109–15, 117, 129–30, 146, 151; letter writing, 119–20; loophole in law, 117, 126, 129, 142; pan-Indian solidarity, 116–18, 130, 132; petitions, 105, 108, 119–20, 143; political, 106, 115, 117–21, 129–30, 137–38, 151; protest, 105, 117–18, 120; testimony in court, 110, 113, 115; testimony on proposed legislation, 106, 116–17, 120, 125, 127, 131, 147; visit congressional representatives, 120–21

peyote, support for, 3, 9, 28, 36, 41, 49, 52–53, 56, 58–59, 81, 89–90, 94, 101, 106, 109–10, 112, 114–21, 124–25, 127, 133–34, 137–39, 143–45, 147, 149; 1918 congressional hearing, 35, 90, 125, 133; congressional, 49, 59, 137; James Mooney, 11, 28, 53–54, 57–58, 81, 89, 110, 112, 125, 133–34, 139, 180n3, 198n37; Native non-Peyotists, 28, 41, 56, 58, 90, 106, 109, 118, 144; Oklahoma congressional representatives, 58–59, 94; Oklahoma legislature, 38, 49, 127; petitions, 105, 119, 143; state court, 149; whites, 3, 41, 53, 57–59, 106, 109–10, 124, 133–34, 137

Peyote Church of Christ, 135

peyote lobby, 53, 106, 115, 117–18, 120–23, 126, 130, 133

Peyote Woman, 31–32

Peyotism, 1–3, 6, 8, 10, 16, 19–20, 23–25, 28–33, 35–36, 38–42, 45–48, 50, 52, 54–60, 66, 69, 72–73, 78–79, 81, 83, 85–90, 96–97, 107–14, 123, 129–36, 139, 142–44, 147, 149–51; Americanized, 23, 26; "false religion" v. legitimate, 129, 133, 144, 148; pan-Indian religion, 3, 9, 19, 25, 31–32, 34, 106, 116–17, 127, 133–34; phenomenological, 132, 144, 151; Native American religion, 1, 7–8, 11, 15, 18, 20, 29, 34–36, 38, 48, 64, 134; Otoe Peyotism, 130; visions (also revelations), 15, 18, 21, 23, 29, 86, 132–33; women, 11, 31–32

Peyotists, 1, 3–7, 9, 11, 15, 22–23, 28–30, 32–38, 41, 46, 48–50, 52–59, 63, 65–67, 69, 71–74, 76–82, 86–87, 89, 91–94, 96, 99, 101, 105–9, 111–24, 126–39, 141–49, 151; Christian Peyotists, 48, 108; non-Peyotists, 2–3, 8, 41, 86–87, 98, 106, 138–39

Pine Ridge Reservation, 113, 135

Pinero, 26

Pipestem, George, 134

Poco, Marcus, 46, 76–77

politics (also political), 4–5, 50, 52, 55, 59–61, 64–65, 77, 90, 97, 99, 103, 105–6, 115–24, 126, 130, 133, 137, 143, 145, 151; Democrats, 118; lobbying, 9, 49, 53, 106, 115, 117–18, 120–23, 126, 130, 133; racial politics, 95, 97, 117–18

polygamy, 46, 116, 123, 129, 132, 142–43

Ponca (indigenous tribe), 28, 72, 108, 134

Ponca Agency, 107

post office, 67, 78, 84, 148; mail, 73, 78, 84, 148; Post Office Appropriation Act, 84

Prairie Band Potawatomi (indigenous tribe), 28

Prentiss, Julia, 131

Price, H. L., 49

progress, 19, 36, 39, 44, 54, 78, 92, 114, 122, 126

Progressive Era, 7, 36, 81, 83, 90, 95, 99–100

Protestant (also Protestantism), 3, 15–16, 21, 39, 41–45, 47–48, 53–60, 106, 121, 129, 131, 140–41, 145–46, 150, 202n97

public health, 92

Pure Food and Drug Act, 83, 92–93, 98

Quapaw (indigenous tribe), 28

race, 4–6, 8, 19, 36, 41, 43–45, 50, 55, 73, 78–81, 86–89, 95–98, 100, 106, 112, 116–17, 124, 128, 134, 146–47, 155n13; assimilation, 8, 45, 50–51, 65, 117, 141, 148; racial mixing, 96; social construction of, 5, 10, 78–80, 96, 106, 116, 147

INDEX

railroads, 25, 64, 67–69, 71, 77, 95; Fort Worth and Denver City Railway, 69; International–Great Northern Railroad, 69; Missouri, Kansas, and Texas railroad companies, 69; National Railroad of Mexico, 67, 69; Rio Grande and Eagle Pass Railroad, 67; Texas Mexican Railroad, 67, 69
Rave, Harry, 132
Rave, John, 32, 48
Real Bull, James, 113
Red Nest, William, 113
Red River, 72, 109
reformers, 2, 19, 30, 34–37, 39–41, 44, 49, 55, 80–81, 83, 85–94, 96, 99, 100, 106–7, 113, 121, 123, 133, 138, 141
religion (also religious), 4–7, 10, 15, 20, 35–39, 42, 45, 47–50, 53–58, 60, 63, 65–66, 70–71, 73–74, 77–85, 89–93, 95–97, 99–101, 105–6, 108–9, 113–15, 119–23, 126–51, 157n6; attacks on Native American religion, 19, 82, 91–92, 97, 132–33, 137, 145, 150, 163n72; cosmology, 6, 16, 33, 35, 38–39, 48; God (also Dive, Holy Other, Creator), 5, 16–18, 28–29, 31, 37, 42–43, 105, 114, 127, 131–32, 144–45, 147, 151, 162n54; Native American religion, 39–40, 48–49, 54, 57–58, 64, 78, 82, 123, 127, 131–32, 134, 138–39, 143, 146; Religious Crimes Code, 19, 82; religious experience, 16, 18, 31, 34–36, 56, 119, 144, 151, 157n6; religious practice, 3–4, 16, 20–21, 26, 35, 40, 42, 53, 56–58, 63, 65, 70–71, 74, 77, 70, 81, 83, 90–93, 96–97, 105–6, 109, 113, 115, 127–29, 132–39, 142–44, 151; sacred-profane dichotomy, 8, 16–18, 22, 36–37, 41, 60, 80, 83, 89, 93, 133, 137–39, 142–43, 150, 154n7; secularization, 4, 8, 36, 60, 80, 99, 101, 121, 138, 151; social construction of, 6, 8, 10, 35, 106, 115, 126, 147; Western, 38, 48, 54, 108, 115, 137,
148, 157n6; variety (also pluralism), 108, 121, 127, 129, 144
religious exemption, 90, 141–42, 149–50
religious freedom (also religious liberty), 1, 3–4, 6–7, 9, 34, 41, 50, 57, 106, 114–15, 118, 121, 126–29, 133–34, 137–38, 141–50, 201n82; Constitution (also First Amendment), 4, 7, 39, 41, 115, 121, 127–29, 133–34, 136–37, 141–44, 146–47, 149–50, 191n46; limits to, 142–44; *Oregon v. Smith*, 150, 203n15; rights, 38–39, 56–57, 101, 113–15, 118, 123, 126, 133, 138–39, 143, 145, 147; suppression, 58, 114–15
Republican, 76, 142
reservation(s), 7–8, 10–11, 15, 18–19, 24–26, 28, 30, 43, 45–46, 49, 53–54, 58, 63–65, 67, 69, 71–72, 74–76, 79, 81–84, 87, 94, 105, 107, 110, 113–14, 117, 120, 128, 130, 135, 148, 161n51; bordered lands, 64–65, 67, 69, 71–74, 79; federal land, 114
rhetoric (also discourse), 4–5, 8–9, 79, 83–86, 90–92, 94–96, 98–101, 109–12, 117–18, 126–30, 136–39, 143, 146, 153n2, 184n58
Riggs, A. L. 52
Rio Grande, 8, 17, 20, 22, 65–67, 70, 78, 92, 98
Road, Paul, 112
roadman, 29, 31, 130
Roe, Mary, 101
Roe, W. C. 47
Roe Cloud, Henry, 101
Roosevelt, Theodore, 74, 107, 116
Rosebud Reservation, 135
Russellites, 131

Sac and Fox (indigenous tribe), 28, 130, 196n18
Sac and Fox in Kansas (indigenous tribe), 28
sacrament, 5, 9, 114, 121, 128–29, 138–44, 146, 148, 151, 200n67; bread, 138, 141–42; wine, 138–43
Safford, William E. 53, 97

INDEX

Sahagún, Bernardino de, 21, 159n25
Salish (indigenous tribe), 131
sanitation, 94, 116
San Luis Potosí, 23, 65
sartorial. *See* clothing
science, 42–43, 45, 57, 81, 84, 94, 110
Seger Agency, 112
Sells, Cato, 56, 84
Seminole (indigenous tribe), 28
Seneca-Cayuga (indigenous tribe), 28, 41, 52
Shahan, Thomas, 139
Shawnee (indigenous tribe), 28
Shawonotty, Miss, 11
Shell, Charles, 109, 111
Shoshone (indigenous tribe), 28, 33, 136
Sioux (indigenous people), 28, 33, 126
Skokomish (indigenous tribe), 131
Slick, Mrs. Sam, 11
Sloan, Thomas, 52, 114
Slocum, John, 131
Slocum, Mary, 132
Smithsonian Institute, 57, 133
Smoking Opium Exclusion Act, 96
Sniffen, Matthew, 57
Snyder, Homer P., 127
Society of American Indians (SAI), 2–3, 8, 41, 50–53, 89, 93–94, 100, 114, 124, 128, 133, 158n17
Sookwat, Mam, 135
Sorrells, Edwin Theodore, 119
South Dakota, 28, 54, 59, 113–14, 135
Southern Paiute (indigenous tribe), 28
Spanish (also Spain), 20–22, 24, 36, 40, 48, 70
Springer, Joseph, 138
Squaxin Island (indigenous tribe), 131
Standing Bird, 112, 119
Standing Elk, 116
Stewart, R. P., 114
Stray Calf, Austin, 114
Sun Dance, 19, 26, 50, 82, 163n72
Sunday school, 59–60
superstitions, 39, 45, 48, 91, 94

Swanton, John, 57
synesthesia, 17–18

Taft, William Howard, 116
Taos (indigenous tribe), 28
Tarahumara (indigenous tribe), 23, 93
Taylor, Reuben (also Istofhuts), 108–9, 111–12, 147
Tejano, 79
Tennessee, 96
Tepehuano (indigenous tribe), 23
Texas, 8, 20, 24, 26, 63, 65–66, 69–75, 77, 85, 93, 49; Eagle Pass, Texas, 67, 75, 77; El Paso, Texas, 8, 67, 73, 75; Encinal, Texas, 66–67; Hebbronville, Texas, 66–67; Laredo, Texas, 8, 59, 63, 66–67, 69–72, 75–76, 79, 149, 176n47, 177n53; Los Ojuelos, Texas, 66–67, 71, 174n20; Mirando City, Texas, 66–67; Torrecillas (Oilton), Texas, 66–67; Vernon, Texas, 69, 72
Thomas, Elmer, 59
Thompson, William H., 50
Thompson, W. W., 94
Tonkawa (indigenous tribe), 24, 28, 72
Tyler, Leonard William (also Magpie), 107–8, 119, 189n12

Uintah and Ouray Agency, 94
United Society of Believers, 131
United States, 26, 28–29, 55, 57, 59, 63–67, 69, 72–76, 78–79, 93, 95–96, 99, 107, 120, 122, 128, 136, 141, 147–48, 150; empire, 64, 122; US Court of Claims, 52
University of Oklahoma, 110
Utah, 28, 54, 74, 94, 124, 136
Ute (indigenous tribe), 28, 33, 124

Valentine, Robert, 77, 94
Villegas, Joaquín, 70–71, 176n43
Villegas, Leonor, 70
Villegas, Leopoldo, 70–71, 176–77n50

Villegas, Lorenzo, 71
Villegas, Quintín, 70–71, 176n50
voting (also vote), 59–60

Walker, Thomas, 119
Warden, Cleaver, 135
Washburn, H. C., 110
Washington, 28, 132, 136
Washington, DC, 55, 106, 111, 120, 122, 124–25, 130, 133–34
Washo (indigenous tribe), 28
Welch, Herbert, 36
Welch, Thomas, 140
Wells, Otto, 46, 55, 119
Wells Fargo Express company, 74–75
White, E. E., 46
White Crane, Sidney, 134
White Face Bull, 107
Whitehorn, Charles, 130
Whitewolf, Jim, 134
Wichita (indigenous tribe), 28, 32, 116
Wiley, Harvey, 35
Wilson, John, 32–33, 48, 133
Win-you, Mrs., 11
Winnebago (indigenous tribe), 28, 32–33, 52, 77, 119, 130, 132, 135

Wisconsin, 28, 77, 113, 130, 136
Woman's Christian Temperance Union (WCTU), 83, 85, 89
Woodruff, Wilford, 132
Woodson, A. E., 86
Woody, Jack, 149
work ethic, 86–87; economic dependency, 86–88; idleness, 86–88; labor, 86–88
World War I, 7, 60, 64, 99, 128, 142, 144–45, 195n3; code talkers, 128, 195n5; patriotism, 128, 144, 195–96n6
World War II, 148
Wormser, Ferdinand, 70, 79
Wormser, Julius, 70, 79, 177n53
worship, 1, 6–7, 16, 25, 29–30, 35, 39–40, 42, 47, 56, 100, 105, 114, 127–29, 136–37, 140, 143–45, 147
Wounded Knee. *See* Ghost Dance
Wyoming, 28, 54, 115

Yankton Reservation, 135
YMCA, 49–50
Young, Brigham, 133

Zitkala-Ša. *See* Bonnin, Gertrude Simmons

The manufacturer's authorized representative in the EU for product safety is Mare Nostrum Group B.V., Mauritskade 21D, 1091 GC Amsterdam, The Netherlands
email: gpsr@mare-nostrum.co.uk

www.ingramcontent.com/pod-product-compliance
Lightning Source LLC
LaVergne TN
LVHW012317240725
817018LV00020B/209/J